TIGER
FIRE

WRITTEN & EDITED BY

TIGER VALMIK
FIRE THAPAR

500 YEARS OF THE TIGER IN INDIA

ALEPH

THIS BOOK IS DEDICATED TO ALL THOSE WHO SERVE WILD
TIGERS IN ORDER TO ENSURE THAT FUTURE GENERATIONS
CONTINUE TO ENCOUNTER THEIR MAGIC.

ALEPH

ALEPH BOOK COMPANY
An independent publishing firm
promoted by *Rupa Publications India*

First published in India in 2013
by Aleph Book Company
7/16 Ansari Road, Daryaganj
New Delhi 110 002

Published in paperback in 2017

ISBN: 978-93-84067-24-3

1 3 5 7 9 10 8 6 4 2

Book design by Bena Sareen (with Ajanta Guhathakurta).

Printed and bound in India by

CONTENTS

The Rocks of Nalghati

A NOTE ON THE BOOK

I was delighted when the hardcover edition of *Tiger Fire* (a sumptuous book that was the culmination of my lifelong obsession with the world's most charismatic big cat) sold out. When we decided to publish a paperback edition, my publishers and I decided to make it more affordable by leaving out some of the photographs, while retaining enough pictures and art to profusely illustrate the text. I hope the book will remain in print for a long time to come and show readers what a magnificent part of the natural world the tiger is. Sadly, we don't seem to realize this as we continue to push the tiger towards extinction. If the tiger goes, our loss will be incalculable. India is home to more than 60 per cent of the world's wild tigers, so it seems reasonable to assume that our country will be the last stronghold of tigers. How are we going to save it? Any solution that hopes to succeed will need to involve both the government and the non-governmental sector.

Where government is concerned, there is urgent need to reform the administrative measures and policies that govern the management of wild tigers. The apex body of tiger conservation in this country, the National Tiger Conservation Authority (NTCA) needs to be overhauled. Those charged with decision-making need to be tutored by experts so they are able to devise useful and workable solutions to managing the country's tiger population. There is no point to having all-India guidelines; rather a great deal more responsibility needs to devolve on the various states as they are the ones which have tiger populations that need to be protected. State governments should not be alienated by the NTCA. At the moment, the NTCA has an arrogant attitude towards other wildlife conservation bodies and it is essential that this changes. Also, the tourism policy devised by the NTCA needs to be revamped. It should take its cue from the effective wildlife tourism programmes that are being run in various parts of Africa.

It is critical that the non-governmental sector is roped in to help with protecting our tigers. The efforts of government and NGOs need to be harmonized, and public-private partnerships need to become the norm not the exception. This is something I've said many times before, but it is a belief I will never stop sharing as it is the most effective way in which to save what is one of the most precious aspects of our heritage. It will be a sad day for India and the world if the last tigers that roam our wilderness are killed. It is a day that I hope will never dawn.

VALMIK THAPAR NEW DELHI JANUARY 2017

A NOTE ON THE HARDCOVER EDITION

When I began to think of writing and putting together *Tiger Fire,* what I saw in my mind's eye was the definitive book on the Indian tiger. I had been obsessively involved with this magnificent animal for nearly forty years, an obsession that had resulted in over twenty books, thousands of pictures and several documentaries and films. Now, I wanted to bring together the best work and writing of all those who had engaged with the animal across the centuries. Accordingly, I began to pore over the hundreds of rare books, photographs and art on the tiger in my collection, accumulated over a lifetime (many of them available nowhere else in the world even in this age of unbridled digitization), to put together the ultimate book on the tiger. By bringing together the observations and insights of these men and women who knew the tiger so well I was hoping to bring alive every nuance of this amazing creature. Further, I was hoping to introduce the reader to those who are devoted to keeping the tiger alive as well as explain the crisis that envelopes it today, and what needed to be done if it has to survive in the wild.

Despite all the volumes that I have written on the animal I have served all my life, as *Tiger Fire* began to take shape, I couldn't help being swept away by the sheer grandeur, scale and majesty of its content. Such a book happens only once in a lifetime, and I am glad I was given the opportunity to put it together in homage to that most awesome and splendid creation of nature—the tiger.

David Davidar has been an inspiration in putting this book together with his team—Aruna, Trisha, Prerna and Bena Sareen. It has been a gigantic task and I must thank my wife Sanjna for her encouragement all through its creation. There is a very long list of photographers I have to thank for the incredible images they have generously shared with me—they find special mention in the list of credits at the back of the book.

I would also like to thank Hajra Ahmad for her assistance in finding the early narratives, Dharmendra Khandal for identifying a bunch of young photographers, Vicky Luthra for his intensive efforts in the photo studio and Kim Sullivan, not just for her amazing pictures but also for the enormous effort she took to find the right ones for the book.

It is my sincere hope that the hearts and minds of readers are stirred by the magnificence of the creature they find in the pages of this book. If they are moved in some way to help with its survival in the wild, then the purpose of *Tiger Fire* would have been served.

VALMIK THAPAR NEW DELHI JUNE 2013

INTRODUCTION

 Summer in Ranthambhore. There is still about half an hour to sunrise but the sky has begun to lighten and all around me the tall grass, the low hillocks, the scrub, and the rocky outcrops have begun to glow a golden yellow. There's an alarm call from a sambar close by, and then I see what I have come looking for, a huge male tiger, walking along the path towards me, his steps relaxed and unhurried, but carrying within them the promise of explosive power. On he comes, the great muscles of his shoulders moving under the skin with every stride, the yellow eyes in his massive head never leaving the vehicle in his path. Although I've watched wild tigers from up close for decades, there is still no sight that moves me as much. A moment longer, there is light in the sky now, it catches his coat, the colours explode in orange and gold, his eyes burn, and then he leaps smoothly, silently, into the grass and is gone, a long streak of flowing liquid fire.

I have been devoted to the tiger all my adult life, right from the time I encountered one in the exquisite forests of Ranthambhore in 1976 to the present day. My early encounters—recounted in the third section of this book—were so exciting that the everyday trappings of life could not match up to them. As I was drawn further into the world of wild tigers, my store of knowledge about this amazing, elusive beast grew. Working with my guru, Fateh Singh Rathore, I observed and recorded the secret life of tigers—something that had seldom been done before. In fact, the Ranthambhore tigers that we watched and wrote about and photographed and filmed reshaped the natural history of wild tigers in the eyes of the world. For us, it was a pleasure like no other, and through our range of books and films, we shared our experiences with wildlife enthusiasts across the world.

As I've said in my note to the hardcover edition, it occurred to me, that although the tiger was probably the most written about wild animal in India, and certainly among the most written about anywhere, among the hundreds of books published on the animal in my collection (including those I'd written) no one volume gave tiger enthusiasts and interested readers a wide-ranging and in-depth selection of the extraordinary writing and pictures that the animal had inspired over the centuries. Once I had decided I would do something about it, for the next three years I read, excerpted, edited, and ranged far and wide in search of material on the tiger, for, as I have explained, what I wanted to do was produce a book that would be a lasting testimonial to one of nature's supreme creations.

Tiger Fire is organized chronologically, more or less, and could be said to be three books rolled into one (I say this because each of these sections could easily be published as a book in its own right) with a short introductory section to set the scene and a coda to wrap things up. First, comes 'Origins', in which I talk about the scientific classification and evolution of the tiger as well as the impact it has had on Asia's social fabric over the years. The second section, 'The Tiger in Time', runs from the sixteenth to the early twentieth centuries and brings together the finest writing on the tiger during this period by a variety of writers. Some of them, like the Mughal emperors Babur and Akbar, and latter-day hunters and shikharis-turned-naturalists like F. W. Champion, Hugh Allen, Kenneth Anderson, and the most famous of them all, Jim Corbett, are well-known, but most of them died unsung. The only things that unify the writers in this section are the remarkable nature of their prose and the originality of their observations on the animal. You will read about humans hunting tigers, tigers killing humans, tigers hunting prey, tigers in love, tigers at play, and all manner of other extraordinary stories about this magnificent beast. The third section, 'The Secret Life of the Tiger', brings together the best of my early writing from the books I've published.

The survival of the tiger in the wild is critical to the well-being of mankind in general because of what it stands for, and its extinction will mark the beginning of the end not just for India but for much of humanity. If anyone has ever doubted this, it would be instructive to note the findings of a recent poll carried out by a well-known natural history channel across seventy-three countries in which respondents chose the tiger as the world's favourite animal over all other choices including the dog and the cat. Now imagine a world in which this charismatic animal no longer exists. Because of us. There is no time to be lost. Every one of us needs to help and this is why I am hoping that this book will engage you, beguile you, and inspire you to join the fight to ensure the survival of the tiger.

~

BOOK ONE

ORIGINS

——

Tigers evolved from the now extinct treetop carnivores called Miacids some fifty million years ago. The Miacids resemble today's pine martens.

THE EVOLUTION OF THE TIGER

The binomial nomenclature of the tiger, the largest of the big cats, is *Panthera tigris*. The lion, leopard and jaguar also belong to the *Panthera* genus—the name given to the big cats that have a special roar, made possible by the vibration of the thickened vocal folds just below the vocal cords in the larynx. *Tigris* is the species name that differentiates the tiger from other members of the genus: *Panthera leo* (lion), *Panthera pardus* (leopard), and *Panthera onca* (jaguar); it is classical Greek for 'arrow', a name also given to the straight and swift Tigris river.

The origins of the tiger trace back some fifty million years, fifteen million years after the mass extinction of dinosaurs and flying and swimming reptiles, an extinction that paved the way for mammals. The tiger's earliest ancestors were miacids—tree-climbing creatures that bore a resemblance to today's pine martens.

The direct ancestors of today's big cats were the Pseudaelurines, which lived about twenty million years ago. Molecular techniques used to compare the genetic similarities among the modern-day members of the *Panthera* genus have determined that it was the tiger that first diverged from the common *Panthera* ancestor; the lion, leopard and jaguar evolved much later and have a stronger genetic resemblance to one another than with the tiger.

The period popularly termed the ice age, which occurred between 1.6 million and ten thousand years ago, was actually a series of ninety or more cold cycles intermixed with warmer periods. About two million years ago, our ancestor, *Homo habilis*, began to evolve into *Homo erectus* and eventually began moving out of Africa. The modern *Homo sapiens* did not exist until about forty thousand years ago and many believe that they evolved from archaic humans nearly two hundred thousand years ago in Africa. The existence of tigers at this time cannot be definitely proved by the distribution of tiger fossils, which provide most of the evidence scientists and researchers have used to piece together our understanding of the tiger. The reason for this is that tigers and lions look very similar when stripped of their stripes and manes, and incomplete, badly weathered skeletons have made the job of identification exceedingly difficult. Moreover, tigers tend to live in dense forest, with lots of moisture, heat and mud—conditions which don't help fossil formation.

The earliest tiger fossils are one to two million years old and have been found in China, Java, and Sumatra. Those in Russia have been traced back seven hundred thousand years, and those in India are only ten thousand years old. Though a few fossils have been found in Beringia, the strip of land that connected Asia to North America during the ice ages, there is no evidence that tigers entered North America, although recent fossil evidence suggests that they existed in Borneo as recently as a few hundred years ago.

From the existing, scant fossil evidence, scientists have formed two alternative theories. The most accepted version is the Asian theory. It asserts that more than two million years ago, when early man had yet to venture out of Africa, tigers separated from their big-cat cousins in East Asia, with the South China form being the original template. They split up in two directions. One group travelled north to Russia while the second spread south-east to the Indonesian islands and south-west to India. The second theory debates the notion that there was a single point of origin in China, as natural selection acting on an isolated but geographically widespread population could also result in its simultaneous evolution elsewhere.

The last major ice age ended approximately twelve thousand years ago. During that time, people and animals had been able to cross from continental Europe to Britain by foot. Now, the ice at the poles melted, and the North and Irish seas and the English Channel became too deep to cross. The land became warmer and trees grew, creating forests across Britain. European lions, which had been common for nine hundred thousand years, became extinct. The Sahara received more rain and became habitable. In North America, sabre-toothed cats and the American lion were becoming extinct. It is at this time, as fossils discovered at the Kurnool cave deposits in Andhra Pradesh tell us, that the tiger first entered India.

Their relationship with humans can be traced back five thousand years, as the discovery of rock paintings from that period in Indian cave sites show. These paintings depict men and various animals, including the tiger, either resting or running, and many of the hunting scenes feature tigers. The peoples of the Indus Valley civilization were the first to use the tiger as an important symbol in their cultures. Tiger engravings on seals have been found. They are believed to have marked the ownership of property and were also worn as amulets.

More than a thousand years ago, the Roman Empire was at its peak. The use of Caspian tigers in their games and in massacres in their amphitheatres introduced the first significant threat to the tiger's existence. Whatever scant fossil evidence has been found of this period, suggests that the tiger population maintained a wide distribution and equilibrium, with humans being far less numerous and lethal than they are now.

The tiger population began to go into decline more than a century ago, when the proliferation of firearms and cars facilitated hunting for sport and medicinal purposes. People also began hunting the tiger's prey and encroaching upon its natural habitats, converting them to agricultural lands. In the fifty years between 1875 and 1925, eighty thousand tigers were killed in India alone and an equal number were probably injured and died later of their wounds.

Today there are an estimated three thousand to three thousand five hundred tigers in the wild. They span eighteen countries, from the snowy lands of eastern Russia to the sweltering jungles of Sumatra. Tigers live in temperatures that range from -33°C (-28°F) in the northern extreme of their range to 50°C (122°F) in the southern part, and at altitudes that range from sea level to three thousand metres (more than ten thousand feet). Vegetation

Tigers have evolved with enough power to tackle and bring down elephants and rhinos when necessary.

also varies greatly. Tigers are incredibly versatile animals, requiring only dense vegetative cover, large ungulate prey, and water to survive.

Tigers living in the north are generally larger and paler, with thick, shaggy coats, while those in the south, which live in jungle and heat, are smaller, darker and have shorter fur. Tigers were originally divided into eight subspecies, often with country-specific names, but recent research, led by Andrew Kitchener, has reduced the number of tiger subspecies to three.

Today, the world's current population of tigers represents five of the original eight subspecies: the Amur (*Panthera tigris altaica*), the Bengal (*Panthera tigris tigris*), the Indo-Chinese (*Panthera tigris corbetti*), the South China (*Panthera tigris amoyensis*) and the Sumatran (*Panthera tigris sumatrae*). The first four are classified as the Asia tiger (*Panthera tigris tigris*), the last as the Sunda Islands tiger. At least three of the original eight subspecies are now extinct—the Caspian tiger, the Javan tiger and the Balinese tiger. South China tigers have not been seen in the wild for several decades, and though footprints and kills have been found, it is generally believed that they are either extinct, or close to extinction.

The tiger, considered one of the world's most dangerous predators, is

The tiger's leap gives it such momentum that it can easily topple the nilgai.

situated firmly at the top of the food chain. In order to survive, it needs to consume at least one deer-sized animal each week, and its anatomy has evolved to make it a perfect hunter.

The tiger's skeleton facilitates both speed and strength. Their long hind legs enable them to leap forward ten metres (32.5 feet) while their small collarbone increases the length of their stride. Their forelegs, the muscles of which are supported by solid forelimb bones, give tigers incredible power, and the closely bound ligaments in their feet help them survive the impact of landing, which is crucial to their ability to sprint. Tigers also have a short, rounded skull which makes their jaws more powerful. Their jaws cannot move from side to side, which adds strength to their bite, and their septum is made of bone, unlike humans and many other animals whose septum comprises only a membrane; this increases the strength of their skull. Tigers have thirty teeth, the largest canines of all the big cats, measuring 6.4 to 7.6 centimetres (2.5 to 3 inches) long. These canines consist of nerves that are extremely sensitive to pressure, which increases the accuracy of their bite, enabling them to locate and sever the spinal cord. The tiger's tongue is rough and covered with many minuscule, sharp objects known as papillae, which helps it to remove feathers, fur and lick meat clean off the bone.

Claws play a significant role in the tiger's hunting abilities. A tiger's claws can be as long as ten centimetres (four inches), and they help the tiger to hold its prey down before the deadly bite. Tigers have four claws on each

VALMIK THAPAR

The tiger's grip from its thirty teeth allows it to carry or drag large prey across long distances.

paw, as well as a dewclaw on the front ones which aid it in gripping prey and climbing. Claws are kept retracted when not in use—tigers walk on their toes, which have big soft pads to help them move without any noise.

The tiger's whiskers, too, help its sense of touch. The whiskers on its face are embedded in capsules of blood. When they brush against something, the root of the whisker moves, amplifying the movement, causing the nerves to send a signal to the brain.

The tiger's tail, often more than a metre long, also aids it in hunting— it gathers force when swung, helping the animal to balance if it has to make a sudden turn during a chase. It also helps in communication: a tiger waves a raised tail upon meeting an acquaintance, but holds it low with an occasional twitch, or swings it violently if it is feeling aggressive.

Tigers have short, relatively uncomplicated guts, since meat can be converted to protein more easily than grass. They also have small, light abdomens which help in the acceleration of their speed. Zoologist George Schaller made a study of the scats of emaciated tigers, and discovered the presence of grass and tapeworms, concluding that tigers sometimes eat grass in order to rid their intestines of parasites. Their digestive system is remarkable—other studies have shown that their stomachs can cope with porcupine quills and bear claws.

The tiger's magnificent stripes provide it with an excellent camouflage. It has been suggested that the reason white tigers are so rare in the wild is because they lose the ability to conceal themselves and thus seldom survive to birth cubs. The tiger's fur traps air, insulating its body to a steady temperature of 37°C (99°F). Longer fur helps heat retention, which is why tigers in colder climates have longer fur than those that live in the hotter southern regions. Tigers shed their fur twice a year, their summer coat being shorter than their winter coat. They use their tongue to groom themselves. The tongue is also important in healing injuries as licking wounds coats them with antiseptic saliva. The colour of a tiger's coat ranges from pale yellow, such as is seen on tigers in cold, northern climates, to the deep orange more commonly found in the south. Since the colour range within a subspecies varies widely, it is not regarded as a definitive species characteristic.

Like all cats, tigers have excellent sight in the dark. Their eyes have sensitive cells that absorb light. The retina contains two different kinds of cells: rods and cones. Rods respond to low levels of light, and cones, which are used in colour vision, respond to high levels. Tigers have more rods than cones, and as a result, they have superior night vision, which is useful for hunting, at the expense of colour vision. A reflective retinal layer known as the tapetum lucidum causes their eyes to glow in the dark and also facilitates night vision. Tigers have binocular vision—their eyes create a sort of 3D image—which is crucial to their ability in calculating their distance from their prey and striking with accuracy. A 'visual streak' close to the centre of the eye makes them extremely sensitive to movement, much more than humans.

Tigers, like other carnivores, have a small pouch on the roof of their mouth called the Jacobson's organ which allows them to analyze and identify scent. Although their sense of smell is not crucial to hunting, it is extremely important for communication. Adult tigers are solitary animals, and their sense of smell helps them to make sense of what is going on in their surroundings. For instance, they use scent to mark their territory or to find a mate at the appropriate time.

The tiger's most highly developed sense is its ability to hear. Tigers have large ear flaps, or pinnae, that help them to catch various kinds of sounds, as well as to locate the precise origin of these sounds. Sensitive to both high frequency and low frequency sound waves, their hearing range is far more extensive than that of humans. Like elephants and whales, they often communicate by infrasound which can travel over long distances and thick forest cover because of its ability to pass straight through solid objects such as trees and mountains.

Everything about the tiger's anatomy has contributed towards making it a supreme hunter.

The tiger was always associated with the goddess and was her vehicle atop which she could destroy evil.

THE CULT OF THE TIGER

Ancient Indian and South Asian history was full of tigers, of course, but an enormous cult of the tiger arose across the rest of Asia as well, including parts of Siberia. The tiger became an integral part of the life of traditional communities, and its influence on religious cults and legends, on art and literature, and on a widespread way of life was unmatched by any other non-domesticated animal. Wherever it existed, it left its impression on the psyche of the people. The Warli tribal gods existed because of the animal. Phallus-shaped wooden and stone images of the tiger, often daubed in red to indicate their extreme sanctity, were placed everywhere as symbols of fertility, not just for crops but also for marriage and the birth of children. There were festivals to the tiger god all across India, and there were frequent ritualistic dances in which dancers painted themselves with tiger stripes and then propitiated the tiger god. The tiger commanded great fear and respect across different religions. A legend of a compassionate prince giving his body to save the life of a starving tigress and her cubs is found in several sacred Buddhist texts.

Thousands of miles away in Siberia, the Udege tribal people also honoured the tiger as their god. To the Udege, the tiger is the spirit of the taiga (evergreen forests) and guardian of the trees and mountains, a divine force of nature. Similarly, many Koreans still believe that their land is blessed by the blue dragon and the white tiger and that the image of the tiger repels evil spirits and protects people's fortunes. Much the same was felt in China. Many believe that the tiger first originated in China and then spread across Asia. At one time, most Chinese believed the breath of the tiger created the wind. Edward Schafer in his book, *The Vermilion Bird* (1967), states, 'Chinese literature from the earliest times is full of tiger stories—man-eating tigers, were-tigers, symbolic tigers, anti-tiger spells, tiger hunts—tigers in China are like mice in a cheese factory.' Three thousand years ago, during the Shang dynasty, people in the Shaanxi province believed that the tiger symbolized regeneration. A bride would receive two dough tigers when she first arrived at her husband's house (a tradition that continues to this day). In Chinese medicine, the body of the tiger was believed to hold miraculous cures. Nearly any kind of disease could be overcome by 'eating the tiger'. Tribal communities believed that the white tiger was a part of the Milky Way and from there he protected the earth. Just as the goddess Durga rides a tiger in her attempt to defeat evil, the Taoist leader in China is shown riding a tiger in his search for a dragon-tiger elixir for eternal life. Indeed, the parallels in tiger belief between China and India are extraordinary.

Tigers were also a symbol of power in China, and their image conferred both strength and courage. The male tiger, as the god of war, was responsible for fighting demons. Chinese soldiers dressed in imitation tiger skins with tails for protection. The tiger was the guardian of China, the protector against evil, and the protector of the living and the dead. Tiger-striped pillows still keep away nightmares, and children don tiger-patterned hats, collars and shoes to keep away evil. The richness of tiger symbolism in China has no equivalent in the belief systems of Christian Europe.

Wherever the tiger lived, its cult enveloped people. In the forests of Vietnam, Laos and Cambodia, the tribal Mnong believed that the tiger was first among animals and had intense supernatural powers, including the ability to transform into a human being. The Mnong, much like the Warlis in India, connected the worship of the tiger to the worship of grain, and they believed this resulted in rich harvests from fertile soil. All across Malaysia and Indonesia, people believed in the tiger shaman who could evoke the tiger and then perform miraculous cures on any patient's body in order to repel sickness and disease. They also believed in 'were-tigers' who are spirit people who can change into tigers and then back into humans. Were-tigers were protective spirits who kept a link between the past and the present, as for most forest people the souls of

Tigers with one head. The cult of the tiger spread across Asia and became a part of the myth and belief of all forest people. The tiger was like a god and was worshipped in India, China, Siberia and across Southeast Asia.

ancestors were thought to reside in the tiger. The cult of the tiger linked beliefs throughout the land of the tiger, from the Manchurian taiga to the Indian forest and the Sumatran jungle.

More than one billion people live in twenty-first-century India. It also boasts nearly half the world's tiger population, half the world's Asiatic elephant population, and an array of other living creatures. One might argue that these animal populations might not have survived at all if these people had not maintained a core belief in nature's power. The Asiatic elephant invoked the spectre of Ganesha, the elephant god; the tiger was the vehicle of Durga.

I firmly believe that true conservation values exist in a nation because of the religions, rituals, myths and legends that abound in the traditions of the people. Enormous damage has been done to the tiger in the last fifty years as changes have affected the cultural fabric across Asia, and this process has accelerated rapidly in the last fifteen years as new economic models increasingly dot the landscape. One of the primary reasons that the future of the tiger is now in question has to do with our apparent inability to integrate the needs of business (and the human communities it serves) with the preservation of our natural environment.

BOOK TWO

THE
TIGER
IN TIME

—

THE SIXTEENTH TO THE NINETEENTH CENTURIES

There is no better way to begin telling the history of tiger encounters than with accounts from the Great Mughals. Nearly 500 years ago, Emperor Babur came across his first tiger, and since the Mughals had a great interest in flora and fauna, it led to some of the first narratives about tigers in history. Akbar's tiger encounters were diverse and varied and the detailed records of his time revealed a great deal about the behaviour of the tiger. I have tried to find the most exciting of these accounts and kept away from those that were probably stage-managed.

As the seventeenth and eighteenth centuries rolled on, ever more travellers landed on Indian shores and discovered the magical world of the country's forests and wildlife. The narratives changed and became more descriptive. By the eighteenth century, the British were busy making inroads into what were then the most impenetrable forests of India. They exploited these forests for timber and minerals but the wilderness also created the sportsman who, on discovering the tiger, became addicted to hunting it. The narratives changed once again as people like Thomas Williamson and William Rice wrote books that enthralled readers across the world. By the end of the nineteenth century, the hunter flourished—wiping out almost seventy to eighty thousand tigers between 1875 and 1925 alone—but, at the same time, the first attempts at conservation had begun.

The accounts in this section are arranged chronologically for the most part and refer specifically to tiger encounters that took place up to the end of the nineteenth century. Dates at the end of every excerpt refer to the date of first publication of the book from which the excerpt is taken but in some cases the event that is being described would have taken place much before the publication of the work, and therefore appears in this section.

~

On Thursday we went out to the riverbank as the sun was coming up. That day we ate ma'jun. How strange the fields of flowers appeared under its influence. Nothing but purple flowers were blooming in some places, and only yellow ones in other areas. Sometimes the yellow and the purple blossomed together like gold fleck. We sat on a rise near the camp and just looked at the fields. Like a painting, on all sides of the hill, yellow and purple flowers in regular clumps were arranged in a hexagon shape. On two sides there were somewhat fewer numbers, but as far as the eye could see were fields of blossoms. In the spring there are beautiful flowers in the vicinity of Peshawar.

We marched out of that camp at dawn. As we approached, a tiger emerged from the riverbank, growling. As soon as the horses heard its sound they took their riders off in all directions and hurled themselves into the gullies and pits. The tiger turned around and went back into the thicket. We ordered an ox put into the bushes to flush the tiger out. It worked: the animal again came out growling, and the men shot at it from all sides. I too shot an arrow. Khalu Piyada stabbed it, whereupon the tiger bit off the end of the lance. Having endured so many arrow wounds, the tiger slunk back into the underbrush. But Baba Yasavul drew his sword and approached the tiger, giving it a blow on the head. When Ali of Seistan struck at its waist, the tiger threw itself into the river, where the men were finally able to kill it. When it was brought out of the water, we ordered it skinned. {1589} {1996}

---

*The Baburnama, *the autobiography of Emperor Babur (the founder of the Mughal Empire in the sixteenth century), from which this extract is taken, is full of observations on flora and fauna as he, like many of his successors, had a keen interest in nature.*

TIGER HUNTING IN THE REIGN OF AKBAR* | ABU'L-FAZL

They make a large cage, and having fastened it (on the ground) with strong iron ties, they put it in places frequented by tigers. The door is left open; but it is arranged in such a manner that the slightest shaking will cause it to close. Within the cage they put a goat, which is protected by a screen so constructed that the tiger can see the goat, but not get hold of it.

*Emperor Akbar, the greatest of the Mughal line (1542-1605), commissioned Abu'l-Fazl, one of his trusted ministers, to write the Akbarnama, *his official biography, which eventually ran into three volumes.*

VALMIK THAPAR

Hunger will lead the tiger to the cage. As soon as he enters, he is caught.

Another method—They put a poisoned arrow on a bow, painted green, in such a manner that a slight movement will cause the arrow to go off. The bow is hung upon a tree, and when the tiger passes, and shakes it a little, the arrow will hit the animal and kill it.

Another method—They tie a sheep to a place in a road frequented by tigers, putting round about the sheep on the ground small blades of grass covered with glue. The tiger comes rushing forward and gets his claws full of the glue. The more he tries to get rid of it, the more will the glue stick to his feet, and when he is quite senseless and exhausted, the hunters come from the ambush and kill him. Or they take him alive, and tame him.

His Majesty, from his straightforwardness, dislikes having recourse to such tricks, and prefers with bows or matchlocks openly to attack this brute, which destroys so many lives.

Another method—An intrepid experienced hunter gets on the back of a male buffalo and makes it attack the tiger. The buffalo will quickly catch the tiger on its horns, and toss it violently upwards, so that it dies. It is impossible to describe the excitement of this manner of hunting the tiger. One does not know what to admire more, the courage of the rider, or his skill in standing firm on the slippery back of the buffalo.

One day, notice was given that a man-eating tiger had made its appearance in the district of Bārī. His Majesty got on the elephant Nāhir <u>Kh</u>ān, and went into the jungle. The brute was stirred up and striking its claws into the forehead of the huge animal, it pulled its head close down to the ground, when the tiger was killed by the men. This occurrence astonished the most intrepid and experienced hunters.

On another occasion, His Majesty hunted near Toda. The tiger had stretched one of the party to the ground. His Majesty aimed at the brute, killed it, and thus saved the life of the man. Once during a *qamargha* chase, a large tiger was stirred up. The animal attacked His Majesty, when he shot it in time through the head and killed it.

Once a tiger struck his claws into a man. All who witnessed it despaired of his life. His Majesty shot the tiger through the body and released the unfortunate man.

A remarkable scene took place in the forest of Mathura. Shujāʾat <u>Kh</u>ān... who had advanced very far, got suddenly timid. His Majesty remained standing where he was, and looked furiously at the tiger. The brute cowered[1]

---

[1] *This is one of Akbar's miracles.*

down before that divine glance, and turned right about trembling all over. In a short time it was killed.

The feats of His Majesty are too numerous to be imagined; much less can a Hindustani, as I am, describe them in a dignified style.

He slays lions, but would not hurt an ant.
He girds himself for the fray but the lion drops his claws from fear.[2]
{1871}

THE SHĀHINSHĀH AND THE WOUNDED TIGER
ABU'L-FAZL

While doing so the huntsmen pointed out a tiger-jungle and H. M. the Shāhinshāh went there to hunt the beast. When he came near the reed-bed, suddenly a formidable tiger came out. The courtiers lost control of themselves and pinned the animal to the earth with life-taking arrows. H. M. the Shāhinshāh did not approve of such haste, and commanded that no one should, without orders, surround any wild beast that came out of the jungle. While H. M. was saying this, another tiger, as formidable as the first one, came out and moved towards him. When the attendants saw this, their hair stood up on their bodies, but on account of the sacred command no one ventured to advance to kill the tiger. H. M., mounted as he was, watched the tiger's eye and shot an arrow at him. The tiger, wounded as he was, daringly advanced, and came out on the high ground and sat there in his wrath. H. M. got off his horse and stood there, while the brave tiger-throwers drew a circle round him. H. M. took aim with a gun and fired at the tiger, so that the ball entered at the corner of his mouth and grazed the skin below the ear. H. M. was endeavouring to discharge another bullet, and was seeking for an opportunity, but to whatever side he turned, the tiger was on the watch there, and a fitting opportunity for shooting did not present itself.

I have heard from the holy lips of the Shāhinshāh that H. M. Jahānbāni Jinnat-Āshiyāni used to relate that God had so ordained it that when a number of persons went tiger-shooting the tiger always kept his eyes on the person who was destined to shoot him. H. M. told me that he had noticed this on many occasions when he went out shooting, and found it come true. In fine, when he could not get an opportunity he bade Dastam Khān advance, so that on the tiger's attention being drawn to him, H. M. might get a shot. 'Ādil...who had been chidden (for shooting the first tiger) thought that the order to advance was given to all the attendants, and he too went from behind H. M. with a bow and arrow in his hand. The tiger turned towards 'Ādil, and when he came near, 'Ādil shot, and by force of destiny he made a miss. The tiger came on and struck him with his two paws. That strong man attacked the tiger, and put his left hand into his mouth, while with the other he drew his dagger. As fate destined something different, the dagger was fastened to the hilt, and while he was unfastening it the tiger chewed his hand. Then he drew his dagger and inflicted two wounds on the tiger's mouth. Then the tiger seized his right hand with his mouth. Meanwhile the brave men in attendance rushed in from all sides and disposed of the tiger with their swords, and at the same time 'Ādil received a sword-wound. That tiger-hearted brave man lay in agony for four months and at last the poison of the wounds caused his limbs to mortify, and he died in Agra. It would seem that this was a retribution for his disrespect to his father.' {1590-1596} {1902-1939}

EMPEROR AKBAR HUNTING SIX TIGERS | ABU'L-FAZL

The royal cavalcade proceeded towards the centre of sovereignty. His Majesty went on, stage by stage, hunting and shooting, but also going on rapidly. When his crescent standards cast their raids on the territory appertaining to the fort of Narwar, a tiger such as might terrify the leopard of heaven[3] came out of the forest with five cubs and on to the track by which the cavalcade was proceeding. His Majesty the Shāhinshāh, who had the strength of the lion of God in his arms and the coat of mail of the divine

---

[3] *Palang-i-gardūn. Perhaps A. F. means the constellation Leo, or he may mean that of the lynx or of the cameleopard.*

protection on his breast, went alone and without hesitation in front of that iron-clawed, fiery-natured wild animal. When the spectators beheld this the hair on their bodies stood erect and sweat distilled from their pores. His Majesty with swift foot and alert arm attacked the brute and killed it by one stroke of his sword.

Gainst him whom God defends
Who is there that dares contend
If he assail a tiger or other beast of prey
He easily strips their skins from their bodies.

The wild beast, so great and terrible, fell bleeding to the dust before the strength of his arm and the might of his courage, and a shout arose on all sides. This was the first beast of prey which His Majesty personally attacked. Its cubs were killed by the swords and arrows of a number of brave men who were in attendance on the sublime stirrup. {1590-1596} {1902-1939}

SHAH JEHAN HUNTS TIGERS WITH
ELEPHANTS AND BUFFALOES
NICCOLAO MANUCCI

The following is an account of one of Shah Jehan's tiger hunts written by Manucci, who lived at his court for a number of years. 'His ordinary amusement,' says the writer[4], 'was tiger hunting, for which he kept ferocious buffaloes with very big horns. These fought with each other or with tigers, and they are very brave animals, and skilful in the sport above referred to.

'When the king desires to go out hunting the huntsmen are warned. These men see to the finding of the tigers and send out into the jungle asses, cows, sheep and goats to prevent the tigers from changing their haunts. The king goes out on his tallest elephant and the other princes likewise on elephants acquainted with the requirements of this sort of fight. They sit in uncovered howdahs, each one with his matchlock. Then they encircle the jungle with high nets, leaving only one opening, through which the king and huntsmen enter. Around the net on the outside stand a number of soldiers, who cannot wound the tiger when it comes near the net, nor can the tiger injure them, for in no manner can it break the net and get out. The order in which the king moves is as follows: In front go the buffaloes, sometimes more than one hundred in number, all in a row. On each one is mounted a man with his legs guarded by leather, and having a broadsword in one hand and holding with the other the reins, which are passed through the buffaloes' nostrils. Behind them comes the king on an elephant, and after the king the princes and the men in highest favour. When they get into the jungle where the tigers are, the buffaloes advance slowly in the formation of a half moon, until the tigers are in sight. After locating the tigers by sight and smell, a circle is formed, leaving them in the centre. In this way, the tigers finding themselves caught, search for an exit. Unable to get away, each one makes its spring in the direction that it sees best. When this spring takes place the man who is mounted on top jumps off with agility, and the buffaloes seize the tigers on their horns with great dexterity and, shaking their heads, tear them to pieces. If any one of the tigers escapes the horns or refuses to stir from it into its place, the king fires his gun and kills it, or gives an order to kill it.

'Sometimes they go out to these hunts without taking any buffaloes,

---

[4]Storio do Mogor, *or* Mogul India, *1653-1708, by Niccolao Manucci, translated with introduction and notes by William Irvin, B.C.S. (Retd.), vol. I, p. 191.*

but riding on elephants as I have before said. This way of hunting has much more risk for the hunters. Once it happened to King Shah Jehan that a badly wounded tiger bounded up and hung on with its claws fixed in the elephant's head. The elephant-driver fell to the ground from fright. The king seeing himself in this urgent danger, clubbed his matchlock and hit the tiger on the head with it, but the tiger did not let go, and the elephant finding he could not make use of his trunk, ran furiously till he found a tree, against which he crushed the tiger. It was on this account that Shah Jehan gave orders for the head of the elephants to be protected in future down to the end of the trunk with a covering of thick leather, studded with sharp nails. In addition to the huntsmen, there is always an official present whose business is to take possession of the tiger's whiskers; and therefore as soon as the tiger is dead, they put on his head a leather bag, coming down as far as the neck. Having tied the bag the officer attaches to it his seal. After this the tiger is carried in front of the entrance to the royal tents, when the official appears who has charge of the poisons, and removes the whiskers which are employed as venom.' {1983}

EMPEROR JĀHĀNGIR'S TIGER | JĀHĀNGIR

On the twenty-fifth they brought a tiger from my private menagerie to fight with a bull. Many people gathered together to see the show, and a band of Jogis (religious mendicants) with them. One of the Jogis was naked, and the tiger, by way of sport, and not with the idea of rage, turned towards him. It threw him on the ground and began to behave to him as it would to its own female. The next day and on several occasions the same thing took place. As no such thing had ever been seen before and was exceedingly strange, this has been recorded. {1605-1624} {1909-1914}

In hunting the cheetahs, Anūp Rāy, who is one of my close attendants, was heading the men who were with him in the hunt at a little distance from me and came to a tree on which some kites were sitting. When his sight fell on those kites he took a bow and some pointless arrows (*tukkā*) and went towards them. By chance in the neighbourhood of that tree he saw a half-eaten bullock. Near it a huge powerful tiger got up out of a clump that was near and went off. Though not more than two gharis of day remained, as he knew my liking for tiger-hunting, he and some of those who were with him surrounded the tiger and sent someone to me to give me the news. When it reached me I rode there at once in a state of excitement and at full speed, and Bābā Khurram, Rām Dās, I'timād Rāy, Hayāt Khān and one or two others went with me. On arriving I saw the tiger standing in the shade of a tree, and wished to fire at him from horseback but found that my horse was unsteady, and dismounted and aimed and fired my gun. As I was standing on a height and the tiger below, I did not know whether it had struck him or not. In a moment of excitement I fired the gun again, and I think that this time I hit him. The tiger rose and charged, and wounding the chief huntsman, who had a falcon on his wrist and happened to be in front of him, sat down again in his own place. In this state of affairs, placing another gun on a tripod, I took aim... Anūp Rāy stood holding the rest, and had a sword in his belt and a baton (*kutaka*) in his hand. Bābā Khurram was a short distance off to my left, and Rām Dās and other servants behind him. Kamāl the huntsman (*qarāwul*) loaded the gun and placed it in my hand. When I was about to fire, the tiger came roaring towards us and charged. I immediately fired. The ball passed through the tiger's mouth and teeth. The noise of the gun made him very savage, and the servants who had crowded together could not stand his charge and fell over one another, so that I, through their pushing and shock, was moved a couple of paces from my place and fell down. In fact, I am sure that two or three of them placed their feet on my chest and passed over me. I'timād Rāy and the huntsman Kamāl assisting me, I stood up. At this moment the tiger made for those who were on the left-hand side. Anūp Rāy let the rest slip out of his hand and turned towards the tiger. The tiger, with the same activity with which he had charged, turned on him, and he manfully faced him, and struck him twice with both hands on the head with the stick he had in his hand. The tiger, opening his mouth, seized both of Anūp Rāy's arms with it, and bit them so that his teeth passed through both, but the stick and the bracelets on his arms were helpful, and did not allow his arms to be destroyed. From the attack and pushing of the tiger Anūp Rāy fell down between the tiger's fore-feet, so that his head and face were opposite the tiger's chest. At this moment Bābā Khurrām and Rām Dās came to the assistance of Anūp Rāy. The prince struck the tiger on the loins with his sword, and Rām Dās also struck him twice with his sword, once on the shoulder blade. On the whole it was very warm work, and Hayāt Khān struck the tiger several blows over the head with a stick he had in his hand. Anūp Rāy with force dragged his arms out of the tiger's mouth and struck him two or three times on the cheek with his fist, and rolling over on his side stood up by the force of his knees. At the time of withdrawing his arms from the tiger's mouth, as his teeth had passed through them, they were partly torn, and both his paws passed over his shoulders. When he stood up, the tiger also stood up and wounded him on the chest with his claws, so that those wounds troubled him for some days. As the ground was uneven, they rolled over each other, holding on like two wrestlers. In the place where I was standing, the ground was quite level. Anūp Rāy says that God Almighty gave him so much intelligence that he bore the tiger over deliberately to one side (in the original, that side)[5], and that he knew no more. At this time the tiger left him and was making off. He in that state of bewilderment raised up his sword and followed him and struck him on the head. When the tiger turned his face round, he struck him another blow on the face, so that both his eyes were cut, and the skin of the eyebrows, which had been severed by the sword, fell over his eyes. In this state of affairs, a lamp-man of the name Sālih, as it was time to light the lamps, came in a hurry and by a blind chance came across the tiger. The tiger struck him one blow with his paw and knocked him down. To fall and give up his life were the same thing. Other people came in and finished the tiger's business.

~

On Saturday, the tenth, the huntsmen represented that there was in that neighbourhood a tiger that greatly troubled and injured the ryots and wayfarers. I immediately ordered them to bring together a number of elephants and surround the forest and at the end of the day myself rode out with my ladies. As I had vowed that I would not injure any living thing with my own hand, I told Nūr-Jahān to shoot at him. An

[5] *The meaning seeming to be that Rāy rolled the tiger over to the side furthest from Jahāngīr.*

elephant is not at ease when it smells a tiger and is continually in movement, and to hit with a gun from a litter (*'imārī*) is a very difficult matter, insomuch that Mīrzā Rustam, who, after me, is unequalled in shooting, has several times missed three or four shots from an elephant. Yet Nūr-Jahān B. so hit the tiger with one shot that it was immediately killed.

~

On the seventh, as the huntsmen had marked down four tigers, when two watches and three gharis had passed I went out to hunt them with my ladies. When the tigers came in sight Begam submitted that if I would order her she herself would kill the tigers with her gun. I said, 'Let it be so.' She shot two tigers with one shot each and knocked over the two others with four shots. In the twinkling of an eye she deprived of life the bodies of these four tigers. Until now such shooting was never seen, that from the top of an elephant and inside of a howdah (*'imārī*) six shots be made and not one miss, so that the four beasts found no opportunity to spring or move.[6] As a reward for this good shooting I gave her a pair of bracelets (*pahunchī*) of diamonds worth 100,000 rupees and scattered 1,000 ashrafis (over her). {1909-1914}

[6]*Note by Sayyid Ahmad: They say that a poet recited this impromptu couplet—*

> *Though Nūr-Jahān be in form a woman,*
> *In the ranks of men she's a tiger-slayer.*

Hither many shippes come from all partes of India, Ormus, and many from Mecca; heere be manie Moores and Gentiles. They have a very strange order among them. They worshippe a cowe, and esteeme much of the cowes doung to paint the walles of their houses. They will kill nothing, not so much as a louse for they holde it a sinne to kill any thing. They eate no flesh, but live by rootes and ryce and milke. And when the husbande dieth, his wife is burned with him, if shee be alive if shee will not, her head is shaven, and then is never any account made of her after. They say if they should be buried, it were a great sinne, for of their bodies there would come many wormes and other vermine, and when their bodies were consumed, those wormes would lacke sustenance, which were a sinne; therefore they will be burned. In Cambaia they will kill nothing, nor have anything killed; in the towne they have hospitals to keepe lame dogs and cats, and for birds. [RALPH FITCH]

~

Agra is a very great citie and populous, built with stone, having faire and large streetes, with a faire river running by it, which falleth into the Gulfe of Bengala. It hath a faire castle and a strong, with a very faire ditch. Here bee many Moores and Gentiles. The king is called Zelabdim Echebar; the people for the most part call him the Great Mogor. From thence we went for Fatepore (Fatehpur Sīkri), which is the place where the king kept his court. The towne is greater than Agra, but the houses and streetes be not so faire. Here dwell many people, both Moores and Gentiles. The king hath in Agra and Fatepore (as they doe credibly report) 1,000 elephants, thirtie thousand horses, 1,400 tame deere, 800 concubines: such store of ounces, tigers, buffles, cocks, and haukes, that is very strange to see. He keepeth a great court…[RALPH FITCH]

~

But lest this remote countrey should seeme like an earthly Paradise without any discommodities, I must needes take notice there of many lions, tygres, wolves, jackals (which seeme to be wild dogs), and many other harmefull beasts. In their rivers are many crocodiles, and on the land over-growne snakes, with other venimous and pernicious creatures. In our houses there we often meete with scorpions, whose stinging is most sensible and deadly, if the patient have not presently some oyle that is made of them, to anoint the part affected which is a present cure. The abundance of flyes in those parts doe likewise much annoy us for in the heate of the day their numberlesse number is such as that we can be quiet in no place for them. They are ready to cover our meate assoone as it is placed on the table; and therefore wee have men that stand on purpose with napkins to fright them away when as wee are eating. In the night likewise we are much disquieted with musquatoes, like our gnats, but somewhat lesase. And in their great cities there are such aboundance of bigge hungrie rats that they often bite a man as he lyeth on his bed. [EDWARD TERRY]

~

Sinnergan[7] is a towne sixe leagues from Serrepore, where there is the best and finest cloth made of cotton that is in all India. The chiefe king of all these countries is called Isacan, and he is chiefe of all the other kings, and is a great friend to all Christians. The houses here, as they be in the most part of India, are very litle, and covered with strawe, and have a fewe mats round about the wals, and the doore to keepe out the tygers and the foxes. Many of the people are very rich. Here they will eate no flesh, nor kill no beast; they live of rice, milke, and fruits. [RALPH FITCH] {1921}

[7]*Sonārgāon, the capital of Eastern Bengal…situated fifteen miles east of Dacca.*

But the most striking and peculiar beauty of *Bengale* is the innumerable islands filling the vast space between the two banks of the *Ganges*, in some places six or seven days' journey asunder. These islands vary in size, but are all extremely fertile, surrounded with wood, and abounding in fruit-trees, and pine-apples, and covered with verdure a thousand water-channels run through them, stretching beyond the sight, and resembling long walks arched with trees. Several of the islands, nearest to the sea, are now abandoned by the inhabitants, who were exposed to the attacks and ravages of the *Arracan* pirates, spoken of in another place. At present they are a dreary waste, wherein no living creature is seen except antelopes, hogs, and wild fowls, that attract tigers which sometimes swim from one island to another. In traversing the *Ganges* in small rowing boats, the usual mode of conveyance among these islands, it is in many places dangerous to land, and great care must be had that the boat, which during the night is fastened to a tree, be kept at some distance from the shore, for it constantly happens that some person or another falls a prey to tigers. These ferocious animals are very apt, it is said, to enter into the boat itself, while the people are asleep, and to carry away some victim, who, if we are to believe the boatmen of the country, generally happens to be the stoutest and fattest of the party. {1916}

CHASING A TIGER IN ASSAM

FITZ WILLIAM THOMAS POLLOK

At last, about three o'clock, there was a yell, and several boats went in full chase of what proved to be a tiger. We were nearly the last, and I urged my men to pull, as I wanted to see a tiger speared in this way. All the Assamese boats were vying with one another and trying who should get up first, and yelling most discordantly. We were nearing fast, when a man in the leading boat threw a spear, which apparently missed; another was thrown which struck the tiger. It immediately roared or growled and turned towards the boat, but was greeted with a shower of spears which turned it. It was swimming in deep water, but not far ahead it was quite shallow, and the object of the men was to kill it before it could get there. They not only threw their spears, but using them as lances thrust away at its beautiful hide. Once it got hold of the side of the boat and nearly upset it, but got a blow from a dhaw that laid open the head and made it let go. Still the tiger, though covered with wounds and dyeing the water all round with its blood, swam strongly; but what with its roaring, growling, and now and then gurgling as it was thrust under water, and the yells and screams of its assailants, the scene was an exceedingly savage one. By this time I was close up; the tiger got to the shallow[s], ran a little way, and then charged at the prow of the boat. Fearing some injury, I thought it was now time for me to interfere, so I fired, but from the unsteadiness of my boat, my first shot missed. By this time the tiger had seized the prow of the boat and was worrying it, taking no notice of the men. Telling my men to leave off rowing and to steady the boat, I put my second shot through the tiger's head, which killed it on the spot. It turned out to be a tigress, 8 feet 3 inches, but its skin was utterly ruined, owing to the numerous spear-wounds. {1879}

I once was in the woods with my fuzee, to try if I could kill a deer, but a small Rain happened to fall that damped my powder, which was only wrapped up in paper and, my gun being useless, I was making towards the plain where our factory stands, and falling on a foot-path from the mountains towards the plain; I kept in that road, and had not gone far, till I espied a tiger of the largest size standing in the same path, with his face towards me. As soon as he saw me he squatted his belly to the ground, and wagged his tail, crawling slowly towards me. I thought it would be in vain to flee, so I stepped leisurely forward, till I came within ten yards of him; I then clubbed my fuzee, and made what noise I could to frighten him, and he out of civility, rushed in amongst a thicket of bushes, and left me the road, which I did not think fit to accept of, but got in among the bushes on the opposite side to him (I dare say) much more frightened than he was. {1727}

EARLY DESCRIPTIONS OF WILD INDIA
SIR THOMAS ROE AND DR JOHN FRYER

Thus we came to Barsta, a despicable Country Town, Seven Course more; it is in possession of the Combies, who are not strong enough to aid their Herds against the devouring Jaws of the Wild Beasts, a young Buffola being seized the Night before, out of the Tabernacle they lodged me in; wherefore they cautioned me to keep Fires all Night, lest the Horse might lose one of his Quarters, or our Oxen might serve them for a Supper; I added to the Fires a strict Watch, whose mutual answering each other in an high Tone, was deafen'd by the Roarings of Tigres, Cries of Jackals, and Yellings of Baloos, or overgrown Wolves: At Cock-crow (the Lions Charm) we parted hence, and observed the Sheds here were round thatch'd, and lined with broad Leaves of Teke (the Timber Ships are built with), in fashion of a Bee-hive: These Combies are the Wood-men. About Seven we overtook our deep Creek, and being somewhat swelled by the Rains, we followed its Current till we found it passable; about Eleven, we returned to Gullean. {1873}

THE TIGER AND THE DEER

SIR THOMAS ROE AND DR JOHN FRYER

It was a Tigre of the Biggest and Noblest Kind, Five Feet in Length beside the Tail, Three and an half in Height, it was of a light Yellow, streaked with Black, like a Tabby Cat, the Ears short, with a few Bristles about the Lips; the Visage Fierce and Majestick, the Teeth gnashing, Two of which she brake against the Stones for anguish, the Shoulders and Fore-legs thick and well set, the Paw as Large as the biggest Fist stretched out, the Claws thick and strong.

The Boy Shot it in the Night from a Chouse, or Estarzo, as it came to Drink, supposing it to have been a Deer; the first Shot was that under the Shoulder, which made her spring Three times an incredible Height, at the last of which she fell into the Chouse from whence she saw the Flash, where with the English Boy were a Comby and a Comby Boy of Eight Year old, asleep a little on one side; she pawed the Straw with her feet, while all but the Child asleep fled; but being wrung by her pain, she soon left the place with an horrible Noise that made the Woods tremble, all which awaked not the Lad, nor had it any Harm. {1873}

It is memorable what is attested, by these Woodmen, of the Tigre, that when he intends to Prey on the Monkies (with which these Woods abound) he uses this Artifice or Stratagem; the Monkies at his first approach give warning by their confused Chattering, and immediately betake themselves to the highest and smallest Twigs of the Trees; when the Tigre seeing them out of his reach, and sensible of their fright, lies Couchant under the Tree, and then falls a Roaring, at which they trembling let go their hold, and tumbling down he at leisure picks them up to satisfy his Hunger: They are his accustomed Repast, seldom making Man his Meal, and they are judged (as St. Paul's Parbarians did him) guilty of some horrid Crime that such Vengeance overtakes; the Woods and Mountains yielding them variety of other Food. The Tigre is dull Scented, and not long Nimble, Three Leaps Tiring him, otherwise it's probable he would make more havock than he does. The She brings forth but once in Twelve Years, and then but a single Cub; they are Ingendring Three Months, in which time their Fury as well as Lust rages upon one another; thus has Providence suppressed the Growth of this master less Creature: Besides, if the Proverb be true, the Bitch brings forth but once in her life, or very rarely more. {1873}

The Woods of this Kingdome are well replenished with wild beasts, most Especially with Tygers and Bears of Vast largenesse, and the most fierce of any in the knowne world: those about the Ganges are Soe accompted. They are of Such a bloody Salvage Nature, that if they meet with a Cow, a deere, or any Other Annimal that hath been newly killed by Shot, or what else, they will not meddle therewith, but will rather Suffer most rageinge hunger, by reason they had not the killing of it themselvs.

~

There are Severall wild Elephants in the Woods here, but more Especially Tygers. Once when I was up att Luppoone, Severall of the Natives went out (by Order of the Radja), and Set a trapp for a Tyger that often resorted to a place where the Radja's goats were kept, which are not very plenty here. However they tooke one of the Smallest and place[d] him for a baite to Trapan the Tiger, and caught him alive by the leggs, which done they Seized fast his mouth as alsoe his paws, and brought him to the Radja's house. He Sent for me to looke Upon him, and although I thought the Sight of a Tyger noe novelty to me (that had Seene soe many), yet this proved one, by reason of his colour which was cole black, and although his body was but of an Ordinary Size, much lesse then Some I have Seen in Bengala, yet his teeth and claws were the largest that ever I saw, which caused mee to looke much upon them, and the Radja perceiveinge that, ordered one of his Soldiers to knock out the teeth and claws, and gave them to me, which I thankfully received and as a great raritie. {1905}

But, as I have already observed, it is dangerous to visit this delightful scenery without a large party of armed men, both on account of the Bheels and savage animals with which they abound: the number of tigers, leopards, and panthers is immense. During the viceroyship of the Mogul princes in Guzerat, and also at a later period among some of the Mahratta chieftains, it was customary for these great men, and their numerous attendants, to pitch their tents in unfrequented tracts, for the purpose of hunting those ferocious beasts. Their encampments, especially of the Moguls, were extensive and magnificent; there they entertained their friends in a sumptuous manner during the continuance of the hunt, which sometimes lasted several weeks.

I have occasionally joined the European parties in their tiger hunts, as particularly mentioned in the wilds of Turcaseer. The forests on the confines of Bhaderpoor, are equally wild and infested with beasts of prey. As I can offer nothing so interesting upon this subject as a description of a tiger hunt in Bengal, the subject of a letter from Sir John Day to Sir William Jones, which I have had for many years in my possession, I shall not apologize for inserting so highly-finished a picture of this royal sport; which was given to me by a very intimate friend of the writer, and has not to my knowledge appeared in print.

DESCRIPTION OF A TIGER HUNT, UPON THE BANKS OF THE GANGES NEARCHINSURA IN BENGAL; IN APRIL 1784:
Matters had been thus judiciously arranged: tents were sent off yesterday, and an encampment formed within a mile and a half of the jungle which was to be the scene of our operations; and in this jungle the thickets of long rank grass and reeds are in many places fifteen feet high. At one o'clock this morning thirty elephants, with the servants, and refreshments of all kinds, were dispatched; at two we all followed in fly-palanquins; at a quarter after four we reached the encampment, and having rested near two hours, we mounted our elephants, and proceeded to the jungle...

At the grey of the dawn we formed a line of great extent, and entered a small detached jungle. My elephant (sorely against my grain, but there was no remedy, for my driver was a keen sportsman, and he and I spoke no common language), passed through the centre, but happily no tiger had at that hour nestled there. I saw, however, as I passed through it, the bed of one, in which there were an half-devoured bullock and two human skulls; with a heap of bones, some bleached, and some still red with gore.

We had not proceeded five hundred yards beyond the jungle, when we heard a general cry on our left of "Baug, baug, baug!" On hearing this exclamation of "tiger!" we wheeled; and forming the line anew, entered the great jungle, when the spot where a single tiger lay having been pointed, on the discharge of the first gun a scene presented itself confessed by all the experienced tiger hunters present to be the finest they had ever seen. Five full-grown royal tigers sprung together from the same spot, where they had sat in bloody congress. They ran diversely; but running heavily, they all couched again in new covers within the same jungle, and all were marked. We followed, having formed the line into a crescent, so as to embrace either extremity of the jungle: in the centre were the houdar (or state) elephants, with the marksmen, and the ladies, to comfort and encourage them.

When we had slowly and warily approached the spot where the first tiger lay, he moved not until we were just upon him; when, with a roar that resembled thunder, he rushed upon us. The elephants wheeled off at once, and (for it is not to be described by any quadruped-motion we know, I must therefore coin a term for the occasion) shuffled off. They returned, however, after a flight of about fifty yards, and again approaching the spot where the tiger had lodged himself, towards the skirts of the jungle, he once more rushed forth, and springing at the side of an elephant upon which three of the natives were mounted, at one stroke tore a portion of the pad from under them; and one of the riders, panic struck, fell off. The tiger, however, seeing his enemies in force, returned, slow and indignant, into his shelter; where, the place he lay in being marked, a heavy and well-directed fire was poured in by the principal marksmen; when, pushing in, we saw him in the struggle of death, and growling and foaming he expired.

We then proceeded to seek the others, having first distinguished the spot by pitching a tall spear, and tying to the end of it the muslin of a turban. We roused four in close succession, and with a little variation of circumstances, killed them all; the oldest, and most ferocious of the family, had, however, early in the conflict, very sensibly quitted the scene of action, and escaped to another part of the country.

While the fate of the last and largest was depending, more shots were fired than in the three other attacks; he escaped four several assaults, and taking post in different parts of the jungle, rushed upon us at each wound he received with a kindled rage, and as often put the whole line to flight.

In the last pursuit he singled out the elephant upon which Lady Day was; and was at its tail, with jaws distended, and in the act of rising upon his hind paws to fasten on her, when fortunately she cleared the jungle and a general discharge from the hunters having forced him to give up the chase, he returned to his shelter. The danger, I believe, was not very great; but it was sufficient, when she shall be again invited, to make her stay with Lord Chesterfield, when they attempted to allure him to a second fox-hunt *"I have been."*

The chase being over, we returned in triumph to our encampment, and were followed by the spoils of the morning, and by an accumulating multitude of the peasants from the circumjacent villages, who pressed round an open tent in which we sat at breakfast, with gratulations, blessings, and thanksgivings. The four tigers were laid in front; the natives

viewed them with terror, and some with tears.

An old woman, looking earnestly at the largest tiger, and pointing at times to his tusks, and at times lifting his fore-paws, and viewing his talons, her furrows bathed in tears, in broken and moaning tones narrated something to a little circle composed of three Brahmins and a young woman with a child in her arms. No human misery could pierce the phlegm and apathy of the Brahmins, and with them there was not a feature softened; but horror and sorrow were alternately painted in the face of the female; and, from her clasping at times her child more closely to her breast, I guessed the subject of the old woman's story, and upon inquiry I found that I was right in my conjecture. She was widowed and childless; she owed both her misfortunes to the tigers of that jungle, and most probably to those which then lay dead before her; for they, it was believed, had recently carried off her husband and her two sons grown up to manhood, and now she wanted food: in the phrenzy of her grief she alternately described her loss to the crowd, and in a wild scream demanded her husband and her children from the tigers; indeed it was a piteous spectacle! {1834}

AN ELEPHANT'S RESPONSE TO A TIGER'S PRESENCE
WILLIAM BLANE

Sometimes, when he can be traced to a particular spot where he couches, the elephants are formed into a circle round him, and in that case, when he is roused, he generally attacks the elephant that is nearest to him, by springing upon him with a dreadful roar, and biting at, or tearing him with his claws: but in this case, from his being obliged to shew himself, he is soon dispatched by the number of shots aimed at him; for the greatest difficulty is to rouse him, and get a fair view of him. The elephants all this time are dreadfully frightened, shrieking and roaring in a manner particularly expressive of their fear: and this they begin as soon as they smell him, or hear him growl, and generally endeavour to turn back from the place where the tyger is: some of them, however, but very few, are bold enough to be driven up to attack him, which they do by curling the trunk close up under the mouth, and then charging the tyger with their tusks; or they endeavour to press him to death by falling on him with their knees, or treading him under their feet. If one tyger is killed, it is considered as a good day's sport; but sometimes two or three are killed in one day, or even more, if they meet with a female and her cubs. {1788}

In the *Sunderbunds*, the tigers are particularly fatal to the wood-cutters and salt-makers, who resort there in the dry season; they will not only seize on them in the islands, but even swim to the boats at anchor, and snatch the men from on board. The Pietists, who annually visit one particular island for the sake of washing themselves in the sacred water, often fall victims to these terrible animals: they have such power as to carry off a man with the utmost facility; they will even go full speed with a buffalo, which they will seize out of the field or pasture. In my *Hist. Quad.* i. p. 279, I have given a melancholy instance of their springing among a party of gentlemen and ladies recreating themselves on the islands of the *Ganges*, and carrying away one of the company; such accidents are not uncommon. Another party in the beginning of this century was more fortunate: the company were seated under the shade of trees on the banks of a *Bengalese* river; a lady among them observed a tiger preparing to take its fatal spring and with amazing presence of mind laid hold of an umbrella, and furling it full in the animal's face, terrified it so that it instantly retired. This lady afterwards fell into distress, but was gratefully relieved by the whole party, as each individual might suppose that his particular existence might have been owing to her. I am told that the tigers are sometimes plagued with flies, which settle about their eyes, and frequently make them almost blind; these wander remote from their usual haunts, and give themselves up to destruction. Large rewards are given for destroying of tigers in general; the skins, the claws, and the teeth, are articles of exportation.

The colours of these animals differ to their age or state of health; the ground color of a young or vigorous beast is almost of a brilliant orange; the black intense, and the little white it has is most pure. In old or fickly beasts the black is dull, and the yellow fades to a sandy hue. {1798}

CHRISTMAS DINNER IN THE JUNGLE

JAMES GORDON ELLIOTT

Forsyth was firmly of the opinion that although every sensible man in India spends his Christmas in the jungle he need not forgo the traditional fare.

'We spent a Christmas of considerable joviality in that remote wilderness, dinner consisting of a peacock and sambar tongue, supported by roast haunch of red deer venison, as *pieces de resistance*, with cheetal cutlets and fillets of nilgai veal as *entrees*, followed up by boiled quails and roasted teal, and concluded by the orthodox plum-pudding and mince pies out of tins. Sundry glasses of whiskey toddy, imbibed round a rattling bonfire in front of the tents, were fully justified by the really severe cold after sunset.'

No one went into the jungle without a good supply of claret, and it is by no means uncommon to read of an exceptional day's sport being celebrated by cracking a couple of bottles of well-iced champagne. {1973}

A TIGER ATTACKS A BOAT IN THE SUNDARBANS

HENRY BEVAN

'I send you an account of what took place on board the Experimental Flat, when at anchor astern of the Diana steamer, three hundred yards from the shore, in the river Arpungasseer (Sunderbunds).

'I turned in at ten o'clock, and about three-quarters of an hour after, was awoke by a disturbance on deck, which, from the men rushing backwards and forwards, appeared to me to be an attack on the vessel by dacoits. I immediately jumped out of bed, drew my sword, and was rushing up the hatchway, when I received a tremendous blow on the head and neck; at the same time my clothes were torn from my back, I was knocked down the hatchway, and found myself instantly covered with blood. Seeing a dark object hanging over the hatchway, and from the blow, I was confirmed in the idea that we were attacked; and the scuffle and disturbance still continuing, I thought we were in a very fair way of losing the treasure, and our lives. About a minute afterwards, when I had in some measure recovered from the stunning effects of the blow, I heard Capt. Linquist, commander of the steamer, calling me as loud as he could. I then made a second rush, and, on arriving on deck, saw by the assistance of the torches the men had by that time procured the body of my unfortunate bearer, lying along the starboard side of the hatchway, horribly mangled by a tiger. The animal had seized him, while sitting smoking his hubble-bubble near two sepoys, who were likewise sitting fishing by the larboard after-gangway. The unfortunate man was perfectly dead, having his neck completely bit through and through, besides a severe wound on the right breast. The animal had first got on the dingy belonging to the steamer, which was fastened on the after-gangway, and thence on the flat. One of the men belonging to the dingy, and who was then in her, was in such a fright that he followed the tiger up, and in passing him got a severe wound under the right arm, and some scratches on the back. On examining my own hurts, I found that they were two scratches on the right side of my neck, one on the right ear, one down the head, one over the right eye, and my face terribly bruised. The animal had left the print of his right paw, with the blood of the unfortunate man, on the back of my shirt as he tore it off. Had I been one step higher up the hatchway, I must have been killed, as he had, in making the blow, cut the top step the eighth of an inch deep about two-inches-and-a-half from the edge, with one of his claws. Fearing that, from having tasted blood, it was more than probable he would pay us another visit should we remain, we weighed anchor, and steamed up five miles, where we anchored for the remainder of the night.

'I think it right to state, that Lieut. Marshall is a gentleman of the highest honour and veracity, and that there cannot be any room to suspect his statement of exaggeration.' {1839}

SENSING WATER CURRENTS | THOMAS WILLIAMSON

A gentleman who was for many years in the salt department at *Culnah* and *Joynaghur*, and whose veracity was indubitable, among many anecdotes relating to tigers, assured me such was their cunning, that, often previous to entering the water, for the purpose of swimming over to attack the *molungies*, they would put in a paw to feel the tide: after which they would proceed at a trot up or down the side of the stream, according as the state of the current dictated, when, dashing in, they would rarely fail to land in the situation most favourable to their purpose! I have heard that foxes will do the same. I see nothing unnatural in such conduct. {1807}

BATTLING A TIGER | THOMAS WILLIAMSON

No sooner did the tiger shew himself, than Captain Rotton, with great readiness, bending his body a little to the left, took aim at him as he stood up, crosswise, almost close to the elephant's head. The elephant no sooner espied his enemy, than he knelt down, as is common on such occasions, with the view to strike the tiger through with his tusks. At the same time the tiger, sensible of the device, as suddenly threw himself on his back; thereby evading the intended mischief, and ready to claw the elephant's face with all four feet; which were thus turned upwards. Now, whether Captain Rotton had not been in the habit of joining in such rapid evolutions, or that the elephant forgot to warn him to hold fast, we know not; but, so it happened, that the delicate situation in which he was placed, while taking his aim, added to the quickness of the elephant's change of height forward, combined to project him, without the least obstruction, from his seat, landing him plump on the tiger's belly! This was a species of warfare to which all parties were apparently strangers. The elephant, however fearless in other respects, was alarmed at the strange round mass, the Captain being remarkably fat, which had shot like a sack over his shoulder; while the tiger, judging it to be very ungentlemanlike usage, lost no time in regaining his legs, trotting off at a round pace, and abandoning the field to the victorious Captain. {1807}

THE MAGNIFICENT FOREST | REGINALD HEBER

At length we got off, and after coasting the lake for one mile, went for about thirteen more by a most steep and rugged road, over the neck of Mount Gaughur, through a succession of glens, forests and views of the most sublime and beautiful description. I never saw such prospects before, and had formed no adequate idea of such. My attention was completely strained, and my eyes filled with tears, everything around was so wild and magnificent that man appeared as nothing, and I felt myself as if climbing the steps of the altar of God's great temple. The trees, as we advanced, were in a large proportion fir and cedar, but many were ilex, and to my surprise I still saw even in these Alpine tracts, many venerable peepul trees, on which the white monkeys were playing their gambols. A monkey is also found in these hills as large as a large dog, if my guides are to be believed. Tygers used to be very common and mischievous, but since the English have frequented the country, are scarce, and in comparison, very shy. There are also many wolves and bears, and some chamois, two of which passed near us. {1971}

VALMIK THAPAR

A small species of Delbergia, of a dark colour with reddish veins, exceedingly brittle, are common in these hills. It is a singular circumstance that most of the trees contain large stones in their centre or heart, and there is not the least appearance of the bark having been injured therefore these stones must be generated in the trees...

In the month of April, nearly all the shrubs, and many of the large trees, are covered with blossoms of various tints, delightful to the eye, whilst the organ of smelling is not less gratified by the fragrant perfume which impregnates the whole atmosphere, and is often too powerful to be pleasant. At other times, a straight road may be seen for many miles, with a thick wood on each side, cut down to the distance of fifty yards, forming a most magnificent and regular avenue.

Sometimes you pass through hollows, dreary and dismal, exciting in the traveller sensations not the most pleasing. The idea immediately occurs of their being the haunts of tigers, the prints of whose feet he will actually see in the sand, yet rarely have a view of the animals themselves, as they are remarkably wary, and, on hearing the least noise, skulk into the thick cover, or behind some bush or rock, where, being themselves concealed, they see everything which passes, and, from this their hiding place, often rush unexpectedly on the weary traveller.

At every village near the ghauts are stationed *Ghautwars*, who accompany travellers through the *ghauts*. They have a strange appearance, being generally covered with the skin of a tiger, leopard, or some other animal, and carry with them a bow and arrows, ornamented with peacock's feathers, or a cow's tail, a large shield also ornamented, a spear or a match-lock gun and sword. These people give the travellers confidence, but very little protection.

~

Some idea may be formed how numerous the tigers must have been at one period in Bengal, from the circumstance that one gentleman is reported to have killed upwards of three hundred and sixty. I heard Mr Henry Ramus, at the time he was Judge of the circuit of *Bahar*, declare that he had killed that number, and I was told that others fell by his hand before his death. He kept a particular account of every one which he killed, of which I suppose his friends are now in possession. {1827}

The moon was near the full, and was shining splendidly over the scene, rendering the use of our torches almost superfluous: altogether, I never beheld anything in nature more mystically grand. The abrupt precipices which enclose the pass, looming doubly prominent in a broad flood of solemn light, appeared to stretch their hanging crags and nodding trees towards each other over the thick obscurity of the narrow passage, giving it the effect of a gigantic cavern. At the foot of the nearest projection, a band of wandering *moozaffirs* (peddling merchants) had pitched their little camp, marked by a blazing fire, before which their naked figures were to be seen passing to and fro, like the flitting spirits of a supernatural world.

While still occupied in admiration of this imposing scene, a magic oblivion stole gently over my senses, and carried me more completely away into the regions of enchantment and romance, where the busy imagination, freed from the shackles of the material world, could sport and revel among the wild images of its own creation. I wandered amid the mazes of a dense forest, where I continued during many pleasant hours, delighting in mild zephyrs and limpid rills; when, suddenly, I was attacked by a terrible tigress, larger than Merat church, and more savage than the Begum Sumroo. A desperate struggle ensued, and I was still panting with the encounter, as my heart thumped loudly against my ribs with terror and excitement, when bump came my palki to the ground, at the end of the stage, just in time to save me from being swallowed alive. {1837}

The vessels sailing along the opposite shore appeared hull-down, and the tops of the trees alone gave evidence of the land. The Burrampooter or Bharampootra—whichever name it rejoices in—although it cannot boast the sanctity of the Ganges, must be acknowledged to be the first river of India. It is supposed to derive its source—like the Rhine and Rhone—from the same group of snowy mountains as the Ganges: after making a sweeping course of upwards of one thousand six hundred miles, it again approaches its sacred sister, and the twin rivers pour forth, at the same point, their munificent tribute to the Bay of Bengal.

~

In the afternoon of the following day we anchored in Sauger Roads, at the mouth of the Hooghly. The island of Sauger, in spite of the efforts made to reclaim it, is still a most desolate jungle; and vegetation is there so rapid as to defy all chance of effectually clearing it. Sauger is famous for the size and ferocity of its tigers; and it was on its shores that Major Munro, of menagerie memory, was carried off by one of these animals. They owe their impunity from the sportsmen of Calcutta to their island position alone, which precludes the introduction of elephants.

~

The anchors, which are strangely clumsy machines of bamboos weighted with stones and bound with cocoa ropes, are required at this stage of our voyage, by reason of the risk attendant upon the usual system of luggowing, from the tigers which infest the jungles bordering the streams. During the passage of the Sunderbunds (beautiful forests), to which Culna may be said to be the northern entrance, the dandies, having Major Munro's fate before their eyes, can rarely go ashore to cook their evening meal; the budgerows casting anchor in the middle of the stream, where the luxurious traveller may lounge securely, smoke his moonlight chillum, and listen to the roars of prowling tigers. At this hour, when all nature sleeps, every leaf is at rest, and no harsher sound than the gentle rippling of the water round the prow of the boat disturbs the soft silence of an Indian night, there is something peculiarly awful and startling in the sudden, short, furious, and perhaps near-at-hand voice of the jungle tyrant, whose yellow skin and glaring eyes may sometimes be distinguished through the imperfect light, as he hungrily surveys the floating ark, whose tenants, though barely a dozen paces from his station, are safe from his attacks.

Near this spot, two years ago, on the return of Head-quarters from the siege of Bhurtpore, two boatmen, belonging to an office budgerow, who had rashly determined on the enjoyment of a meal ashore, were themselves made a meal of, ere they had leisure to complete their own. [1832]

VALMIK THAPAR

HUNTING FOR SPORT | VICTOR JACQUEMONT

A few broken legs, and shattered shoulders, are so much a matter of course in Indian hunting, that none is ever undertaken without a surgeon. As for hunting lions and tigers, it is (for gentlemen, I mean) a most harmless amusement, since the game is never sought on horseback, but only on an elephant. Each hunter is perched, like a witness in an English court of justice, in a strong and lofty box, fastened upon the animal's back. He has a little park of artillery near him: namely, a couple of carbines and a brace of pistols. It sometimes happens, but very seldom, that the tiger, when brought to bay, leaps on the elephant's head, but that does not concern us; it is the affair of the conductor (mahout), who is paid twenty-five francs a month, to run the risk of such accidents. In case of death, the latter has at least the satisfaction of a complete revenge, for the elephant does not play the clarionet unconcernedly with his trunk, when he feels he has a tiger for his head dress; he does his best, and the hunter assists him, with a ball point blank. The mahout is, you see, a sort of responsible editor. Another poor devil is behind you, whose duty it is to carry a parasol over your head. His condition is still worse than that of the mahout; when the elephant is frightened, and flies from the tiger, which charges him and springs on his back, the true employment of this man is to be eaten in the gentleman's place. {1834}

VALMIK THAPAR

THE SPLENDID FOREST | JAMES INGLIS

The general colour of the forest is a dingy green, save when a deeper shade here and there shows where the mighty bhur uprears its towering height, or where the crimson flowers of the *seemul* or cotton tree, and the bronze-coloured foliage of the *sunpul* (a tree very like the ornamental beech in shrubberies at home) imparts a more varied colour to the generally pervading dark green of the universal sal.

The varieties of trees are of course almost innumerable, but the sal is so out of all proportion more numerous than any other kind, that the forests well deserve their recognised name. The sal is a fine, hard wood of very slow growth. The leaves are broad and glistening, and in spring are beautifully tipped with a reddish bronze, which gradually tones down into the dingy green which is the prevailing tint. The *sheshum* or *sissod*, a tree with bright green leaves much resembling the birch, the wood of which is invaluable for cart wheels and such-like work, is occasionally met with. There is the *kormbhe*, a very tough wood with a red stringy bark, of which the jungle men make a kind of touchwood for their matchlocks, and the *parass*, whose peculiarity is that at times it bursts into a wondrous wealth of bright crimson blossom without a leaf being on the tree. The *parass* tree in full bloom is gorgeous. After the blossom falls the dark-green leaves come out, and are not much different in colour from the sal. Then there is the *mhowa*, with its lovely white blossoms, from which a strong spirit is distilled, and on which the deer, pigs, and wild bear love to feast. The peculiar sickly smell of the *mhowa* when in flower pervades the atmosphere for a great distance round, and reminds one forcibly of the peculiar sweet, sickly smell of a brewery. The hill *sirres* is a tall feathery-looking tree of most elegant shape, towering above the other forest trees, and the natives strip it of its bark, which they use to poison streams. It seems to have some narcotic or poisonous principle, easily soluble in water, for when put in any quantity in a stream or piece of water, it causes all the fish to become apparently paralyzed and rise to the surface, where they float about quite stupified and helpless, and become an easy prey to the poaching 'Banturs' and 'Moosahurs' who adopt this wretched mode of fishing.

~

Along the banks of the streams vegetation gets very luxurious, and among the thick undergrowth are found some lovely ferns, broad-leaved plants, and flowers of every hue, all alike nearly scentless. Here is no odorous breath of violet or honeysuckle, no delicate perfume of primrose or sweetbriar, only a musty, dank, earthy smell which gets more and more pronounced as the mists rise along with the deadly vapours of the night. Sleeping in these forests is very unhealthy. There is a most fatal miasma all through the year, less during the hot months, but very bad during and immediately after the annual rains; and in September and October nearly every soul in the jungly tracts is smitten with fever. The vapour only rises to a certain height above the ground, and at the elevation of ten feet or so, I believe one could sleep in the jungles with impunity; but it is dangerous at all times to sleep in the forest, unless at a considerable elevation. The absence of all those delicious smells which make a walk through the woodlands at home so delightful, is conspicuous in the sal forests, and another of the most noticeable features is the extreme silence, the oppressive stillness that reigns.

The hornbill darts with a succession of long bounding flights from one tall tree to another. The large woodpecker taps a hollow tree close by, his gorgeous plumage glistening like a mimic rainbow in the sun. A flight of green parrots sweeps screaming above your head, the *golden oriole* or mango bird, the *koel*, with here and there a red-tufted *bulbul*, make a faint attempt at a chirrup; but as a rule the deep silence is unbroken, save by the melancholy hoot of some blinking owl, and the soft monotonous coo of the ring dove or the green pigeon. The exquisite honey-sucker, as delicately formed as the petal of a fairy flower, flits noiselessly about from blossom to blossom. The natives call it the 'Muddpenah' or drinker of honey. There are innumerable butterflies of graceful shape and gorgeous colours; what few birds there are have beautiful plumage; there is a faint rustle of leaves, a faint, far hum of insect life; but it feels so silent, so unlike the woods at home. You are oppressed by the solemn stillness, and feel almost nervous as you push warily along, for at any moment a leopard, wolf, or hyena may get up before you, or you may disturb the siesta of a sounder of pig, or a herd of deer.

Up in those forests on the borders of Nepaul, which are called the *morung*, there are a great many varieties of parrot, all of them very beautiful. There is first the common green parrot, with a red beak, and a circle of salmon-coloured feathers round its neck; they are very noisy and destructive, and flock together to the fields where they do great damage to the crops. The *lutkun sooga* is an exquisitely-coloured bird, about the size of a sparrow. The *ghurāl*, a large red and green parrot, with a crimson beak. The *tota*, a yellowish-green colour, and the male with a breast as red as blood; they call

it the *amereet bhela*. Another lovely little parrot, the *taeteea sooga*, has a green body, red head, and black throat; but the most showy and brilliant of all the tribe is the *putsoogee*. The body is a rich living green, red wings, yellow beak, and black throat; there is a tuft of vivid red as a topknot, and the tail is a brilliant blue; the under feathers of the tail being a pure snowy white.

At times the silence is broken by a loud, metallic, bell-like cry, very like the yodel you hear in the Alps. You hear it rise sharp and distinct, 'Looralei!' and as suddenly cease. This is the cry of the *kookoor ghēt*, a bird not unlike a small pheasant, with a reddish-brown back and a fawn-coloured breast. The *sherra* is another green parrot, a little larger than the *putsoogee*, but not so beautifully coloured.

There is generally a green, slime-covered, sluggish stream in all these forests, its channel choked with rotting leaves and decaying vegetable matter. The water should never be drunk until it has been boiled and filtered. At intervals the stream opens out and forms a clear rush-fringed pool, and the trees receding on either bank leave a lovely grassy glade, where the deer and nilghau come to drink. On the glassy bosom of the pool in the centre, fine duck, mallard, and teal, can frequently be found, and the rushes round the margin are to a certainty good for a couple of brace of snipe.

Sometimes on a withered branch overhanging the stream, you can see perched the *ahur*, or great black fish-hawk. It has a grating, discordant cry, which it utters at intervals as it sits pluming its black feathers above the pool. The dark ibis and the ubiquitous paddy-bird are of course also found here; and where the land is low and marshy, and the stream crawls along through several channels, you are sure to come across a couple of red-headed *sarus*, serpent birds, a crane, and a solitary heron. The *moosahernee* is a black and white bird, I fancy a sort of ibis, and is good eating. The *dokahur* is another fine big bird, black body and white wings, and as its name (derived from *dokha*, a shell) implies, it is the shell-gatherer, or snail eater, and gives good shooting. {1878}

THE TIGER AT CAMP | JAMES INGLIS

Suddenly there was a hush. Every sound seemed to stop simultaneously as if by pre-arranged concert. Then three men were seen rushing madly along the elevated ridge surrounding one of the tanks. I recognised one of my peons, and with him two cowherds. Their head-dresses were all disarranged, and their parted lips, heaving chests, and eyes blazing with excitement, shewed that they were brimful of some unusual message.

Now arose such a bustle in the camp as no description could adequately portray. The elephants trumpeted and piped; the *syces*, or grooms, came rushing up with eager queries; the villagers bustled about like so many ants aroused by the approach of a hostile foe; my pack of terriers yelped out in chorus; the pony neighed; the Cabool stallion plunged about; my servants came rushing from the shelter of the tent verandah with disordered dress; the ducks rose in a quacking crowd, and circled round and round the tent; and the cry arose of 'Bagh Bagh! Khodamund! Arree Bap re Bap! Ram Ram, Seeta Ram!'

Breathless with running, the men now tumbled up, hurriedly salaamed, and then each with gasps and choking stops, and pell-mell volubility, and amid a running fire of cries, queries, and interjections from the mob, began to unfold their tale. There was an infuriated tigress at the other side of the nullah, or dry watercourse, she had attacked a herd of buffaloes, and it was believed that she had cubs.

It was the wildest sight I have ever seen in connection with animal life. The buffaloes were drawn together in the form of a crescent; their eyes glared fiercely, and as they advanced in a series of short runs, stamping with their hoofs, and angrily lashing their tails, their horns would come together with a clanging, clattering crash, and they would paw the sand, snort and toss their heads, and behave in the most extraordinary manner.

The cause of all this commotion was not far to seek. Directly in front, retreating slowly, with stealthy, prowling, crawling steps, and an occasional short, quick leap or bound to one side or the other, was a magnificent tigress, looking the very personification of baffled fury. Ever and anon she crouched down to the earth, tore up the sand with her claws, lashed her tail from side to side, and with lips retracted, long moustaches quivering with wrath, and hateful eyes scintillating with rage and fury, she seemed to meditate an attack on the angry buffaloes. The serried array of clashing horns, and the ponderous bulk of the herd, seemed however to daunt the snarling vixen; at their next rush she would bound back a few paces, crouch down, growl, and be forced to move back again, by the short, blundering rush of the crowd.

All the calves and old cows were in the rear of the herd, and it was not a little comical to witness their ungainly attitudes. They would stretch their clumsy necks, and shake their heads, as if they did not rightly understand what was going on. Finding that if they stopped too long to indulge their curiosity, there was a danger of their getting separated from the fighting members of the herd, they would make a stupid, headlong, lumbering lurch forward, and jostle each other, in their blundering panic.

It was a grand sight. The tigress was the embodiment of lithe and savage beauty, but her features expressed the wildest baffled rage. I could have shot the striped vixen over and over again, but I wished to keep her for my friends, and I was thrilled with the excitement of such a novel scene. {1878}

VALMIK THAPAR

In most of our hunting parties on the Koosee, we had some twenty or thirty elephants, and frequently six or eight howdahs. These expeditions were very pleasant, and we lived luxuriously. For real sport ten elephants and two or three tried comrades—not more—is much better. With a short, easily-worked line, that can turn and double, and follow the tiger quickly, and dog his every movement, you can get far better sport, and bring more to bag, than with a long unwieldy line, that takes a considerable time to turn and wheel, and in whose onward march there is of necessity little of the silence and swiftness which are necessary elements in successful tiger shooting.

I have been out with a line of seventy-six elephants and fourteen howdahs. This was on 16th March 1875. It was a magnificent sight to see the seventy-six huge brutes in the river together, splashing the water along their heated sides to cool themselves, and sending huge waves dashing against the crumbling banks of the rapid stream. It was no less magnificent to see their slow stately march through the swaying, crashing jungle. What an idea of irresistible power and ponderous strength the huge creatures gave us, as they heaved through the tangled brake, crushing everything in their resistless progress...

In the captain's howdah are three flags. A blue flag flying means that only tiger or rhinoceros are to be shot at. A red flag signifies that we are to have general firing, in fact that we may blaze away at any game that may be afoot, and the white flag shews us that we are on our homeward way, and then also may shoot at anything we can get, break the line, or do whatever we choose. On the flanks are generally posted the best shots of the party. The captain, as a rule, keeps to the centre of the line...

In the howdah we carry ample supplies of vesuvians. We light and drop these as they blaze into the dried grass and withered leaves as we move along, and soon a mighty wall of roaring flame behind us, attests the presence of the destroying element. We go diagonally upwind, and the flames and smoke thus surge and roar and curl and roll, in dense blinding volumes, to the rear and leeward of our line. The roaring of the flames sounds like the maddened surf of an angry sea, dashing in thunder against an iron-bound coast. The leaping flames mount up in fiery columns, illuminating the fleecy clouds of smoke with an unearthly glare. The noise is deafening; at times some of the elephants get quite nervous at the fierce roar of the flames behind, and try to bolt across country. The fire serves two good purposes. It burns

up the old withered grass, making room for the fresh succulent sprouts to spring, and it keeps all the game in front of the line, driving the animals before us, as they are afraid to break back and face the roaring wall of flame. A seething, surging sea of flame, several miles long, encircling the whole country in its fiery belt, sweeping along at night with the roar of a storm-tossed sea; the flames flickering, swelling, and leaping up in the dark night, the fiery particles rushing along amid clouds of lurid smoke, and the glare of the serpent-like line reddening the horizon, is one of those magnificent spectacles that can only be witnessed at rare intervals among the experiences of a sojourn in India. Words fail to depict its grandeur, and the utmost skill of Doré could not render on canvas, the weird, unearthly magnificence of a jungle fire, at the culmination of its force and fury. {1878}

THE TIGER AND THE RHINO | WILLIAM KNIGHTON

The steady guard of the larger animal and the stealthy, cat-like attack of the smaller—the lowered snout of the one and the gleaming tooth of the other—the cocked horn, kept valorously in an attitude of defiant guard, and the bullet head, with its gleaming eyes, together with the brawny claws—were all things to be watched and to interest. The rhinoceros, however, is secure from attack on his back, and when the tiger springs, his claws get no hold in the plate-like covering of his antagonist. Should the rhinoceros be overthrown by the tiger's weight, then the fate of the former is sealed; he is ripped and torn up and gnawed from beneath, as a tiger only can rip, and tear up, and gnaw; I have heard of, but have never witnessed, such results following the tiger's assault.

In nine cases out of ten the rhinoceros gains the advantage; the tiger springs, and springs, and springs again, still baffled by the voluminous armor-like skin of his antagonist, until, at some moment or other, the rhinoceros seizes his opportunity, and succeeds in inflicting a severe wound with his formidable horn. The tiger then declines the combat, and easily escapes its unwieldy enemy, should the rhinoceros take it into his head to attack. {1855}

THE TIGER THAT KILLED A CHEETAH | WILLIAM RICE

One day...while thus tracking a tiger, as silently as possible, we found that the brute must have been moving off a long way just in front of us, for we came upon his fresh prints over the marks made by a flock of goats that had been driven along a road only a few minutes before. This proves how easily the "large game" moves about, even in the day time, during such cool weather. On still further following this tiger's tracks, we came upon a dead "hunting cheetah" (or hunting leopard) that had just been killed by the tiger, he having, no doubt, surprised the "cheetah" asleep, for the marks of the tiger's claws, from which blood still was flowing, were quite plain on the body.

This animal (harmless enough except for deer) he must have killed in mere wantonness. On another occasion we found a hyaena that had been thus murdered by a tiger, perhaps for heedlessly passing too close to him. The paw alone had been used to kill these victims, for there were no teeth marks. It struck me as rather odd to find a "hunting cheetah" in the hills, for these animals live mostly in the plains, where they hunt deer or antelope in parties of four or five together, in the same manner as the wolves do, secreting themselves in bushes at different points while one of their number chases the buck. On its passing the ambuscade they pounce out upon the little gazelle, or take up the running in turn as it races past them. {1857}

THE TIGER'S FOREST | LEOPOLD GRIMSTON PAGET

I had often longed to see the luxuriance of tropical vegetation in the dense masses of a *real jungle*, and now I must say that its beauty far surpassed my most vivid imaginings. The variety of foliage, in colour of every shade, from brightest green to brilliant scarlet, the large size of many of the leaves, and the graceful pendant branches, connected by creepers and parasites, hanging from every spray, forming a tangled mass, with sunbeams glinting through it; these, and the splendid wild flowers on every side, formed a scene almost *unreal* in its beauty, though the roar of a cheetah, close to our path, reminded one of the fierce inhabitants of these lovely bowers. I was sorry I did not see the creature, but we came across the trail of a huge boa constrictor in the dusty road, nearly two feet wide, and a short time ago one was killed near here, measuring seventy-six feet long! Quantities of the silk-cotton trees grow by the roadside, with their splendid white flowers, which are collected by the people in heaps as they fall off. {1865}

THE FEROCIOUS TIGER | C. E. GOULDSBURY

I called to him to get on the elephant at once, but the words were hardly
out of my mouth when there was a deafening roar, and the next moment
a huge mass of black and yellow sprang from the hole right on to the poor
old man. The latter kept his head, and, with marvellous coolness, fell flat
on his face as he saw the beast coming, thinking he would spring past and
over him.

But the tiger naturally was not in the best of tempers. He had been
driven off his kill, and had been considerably hustled and worried, and he
meant business now; so instead of springing over, he deliberately jumped on
the unfortunate man. Then followed a scene the recollection of which haunts
me still. Being some twenty feet above I could not see very clearly what was
actually going on, as the huge body of the tiger completely covered the old
man, but the loud angry growls of the brute and the manner in which he
appeared to be biting and tearing with his teeth and claws was too horrible
to witness, more especially as I was powerless to render any assistance. To
fire was impossible, and it would have been madness to have attempted it,

VALMIK THAPAR

as I could not possibly have hit the tiger without hitting the man. Moreover, unless I could kill him instantaneously, I should only infuriate him more, and with the brute moving every second, it was impossible to make sure of hitting him in a vital part. The temptation, however, to do so was hard to resist. The rifle was in my hand and at full cock; I brought it to my shoulder, my elephant was as steady as a rock, and I was just about to risk a shot at the tiger's head, when providentially it occurred to me that a sudden noise might cause him to release his victim; so calling upon the mahout (elephant driver) and my orderly sitting behind me to join, we yelled and shouted with all our might, and so hideously appalling must have been the noise we made that we had hardly begun when the tiger sprang off the man and into the jungle. All that I have described occupied actually about two minutes—probably less. {1916}

The two tigers were in the piece of jungle to my left, but as I was watching them, one suddenly disappeared, and some five minutes later, I caught sight of it for an instant peering out of the opposite cover!—having evidently crossed over through the heavy jungle behind me, as I must otherwise have seen it crossing.

Meanwhile the buffalo—apparently finding the grass in the glade to their liking—had stopped and commenced grazing, when suddenly, from the spot where I had first seen them, out rushed a tiger with a roar so loud and terrifying that the buffalo, taken completely unawares, seemed quite demoralized for the moment, and before they had time to recover and assume their ordinary defensive attitude, the tiger in the opposite cover—where it had lain concealed—now attacked them too!

The scene that now followed is almost impossible to describe—not only because of the rapidity with which it was enacted, but in the confusion that ensued it was difficult to follow the sequence in which the events took place.

The buffalo, notwithstanding the unexpected second attack, made some attempt to concentrate, but the tigers were too quick for them, the first had already seized its victim, and having brought it to the ground, was biting at its throat, while the second, without a moment's hesitation, sprang upon another, and seizing it by the neck with teeth and claws, seemed to kill it instantaneously but this was the extent of their ravages, for the herd had at length succeeded in packing together, presenting a formidable array of lowered heads and pointed horns against which no soft-skinned animal like a tiger could possibly prevail, nor did they attempt to, but, growling savagely the while, confined their attentions to the two they had killed. {1916}

We had proceeded in this manner about two hundred yards when we came to a small clearing some thirty yards wide. Traversing this we were about to re-enter the jungle, when, without the smallest warning, the tiger, with a roar appalling in its volume and ferocity, sprang at the elephant's head.

Rendered wary by the extreme suddenness of his previous appearance, I was fortunately prepared, and, as he sprang, fired both barrels almost simultaneously, the next moment tumbling backwards into the howdah, as the elephant, turning sharp round, made off for all he was worth in the direction from which we had come.

Now came the most unpleasant half-hour I have ever gone through. The jungle, as already stated, was what is known as tree jungle, and therefore one to be traversed with extreme care and caution, and of necessity very lowly, when in a howdah. The reader may, therefore, imagine my feelings when, on recrossing the small clearing, we dashed into the cover at railway speed, regardless alike of branches, thorns, and creepers, and tore through them at a rate which, though necessarily reduced, was yet sufficient to sweep off howdah, guns and riders, landing the latter, perhaps, into the very mouth of the tiger, who, for all we knew, might be pursuing us!

How we escaped being brained, or at least swept off, I have no conception, for, as in most situations of the kind, it all seemed to happen so

quickly that we never quite knew what actually did happen. One very vivid recollection, however—which a bump the size of an egg on my forehead helped me to recall for some days after—was a violent collision with a large branch. The bump aforesaid was not the only evidence of this *rencontre*, for on looking for my pith hat afterwards, all I could find of it was the rim, the crown being found later in the branches of a tree! We had also apparently collided with one or two other hard substances, for my coat was badly torn about the shoulders, both of which felt extremely sore. {1916}

VALMIK THAPAR

JUNGLE LIFE | WALTER CAMPBELL

I pray you, Friend, to fancy yourself returned from a fatiguing ramble in
the forest, hot and dusty, but elate with success; that you have enjoyed
a refreshing bath, and that, having exchanged your hunting dress for light
linen clothing, and thrust your wearied feet into a pair of embroidered
Indian slippers, you are seated in a large airy tent, the canvas walls of which
are raised on one side to admit the refreshing breeze. The table is covered
with the finest damask, and loaded with goodly viands, intermixed with
plate and sparkling crystal. Take, for example, a haunch of venison that
would do no discredit to the best park in England; a cold wild boar's head
soused in vinegar; wild boar chops, combining the flavour of venison with

that of the most delicate pork; a noble venison pasty, over which Friar Tuck would have pronounced a benison with watering lips; stews, curries, and ragouts, composed of every variety of small game, and cunningly devised by Elliot's incomparable *artiste*, the Portuguese 'babachee'; marrow-bones of bison and deer, and a dozen other sylvan dainties too numerous to mention. A host of native servants clothed in white muslin, with scarlet turbans and sashes, stand around, watching with anxious looks to anticipate your slightest wish; and in a remote corner you may observe a dusky figure (the high-priest of Bacchus) squatted on his heels, and intent on cooling to the exact pitch some dozen long-necked bottles that conjure up visions of ruby claret and sparkling champagne. The bronzed features of your companions, glowing with healthful excitement, and beaming with good fellowship, smile around the hospitable board. And the gay scene is lighted up by a profusion of wax candles in tall glass shades, to protect them from the gentle breathing of the night air, which, playing round the tent, fans your heated blood into refreshing coolness.

Fancy yourself snugly ensconced in an arm-chair, recounting your own adventures, and listening to those of your brother sportsmen. Fancy the interesting discussions, the comparing of notes and drawings that takes place between the scientific members of the party, and the good-humoured jokes that are bandied among the less learned but lighter-hearted youngsters. Fancy all this, friend, and say if you can imagine anything more delightful than the mode of life of an Indian hunting party...

After dinner we adjourn to the outside of the tent, to sip our coffee and smoke our hookahs; and retire at an early hour, with cool heads, to ensure steady nerves in the morning.

Having bathed and refreshed ourselves, breakfast is the cry; and, at the word, a host of obsequious natives appear, bearing curries and pillaws, eggs, omelettes, dried fish, sardines, and venison cutlets, claret, green tea, and coffee, iced water and fruit, and other luxuries which none but an Indian breakfast can boast. {1864}

THE TIGER AND THE WILD HOG | WALTER CAMPBELL

We had just passed the thicket, and were making a short turn round the end of it; when, to my utter dismay, I found myself face to face, and within twenty yards of a royal tiger, busily engaged in tearing up the carcass of a wild hog he had just killed. My hair almost stood on end, as the brute raised his enormous head, smeared with blood, and glared upon us with his malignant green eyes. Mohadeen dropped his cheroot, and remained motionless as a statue, with his keen eye steadily fixed upon that of the tiger. I knew enough of the nature of the animal to be aware that it was more dangerous to retreat than to stand fast but thinking that a charge was now inevitable, I was determined to have 'the first word of flyting,' as we say in Scotland, and was about to raise my rifle, when Mohadeen, without removing his gaze from the tiger, laid his hand upon my arm, and kept it down with a firm grasp. The tiger growled and shewed his teeth, but unable to withstand the fascination of the human eye, he gradually withdrew the paw, which jealously clutched his prey, crouched together, as if appalled by the steady gaze of the savage, turned slowly round, and uttering a sulky growl, slunk away into the long grass. No sooner was his back turned, than Mohadeen, clapping his hands to his mouth, sent forth that peculiar wild yell, which appears to strike terror to the heart of the most savage animal, and we instantly heard the stealthy tread of the tiger change to a bounding gallop, as he fled in dismay from that unearthly cry. [1864]

MAN AND TIGER | WALTER CAMPBELL

Before dismissing the subject of tiger-hunting, I cannot resist introducing a ludicrous adventure told me by an old Kandeish sportsman, in whose own words I shall endeavour to relate it.

"We were closing in upon a wounded tiger, whose hind leg was broken. Some Bheels, who had run up the trail to a patch of high grass, were drawing back, now that their game was found, when the brute started up behind the elephant, and charged the nearest man, a little hairy, bandy-legged, square-built oddity, more like a satyr than a human being. Away spun the Bheel for the nearest tree, with the wounded tiger roaring at his haunches. By the Prophet, sir, it would have done your heart good to see the springs the active little sinner made. Just in time he reached the tree, and scrambled into a branch, hardly out of reach. There he sat, crouched up into the smallest possible compass, expecting every moment to be among the Houris. The tiger made several desperate efforts to reach him, but the broken hind leg failing, he dropped back exhausted. It was now the Bheel's turn. He saw that he was safe, and accordingly commenced a philippic against the father and mother, sisters, aunts, nieces, and children, of his helpless enemy; who sat with glaring eyeballs fixed on his contemptible little reviler, and roaring as if his heart would break with rage. As the excited orator warmed by his

own eloquence, he began skipping from branch to branch, grinning and chattering with the emphasis of an enraged baboon; pouring out a torrent of the most foul abuse; and attributing to the tiger's family in general, and his female relatives in particular, every crime and atrocity that ever was or will be committed. Occasionally he varied his insults by roaring, in imitation of the tiger; and at last, when fairly exhausted, he leant forward till he appeared within the grasp of the enraged animal, and ended this inimitable scene by spitting in his face. So very absurd was the whole farce, that we who were at first shoving up the elephant, in alarm for the safety of our little hairy friend, ended by laughing till our sides ached; and it was not without reluctance that we put an end to the scene by firing a death-volley." {1864}

Elliot ordered the 'mahout' to urge the elephant forward at his utmost speed. I shall never forget the excitement of that moment. My brother and I, both novices in tiger-hunting, were almost in a rabid state; and in our anxiety to rescue the doomed wretch from his impending fate, we stamped with impatience, and abused the driver for not exerting himself sufficiently, although he was plying the goad with all his strength, making the blood flow, and extorting a scream of pain from the unfortunate elephant at every stroke.

But all was in vain. Before we were halfway down the hill, the tiger had caught sight of the poor helpless drunkard, standing directly in his path, and his doom was sealed. He might still have made an effort to escape, for he had a long start; but he appeared paralysed by fear when he saw the tiger making directly towards him with terrific bounds. The brute was upon him with the speed of light. We saw him rear for an instant over his victim, who attempted to defend himself with his sword and shield. One savage roar rang through the soul of the stricken wretch, and he was dashed to the ground, amidst a cloud of dust, through which we could just distinguish the agitated forms of the tiger and the wretched man, writhing like a crushed worm in his grip. It was over in an instant. The tiger trotted off, sulkily, to a small patch of thorny bushes, and being now excited to madness by the taste of blood, stood boldly awaiting our attack.

The elephant was pushed forward with all speed, the tiger roaring furiously as we advanced, and the moment his splendid head appeared, a volley from six barrels sent him back staggering into the centre of the bush. He rallied instantly, and made a brilliant charge close up to the elephant's trunk, when he was again turned by a well-directed volley from the spare guns, and retreated growling to his lair.

We now retired a short distance to reload; and when we advanced again, the tiger, although bleeding at every pore, rushed forth to meet us, as savage as ever. He was again turned before he could spring on the elephant, and again dragged forward his bleeding body to the charge, roaring as if his heart would burst with impotent rage. We now let him come up quite close, so that every ball might tell, and gave him shot after shot, till he crawled back exhausted into the bushes. We followed him up, and in a last expiring effort to reach the elephant, he was shot dead, while struggling to make good his charge. He was game to the last, and Elliot, who has killed many tigers, says he never saw one die more gallantly. {1864}

A TIGERS IN THE HOUSE

CUSTOMS OFFICER FROM THE NORTH-WEST
PROVINCES OF INDIA

As he was about to tell his friend where would be a good place to have a hankwa, a servant came running in to say that two tigers were coming directly towards the bungalow, and were close to it then.

Not believing the man's word, the planter got up and went to the door to see for himself, the servant meanwhile vanishing. Hardly had he looked out, when, stepping back quickly, he told his friend instantly to climb up the other side of the bungalow, get on the cross beam, and not stir for his life.

Seeing the planter climbing, the friend climbed too, and both had scarcely got seated when a large tiger showed itself in the verandah, at the door of the room. The brute gave a look in, but, not satisfied, came in half its length, and after a searching look around, and a stare aloft, it upset a stool that happened to be close to the door.

The noise that the stool made in falling startled the tiger, causing it to make a quick step back into the verandah, and this sudden action alarmed the tigress, which was close behind, causing her to spring off the verandah into the compound and walk off. The tiger, seeing its mate going away, tried to recall her by a sort of low growl, but instead of returning she broke into a trot, and the tiger after her.

When the tiger came up to its mate there was a matrimonial squabble between them, the two growling at each other, and clapper-clawing in a sort of friendly way. The noise they made showed them to be at a safe distance, and then the planter and his friend descended from their elevated positions.
{1874}

While engaged over their breakfast, the butler reported that a man had brought a porcupine for sale, if the gentlemen would like to have it…

The porcupine, after being cut open, cleaned, and stuffed with proper seasoning, is enveloped, quills and all, in a thick paste of coarse atta (flour with the pollard and bran in it); the cook then digs a hole in the ground, and smoothing it all round with thin mud, puts in a quantity of live coals. When the hole becomes well heated, the ashes are withdrawn, more live coals put in, and the porcupine on them, and all covered up with live coals and wood. After a sufficient time has elapsed to allow for the porcupine to be properly cooked, the black mass is taken out of the hole and cut open, the head is then cut off, and the skin (the quills coming with it) peeled off easily, the rest being sent to the table, looking and tasting very much like a well-fed, sucking porker…

The butler was then ordered to bring the sambhur meat and receive orders for dinner, directing him also to have plenty of hot water got ready at once. When the sambhur was brought, the president directed the horns of the head to be knocked off, and the eyes and tongue removed, the latter to be put in pickle; the shins, after removing the hocks, were then cut off from the knee-joint, and the head and shins plunged into hot water to wash and scald them. After soaking until the stronger hairs were removable by hand, the head and shins were taken out, carefully shaved with a razor, and again well washed with hot water. Next, the head and shins were broken, the brain of the head and marrow of the shins extracted, and, after placing the whole in a large dekchee (Indian copper cooking vessel) or saucepan, with some salt, and enough water to cover it all an inch deep, the cook had strict orders to let it boil for one hour, and then merely simmer for five hours, or about six hours altogether (adding now and then boiling water enough to keep the contents just covered), when the president, tasting it, put in a few drops of sundry herb essences, and a pinch or two of celery salt, with pepper and more salt to taste…

Knowing that the party would be very thirsty after their shooting ramble, the caterer, to give them a refreshing surprise, had a quantity of tamarind-and-honey sherbet prepared, which was pronounced delicious by all, and entirely superseded Bass and other drinks…

The smoked deer's tongues, venison steaks, fried fish, curry, and jerked neelgye made into bhurta, left nothing to be desired.

The bhurta gave general satisfaction as a capital zest, and is made as follows—Smoke-cured lean of any kind of meat, or fish, is scraped or pounded fine, young onions and green chillies, or capsicums (in quantity according to individual taste), cut up small, with a pinch of salt, is then added, and all mixed well together. The remainder of any kind of cold boiled or roast meat is frequently utilized in this way. This zest is usually eaten with curry and rice, but spread on bread and butter is not bad...

The soup gave decided satisfaction, especially to their guest, and was followed by hunter's pie, hunter's stew, roast saddle of venison with tamarind sauce, deer's tongues with ham, venison cutlets with tomato sauce, and three or four kinds of curries, winding up with some peculiar Indian pies, and other sweet preparations, until the malcontents were not only satisfied, but were pleased to declare that the caterer, khansamah, and all concerned had surpassed themselves, that such a dinner would not soon be forgotten, and that they only hoped none of them might have the nightmare. {1874}

This most dangerous of all accidents occurring among trees, was attended with the not unusual result—the howdah was crushed against an overhanging branch, and swept from the elephant's back. Major A. and the native in the khawas—that is the back seat of the howdah—were likewise swept away, but seizing the branch, hung suspended as the elephant passed from under them. The native being light and active swung himself on to the branch and was safe. Major A. not having so secure a hold, and probably not being so agile, was unable to do so, and after hanging suspended for a few moments, vainly attempting to get on to the branch, at length dropped to the ground, and, as ill luck would have it, fell on to the wounded tiger's back, which was lying under the tree. Being wounded in the spine the tiger was unable to move his hind-quarters, and could not rise, but retaining all his vigour in the fore part of the body and limbs, struck at and drew Major A. within his grip, and, infuriated with rage, wreaked his fury on the unfortunate gentleman; seizing him first by one leg he severely lacerated it, then leaving that, he seized the other, and bit it more severely. Major A. was utterly unable to get away from the infuriated animal, and spent some dreadful moments in this awful position. His companion, whose elephant had also taken fright, shortly after reappeared on the scene, and gave the wounded tiger the *coup de grâce*. Major A., frightfully wounded and exhausted by loss of blood, was then carried some distance into the nearest station, where it was found necessary to amputate one leg. Notwithstanding his serious injuries and the capital operation, he recovered, and…lived to return to England. {1875}

THE TUSSLE WITH THE CROCODILE | JOSEPH FAYRER

It is said that the tiger sometimes attacks the alligators, or gurriáls, as they lie basking on the banks of the rivers, or on sand-banks, the margins of which are often fringed with the tamarisk, long grass, or other congenial cover. This may be possible when other food has failed, and it is said that it occasionally happens that he falls a victim in the attempt, more than one instance being recorded of his having been seized by the powerful jaws of the alligator, dragged into the river, and drowned. There is a fine illustration of a tiger being so treated by a large alligator, in a picture by Wolf, recently published. As the tiger is found on the margins of swamps and rivers which teem with these great saurians, it is possible that such an incident may occasionally occur, though I confess I feel inclined to relegate it to the category of travellers' stories. It is said also that he is sometimes surprised and destroyed by the great python (P. Mollurus) of the Indian jungle and swamps; and though I have no knowledge of, or scarcely any belief in such an occurrence, I think it not absolutely impossible; for I have seen and helped to kill a python nearly twenty feet in length, which probably would have been equal to the destruction of a tiger, had it been so inclined, and had the opportunity occurred. {1875}

THE RECORDS AND THE SUPERSTITIONS | JOSEPH FAYRER

Speaking of the destruction of life by wild animals, Captain R. says, in Lower Bengal alone, in a period of six years ending in 1866, 13,400 human beings were killed by wild animals, whilst 18,196 wild animals were killed in the same period at a cost of 65,000 rupees; and it appears, moreover, that the Government reports show that in these six years ending in 1866, 4,218 persons were killed by tigers, 1,407 by leopards, 4,287 by wolves, and the remainder by other animals; the tiger and wolf thus claiming nearly equal shares. The worst district in Bengal Proper is that of Rungpore, in the Rajshahye Division, the yearly loss of life being between fifty-five and sixty persons. In Bengal Proper alone about 1,200 tigers are killed annually; of these four per cent are cubs. Next to Bengal come the Central Provinces, and then certain parts of Madras.

> The Chief Commissioner's reports of the Central Provinces show that in 1866-67, 372; in 1867-68, 289; in 1868-69, 285 persons were killed by tigers.

The natives of India, especially the Hindoos, hold the tiger, as they do the cobra, in superstitious awe. Many would not kill him if they could, for they fear that he will haunt them or do them mischief after death. Some they regard as being the tenement of a spirit, which not only renders them immortal, but confers increased powers of mischief. In many parts of India the peasants will hardly mention the tiger by name. They either call him, as in Purneah, gidhur (jackal), janwar (the beast), or they will not name him at all; and it is the same in the case of the wolf. But though they will not always themselves destroy him, they are quite willing that others should do so, for they will point out his whereabouts and be present at his death; and the delight evinced thereat is intense, for it often relieves a whole village from an incubus of no slight weight, and saves the herdsman from his weekly loss of cattle. The conversation and remarks made by these villagers round the fallen tiger are often very amusing and characteristic. {1875}

"The writer of 'Three Months in the Forests of Travankor' describes the following scene in the forest—'Threading our way carefully, single file, along the narrow track, now cutting a path through the dense jungle with our hunting knives (essential appendages to an expedition such as ours), again getting to a clearer space where the fresh breezes fanned our heated brow, and glimpses of wooded hills and slopes and valleys appeared through the trees, but still proceeding steadily upwards, we at length came to an open space on the verge of a steep and precipitous hill side, where we sat down to rest and enjoy the beauty of the scene. On one hand towered the mighty forest trees rising tier above tier to the blue heavens; on the other, a yawning precipice sloped down to where a mountain torrent settled among great boulders of rock far below us. While we were gazing in quiet admiration of the scene, a rustling of the trees and sounds of hurried footsteps rapidly approaching, made us turn hastily round, and a magnificent sight greeted our astonished eyes. A noble stag, his antlers thrown back in the act of listening, his nostrils dilated in terror, was flying down the path straight towards us, and in another instant the cause of his terror became apparent. A splendid tiger was following in his path, rushing down the narrow gorge, leaping over every obstacle that barred his way, and momentarily gaining on his prey. The stag flew on, not seeing us in his wild haste, until he was so close we could almost have touched him, when his terrified gaze fell upon us, standing rifle in hand, though we refrained from firing, seeing the tiger behind. To go on was death from our bullets, behind the tiger was close upon him, and without an instant's hesitation he turned and took a flying leap over the precipice, the tiger (who had never once caught sight of us, so intently was he gazing at his prey), following in his excitement, and in a moment both the noble animals were lost to sight among the branches of the trees, where they must have been dashed into a thousand pieces before they reached the bottom.'" {1875}

TIGERS FIGHT OVER A KILL | H. A. LEVESON

On one occasion we witnessed a grand combat between two tigers for the possession of a deer, and this episode forms the subject of our sketch. Our goat-boy saw a tiger strike down a buck whilst watching his charge, and scared him from his prey by shouting at him and throwing stones. When the coast was clear, he gave us the information, and towards evening we took post behind some rocks, that commanded the spot. We had hardly spread our rugs to make ourselves comfortable when we heard a rustling in the bushes, and a fine male tiger came crouching along the edge of the water, smelling the ground like a pointer on scent. Although he was within point-blank range, and offered an easy shot, his proceedings seemed so unusually strange that we forbore to pull trigger, and watched his manoeuvring for some minutes. At last he perceived the dead deer, and made his way up to it with great caution, sniffing the air at every step he took, as if he could detect some danger threatening. Scarcely had he time to smell his windfall when with a ferocious roar a second tiger sprang from some cover close at hand, and a tremendous fight ensued which we watched with intense interest for several minutes. The second comer, which was much the largest tiger, was gaining the mastery, as he had his opponent hard and fast by the throat, when we fired a right and left simultaneously, and ended the fight... {1877}

RARE ENCOUNTER BETWEEN TIGER AND GAUR

H. A. LEVESON

Whilst hunting in the jungle between the Bowani River and the Goodaloor pass at the foot of the Nedineallah Hills, my friend Burton and I witnessed a most gallantly contested fight between a bull bison and a tiger which is worth recording. Night had scarcely set in when a loud bellowing noise was heard, followed by an unmistakable roar which caused no little commotion amongst the horns and bullocks that were picketed round our tents, and from the ominous sounds that followed we knew that a mortal combat was raging at no great distance from our bivouac...

We came to an opening in the woods where we saw a huge bull bison, evidently much excited, for his eyes flashed fire, his tail straight on end, and he was tearing up the ground with his forefeet, all the time grunting furiously. As we were all luckily well to leeward, the taint in the air was not likely to be winded, so I made signs to Chineah and Googooloo to lay down their guns and climb into an adjacent tree, whilst Burton and I, with a rifle in each hand, by dint of creeping on hands and knees, gained a small clump of bush on a raised bank, not more than thirty yards distant, from whence we could see all that was going on. When we first arrived the tiger was nowhere to be seen, but from the bison's cautious movements I knew he could not be far off. The moon was high in the heavens, making the night clear as day; so not a movement could escape us, although we were well concealed from view.

Several rounds had already been fought, for the game had been going on a good twenty minutes before we came up, and the bison, besides being covered with white lather about the flanks, bore several severe marks of the tiger's claws on the face and shoulders. Whilst we were ensconcing ourselves comfortably behind the cover, with our rifles in readiness for self-defence only—for we had no intention of interfering in the fair stand-up fight which had evidently been taking place—a low savage growling about fifteen paces to our right attracted our attention, and, couched behind a tuft of fern, we discerned the shape of an immense tiger watching the movements of the bison, who, with his head kept constantly turned towards the danger, was alternately cropping the grass and giving vent to his excited feelings every now and then by a deep tremulous roaring, which seemed to awaken all the echoes of the surrounding woods. The tiger, whose glaring eyes were fixed upon his antagonist, now and again shifted his quarters a few paces either to the right or the left, once coming so near our ambuscade that I could almost have touched him with the muzzle of my rifle; but the wary old bull never lost sight of him for a second, but ever followed his movements, with his head lowered to receive his attack. At last the tiger, which all along had been whining and growling most impatiently, stole gently forward, his belly crouching along the ground, every hair standing on end, his flanks heaving, his back arched, and his tail whisking about and lashing his sides; but before he could gather himself together for a spring, which might have proved fatal, the bison, with a shriek of desperation, charged at full speed with his head lowered, and the horns pointed upward, but overshot the mark, as his antagonist adroitly shifted his ground just in time to avoid a vicious stroke from his massive horns, and, making a half-circle, sprang a second time, with the intention of alighting on his broad neck and shoulders; this the bull evaded by a dexterous twist, and before his adversary could recover himself, he again rushed at him, caught him behind the shoulder with his horns, and flung him some distance, following up to repeat the game, but the tiger slunk away to gather breath.

Round after round of the same description followed, allowing breathing time between each, the tiger generally getting the worst of it, for the bull sometimes received his rush on his massive forehead and horns, and flung him a considerable distance, bruised and breathless, although the skin seemed too tough for the points to penetrate; once, however, I thought the bison's chance was all over, for the tiger, by a lucky spring managed to fasten on his brawny shoulder, and I could hear the crunching sound as his teeth met again and again in the flesh, whilst the claws tore the flank like an iron rake. With a maddening scream of mingled rage and pain, the bull flung himself heavily on the ground, nearly crushing his more nimble adversary to death with his ponderous weight; and the tiger, breathless and reeling with exhaustion, endeavoured to slink away with his tail between his legs, but no respite was given, his relentless foe pursued with roars of vengeance, and again rolled him over before he could regain his legs to make another spring. The tiger, now fairly conquered, endeavoured to beat a retreat, but this the bison would not allow, he rushed at him furiously over and over again, and at last getting him against a bank of earth pounded him with his forehead and horns, until he lay motionless, when he sprang with his whole weight upon him, striking him with the fore feet, and displaying an agility I thought incompatible with his unwieldy appearance. I have attempted to depict "the last round" in my sketch.

The game, which had lasted over a couple of hours, was now over, for the tiger, which we thought, perhaps, might be only stunned, gave

unmistakable signs of approaching dissolution. He lay gasping, his mouth half-open, exposing his rough tongue and massive yellow teeth; his green eyes were fixed, convulsive struggles drew up his limbs, a quiver passed over his body, and all was still. His conqueror was standing over him with heaving flanks, and crimsoned foam flying from his widely distended nostrils; but his rolling eye was becoming dim, for the life-blood was fast ebbing from a ghastly wound in his neck, and he reeled about like a drunken man, still, however, fronting his dead antagonist, and keeping his horns lowered as if to charge. From time to time he bellowed with rage, but his voice became fainter, and at last subsided into a deep hollow moan; then his mighty strength began to fail him, and he could not keep his legs, which seemed to bend slowly, causing him to plunge forward. Again he made a desperate effort to recover himself, staggered a few paces, and with a surly growl of defiance fell never to rise again, for, after a few convulsive heavings, his body became motionless, and we knew that all was over.

On examination we found the throat of the bison so lacerated that the windpipe was exposed, and several large arteries cut, an ear bitten off, and the flesh on the shoulder actually torn away in strips. The tiger, on the other hand, had one eye gouged out, several ribs broken, and the lower part of the belly ripped open, from which wound the intestines were protruding. I ordered Chineah and Googooloo to collect some dry wood, and light a large fire to keep the jackals and hyenas away, which, being done, we returned to our camp, and were soon in the arms of Morpheus. [1877]

On getting up we saw the natives going towards the spot where we had killed the tiger, apparently very busy about something. At the same time several of the villagers came running to the camp, crying out—

"Come, saibs, come, the tiger is near; come shoot him."

Springing to our feet we took our guns and followed ."The tiger will be off before we reach the spot," I observed to the major.

'No fear of that," he replied, "didn't you hear them say that the tiger had been caught in a trap? They have employed a mode I have heard of, but never saw practised, and very much doubted of its success. The animal has been captured by bird-lime. Their plan is to smear with it a number of broad leaves of a tree resembling the sycamore, and to place them in the animal's way with the prepared side uppermost. On putting its paw on one of the leaves it remains sticking, when, on endeavouring to shake it off, it treads on several more, and then rubs them against its face, which is consequently smeared with the ropy stuff getting into its eyes and nose and gluing its eyelids together. Bewildered, it then rolls on the ground, covering its head and face with leaves until it is completely hoodwinked. We shall soon see whether I am right in my conjectures."

I could scarcely believe the account the major gave. In a short time we heard the tiger roaring, when the natives, who had at first advanced boldly enough, scattered on either side, while they pointed out the animal, its whole head covered with leaves, which it was making frantic endeavours to tear off without attempting to escape. It was thus completely in our power. "Now, Rice, there is something for you to shoot at," said the major, keeping his gun on his shoulder. "If you miss, Curry or Desmond may exert his skill." Rice advanced a few steps and fired. The bullet hit, but the tiger continued its efforts to free itself from the leaves, taking no notice of its wound. {1884}

As I had no gun, I took one of the pistols, with poor Staunton's sword, and set out, accompanied by the little Ghoorka, in the hopes of knocking over a few birds, for I could not expect to kill any larger game. My companion was a short distance ahead of me, in an open part of the jungle, when I heard a roar, and presently caught sight of a huge tiger, creeping out from among the bushes. I expected to see the Ghoorka retreat to a tree near at hand, up which he might quickly have ascended; instead, however, of doing so, he firmly stood his ground, eying the tiger. Had I possessed a rifle I should have remained where I was, but as there was close to me a tree with easily accessible branches, I stepped back until I got behind it, when, grasping one of the lower boughs, I swung myself up as rapidly as I could, until I was beyond the tiger's reach. I did not feel that I was deserting my companion, because I saw that he was in no way afraid of the tiger. I guessed, indeed, that he could manage the brute quite as well by himself as with any assistance I might give him.

I was not mistaken. The Ghoorka, waving his hookery—the only weapon he possessed—then shouted, and, stopping for an instant, stepped back a pace or two to induce the tiger to come on. I watched him anxiously.

Out sprang the tiger, when with wonderful agility the Ghoorka leaped to the left, delivering a blow which cut off the animal's right paw as it bounded on. On reaching the ground it looked round at its foe, and now, furious with pain and rage, made another spring at the Ghoorka; but he was as active as the tiger, and had also sprung round so as to be on the side of the disabled paw, with which it endeavoured to strike at him, but the blow was harmless, and was again avoided.

The tiger, roaring and excited to the greatest fury by the pain it was enduring, once more sprang at the man; but as it did so he delivered a stroke at its throat which well-nigh severed its head from its body. But the brute was not dead, and, still animated by rage, it was preparing for a last effort. As the Ghoorka stood watching it with his brilliantly black eyes, it made a final spring, this time to receive a blow on the back of the neck, which severed its spine. Over it rolled, and lay motionless.

"You may come down, saib!" shouted the Ghoorka, as he wiped his hookery on the grass; "The tiger will harm no one now. You did wisely to get out of its way, for by remaining on the ground you would only have impeded my movements, and would very likely have been seized by the tiger before I could rescue you."

I agreed in this, and complimented him especially on his achievement, of which, however, he seemed to think but little.

We greatly astonished our friends in camp when we returned with the tiger's head and skin, for as they had not heard a shot they could scarcely believe that so fierce an encounter had been going on close to them. {1884}

She disappeared for a second, and then with unerring aim hurled herself on to the head of my elephant. Her fangs were buried deep in the soft pads on his crown, where one is wont to prod him with the ankus. I could have touched her muzzle with my hand. I had no weapon but my gun, and she was too close for me to get it up to my shoulder. I had just time to admire the brilliancy of her attack, when I found myself, I know not how, flying through the air in her company. The elephant had given a prodigious shake, and got rid of us both at once. My feet were torn from the kelawa or neck-band in which the mahout's feet are secured. Many of the strings broke, and some of the eyelet hooks of my boots were torn out at the same time. Yet, strange to say, I was not in the least hurt, and had an eye for all that was going on. For a second I saw myself in the air with the tigress, and almost simultaneously found myself sitting quite comfortably in a nest of long fine grass, within a yard of my infuriated enemy. I knew she was there, for I had received no shock, and had at once listened for her backward rush into the heart of her stronghold. Not the faintest sound of any kind, however, had greeted my attentive ear. The crashing and grunting of the elephants, who had all taken to ungovernable flight through the dense forest, soon ceased to be audible. Not even a bird was twittering in the heat of the midday sun. All was silent; there was nothing to disturb my reflections! {1885}

THE FURIOUS TIGRESS | JULIUS BARRAS

Those in the trees could see her as she charged on to the elephant, Noor Jehan, who, however, escaped with only a slight scratch, for the tigress wheeled round and flew towards the hindmost elephant, Buddul Pyaree, whom she seized first by the shoulder, and then fixed on to her hind leg, making her teeth meet through the flesh. This I saw myself through an opening of the trampled herbage. Buddul Pyaree behaved with such masculine courage on this occasion that I was very sorry she was not one of the animals told off for my use. She sat down on her foe, whom she got well under her, and nearly smothered in the mud. All the people on the elephant's pad fell off during this process, and came running up towards the main body. One of them, called Seesoo, had even got a scratch from the tiger's claw on his temple, so he had had a narrow escape. In another second or two, the elephant rose and came rapidly shuffling towards us. The tigress then sat up for an instant blackened with mud, and looking more ferocious than ever. She again disappeared into the very same thicket of rushes whence she had delivered her attacks on me. {1885}

TIGERS ON TREES | F. B. SIMSON

Tigers, as a rule, do not climb up trees, as leopards often do; there is no reason why they should not, and tigers have been several times shot on trees in the district of Purneah. I have seen these trees; they are situated in the moist undulating plains which are always inundated when the Ganges rises to its greatest height. These wide and desolate pergunnahs contain a certain amount of game which, when the grass is high and unburnt, may be said to be in safety, but when the inundation is really high it is only the few highest spots which are uncovered with water. To these every species of living thing resorts that has not already provided against death by drowning. In Southern Sylhet the appearance of these watery plains when the water is unusually deep must be about the nearest resemblance to the scriptural deluge conceivable. I have sailed across these places when the human inhabitants only existed on artificial mounds crowded with huts, filled to overflowing with human beings huddled together for the short time, waiting for a fall of twelve or eighteen inches in the flood. To each hut you would see a canoe or two fastened. In some places on the top of similar mounds a few trees would be seen, their bases standing in the water and their branches waving over it; these branches were covered with an extraordinary collection of living creatures—snakes and lizards on every branch, rats and animals of the cat tribe, squirrels and wading or short-winged birds, curious unknown insects, turtles and crab-like creatures unknown to me. As the boat came near, the snakes and the rats would leave the trees and come swimming towards it.

We used generally to be going too fast, and the animals were left in our wake, but we had to kill many snakes and rats if they were likely to come up to the boats. At such times tigers used to live for the ten days or fortnight on trees; and at Purneah, when their doings were reported, they used to be shot on the branches. These beasts fed apparently on turtles and young crocodiles, on fish and on animals which came to the mounds for refuge, and on carcases of drowned creatures which came floating by. Tigers can swim well and I dare say they used to swim from these trees and return to them. I never saw any thing of this myself, but I know the country and more than one gentleman who shot tigers on these trees. {1886}

THE MAHOUT AND THE TIGER | F. B. SIMSON

There were no more tigers in this patch, so before going on we had to pad these three; this took a long time. Then we made a beautiful line to beat the next great jungle of similar jhow-trees. The three elephants, each with a tiger on the guddies, looked lovely. I wish an artist could have depicted the party about a quarter of an hour afterwards, when an active tiger bounded over the top of the jhow with loud roar and arched back, tail up, and ears laid back; he jumped fifteen feet in the air. This was merely to enable him to see exactly what was going on. In his next bound he was right on to the head of my old elephant 'Shamkholly'. He did not pull the

VALMIK THAPAR

elephant down, and the mahout struck the tiger on the head with all his force with the heavy elephant-goad; this made him let go, and as he moved off we fired and he was killed. This was number four; but there was another yet. We beat steadily on, and after some delay got our fifth tiger. I never shot five tigers at any other time. {1886}

'A few months ago, while going to look for ibex, I was passing over the large hill in front of the Avalanche bungalow on the Kondahs. Suddenly my gun-carrier asked me for my glass, and whispered that he could see a tiger crossing a bare ridge about half-a-mile off; his assistant corroborated this, but, even with the glass, I could not succeed in making out what these two men had discovered with the naked eye—and I own I thought the men were attempting to deceive me in order to restore my temper, which had been sorely ruffled by them the day before. They insisted that they saw a large tiger and not a panther, as I suggested it might be, and, when it passed out of view, agreed that we should probably come on it again by skirting another spur of the hill. I consented to this, although without placing the slightest faith in what they said.

'Presently, however, there was no doubt that they were right, for about five or six hundred yards from us appeared a tiger, a magnificent hill animal. He was quietly crossing a bare and rocky ridge, evidently looking out keenly for his breakfast, and taking advantage of every inch of cover, much as a cat in a cabbage garden looks out for sparrows. He sank nearly to a crouching position before attempting to top any ridge or hillock, and thus, with all but his head concealed, cautiously surveyed the ground in his front; to us on his flank he was perfectly visible. It may have been by chance, but, as he was then working, he was able to take as much advantage of the wind as the most scientific deer-stalker could have done. Twice he crouched in a half-sitting, half-recumbent posture, and gazed long and anxiously over the valley between us at the brow of the spur whereon my two men and I were stretched as flat as we could lay ourselves. He evidently suspected that there was something uncanny there, but luckily the wind was blowing strong from him to us, and moving the scanty grass sufficiently to puzzle his vision. The light shone full upon him, and in the clear mountain atmosphere which always causes objects to appear nearer than they really are, even without the glass, one could almost have counted the stripes on his sleek and glossy coat. He must have remained in view for many minutes as he quietly passed along the mountain side; and when he disappeared my men, with admirable knowledge of ground, took me as fast as we could run to a spot which would, they said, cross his path. He must have increased his pace during this interval, or he may have discovered there was something wrong in the air, for, notwithstanding that we had only a short way to go in comparison to his, he was at a rapid trot, or *run* would be a more correct term for the pace, and coming direct for us, just topping one hillock as our eyes rose to a level with the summit of the opposite one; we were in Indian file, and dropped down on the grass without a whisper. This attracted his attention—but he could not make us out, and, probably taking us in our grey shooting clothes for pigs, or ibex at rest, commenced stalking us most carefully. He was about one hundred and thirty yards from us with one of the most beautiful Kondah glens between; on his hill, and about fifteen or twenty yards in his front, was a single rhododendron, about the same distance on mine was a small clump of three or four of those lovely shrubs, then glowing in all the glory of their deep red blossoms. He dropped on his belly at once, and thus crept onwards to his bush, while I, making myself as snake-like as possible, contrived to get forward to my clump.

'Thus stalking each other, so to speak, we mutually managed to decrease the distance between us. It was almost in vain, however, for the cunning brute kept his rhododendron stump so pertinaciously before him that, although I had a perfect view of his hind-quarters beyond it, and he was facing me, I could not, though in a most favourable position to aim, get a shot at his chest. I think he would have come on had not one of my men tried to crawl after me; this caused him to jump up.' {1887}

There is a very prevalent notion that the tiger kills his prey with a crushing blow from his forepaw. This is decidedly a mistake, I think. A tiger certainly does use his forepaws to strike down his quarry, but the death-wound is administered by the teeth. The neck being seized in the powerful jaws, and bent back till it is dislocated. {1887}

One day when I was walking out with the Duke of Connaught near Bombay Point, and close to Government House, we saw six wolves in the road about thirty yards in front of us; they looked at us for a few seconds, and then vanished into the jungle.

Tigers abound and do a lot of damage. There is a well-known man-eating tigress about, for which a government reward of one hundred rupees has been offered; but, although she has been 'wanted' now for some years, she has as yet always successfully evaded the numerous shikari who have been after her. We did our best to bag her whilst there, but without success; for, although she killed the beasts we tied up, she never lay up near the dead carcase.

I went out one day, with a large party of friends, to a piece of jungle near Elphinstone Point, and we were very sanguine of success, as she had killed the bait and eaten a great part of it. We were all placed in trees, with comfortable machans rigged up for us, but, when there, we could not see more than half-a-dozen yards around, so that the animal might have easily slipped past between two guns unnoticed. On the second occasion of a kill, I did not go out, and this time the tigress came under Colonel Rawlins's tree. He, unfortunately, was only armed with a Winchester repeating rifle; and, although he fired two shots, and is confident that he hit her, she was never seen again. {1888}

The first of these tragedies is recorded in the *Annual Register* for 1787 in a letter dated from Calcutta on October 12th, 1786, and it is worthy of remark that the record states that 'this melancholy accident shows that a tyger is not always deterred from approaching fire.' A small vessel bound from Ganjam to Calcutta, being longer on the passage than was expected, ran out of provisions and water: being near Sagar Island, the Europeans, six in number, went on shore in search of refreshments. There were some coconuts on the island, in quest of which they strayed a considerable way. Darkness coming on and the vessel being at a distance, it was thought safer to take up a night's lodging in the ruins of an old pagoda than to return to the vessel. A large fire was lighted and it was agreed that two of the number should keep watch by turns, to alarm the rest in case of danger which they had reason to apprehend from the wild appearance of the place. It fell to the lot of one Dawson, late a silversmith and engraver of Calcutta, to be on watch. In the night a tiger rushed over the fire and, seizing Dawson, sprang off with him in its jaws, but struck its head against the side of the pagoda, rebounding with its prey upon the fire over which they rolled over one another once or twice before the man was carried off. In the morning they found the thighs and legs of the unfortunate victim at some distance, mangled and stripped of flesh.

It was unfortunate that the fate of this man was not known to another party who, in the ship *Ardasier Shaw*, anchored off Sagar Island on December 22nd, 1792. Or if they were aware of the tragedy of six years before, they did not grasp the significance of its lesson which proved the uselessness of fire as a protection against a determined man-eating wild beast. Their story was related in a letter from Captain Consar, one of the party, published in the *Annual Register* for 1793. The others were Captain George Downey, Lieutenant Pyefinch, and Mr. Munro of the East India Company's Service, a son of Sir Hector Munro. They all landed on Sagar Island to shoot deer. Captain Consar wrote:

'We saw innumerable tracks of tigers and deer; but still we were induced to pursue our sport and did so the whole day. About half-past three we sat down on the edge of the jungle to eat some cold meat, sent to us from the ship, and had just commenced our meal when Mr. Pyefinch and a black servant told us there was a fine deer within six yards of us. Captain Downey and I immediately jumped up to take our guns; mine was nearest, and I had just laid hold of it when I heard a roar like thunder, and saw an immense royal tiger spring on the unfortunate Munro, who was sitting down; in a moment his head was in the beast's mouth, and it rushed into the jungle with him with as much ease as I could lift a kitten, tearing him through the thickest bushes and trees, everything yielding to its monstrous force. The agonies of horror, regret, and fear rushed on me at once, for there were two tigers; the only effort I could make was to fire at the tiger, though the poor youth was still in its mouth. I relied partly on Providence, partly on my own aim, and fired a musket, saw the tiger stagger and agitated, and cried out so immediately. Captain Downey then fired two shots and I one more; we retired from the jungle and a few minutes afterwards Mr. Munro came up to us all over blood, and fell. We took him on our backs to the boat, and got every medical attendance for him from the *Valentine*, Indiaman, which lay at anchor near the island, but in vain. He lived twenty-four hours after, but in the extreme of torture; his head and skull were all torn and broken to pieces, and he was also wounded by the animal's claws all over the neck and shoulders; but it was better to take him away, though irrecoverable, than to leave him to be devoured limb by limb. We have just read the funeral service over his body and committed it to the deep. He was an amiable and promising youth.

I must observe there was a large fire blazing close to us composed of ten or a dozen whole trees; I made it myself on purpose to keep the tigers off, as I had always heard it would. There were eight or ten of the natives with us, and many shots had been fired at the place, and much noise and laughing at the time, but this ferocious animal disregarded all.

The human mind cannot form an idea of the scene; it turned my very soul within me. The beast was about four and a half feet high and nine feet long. His head appeared as large as that of an ox, his eyes darting fire, and his roar when he first seized his prey will never be out of my recollection. We had scarcely pushed our boat from that cursed shore when the tigress made her appearance, almost raging mad, and remained on the sand as long as the distance would allow me to see her.' {1931}

THE TIGER AND THE PONY | R. G. BURTON

A remarkable story appeared in the Calcutta *Statesman* some 15 years ago. Mr. and Mrs. F. were on their way to Calcutta from Assam, having to drive 35 miles to the station in a dog-cart. The train was due to leave the station at one o'clock in the morning. On their road a tiger had taken up a beat and was so troublesome that all traffic had to be stopped at sunset, as the tiger had taken a number of bullocks out of passing carts. The tiger's patrol was on a three-mile stretch between Kotiatuli Post Office and the station of Chaparmukh on the near side of a river that was bridged. Once across the bridge, travellers were supposed to be safe. At about half-past ten the party left a bungalow where they had dined, nine miles from the station. Mr. and Mrs. F. sat in front, Mr. F. driving, the lady with the child in her arms, and an ayah and syce sitting behind.

They were in an American four-wheeler. The horse and harness were lit up by two brilliant lamps, which shone on the road ahead and lighted up the drain and banks on each side. They reached the river and crossed the bridge, when Mr. F. said to his wife, 'That's all right, you needn't be frightened anymore.' Just as he spoke, his wife said: 'What's that?' In the light cast by the lamp they saw a huge tiger galloping alongside the trap, its back on a level with the tops of the wheels. As they sat looking, mute with awe, the tiger moved on to the pony's head and they next saw its great paws round the pony's neck, the head jerked upwards, and in a moment it fell dead without a movement. The tiger had attacked on the driving side, and it deliberately got hold of the pony just in front of the withers, and began to drag it and the trap with its five occupants across the road, at the edge of which it entered the jungle without much effort. Probably it could not see the occupants of the trap, as the light to some extent blinded it. The trap had not been dragged far off the road when the axle caught the stump of a tree and the procession came to a stop.

Mr. F. then regained his presence of mind. He got out of the trap and said: 'Give me the child.' Even at that critical moment, the mother said: 'Be careful, she's asleep,' and stepped down after her husband. The whole incident occurred so quickly that there was no outcry, and even the talk had been in whispers. The whole party got clear of the trap and started running up the road. They went to an empty house close by. It was autumn and the night was cold, but a fire was lighted and, sleeping and sitting dozing, the long hours slowly passed. At the first streak of dawn the weary father and mother were awakened by the rattle of bullock-carts on the road; when these

VALMIK THAPAR

approached Mr. F. stopped them and told the drivers what had happened. With one or two men he went to the scene of the night's adventure, and there found that the head of the pony had been eaten away. {1931}

A gallant deed was related in the Report of a Survey Officer in the Sunderbans a few years ago. An Indian surveyor was seated at a table at work when an assistant close to him was seized and carried off by a tiger. Without hesitation the surveyor took his brass sight-ruler, weighing about two pounds, and ran after the tiger. He came up with the beast and beat it over the head with the ruler until it dropped its victim and made off. The man was deservedly promoted for his gallantry, but unfortunately the assistant was killed in the first onslaught.

~

Tigers must have been terribly destructive to both people and cattle before the advent of English sportsmen, among whom the district officers were conspicuous and did much to keep down the numbers of these animals. Thus Buchanan Hamilton wrote of the Gorakhpur district, that when the English took possession of the country, tigers were bold and numerous; soon after that event a sentinel was carried off even in the middle of the town of Gorakhpur. But tigers soon became less bold and, several Europeans of the station being keen sportsmen, their numbers had been greatly reduced. There is a terrible account of the year 1769, which was a famine year, when, most of the herbivorous animals having perished, the tigers were famishing, and great numbers infested the town of Bhiwapur, where in a very short time they killed 400 of the inhabitants; the survivors fled, and for some years the town was deserted. A fine sportsman, Mr. Parry Okeden, and his friends, when stationed in Moradabad, killed over 300 tigers between the years 1823 and 1841, as recorded in his diary. {1931}

THE ATTACK | R. G. BURTON

The ground was rough, and they could move only very slowly. They had gone about 180 yards when the ground became too rough for walking on Osmaston's side, and he descended to the bottom of the ravine, Hansard walking parallel with him about 30 yards off on the steep slope. Osmaston described what followed: 'Suddenly I heard a thud, followed by a series of short, snappish, angry growls, and at the same moment I heard groans and cries for help from Hansard, crushed to the ground by the tigress, and struggling, face downward, to get free. The tigress appeared to be tearing his face and neck with her claws. As quickly as I could I levelled the 12-bore at the brute and, although I was very much afraid of hitting Hansard, I knew it was the poor fellow's last chance. So I pulled the trigger, and to my relief saw the brute relax her hold and come rolling down the precipitous slope, which ended in a 15-foot drop, nearly sheer. The tigress never ceased her hideous growling even to the moment when she fell into the ravine and lay there in the water within a couple of yards of me. I was hemmed in on both sides, so I knew if she was still capable of doing damage it was all up with me. I fired the second barrel into her, and springing down the precipitous ravine, a feat which I don't think I could possibly perform a second time, I rushed up the side of the ravine and made for the place where I had seen Hansard lying, his face all gory and apparently dying. I could not, however, find him, and I rushed back to camp, the direction of which I more or less knew, across several spurs and ravines.' Fortunately the prompt and effective action taken by this young and inexperienced officer, who showed a nerve and promptitude beyond all praise, had finished off the tigress and saved his companion who would have been killed had there been a moment's hesitation. {1931}

VALMIK THAPAR

SUPERSTITIONS AND THE VALUE OF A TIGER'S PARTS

R. G. BURTON

Value for medicinal and other purposes is attached by the natives of India to various products of the tiger. The fat is highly valued, and when a tiger is killed, the flesh is boiled down and the fat carefully bottled as an aphrodisiac and as a remedy for rheumatism. The clavicles or 'lucky bones,' rudimentary collar-bones found loose in the flesh of the neck, and the claws are prized as charms and ornaments; the whiskers have to be looked after when a tiger is shot, or they will be surreptitiously plucked out, it is said for use as 'medicine' for poisoning enemies, just as ground glass is commonly used in India as an irritant poison, perhaps given in a cup of tea. The liver is eaten to impart courage, and the tigress's milk is valued as an application for sore eyes. {1931}

Tigers have their place in military history. In the Mahratta War of 1817, man-eaters took their toll of stragglers of the Deccan Army under Sir Thomas Hislop as it marched through the valley of the Tapti River on the way to Mehidpur, just as Herodotus relates that the lions of the Macedonian mountains harried the baggage-camels of Xerxes. After the dispersal of the Pindaris in 1819 at the end of the war, their famous leader, Chithu, deserted by all his followers, at last wandered off alone in the jungles on the banks of the Tapti near Asirgarh, where he was killed and devoured by a man-eating tiger, the remains being recognised by the discovery of the victim's head. {1931}

MAN, TIGER AND A PACK OF WILD DOGS
JOHN DANIEL ST. JOSEPH

It is only in very exceptional circumstances that a tiger will try to go up a tree. He is a bad climber owing no doubt to his great weight which prevents him from obtaining a firm hold of the trunk, especially as cat-like he uses his claws which cannot always get the necessary grip in the soft bark or bast of the stem. He may rush up the trunk for a short height by sheer impetus and lodge in its fork, but more than this it seems he is unable to do. Cubs however are quick in getting up and down trees.

I once heard an account of a tiger being treed by wild dogs. The sight was witnessed by a young Gond who was collecting gum off a tree, and remained quietly in his seat on observing the strange event. The shikari said he could vouch for the lad's telling the truth, and he took me to see the spot. The tree was an old pollard of kalam with a thick knotty trunk about ten feet high, supporting a whorl of shoots at the apex. According to the youth, the tiger came bounding along from the direction of a stream close by, pursued by a pack of twenty or thirty dogs, and ran up the stem and lodged at the top among the nest of shoots that grew out of the head of the trunk. The dogs kept near the tree for about a quarter of an hour and then went back to the stream whence they had come, while the tiger remained up for some time longer and then slid down and trotted off in the opposite direction. It is painful to reflect that the King of beasts should have been humiliated by such vermin, and looking to the odds against him perhaps he was well advised. The dogs must have been pretty hard up to attack a tiger. My own impression was that they had either chanced upon the tiger's kill in one of their hunts, or else had killed near where he was lying up. In either case, the tiger would show his resentment at being disturbed, and the dogs being in great force would naturally endeavour to drive him away...

During stalks and excursions, trees with deep vertical incisions have been pointed out to me as examples of the tiger's escalades, but this was mere supposition and the marks could have been caused by bears, more probably by tigers sharpening their claws.

Something like this befell me while sitting up for a tiger at Ambimata in the Debke forests of the Betul district. The kill was in a ravine some miles from camp. The ground was difficult to beat, so I decided in spite of a late moon, to sit up with my Mohammedan shikari. The machan was prepared in the fork of a pepul tree, about twelve feet from the ground, and overlooking the kill. No sooner was it dark than the tiger turned up

unexpectedly from the back of us, passing under our tree to get to his kill which he commenced to tackle at once. The kill had not been disturbed in the least, and was lying just where the tiger had left it under the spreading boughs of trees growing along the nullah bank. It was so dark in the ravine that try as I would, I could not even get a glimpse of the brute, so the only thing was to wait till the moon rose at about ten o'clock. In the meanwhile the tiger continued to feast unsuspicious of our presence. About an hour passed in almost perfect stillness, broken only by the rippling of water in the stream hard by and the munching of flesh and crackling of bones. Then suddenly there was a slight rustling of leaves caused by a current of air speeding through the valley. This must have wafted our scent to the tiger, for he stopped eating, remained perfectly still for a few minutes and then as if agitated began to walk about all over sniffing the air. Having satisfied himself, he returned to the kill and continued his meal. Half an hour after there came another puff of wind and again he began perambulating further afield. He was absent quite ten minutes and ended by sitting under our tree for a third time and could have barely swallowed a few mouthfuls, when the breeze rose again with a deeper note causing the tiger to make straight for our tree in a few rapid strides. This time he braced himself up against the trunk and began to snuff and snort, barely a foot below the machan then, having made sure of our presence he was off instantly without a sound. It may be imagined what an exciting few minutes we had in the machan. The thick cover over which we were seated made it absolutely impossible to fire vertically downwards, while a fork of the tree closer to the ground presented a veritable ladder for him to get up. But although his claw marks reached up to nine feet, he made no hostile attempt beyond using the stem as a support to enable him to stretch out to his full height and satisfy his curiosity. This experience corroborates what I have said that the ordinary tiger will always try to avoid collision with man even when the advantage rests with him. {1930}

THE TIGER'S BEHAVIOUR AND DIET

JOHN DANIEL ST. JOSEPH

Natives consider [the tigress's] milk very efficacious for certain eye diseases. Shikaris told me it was of a thick, sticky consistency and drops lost while suckling coagulated on the surface like bird-lime, and could be scraped up and utilised days after it had been spilt.

The tiger's fat is in great demand as a cure for rheumatic pains. His claws are used as charms to keep off the evil eye, being suspended round the necks of children or worn as an amulet with other charms encased in a bag. Men and women who practice witchcraft wear them in a string round the neck or waist and arms to render themselves immune from the evil effects of spirits with whom they consort. Ascetics also wear them, doubtless for the same reason. The cartilages from the shoulders are mounted on gold or silver and used as ornaments in various devices. The ends of the tiger's whiskers are considered to be deadly. They are supposed to be useful for bringing about the death of a rival without inviting suspicion on the person who administered the poison. It is said that if the whiskers are chopped very fine and given to the victim in his food the particles will enter the liver and perforate it, causing gradual decline and death. It is because of this that natives are so intend [sic] upon burning the tops of whiskers when a tiger is shot.

A very evident fact about tigers is that the sexes are nothing like as equally represented as they should be, considering the natural conditions under which they live and breed. My own experience shows that the proportion of males to females varies in the ratio of one tiger to every four tigresses. This inequality is in a less measure the result of natural preference which aims at producing more females than males to perpetuate the race but also, in a greater degree, it is due to immature males being killed off by adult tigers either through jealousy or during fits of temper when the two have quarrelled. The latter theory is what aboriginal shikaris hold to, and I think they are correct. We know that the cubs remain with the mother until they are practically full grown. Under the circumstances the tiger naturally resents the presence of another male with the tigress and tries to get rid of him in the soonest time he can. This often means the killing of the younger and weaker beast if it persists in keeping with the tigress. Again, in a quarrel over food or opposition to the tiger, the younger male would have to bear the consequences of his indiscretion. Females are seldom or never attacked by males, even if they should be the aggressors.

The tiger's dietary is very varied. Essentially he is carnivorous, but he does not disdain fruit and buds which he finds palatable. In common with animals and birds he relishes the succulent corolla of the mahua flower, and jungle tribes say that he will occasionally take the pickings of juicy fruits. I know panthers will sip the juice of the common date palm, when the crowns of the stems tapped happen to be near enough to the ground to allow them to reach the cut surface from which the sap exudes. It is therefore very likely that tigers follow their example in places such as the Deccan and Mysore, where the date palm grows in their haunts. As regards flesh, I believe he will eat of every kind under the sun. In the Bori reserve in the Hoshangabad district, I came across a python half devoured by a tiger. The reptile must have been a monstrous size, judging from the dimensions of the parts remaining. The fore part from the head to about the middle of the body was five feet ten inches long with an average girth of seventeen inches; whilst the piece of tail discarded was eighteen inches long and eight inches in girth. The body was frightfully lacerated by the tiger's claws.

Gond and Korku shikaris have told me that the tiger enjoys a meal of frogs, crabs and fresh water shells and that he will walk along the water's edge for miles, tilting up the stones and slabs under which they are usually found, hunting for them. They declared that these creatures, with birds, form the principle food of cubs after they have been weaned. Bird is doubtless seized by various means but I know of one instance where a tigress pounced into a covey of bush quail and knocked over a few with her paws before they had time to scatter. Then most sportsmen must know of instances of vultures knocked over if they ventured on the kill while the tiger was near, although in this case it is not for food but merely to keep them off the kill. Still it affords further evidence that he is equally quick in killing birds as animals.

Like a cat the Tiger is also fond of fish and he will poach for enticing fish at night from decoy pools and drains prepared by aborigine fisher folk. I remember my surprise at hearing of this the first time I came upon these people in the early morning. To their disgust at being outdone by the tiger was added their concern at being themselves detected in the reserve. Their account interested me so much, however, that the human poachers were let off with a warning. In this case the tiger had slashed about in the artificial pool and made it very muddy, possibly with the object of blinding the fish and so rendering their capture easy. The men said that he usually bagged the sanval or fresh water murrell, and eels which are easier to capture owing to their sluggish nature.

Mr Sanderson, in his "Wild Beasts of India", mentions hearing from his

men that a tigress fed her young with undigested meat which she brought
up. I have heard this corroborated by some Gond shikaris. Ram Singh,
of Panchi-Tokra, even declared that to cause her to vomit the tigress ate
grass, like dogs. I believe that tiger cubs do not actually begin to fend for
themselves until they are about a year old, though like cats they commence
much earlier to seize rats, birds and other small creatures. I have disturbed a
cub eating a mongoose near his cave, into which he rang [sic] on seeing me
and my trackers and evidently he had caught and killed it himself. Again, a
cub about a year old was shot by a forest officer in a teak thicket a few miles
out of Badnur in the Betul district. This beast was stuck with porcupine
quills all over the body and forepaws and could hardly move without pain,
and looked very sick. I fancy he had lost his mother and, not being quite up
to the skill of hunting, he had tackled a porcupine, which is not surprising
considering the tempting bait which its slow movements invite, and were
it not for its protective covering the porcupine would be an easy prey and
rendered extinct years ago. A young tiger without a parent's guidance would
naturally tackle such a prey on sight. [1930]

THE NATURAL KILL | JOHN DANIEL ST. JOSEPH

Four kills were made within seeing and hearing distance of my positions. Twice the tigress killed nilgai and once a chinkara doe. The latter practically ran into her jaws. She was being pursued by a buck and quite unsuspicious of danger ahead, went near by where the tigress happened just then to be. The tigress had already spotted them coming, and to avoid being seen had crouched behind the shelter of a bush, and as the doe rushed up she sprang out and laid hold of her by the throat. The buck who was hot in pursuit seeing the sudden turn of events, was scared out of his wits and actually bounded over the tigress and escaped. The cubs which were near the mother at the time tried to follow her example for when she had seized the doe, they sprang out of cover, one after the other, and laid hold of the creature by the loins. {1930}

A tiger will rarely tackle a boar, and he will go for wild dogs only when they are alone or in twos or threes. He avoids porcupines, but a famous old Gond shikari in the Betul district told me that he greatly relishes porcupine's flesh, though only a few tigers will attempt to tackle him, because the little beast has a way of jerking off its quills by some extraordinary manipulation of its body with such precision, that the quills stick fast in its assailant's body, and cause it such discomfort that it abandons its intentions. Apparently the porcupine possesses only few of these quills that can act like darts, for tigers with experience will first engage in feints by a few attempts at attacking the animal in order to draw off the injurious quills, when the creature becomes an easy prey.

Again, a good boar is a difficult antagonist, and tigers prefer to leave him alone. I have heard that a tiger will often stalk a boar for a long distance. He will pounce on him only when he has a chance to grip him by the nape of the neck, as a hold on any other part is nothing like as certain to render him helpless. He grips panther and bear also by the nape of the neck, and these are the only kinds of animal I have seen killed in this way. The reason is obvious. They are strong active beasts with powers of offence quite different from other animals, so that a grip elsewhere would involve a struggle, and the only way of avoiding it is to bear down the victim by gripping him by the nape of the neck. A wrench would not be practicable as their thickset bodies, with short necks, do not allow of the necessary purchase to kill.

I was once privileged to hear a great fight between a tiger and a boar at a short distance from my camp at Baretha Ghat. It was on a night in October and the noise woke the whole camp and made my forester come rushing into my tent. The combat must have started just before three o'clock and lasted till nearly five o'clock. It made a regular pandemonium of growls, coughs and snorts by the infuriated beasts, the tiger engaging in a whir of hideous growls, broken every now and again by a loud, hoarse cough; while the boar maintained a jumble of snorts and growls. As the end came suddenly and quietly we hoped that the combat had ended by a mutual withdrawal, but when we visited the scene of the encounter, the boar was lying dead where he had fought. The tiger had driven him out of a puddle-hole in which he had been wallowing, into a little depression some distance from the bank, and there the boar took up his position. The site was like a potato patch, the thick under-growth being torn up and scattered all round. There were marks of profuse bleeding all over, and little strips of skin both of tiger and of boar. The boar was of the brown variety, not very big, just two and a half feet at the shoulder, and the tusks measured less than nine inches; but he had made a great fight. His whole body had been frightfully lacerated, and possibly he failed owing to loss of blood. He had been gripped by the nape of the neck and borne to the ground till he died. But the tiger must have been in little better case as his subsequent behaviour showed. His fury with the boar was evident from the way he had crunched the boar's head after its defeat. However he was too sick to do more, he could not even move his trophy into cover for it was dropped and left in the open, a few paces from the scene of the struggle. We beat for the tiger, but he did not appear, so...he had left the locality. I would have given much to have even just seen him. All the trackers that could be mustered were put on to locate him, but the undergrowth was much too thick for them.

Besides varying his food the tiger is a connoisseur of the quality of what he eats. He will not kill a lean, decrepit or sickly animal, still less a tough old stager, but he selects his food from those in the prime of life. He relishes the meat of half-grown animals of all species, as well as that of females carrying young, especially during their first fecundation. An incident of the kind came to my notice in a reserve in the Hoshangabad district where I had to supervise markings for fellings. One morning I had preceded the coolies and sat on a knoll with two Korku head-men, watching the sun rise to while away the time till the men arrived, when one of the Korkus called my attention to a tiger. He was going slowly on our left front, quite unsuspicious of our presence, and passed within a few paces on the lee-side of a sambhar hind who was watching us. The tiger saw her and could have brought off the coup in one spring, but he went on. I was puzzled to account for his scrupulous conduct; the Korkus however did not appear surprised and I made enquiries.

At last, after much questioning, the elder man explained that the tiger did not attack the hind because the venison would not be worth eating as she had a young one. There is a general belief among these people that the meat of females for a week or so after they have calved has a bitterish flavour and is unsuitable for eating. Asked how he could tell, he replied that the hind had been watching us from one position ever since we got on to the knoll, and if her young had not been near she would not have stayed so long, nor been so intent in keeping us in view. We began therefore to look about in the grass and sure enough we found a little fawn a few days old. I ought to add that I had just come among these people and had not yet gained their confidence which is perhaps why they prevaricated before giving me the right explanation. {1930}

VALMIK THAPAR

THE TIGER'S HUNTING TECHNIQUE

JOHN DANIEL ST. JOSEPH

Being caught by an early monsoon, I was obliged to take shelter in the forest huts for a few days. One afternoon while seated listening to my clerk read out the vernacular papers, my attention was drawn to a disturbance among a colony of plovers that kept close by a shallow depression marking the course of a stream during the rains. The channel was barely two hundred yards from the huts, and my forester's buffalo was grazing by herself close to it. She was making for the huts, but moving slowly as animals do when grazing, that is, she was facing in our direction. The tiger stalked along the bed of the watercourse which was open and visible from where I was seated on the top of the rise, but as he hugged the bank, he was hidden from my view. My curiosity was however aroused, as I knew the birds would not speak for nothing: so I kept a good lookout while my clerk went on with his reading quite unsuspecting that my attention was riveted elsewhere. In a few minutes, I saw the tiger's head emerge over the bank as if to survey the ground in his front and then I at once realized what he was after. In a second, he was up the bank and lay down for an instant as if to take rest. Then he ran or rather walked with quick long strides keeping his body as close as possible to the ground, parallel to the direction in which the buffalo was standing grazing, and coming up within ten paces on her left side, he sprang alighting within a yard of the creature's head. This was the first intimation the buffalo had of the tiger's presence, and she raised her head in astonishment, but at that very instant the tiger bounced up like a cannon ball, grasping the buffalo's cheek at the angle with his mouth and at the same time seizing her chin with his left paw, he swung round twisting the head up as he went over on the right side of her, but letting go of his hold before he had alighted.

The force practically lifted the buffalo off her forefeet, and she uttered a shrill moan sounding like the whistle from a throttle valve, and lurched forward a few paces and fell. I was too absorbed to say a word and till then no one else seemed to have an inkling of the tragedy that was being enacted in full view of the huts in broad daylight. But the buffalo's moan and struggles at once called the men's attention to the occurrence and despite my endeavours to pacify them, as I was anxious to see the business through, they created a tumult and rushed to the scene. This was too much for the tiger and he vanished by the way he had come. The men tried to raise the buffalo and applied cures to the wounds on her jaw, but the tiger had

done his work too surely, and try as they would to revive her, she could not even sit up and expired after struggling for ten or fifteen minutes. The four canine teeth were embedded in the jaw, two just under the cheek and two just above it, that is the tiger had gripped the buffalo's face at the angle of the lower maxillary bone, while the chin bore slight marks of the tiger's claws. The distance from buffalo to bank of nullah, where the tiger got up, measured twenty-six paces or about eighty feet, of this he ran about seventy feet before springing to the attack. |1930|

THE TIGER AND THE PYTHON

FITZ WILLIAM THOMAS POLLOK

We were far from the haunts of man, and all was solitude, when there was heard a piercing cry, which was unmistakably the death shriek of some miserable creature struck down by a beast of prey. I rushed forward, followed most reluctantly by my two attendants, and found a poor wood-cutter. He was a small, wiry man probably about forty years of age, all but naked, and the breath was scarcely out of his body. As I stooped over him to ascertain whether there was the least hope of his recovery, I found that the back of his skull had been beaten in, as with a sledge-hammer. When I turned round the *Karumba* was making tracks, evidently with a view of giving notice of the misfortune to some villagers, and as I knew if he once got away we should have a posse of men with torches coming for the body, I caught him by the scruff of his neck and told him if he attempted to leave I would break every bone in his body. Now that I had a corpse I meant to utilise it, so I forcibly detained him and made him and the shikarie collect wood and erect a "machan". The body lay with the face uppermost, and had fallen amid some brush-wood close to a stout sapling, while a fair-sized tree commanded the position from a distance of about fifteen yards. There was fortunately a good moon, so soon before dusk we climbed into our perch, the villager muttering that it was sacrilege we were guilty of, and that surely the corpse would arise and slay us. Finally I procured silence by telling the men, if they made the least noise, I would tie them up as living bait. It was a gruesome sight, watching that dead body as the moon shone on its face, exaggerating every feature. I must own, were it not that I considered it a duty to try and rid the country of that awful infliction, a man-eater, I would even at the last moment have gone back to camp.

The time went by but slowly. Eleven o'clock arrived; no appearance of the tiger. Some tall trees cast a shadow over the corpse, but I could not take my eyes off that poor, thin, ghastly upturned face, when, oh, horror! one eye opened, then the other; soon after an arm moved, succeeded by a shiver of the body. Was it going to rise and kill us as the men asserted? It was too absurd. The sight was too much for my companions. They dropped forward in a swoon. Even I, too, felt as if icy cold water was being poured down the back of my neck. Demoralized I was certainly getting, I do not think that I could have borne the gruesome sight much longer, when there was a roar, and a brindled mass sprang at something which was invisible to me. Instantaneously a vast speckled body coiled itself round the brindled matter, there was a struggle, bones seemed to be crunched to bits, the tiger gave a feeble roar or two, and then all was still except an occasional convulsive upheaving. In that fearful effort, the corpse had been shifted so that its wide and sightless orbs no longer stared upwards. That alone was a relief. What had occurred I could not conjecture.[8] The men, when they recovered from their faint, still lay prone with their hands over their faces, muttering that we were now as good as dead. Giving one a slight kick, I asked him what he was afraid of. "'The corpse will kill us," he muttered.

"Why, you fools," said I, "the dead come not to life again. The woodcutter is dead, and something has killed his destroyer. We shall know all about it in the morning. I am going to sleep; you had better do so too."

I knew they were in too great a fright to descend from the machan and seek a village at that time of night, so making myself as comfortable as I could, I turned over on my side and dozed off, giving a convulsive start now and then as I dreamt that the woodcutter was threatening me. But everything has an end. That long, long night at length terminated, and thankful I was to see the dawn of day and hear the jungle fowls proclaim that sunrise was at hand. Losing no time I descended to solve last night's mystery, the sight that met my eyes was marvellous. A huge rock snake, a python, just over twenty-one feet in length, lay coiled round the body of the tiger, whose fangs in turn were imbedded in the back of the snake's head, while the reptile's folds, after enveloping the tiger, had got a purchase by lashing its tail round the adjoining sapling, and so assisted the vast muscular power it possessed in crushing the tiger to death. On examining the corpse of the man, we found saliva or slime over the face and the upper part of the body, and so I have no doubt the snake had thus prepared the human prize for swallowing when the tiger sprang upon it, resulting in the two meeting their deaths as described. The movements of the man's body were doubtless caused by the snake's pressure and by its progress round and about the carcase. The python, though dead some hours, had still sufficient muscular power left to make it appear dangerous. These reptiles are properly called *boa constrictors*, for their power of contraction, when they have a purchase to aid them, is immense, and I have heard the natives tell wonderful tales about their strength, even to their making buffaloes their victims. Snakes may have the power, but as they could not make a meal of a buffalo, they would have no object in assaulting them, unless under similar circumstances to those related above. {1894}

---

[8] *There was a good deal of brushwood and débris about.*

Presently four lassies, the eldest not more than seventeen and the others between fifteen and that age, with trays on their heads and in gala costume, came in view on the opening at the further side of the river's bank. It did not take them a minute to deposit their burdens, take off their thin jackets, lay aside their "thamins", and throw themselves into the river, which nowhere was much above their knees. They amused themselves playing and romping with each other, totally unconscious that there was a man sitting down within thirty yards of them. I was absorbed in the spectacle, for the girls were pretty, in fact you might travel through the length and breadth of Europe and not meet with such perfect figures. But Asiatics, left to nature, strangers to corsets and tight-lacing, develop in a manner unknown to people of colder climes, who, though oftener prettier in the face, are sadly deficient in the contour of the body. The Elders who peeped at Susanna, would have gone raving mad could they have seen the abandon of these four damsels! I had been inwardly chuckling and conceived the idea of jumping up and overwhelming them with confusion, when a movement in the grass attracted my attention. As I said before, I did not think that a hare could have passed without being seen, but though I took my eyes off the fascinating spectacle in the stream, and bent them on the spot, I could see nothing, but once my attention had been called away from the nymphs, my instinct as a hunter predominated. So I seized my rifle, loaded the gun with ball so as to be ready for any contingencies, and silently cocked both weapons. For the space of half a minute nothing moved and nothing was visible; and the girls continued splashing one another and enjoying their douche amidst fits of laughter.

Then there was another slight rustle, yet I could see no living thing. I surmised it might be a snake, or a yit, so thought of replacing the shot cartridges, when another movement riveted my attention. I forgot the girls, my eyes protruding out of my head in a vain attempt to penetrate the mystery, but although the whole time was not more than a couple of minutes, it appeared an hour, before I obtained a view of a brindled mass which, crouching with belly touching the ground, was creeping slowly but surely towards its unconscious victims in the water! Why, thought I, it is a tiger, and probably the man-eater we have heard of. It is stalking the girls, but by G—d, I'll spoil its little game. I could distinctly trace the murderous brute drawing its hind legs under its body preparatory to springing forward, so I thought it time for me to interfere. I could see the two white marks which are so conspicuous on the backs of a tiger's ears, and knew therefore that if I fired exactly between them, that I should hit the back of the head at its junction with the spine—a fatal spot if struck, no matter whether the animal be an elephant, a rhinoceros, a buffalo, or any other living thing. Moreover my position for that shot was most advantageous, for I was shooting downwards. The rifle[9] and I were old comrades. I had killed much game with it and won many a match, so provided my nerve did not desert me and I held the weapon straight, the bullet would not fail me. I had a splendid support, for my feet resting on a rock a little below, enabled me to place my elbows on my knees, so taking a rapid but careful sight, I fired. What happened for the next second or two, I cannot tell, for at the report of the rifle the girls screamed and made for the bank, luckily on the side they had entered the river. The smoke hung, but there was a roar and something flashed past me, and as the smoke cleared away I saw a tiger in the water bounding towards the girls, who, huddled together, appeared paralysed with fright and unable to move. Surely, thought I, I could not have missed. I never fired more coolly or steadily in my life and if struck the brute should be as dead as a door-nail. But the fact remains, there he is, and if I don't disable him within the next minute he'll kill some of those girls. Then I remembered the roar behind me and the flashing of something over me, and wondered whether there could be a second brute, but I had not much time for cogitation. Act I must, and that speedily. Fortunately I had not altered my position; my elbows were still on my knees, and aiming at the would-be destroyer's broad back, I fired. Luckily a gust of wind at that moment blew the smoke aside and I saw the tiger rear up, give a gasp, and then swim steadily forward. I dropped the rifle and seized the gun, but by that time the tiger was all but out of the water, and as he made for the girls I fired and broke a foreleg, but beyond stumbling and giving one snarling roar, he continued on his way. Again I pressed the trigger when over he rolled, almost within touching distance of the women, and as he struggled on the ground, one of them[10] threw her "thamin" over his head, and dragging her comrades with her, retreated backwards into the river, and made for my side of it, as fast as they could. Before the tiger could clear himself of the encumbrance over his head—for he had a foreleg broken and was otherwise hard hit—the girls were scrambling up the hill-side, while I

---

[9]*It was a two-groove No. 10 rifle, by Joseph Lang.*
[10]*She married a noted worker in gold in Tongho and was christened, why I know not, "Orangie".*

again was ready for the would-be homicide. The tiger without a moment's hesitation plunged back into the river. I aimed at his head, the ball struck him just above the nose, but below the brain, and passed through both jaws, breaking them. But the enraged beast would not be denied, and he was dragging his dripping body out of the water, when I hit him in the chest, but the ball did no great harm as it passed downwards and did not penetrate a vital part, as it would have done had I been on the same level. However he now stood still, uttering roar on roar, swaying about so that I hesitated to fire for fear of missing him altogether. The girls in the meantime had rushed past me and I knew they would be up trees before the feline could overtake them in his crippled state, moreover now I was between him and them. I had therefore time to slip in another cartridge, and biding my time, as he turned his side to me, for he could not face the steep ascent of the bank, I struck him in the centre of the shield and knocked him over. As he was not dead, but still gasping and now and then uttering a low growl, I reloaded the rifle and going down put the brute out of pain. Whilst I was standing over my prize, I found that it was a very large tigress. I heard voices some way off, so crossed the river, seized the girls' clothes, ran up the hill, and found them as anticipated perched upon so many branches. Laughing at them as they attempted to screen their nakedness from me, I told them not to be afraid as the tiger was dead, but as a lot of villagers were not far off

they had better don their dresses. So not wishing to add to their confusion, I turned my back on them and walked off, and in a few minutes my boy and about a dozen men appeared, but from a direction quite different from that by which the girls had come, as the latter belonged to another village. {1894}

VALMIK THAPAR

A black example was found dead at Chittagong, North-eastern India, in the year 1846; while a pale whitish specimen, in which the stripes were very opaque and only visible in certain lights, was exhibited alive many years ago at Exeter 'Change, and has been figured in Griffith's "Animal Kingdom". Another nearly white specimen, from Northern India, is recorded by Mr. Howard Saunders in the "Proceedings of the Zoological Society" for 1891. {1896}

THE CHERRAPUNJI TIGER | RICHARD LYDEKKER

In many districts in India, Tigers were (and in some instances still are) extraordinarily numerous and audacious, and the following account by an anonymous author, taken, with some verbal alteration, from the *Asian* newspaper of August 3rd, 1894, of their habits and vagaries in the Cherrapunji Hills, on the north-eastern frontier, will be found of more than common interest. "The station of Cherrapunji," writes the narrator, "stands upon a plateau overlooking the plains, surrounded on the three sides by well-wooded ravines, the slopes, or rather cliffs, of which are so precipitous that Deer are seldom found there, and though the Black Bear now and again turns up he generally prefers other lines of country. The visitor to Cherra, in the cold weather, would have been puzzled to account for Tigers patronising the place, but that is easily explained. As the rains set in, almost the whole of the grazing-grounds along the foot of the hills are submerged, though the houses, when not built on piles, are raised on mounds of mud some three to four feet in height, but it would be impossible to keep cattle in the limited area of the raised *baree*. As the rains approached, therefore, the cattle were driven up to Cherra, upon whose desolate plateau a few inches of rain effects a wonderful transformation scene. These herds were increased by the return of the garrisons of the outposts and stockades for the rains, who also brought their Cows with them, and, as most of the Sepoys owned at least two head, the number of cattle that came up for the benefit of the grass that sprouted so magically after the first shower could not have been far short of 1,200 to 1,500. Hence, washed out of his lair below, and the hillsides being barren, the Tiger has no alternative but to follow his commissariat supplies up the mountain; and numerous as these brutes were, it is a marvel that they did not show up in greater force, considering the ample supply of provisions available. The area of the plateau is restricted, and as the central portion was occupied by houses, the grazing-grounds were mostly on the edges of the ravines. On the east side Tigers would lie just below the level, and creeping to the summit with the mists that roll up from the valleys when the hot sun shone down on the sodden vegetation, scarce a day passed without one or more Cows falling victims. The western side of the flat had long been abandoned as a grazing-ground, for the coal-mine hill was not only covered with thick second growth but honeycombed with limestone caves and coal-galleries, in which the marauders established their quarters; and so many at one time occupied these refuges that the coal-carriers had to go for their requirements in a body, while, when coal was needed for the mess or officers' bungalows, a guard had to be sent with the coolies. Not that the animals were aggressive in the open, but in the dark recesses of the coal-tunnels, they were apt to resent intrusion, being run into a *cul de sac*. In addition to the cover named, there were several spots within the station, such as rifts in the sandstone and under slabs, where the brutes could skulk the whole day long, issuing forth in the gloaming to intercept the cattle wending their way home for the night. A Tiger had, indeed, every advantage in Cherra; he fought shy of the traps erected for his special behoof, and, as no trees can be induced to grow on this storm-swept, rock-strewn heath, and *machans* would be too conspicuous unless you could manage a potshot from the houses, it was difficult to bag one. [...] Tigers were instinctively chary of exposing themselves against the skyline on the ridges; while, owing to the almost incessant rain, clear moonlight nights were the exception; and though few houses were without a trophy in the shape of a hearthrug or two from the hide of the beasts, nearly the whole of these had either been trapped or shot by sheer luck from the bedroom windows or glass-enclosed verandas...

Well, one night in August, when the rain was coming down, as it only knows how to in Cherra, a gentleman was reading in bed, the lamp being on a teapoy placed between his couch and a low window that opened into an unenclosed veranda on the leeside of the house. On the opposite side of the room a bright fire was burning, throwing a strong glare all over and through the window, which had the usual half horizontal curtain. Once or twice the reader's attention was drawn to a slight noise, but on looking up from his book and noticing nothing he resumed his reading, until a most pronounced bump against the upper panes caused him to start up, when, to his no small perturbation, there, with his nose pressed against the glass, which the narrow frame prevented his cheek from breaking, stood a full-grown tiger. How long the brute had been there, and what his ultimate intentions may have been, it is impossible to divine, but that the lamp, which was within two feet of him, and the glare of the window full upon him had no deterrent effect upon the gratification of his curiosity is certain. Although the occupant was not quick enough to seize them, guns ready loaded stood against the mantelpiece.

So extraordinary was the occurrence deemed that the marks of the animal's paws were allowed to remain on the window-sill until the whole station had seen them; and though most of those who could testify to the correctness of this story have passed away, there are, I think, three still in India who, besides myself, can bear witness to the truth of this statement...

But to return to Cherra. Though not aggressive in the daytime the Tigers were rather more familiar than was pleasant, and if, as is mostly the case during the rains, the days were dull and misty, the roads deserted, and your business, or inclination, led you anywhere near the *khud* ten to one but what you would see some sneaking cattle-lifter dodging from rock to rock or peeping cautiously from some deep rift. People perambulating their own compounds were often stalked, but from their [sic] being no recorded instance of accidents, I fancy that Tigers, like the rest of the Cat-tribe, are imbued with that insatiable curiosity that housewives lament in the domestic puss. The compounds were one and all surrounded with stone walls, some three or four feet in height, and one evening, leaning up against the outside of one of these below the messhouse, while talking to the adjutant and a young civilian, our conversation was brought to an abrupt termination by the former officer suddenly taking to his heels, bolting up the messhouse hill as fast as his legs enabled him. Left behind we gazed on each other in blank amazement, looked about us and were about to resume our conversation when our friend, having reached his goal, turned round, and though far too exhausted to utter a word, pointed apparently straight at us. 'Something round the corner, maybe,' said my companion, but as we did not know what it might be, we vaulted inside the wall and peeped over, just in time to see a Tiger creeping stealthily along under cover of the wall towards a deep gully.

A shout soon quickened his movements. It turned out that our friend while talking had caught sight of the brute's face as he peered round the angle of the wall, taking stock of us. Why he did not warn us at the time he started on his flight, he did not seem inclined to explain, but the construction we put on his behaviour was that he preferred saving his own skin at the expense of one or other of us… {1896}

VALMIK THAPAR

A TIGER FAMILY

ROBERT H. ELLIOT

One evening, after the day's work was over, he went out accompanied by a kangaroo dog, and took a seat on the hillside to enjoy the view. Immediately below him ran a jungly ravine, and behind him the hill rose sharply. He had no gun with him, not expecting any game so close to his new abode, and now, to his dismay, a large tiger emerged from the shola at a point between him and his bungalow. As the grass was long at that season, the tiger did not perceive my friend (and, as I have previously shown, tigers, and I believe all animals, do not readily perceive any non-conspicuous object which is not in motion), who, as may be supposed, sat as close and still as possible, and beckoning to the dog, held him fast by the collar. The tiger lay down in the grass, and was presently followed by another tiger, which lay down in front of the first and rolled over on its back. This was pretty well for a beginning, but presently, one after the other, emerged three smaller tigers, which also took their seats in the grass. Here then was a nice family to have between one and one's dinner. The sun presently set, and the prospect of darkness was not encouraging. My friend naturally waited for the tigers to go, and no doubt devoutly hoped that they would not come his way, but time seemed to them to be of no importance, and they showed not the slightest disposition to move. Presently there came on to the ridge of the hill above a jackal, which looked down upon the party and then set up a most unearthly howl. The three smaller tigers, evidently young and inexperienced animals, took no notice of the protestations of the jackal, but the two larger tigers at once got up and took a long steady look at him, and the jackal moved restlessly about and seemed to redouble his efforts to attract the attention of the tigers. The larger tigers now seemed satisfied that some danger was at hand, and to the immense relief of my friend, walked down into the jungle, followed by the three smaller tigers. After waiting a little my friend got up and proceeded homewards, and, he said, "I am not ashamed to own that, after passing the place where the tigers had disappeared from view, I fairly ran for the house." {1898}

STEALING CATTLE | SAMUEL W. BAKER

A few months ago, from the date at which I am now writing, a native came to my camp with the intelligence that a large tiger had suddenly sprung from a densely wooded nullah and seized a cow that was grazing within a few yards of him. The man shouted in the hope of scaring the tiger, when two buffaloes who were near the spot and were spectators of the event at once charged the tiger at full speed, knocked it over by their onset, and followed it as it sprang for safety into the thick bush, thus saving the cow from certain destruction. The cow, badly lacerated about the throat, ran towards its native village, followed by its owner. I lost no time in arriving at the spot, about two miles from camp, and there I found the recent tracks precisely tallying with the description I had received. We organised a drive on the following morning, but the crestfallen tiger had taken the notice to quit, and had retreated from the neighbourhood…

The Brahmaputra is an extraordinary river, as it acknowledges no permanent channel, but is constantly indulging in vagaries during the season of flood; at such times it carries away extensive islands and deposits them elsewhere. Sometimes it overflows its banks and cuts an entirely new channel at a sudden bend, conveying the soil to another spot, and throwing up an important island where formerly the vessels navigated in deep water.

VALMIK THAPAR

This peculiar character of the stream renders the navigation extremely difficult, as the bed is continually changing and the captains of the steamers require a long experience.

During inundations the islands are frequently drowned out, and the wild animals are forced to swim for the nearest shore. Upon such occasions tigers have been frequently seen swimming for their lives, and they have been killed in the water by following them in boats. The captain of the steamer in which I travelled told me of a curious incident during a great inundation, which had covered deeply all the islands and transported many into new positions. Upon waking at daylight, the man who took the helm was astonished to see a large tiger sitting in a crouching attitude upon the rudder, which, as already explained, was 17 feet in length. A heavily-laden flat or barge was lashed upon either side, and the sterns of these vessels projected beyond the deck of the steamer, right and left.

The decks of these large flats were only 3 feet above the water, and the tiger, when alarmed by a shout from the helmsman, made a leap from the rudder to the deck of the nearest vessel. In an instant all was confusion, the terrified natives fled in all directions before the tiger, which, having knocked over two men during its panic-stricken onset, bounded off the flat and sought security upon the deck of the steamer alongside. Scared by its new position and by the shouts of the people, it rushed into the first hole it could discover; this was the open door of the immense paddle-box, and the captain rushed to the spot and immediately closed the entrance, thereby boxing the tiger most completely.

There was only one gun on board, belonging to the captain: the door being well secured, there was no danger, and an ornamental air-hole in the paddle-box enabled him to obtain a good view of the tiger, who was sitting upon one of the floats. A shot through the head settled the exciting incident; and the men who were knocked over being more frightened than hurt, the affair was wound up satisfactorily to all parties except the tiger.
{1898}

A GOOD MAN AND TRUE | SAMUEL W. BAKER

The following experience of a sportsman in the Deccan is from the Secunderabad paper of 14th June 1888—

"Mr. Cuthbert Fraser had a most miraculous escape from a tiger the other day at Amraoti. The lucky hero of this adventure is a District Superintendent of Police in Berar. He is well remembered in Secunderabad as Superintendent of the Cantonment Police before Mr. Crawford. A son of Colonel Hastings Fraser, one of the Frasers of Lovat, he has proved his possession of that nerve and courage which rises to the emergency of danger—on which qualities more than all else the British Empire in India has been built, and on which, after all is said, in the last resort, it must be still held to rest. To quote the graphic account of a correspondent, the escape was about as narrow as man ever had. Mr. Fraser was told by his orderly that a wounded tiger was lying dead with his head on the root of a tree. The orderly having called him up, he went to the spot. Mr. Fraser then sent the orderly and another man with his second gun back, and knelt down to look. Just then the tiger roared and came at him from about eighteen feet off: he waited till the tiger was within five feet of him and fired. As the tiger did not drop, he fired his second shot hurriedly. The first shot had hit exactly in the centre of the face but just an inch too low. It knocked the tiger's right eye out and smashed all the teeth of that side of the jaw. The second shot struck the tiger in the chest, but too low. What happened then Mr. Fraser does not exactly know, but he next found himself lying in front of the tiger, one claw of the beast's right foot being hooked into his left leg, in this way trying to draw Mr. Fraser towards him; the other paw was on his right leg. Mr Fraser's chin and coat were covered with foam from the beast's mouth. He tried hard to draw himself out of the tiger's clutches. Fortunately the beast was not able to see him, as Mr. Fraser was a little to one side on the animal's blind side and the tiger's head was up. Suddenly seeing Mr. Fraser's orderly bolting, he jumped up and went for the man, and catching him he killed him on the spot. Mr. Fraser had lost his hat, rifle, and all his cartridges, which had tumbled out of his pocket. He jumped up, however, and ran to the man who had his second gun, and to do so had to go within eight paces of the spot where the tiger was crouching over his orderly. He heard, in fact, the crunching of the man's bones and saw the tiger biting the back of the head. He now took the gun from his man. The latter said that he had fired both barrels into the tiger—one when he was crouching over Mr. Fraser, and the other when he was over the prostrate body of the orderly.

The man had fired well and true, but just too far back, in his anxiety not to hit the man he would save, instead of the tiger. When afterwards asked if he was not afraid to hit the *Sahib*, 'I was very much afraid indeed,' he replied, 'but *dil mazbut karke lagaya*.' I nerved myself for the occasion, 'A good man and true!' a high officer writes, 'who after firing never moved an inch till Mr. Fraser came to him, although close to the tiger all the while.' {1898}

THE MAN-EATERS OF DOON | MARK THORNHILL

The tiger being an animal so fierce, active and powerful, it may be supposed that of all sports tiger-shooting must be one of the most exciting and dangerous. As ordinarily it used to be practised in large parties, and on elephants, it was really one of the tamest and safest, so safe that accidents were of the rarest occurrence. I remember, however, one very sad one. As it happened in the Doon, and as its incidents were very singular, I will relate them.

A young officer at Dehra heard of a tiger in one of the neighbouring forests. He went out on an elephant in search of it; he took with him only his soldier-servant, a Goorkha. The elephant was not trained for shooting, and it carried no howdah, but only a pad. The tiger was found; the officer fired and hit it. The tiger, mortally wounded, crawled under a tree and there fell. The elephant was urged towards it; being untrained, on coming near the tiger it took fright and became unmanageable. To save themselves, the officer and his servant seized hold of a branch of the tree that stretched above them as the elephant rushed off into the forest.

The Goorkha servant, light, active and loosely clad, swung himself up and sat astride on the branch. The officer, heavier and encumbered by his tighter-fitting dress, was unable to do so, notwithstanding all the efforts of his servant to assist him. He had to remain suspended, holding on by his hands alone. The situation must have been terrible, for the tiger lay below him still alive, and he felt his own strength failing. Presently the grip of his hands relaxed, and he fell.

He felt too much shaken to move, and had his leg within reach of the tiger's jaws. The tiger had just sufficient life remaining to enable him to seize the leg and crunch it. The officer was rescued, and eventually recovered, but it was with the loss of his limb. What made the case sadder was that he was remarkably handsome and a soldier of much promise. The event occurred long before I had charge of the Doon, but at a time when I happened to be at Mussoorie on leave. I tell the story as I then heard it.

I will conclude my account of the tigers by the correction of a very prevalent error in regard to some of them. It is commonly supposed, especially in this country, that the tigers termed 'man-eaters' are tigers of unusual ferocity. It is quite otherwise. They are tigers whose strength and activity have become diminished by age. Unable to catch the deer and wild animals, as before, they approach the villages and prey on the sheep and cattle or, if they happen to meet with any, on the human inhabitants; and this they continue to do when opportunity offers, not from any special partiality for the flesh of man, but because it happens to be easily obtainable.
{1899}

THE TWENTIETH CENTURY

By the turn of the twentieth century, hunting was rampant and the crisis that resulted from it threw up legendary figures like F. W. Champion and Jim Corbett who became pioneers of early conservation initiatives. Champion was a sportsman who preferred photographing animals to hunting them. Corbett was a master tracker and often followed and dispatched dreaded man-eaters. He had mastered the language of the forest and his books were famous around the world. By the late 1930s, influenced by Champion, he took to filming tigers.

Even after India's independence, the rich and the famous continued to slaughter India's wildlife. The maharajas of India indulged in the massacre of tigers, with one record bag even touching 1,100 animals. In the nick of time, the then Prime Minister Indira Gandhi banned tiger hunting in 1969, and by 1974, Project Tiger had been born to protect tigers in the wild.

~

At last, after several days of inaction, we met with our first real excitement, and at the same time I shot my first tiger. He was well known, for three gunners who were in the same place last year had three beats after him—ineffectual beats. He was fond of killing bears—a very uncommon thing; and the villagers told us he had been seen to climb a tree after a bear which scrambled up it to get out of his clutches. He managed to reach the bear, and attacked him. Both fell out of the tree on to the ground, when the tiger promptly killed the bear.

This we did not at the time believe; it is most rare for a tiger to climb trees—in fact, almost unheard of. But it proved to be true. He was what they call a very *bobbery* (pugnacious) tiger, the first news we heard of him being that he had killed and eaten another bear six miles from our camp. We went out and had a beat, and found the remains of poor Bruin [the bear]; the tiger was in the beat, but he broke out through the stops on one side without being fired at. {1900}

I sat on my machan, absorbed in watching the jungle actors pass across my stage. Believe me, I was far from bored with this vigil. The scraggy trees surrounding the swamp were silhouetted against a setting sun that blazed in the west like a ball of incandescent copper. The day insects gradually ceased their irritating humming and biting; and the fairy life of the night, whose dawn is the setting day, came buzzing in myriads from their hiding places like the ballet of an elfin chorus.

A stately crane stepped daintily through the reeds; and fat-breasted little birds of brilliant plumage settled on twigs, twittered and kissed good night, ruffled their gorgeous feathers, and then tucked tiny heads under their wings. Nature was retiring to rest; only the killers were on the prowl.

There is never an armistice in the wild spaces of the earth. It is always war: and war to the death. No quarter is given to any living thing, and only the very fittest and most cunning can escape for long from their ultimate fate.

I breathed deeply, stirred and delighted with all I saw. The swamp air, sweet to my nostrils, almost intoxicated; a cool night wind sprang up and soothed my sun-baked body; and my senses revelled in this picturesque unveiling of Nature's own bed-chamber. Surely no human being could have remained insensible to, or out of tune with, the charms of that perfect picture!

All at once, I was alert. I had heard heavy feet forcing their way through the tangled masses of the jungle. The giant grass ahead of me now swayed and bent down; and, a moment later, a magnificent cow buffalo breasted her way out of that thick mat of grass and undergrowth, and stood out in the open. She had a massive sweep of horns; one of the best I have ever seen on one of her kind. Powerful bulk, terrific shoulders and gigantic head, she made a grand picture. She offered a perfect target; and I had not yet bagged an Indian buffalo. For a fleeting instant or so I hesitated, fingers clutching my rifle. But I wanted that tiger, and so refrained from shooting. Oh, how glad I am today that the tiger was uppermost in my thoughts!

Suspiciously, she sniffed the air; and then, throwing her face skywards, bellowed like a thunderclap. The tree seemed to quiver under me to the vibrations of that majestic challenge to all in the wilds.

A moment later came an answering bellow, as if from miles away. It sounded faint and distant after the volume of her great voice. The cow replied joyously to her mate. She shook her huge head, and then drove the cruel points of her horns viciously into the soft earth. Evidently she was feeling good, and wanted the world to know it.

Leisurely, she walked over to the tiger's kill, and sniffed at it thoughtfully for a minute or two. Again up came her splendid head, and the thunder of her throat burst and shattered the silence of the dying day. It was a sound of challenging defiance: arresting, menacing and utterly provocative.

Suddenly she showed signs of palpable uneasiness. She turned about swiftly, facing the suspected point of danger. Her head was lowered now, eyes peering intently at the edge of the jungle beyond my tree. My own followed the direction of her steady gaze. Almost at once I saw what she had seen.

The tiger was there, just clear of the fringe of the dense jungle. He was skulking along silently, furtively, and with white belly sweeping the grass.

He saw the cow buffalo and halted instantly: motionless save for his twitching, writhing tail. The buffalo scattered the loose earth with a swift stroke of her forefoot, eyes never wavering from that intent watch on her ancient foe. Both animals were alert, and fully on guard. Eyes held eyes, unflinching and savage. There was deadly hate in the whole attitude of each great beast.

Shoot that tiger I would not. I desired now only to see this wonderful jungle drama played out to the final drop of the curtain.

Slowly the striped jungle-cat crept forward more into the open, never once straightening his elastic body, eyes glaring fixedly at the buffalo, and tail swishing the grass angrily. The massive jaw hung half open, low to the ground and dripping saliva. The cow buffalo moved only to keep facing him, neither advancing nor retreating. There was a deadly menace in her whole intense attitude.

Round and round, in an ever-narrowing circle, went the tiger, trying to get in behind the buffalo for a sudden spring on to her back; but she was always too quick for him. You could not teach her much in ring tactics, and her footwork was perfect. She knew every trick of the jungle.

Abruptly the tiger paused and drew himself up into a ball, tail lashing the ground savagely. Then, without sound or warning, his body shot through the air like a rocket. At the same instant, with a thunderous bellow and the fine sweep of horns levelled, the buffalo charged. She met the tiger's body in mid-air. The shock of that impact hurled both to the ground; but, in a flash, they were up again. With a roar and answering bellow, they charged at each other once more. The tiger missed, but his leap landed him behind the buffalo.

With almost incredible agility, he turned and sprang upon her back. Before his terrible fangs could sink deep into her neck, she threw herself over backwards and tried to roll upon him. The move was both astute and effective.

The tiger, in order to save himself from being crushed beneath that massive body, loosened his hold on her. As she regained her feet, he was ready; and now fastened himself on her right shoulder. The cow shook him clear of her and, with a furious bellow, charged full at him. She bowled him over like a ninepin, and then rammed him against the thick trunk of a large tamarisk tree.

Blood was flowing freely from her bellowing mouth, streaming also from the great gashes in neck, shoulder and back made by those cruel talons. She retreated to gain charging distance to finish off her enemy.

The tiger, however, was still fit to fight, though badly gored and crushed. He was game, too. Again he sprang in, and this time landed fair and square between her great horns, his beautifully striped body hanging down and completely smothering her face. His teeth and claws sank deeply into her flesh, blood filled his mouth and ran down the cow's sides in great rivers of carmine. She bellowed aloud in her agony.

Lowering her head almost to the ground, she charged full speed at a big tree trunk. Her burden was still festooned over her face. There came a sickening thud as they met the solid tree. She staggered back and almost sat down on her rump, but quickly regained her poise. A feeble roar told me that the tiger's distress was very great indeed; and that the result of that terrific impact would be his complete undoing. In a limp heap, he collapsed on the ground.

The cow buffalo had delivered a real upper-cut and knocked him out.

I saw her draw back, and carefully measure her mark. A short rush forward, a sharp twist of her cruel horns, and she had gored him again and again. He tried to crawl away into the cover of the jungle growth, and hide from that pitiless onslaught. Now he had had enough: rather more than enough. But there is no referee in the jungle to count "time". He was not to know escape from the relentless law. Only the death of one, or both, could end that fierce combat.

A triumphant bellow of victory shook the swamp-grass and made my machan shiver. The cow buffalo charged home for the final effort. She lifted that mangled, crushed body on her great horns, gave a sharp twist of her head, and threw the big jungle cat, as if he was a wisp of straw, some distance away.

He must have died as he hit the ground. She did not even trouble to follow his body, and make certain that he was killed. She *knew.*

I could not resist a loud shout of: "Bravo!" All through that titantic battle my sympathies had been with the buffalo, even though she had robbed me of my trophy. But no tiger skin in the world could have compensated me for having failed to witness that stupendous fight to the death. It was an opportunity that comes but once to a man in a lifetime: even if then.

The black pall of night descended and shut out that great picture. A young and tender moon shed an ethereal light over the stage, and twinkling stars began to wink at me from the darkening canopy overhead.

The buffalo bellowed again, triumphantly; and was answered immediately from close at hand in the dense jungle. I heard the crash of her thundering departure from the stage to meet her mate in the wings of the forest. The curtain fell soundlessly then, and shut out the last act of that thrilling jungle-drama.

I was glad that she had won: glad with all my heart that the tiger had gone down to such a splendid creature. She had asked no mercy: given none.

I wanted to say something to that dumb heroine in her hour of triumph; but I was tongue-tied. Never till that moment had I realized how narrow are the limits of human speech. There were no words in the cold English language to express adequately all I felt.

The tiger's body I left where it had fallen. It was not mine. {1933}

The Kotwar shikari was the first to see the wounded tiger and he called out to Mr. Bourne to look, at the same time signing with his hands. As soon as the tiger heard the Kotwar's voice it was on him like a flash of lightning and caught hold of the man's neck with its mouth. Mr. Bourne was only ten paces away and he shot it in the stomach. The tiger fell from the Kotwar, but only momentarily was it down, and in another few seconds had sprung upon the Deputy Commissioner, who fired again as it leapt, but missed. Now Mr. Bourne's ammunition was finished and the cartridges were with the peon who had already taken to his heels. With admirable presence of mind and courage, Mr. Bourne jammed the barrel of his rifle into the animal's mouth, but it grabbed it and threw it away, and as it turned again to its victim Mr. Bourne thrust his left hand inside the tiger's mouth. The tiger stood up on its hind legs and put its uninjured leg on Mr. Bourne's shoulder and a terrible struggle ensued. The District Commissioner was a well-built and very brave man and a very strong one, but he could never hold his own against a wounded tiger. He was shouting agonizingly for a gun and cartridges and imploring someone to shoot the tiger, but everyone was too concerned about his own safety and in their haste to get up the trees had left their guns on the ground below. The tahsildar was in the machan and the Police Inspector, the village headman and the Gond shikaris were up as high as they could go and several of them had soiled pants to show for their terror. The District Commissioner was now on the ground, but still fighting gamely, kicking with all his might at the tiger's mouth—it was vital to prevent the tiger catching hold with its mouth. The duel went on for nearly twenty minutes and Mr. Bourne was very severely ripped and gashed, when suddenly the tiger's strength departed because of the extent of its wounds. It fell down beside Mr. Bourne. The men on the tree-tops came down and picking up their rifles fired a few more shots into the tiger and then carried Mr. Bourne to his car and took him to the hospital at Betul. Mr. Bourne was still conscious and directed the operating theatre to be opened up and doctors and nurses sent for immediately, but in spite of all the medical aid given him he died three days later. He had really given his life for the Kotwar, because he might so easily have taken cover when the man was attacked. He was greatly mourned in the district, because in spite of his brusque manner, of which I had had experience, he was extremely kind and generous to the poor of the district. {1963}

ALADDIN'S CAVE | A. MERVYN SMITH

On approaching the side, I suddenly found it sparkling with gleams of gold and green and red light, as if studded all over with gems, from which the light I held in my hand was scintillated and refracted. Turning round, I found a similar twinkling light all round on the walls of the mine, as if ten thousand fireflies had settled all over the sides, only that the light differed in colour, there being sparkles of white and red and green. Was this a veritable Aladdin's Cave, and were all these glints of light flashing from real diamonds, rubies and emeralds!

The adventure of the early part of the day had given me cause to believe that there was at least some foundation of truth in the stories of "The Thousand and One Nights". Could this be the same cave in which Aladdin was shut up by the cruel magician? And were all those diamonds and rubies and emeralds, within my reach? It only wanted a Genius of the Ring to complete the illusion. Great Heavens! What was that? A distinct hiss as of a cat, and then in the distance a gigantic cat itself. As I looked it appeared to grow in size and swell to enormous dimensions. A veritable Genius, and this the enchanted cave! With my heart in my mouth, I hurried back to the mound in the centre of the shaft, and shouted to Permal to join me and bring my gun with him. I had now time to collect my thoughts and try to work out some explanation of this strange adventure. Experience had long ago taught me that diamonds, rubies, and emeralds are never found together in their natural state, and I was also aware that these gems do not reflect light or sparkle to any extent in their uncut condition. Perhaps it might be a mica mine, and the light be reflected from flakes of that mineral. But what about the monstrous cat? Was that the result of imagination, or stern reality? There was no mistaking the hiss and growl, which again emanated from a far corner of the mine on our throwing a stone in that direction. Permal at once declared that he could smell tiger. He kept sniffing about, and said, "*Ullee, davaru* (tiger, my lord)." The strange sparkles of light still kept twinkling around, as if innumerable stars were set in the walls. I noticed, however, that, if we attempted to move, thus agitating the air, the scintillation would be more brilliant. Cutting up several candles into pieces, we soon had a brilliant light about us, and this enabled me to see that the underground chamber was very irregular in shape, about thirty feet wide from east to west, and somewhat longer towards the north. It was from the latter direction that the hissing and growling seemed to come, and Permal declared he could see a large tiger crouching down behind a piece of rock in the far corner. But if it was a tiger, why did it not attack us, as it could not be more than twenty paces away from us? I was inclined to believe it was a hyena, and therefore plucked up heart to have a shot at it, as I would not have ventured to attack a tiger at such close quarters, and on foot. Cocking both barrels, I directed Permal to throw stones at the creature to induce it to break cover; but no, the brute would not move, but continued spitting and growling. I was now convinced it was a hyena, and advanced more boldly until I could just see a dark object behind a rock. I could see the gleaming eyes distinctly, so, taking careful aim, I fired, and then retreated hastily to the mound. We waited some time, but could hear no sound, and the smoke made it more difficult to see. We threw several large stones in the direction, but there was no movement. The hissing, too, had ceased. Re-loading the empty barrel, we again advanced cautiously, and then I made out the body, in the same position apparently. Again aiming carefully, I tried a second shot. There was no missing so large an object within a few paces, so I felt quite sure the creature was hit, but not so sure that it was dead. We retreated once more to the mound, and after some time advanced again to the attack, but not a movement had taken place in the object. Feeling quite sure it was dead, we now got close up and examined it, and found it to be a tiger of the largest size, in a most emaciated condition. {1904}

"I soon noticed that there were two sets of pugs which went together. This led me to believe there were a tiger and a tigress. I went to every kill before the Khols got scent of it and carried away the flesh, as these people eat every kind of flesh, even rats and snakes and carrion, and I carefully noted that the trails all led in one direction—to a rocky hill covered with dense jungle. This was where the tigers had taken up their abode. I soon found that the tigers took a particular path to the river to drink. That was the clue I wanted. I would now have my revenge, and the villagers would see I was a real *baghmaree* [tiger hunter], although only a weaver by caste. *Shabash!* I set my bow to command the path the tiger took when going to the river, and went home quite pleased with myself; but I did not tell anybody that I had set my trap, as I waited for my triumph to be complete. I hardly slept that night, and was away at grey dawn to see the trap. The bow was sprung and both arrows had taken effect as they were not to be found anywhere, while pug marks, blood and signs of struggling were to be seen on the path. I knew the arrows would do their work, for I had put on some fresh cobra poison the previous day. Imagine my feelings, Sahib, when I saw I had triumphed! The bridegroom on his wedding-day, when the village girls anoint him with turmeric and oil; or when you have just secured a pair of strong buffaloes for your plough at half price; or when your field has yielded forty-fold; or when your enemy is dead—mine were all these feelings in one! I felt a hero. I gathered up my bow and ropes and walked to the village a new man. I went straight to the gathering-tree in the centre of the village and sat down. First came one and jibed, 'Well, *tantee* (weaver), is that your loom you have rolled up?' pointing to my bow. 'Make me a *saree*...for my wife, and I will give you half a candy of grain when the crop comes,' said another. Many joined in the laugh, but I waited quietly till the principal men of the village had assembled to talk, when I said, 'Brothers, don't laugh any more, but come with the poor weaver. I have something to show'; and I strode on with the gait of an elephant with the great Maharaj on his back. All the village followed, and I led—straight to the place where I had set my trap, and the trail from there was clear. Not two hundred yards off we found the body of the tiger. It was a white tiger. Pure white: no spot or stripe of any kind. Believe me, Sahib, when I tell you it was white. A great shout went up from the villagers and I was happy. Such moments come seldom.

"After a time the villagers left and only the *shikarees*...of the village remained with me to do *pooja*.... The oldest of the *shikarees* made a slight wound in my head and took some of the blood and rubbed it on the head of the tiger. I walked three times round the body of the tiger, and then touched its body with my forehead while the others looked aside. We now slung the tiger to a pole and took it to the village in triumph. When we got there, the *shikarees'* wives came out and washed my feet with water and *salaamed* to me. You don't want to hear all that—you want to know where the danger came in. I will pass over the triumphs of the day; how the Raja gave me two rupees and a *dhotee*…how the villagers also rewarded me, each according to his means. I was a great man that day. Don't be impatient, Sahib; one likes to talk of one's victories—we are all alike.

"We skinned the tiger, and found it was very old—fifteen years old. How do we know a tiger's age? By the number of lobes in the liver. This one had fifteen distinct marks, one for each year. Panthers have these marks also, but not other animals. All *shikarees* know this, as we always take out the liver for medicine. This is how we judge of a tiger's age, and it is true. We pegged out the skin in the sun to dry, the head being boned and stuffed with straw and the mouth agape. At night we rolled up the skin and placed it on some sticks in an empty cow-shed." {1904}

VALMIK THAPAR

THE FOREST AND THE TIGER | A. I. R. GLASFURD

It is an early December morning in the Sátpúras. The still air of the deep glen of the Sípna is bitterly cold, and dank with surcharged dews that have heavily saturated the long fresh grass and surrounding jungle, and the calm surface of a long pool that lies along the grey bed of the shingly mountain stream is shrouded in clinging white vapour; the temperature of the water, sun-warmed as it is by day, being several degrees higher than that of the atmosphere at dawn.

Overhanging the river-bed from either bank, and helping to wrap the scene in yet deeper shadow, stretches a long, vista-enclosing fringe of great umbrageous trees, their gnarled roots washed bare by the mountain freshets that during the rainy season fill this wide-banked space with an irresistible flood. Close above the pool the steepness of the bank is somewhat worn away, and here a rut-worn cart track descends to cross the broad Sípna, on its way westward from the jungle hamlet of Pili. Beyond the river the forest road is at once lost sight of in long grass and the tall straight trunks of the big-leaved teak trees; it is but a passing glimpse of man's influence in these remote tracts, one of the slender threads he has drawn through the untamed woods.

Far upstream the forest river takes a bend to the right, its shore opposite the abrupt angle piled high with huge rotting tree-trunks and other heavy driftwood swept there by the floods of late September; and through this one break in the enveloping jungle the surrounding teak-clad hills are seen to rise tier on tier, glowing mauve-pink in an early sunlight that has not yet pierced its way to the dark valley itself, their distant woody summits standing sharp-cut against a clear blue sky. High up in the calm morning air a flight of big green parakeets cleaves its way with piercing answering cries.

Building on such a huge and inhospitable scale, Nature here seems to have forgotten man, to have excluded him from this stern wild scheme; and it is with a culprit-like sense of trespass that the solitary intruder finds himself standing in these silent woods. The thickness and mystery of the surrounding all-pervading jungle adds a touch of disquietude. How easily a man might utterly disappear in such solitudes! A few paces into that bamboo cane-brake—the rush of some too suddenly disturbed feline—an unexpected meeting face to face with a startled bear—an incautious step on some comatose lurking Russell's viper—or the rash disturbing of that great bees' nest hanging from yonder bough—and he would be seen no more. Nay, in this insect-crammed, life-teeming tropic land he would in a few hours be completely gone!

Such thoughts, however, seldom trouble the sportsman and naturalist, although they may add to that fascination which all forests exercise over the human mind.

Wherever the broad stretches of shingle are succeeded by sand, or by the moist margins of pools, the tale of the jungle is clearly unfolded. The tracks of creatures that wander by night—and in Indian forests few of the larger fauna move by day—have inscribed a fresh page each twenty-four hours, and it needs but little practice to read what is imprinted thereon. Here the deep and pointed slot of that great woodland stag, the sámbar; there the rounder-toed track of a solitary forest boar, as he picked a leisurely and truculent way under this steep bank; and perchance, also, the lately used mud-wallow, in which the discoloured water has not yet had time to clear. See! a prowling panther passed this way during the night, for his footprints overlie all the marks left by the peafowl and jungle fowl that drink before roosting for the night.

It was on just such a cold-weather morning, soon after dawn, down a retired reach of the forest-penned Sípna, that the brown ground-squirrels set up a sudden shrill squeaking, and a bevy of peafowl in the river-bed stretched their long necks, bright-eyed, alert, with clucking notes of warning. Next moment the big birds made rapidly for the shelter of the jungle, some running as only a peafowl can run, others leaping into a heavy flight in order to clear the high bank above them.

Round a corner, a hundred paces away, stood, where nothing had shown a moment before, a vision of banded black and gold. Above the white of chest and chin, yellow eyes, set in a strangely mesmeric forehead, gazed inquiringly down the deserted vista. The lower jaw, with its cruel fangs just bared, hung slightly opened, and projected in that stern manner symbolic all the world over of uncompromising animalism, the saliva on the retracted black lips glistening in the early light, and gently quivering with the vibrations of a throaty breathing. The head was held level and advanced. The great forepaws had come to rest in the middle of a pace. And behind the muscular ridge of the shoulder-blades the sinewy and rounded back curved away into a low-carried, black-banded tail. From its side came solemnly pacing, with absurdly big ungainly paws, a smaller, blear-eyed, and uncouth replica of itself, followed an instant later by yet another that gambolled awkwardly across the sand to halt and sniff at the edge of the pool close by.

Then the largest of the three came heavily pacing forward, each step making a soft, deep crunching in the yielding sandbank.

It was the tigress and her cubs. They were seeking a lair for the day after the nightly prowl abroad. And something in the attitude of the trio seemed to suggest that they had not walked the night in vain!

Sometimes the cubs would lag behind, but mother would wait for them, her head turned, her jaw ever quivering with her warm breath, or vibrating with a low, affectionate purring that sounded like the deepest throbbing note of an organ. Their proper place was ahead of her, where she might best shepherd their waywardness, or rush to defend them; while the way in which she started at a falling dry leaf—she, the mistress over all but one of the other beasts of this forest—was proof of her unceasing solicitude for their welfare.

In such manner the little family party passed slowly down the winding reaches of jungle river-bed, the frogs leaping hurriedly for the pools at their approach. Now and then a land-crab would go scuttling off sidewise to its hole amid the stones; and perhaps a heavy paw would descend on it. There would be a crunch or two as the succulent morsel disappeared. Here and there a handsome grey jungle-cock, strutting in the open with his sombre hens, would beat a cackling retreat, and set up his alarmed "*Kaaw—wick-a-wack!*" from the neighbouring undergrowth; while at one sharp bend a little *khákar*—the *muntjac* or barking-deer—bounced off coughing in alarm, his white flag of a tail cocked high in sudden affright.

Farther down the Sípna's bed a tributary steep-banked ravine joined it at right angles, and opposite this the tigress and her two young hopefuls came to a halt.

For a time the mother stood there, the tip of her tail curving gently from side to side, her gaze fixed downstream. Then she quietly turned and made slowly towards the little side ravine, waited a moment while her cubs passed ahead under a fallen tree, then followed them. The long dry grass into which they had passed closed slowly over her red rump. Tigress and cubs had disappeared.

After some minutes a crow that had been silently watching with beady eyes from a neighbouring bough cocked its intelligent head, and seemed for an instant to lower a filmy eyelid. It depressed its tail and emitted a thoughtful "*Caw!*" Then it dropped neatly from its perch, and flew low up that same side ravine.

There was no further movement in the jungle. {1905}

THE ALLIGATOR, A NASTY OPPONENT | JOHN FINNEMORE

The tiger himself, unmatched in combat with any other beast of the jungle, sometimes falls a prey to the alligator. Coming to drink at the river, the king of the jungle is seized by the waiting reptile. A terrific struggle follows. Unable to wrench himself from those mighty jaws, the tiger uses his terrible fangs and claws on the alligator's back. Here for once they fail on that coat of horny scales. The tiger does not know that the alligator is soft beneath, and there could be ripped up by his claws of steel, and he continues to spend his strength in vain. Inch by inch he is dragged into the river, and once under water, he is lost. He swiftly drowns, and the alligators feast on his body. [1907]

THE VICIOUS ATTACK ON THE ELEPHANT

S. EARDLEY-WILMOT

It was extremely hot, the gun-barrels were burning to the touch, and both men and elephants felt the sun greatly, so that I wished to go home, and return later in the evening or next morning to recover a beast that was evidently in no way disabled; but I foolishly listened to the clamour of my men, who insisted, as usual, that the tiger was dead, and consented to follow him up almost at once.

As might have been expected, he instantly charged, selecting the small elephant, who as promptly fled, and might indeed have made her escape, as the tiger was merely striking in an undecided manner; but, unfortunately, he inflicted a slight scratch on her hind-leg, and the foolish animal turned on him. She was at once seized as in a vice, the claws of both fore-paws being embedded in her head, and the fangs in the base of her trunk. From this grip there was no escape, and, the tiger continuing to pull in heavy jerks, the elephant came down on her knees. At this stage the driver described a parabola through the air and lay motionless in the grass; while the tiger, still pulling, turned the elephant on her side. I in the meantime stood watching at a few yards off, unable to fire on account of the deep agitation of my own mount, who could hardly be restrained from either fighting or fleeing, and could not be made to stand steady. The tiger ultimately disappeared with one bound into the grass, the prostrate elephant slowly arose, blood pouring from her wounds, while the man lay still, and some minutes elapsed before he staggered bewildered to his feet, picked up his turban, and sought safety on my elephant. It was a melancholy procession that returned to Dhikála, and there was an anxious time to follow in tending the elephant day and night till her wounds healed and she was herself once more. The remains of the tiger were found not far from the spot later on, but I had little interest in the matter, because I felt that, in yielding to the foolish persuasion of my men, I had brought about a disaster that might have been much more serious than it actually was. {1911}

THE BEND OF A STREAM | S. EARDLEY-WILMOT

I once in the Pátli Doon watched a tiger who was interested in some hog-deer grazing in the open plain at about 150 yards distance from the banks of a small stream. He seemed at once to recognize the spot where he would be nearest to his intended prey, and proceeded under the cover of the bank towards it. At a bend in the stream a small crocodile about 7 feet long was lying, evidently fast asleep, and to this the tiger paid no attention, perhaps in his eagerness mistaking it for a piece of driftwood; but when he suddenly became aware of the reptile his discomfiture was amusing: he bounded into the air and ran a few yards, then turned, snarling with ill temper. When this tiger at last found himself in the most favourable position for attack, he spent some time in adjusting himself for the start, arranging and rearranging his feet to obtain perfect balance, and finally shot across the open at full gallop. He had covered the first half of the distance before the deer realized their danger, and was within a few yards before they had got up their speed and fled with startled cries. Their escape was narrow enough to prove that luck might be sometimes against them, and that, though the tiger on this occasion returned grumbling with vexation, he might on another be successful in securing a toothsome meal. [1911]

VALMIK THAPAR

THE TIGER AND THE COOKING POT | J. H. RIVETT-CARNAC

I must now close my tiger stories with one less pathetic than the last, relating to the days when the first houses for Europeans were being built on the now well-covered western slope of Malabar Hill, Bombay. The jungle there was then thick, and wild animals abundant. An officer of the Royal Engineers, who, engaged on the works, had built him a bungalow there, was alarmed one evening, so said my informant, by a terrific row in his cook-house, and rushing thither, found, to his amazement, a tiger in possession of the place. The beast, attracted apparently by the smell of the viands, had entered the house and put his head into a large *deckchi*, or copper cooking pot, containing meat. Having filled his mouth with the viands, the tiger, who had squeezed in his head with difficulty, found it even more difficult to extract his swollen neck from out of the pot and was floundering and blundering blindfolded about the place when the officer opportunely made his appearance. A shot, fired at close quarters, disposed of that tiger. My informant added that he was called in later to see that muzzled tiger, and that the copper pot had got so tightly welded on to the beast's swollen neck, that it had to be chopped off from the carcase! Some will, perhaps, hold that this is a companion picture to the lantern-slide of one's childhood, "The Tale of a Tub," noticed among my Chandah experiences. But when I state that my informant was no other than my dear old friend the late Right Rev. Dr James Wilson, the well-known missionary, the Vice-Chancellor of the University of Bombay, who himself was in at the death, it will be recognised that this is no traveller's tale, but is supported indeed by the highest credible authority. {1910}

Kadra, January 13th

The horses are being marched down to Karwar today, but we don't go till tonight, sailing down the Kali Nadi in a native fishing boat. Poor Solomon. The tiger was roaring all night. How terrified he will be lying shivering in his bullock cart jolting through the jungle.

We were called about three, dressed, breakfasted and came down to the shore, a procession of bobbing hurricane lanterns through the trees. Dogs tightly chained to our waists. No sound of the tiger. Only the crunching of dead teak leaves like broken earthenware under our feet. The false dawn was breaking as we came out of the trees. A blessed coolness breathed on our brows; men's voices, the sound of splashing; we could just distinguish the fishing boat, her sails and her mast darker against the dark sky, and a lantern glowing in the bows. The dogs jumped on board nearly pulling us over, and instantly hurled themselves down on the mattresses prepared for Henry and me in the stern. (Why do bull-terriers do everything with such violence, even lying down?).

The air on one's brow was delicious, the night lovely.

Poor people in England! How dull their lives. Pictures of deserted London streets, a solitary cat, and lonely lamp posts rise before me...but perhaps England in wartime isn't like that.

The false dawn was over, and the true dawn coming up behind our backs, the hills taking shape and the sky lightening so fast we could see the lazy sail was striped tomato and gold. It was filmy with rents so that in patches one could see the grey sky brightening to blue. The light wind dropped, so now with cries the four boatmen were pulling in the sail against the tapering mast. It looked like the netherside of a mushroom. {1949}

One evening, in Assam, a young Englishman was driving along a lonely jungle road. He wished to visit a neighbouring Saheb; and though his servants had warned him that tigers had been frequently seen on that particular road, he had laughed at their fears and told them that the only tiger to be feared was a "man-eater", and that there were no "man-eating" tigers about that district. As usual in the mofussil of India, he was going out to dine and sleep, and his bearer had put up his clothes and his suitcase was stowed into the dog-cart.

The road was a good one and considerably wide, for it was the main thoroughfare in the district and along it tea, jute and all other agricultural products were transported to the river for export to other districts of India and also to Europe. Nevertheless it was bordered on either side by dense jungle, and there were few villages in its vicinity. After sunset it was a road little frequented by villagers and it had the reputation of being tiger-haunted.

There was no moon and as B. had not started much before sunset darkness soon overtook him on the road. As he had no *syce* [attendant] with him he got down to light the trap-lamps and jumped in and drove on again very cheerily. He was not far from where he must turn off the main road to the narrow one leading to his friend's estate, when the pony suddenly took fright at something and bolted. At first B. tried to pull the animal up; but its erect ears and wild snorting showed him that there was cause for alarm. He looked over his shoulder and in the dim starlight discerned the bulk of some animal in pursuit of them. An eerie feeling came over him and he wondered what was going to happen. He sat tight in his seat and let the pony race on. The chase continued and the pony began to show signs of collapse. It was evidently being overcome by fear and, in spite of all B.'s urging, could not keep up the pace, and the pursuing animal gained upon them. B. had just determined to leap from the cart when the pony tripped and fell and B. was shot out of the cart. He fell into the long grass on the side of the road, and had barely collected himself when a dark form sprang upon the pony.

The poor animal neighed with fear but kicked and fought its foe. B. rolled down the side of the road and began to crawl away through the jungle as fast as he could. Long grass and thorny brambles grew on either side of the road and as it was the dry season every movement of his made a crackling and rustling; and often he fancied he heard an animal in pursuit of him, or he would imagine he was about to meet one coming through the jungle towards him. He pressed on as fast as he could, sometimes crawling and sometimes walking, and at last he saw the glimmer of lights and came to some huts. He shouted to the inmates who came to his assistance.

When they discovered a Saheb in such a plight they were full of concern, helped him to their huts, gave him hot milk to drink and washed his wounds. His clothes were torn and his hands and knees bleeding from his flight through the thorny jungle. The sympathising villagers emptied a hut for him to rest in, and when morning came escorted him to the scene of his mishap.

The mangled remains of his poor pony told him that the wild animal had been a very famished tiger. B. returned to his own bungalow a wiser man, and told his servants that, had he taken their advice, he would not have suffered such an adventure or the loss of his pony. He rewarded the villagers for their kindness and hospitality and for a long time his escape was the talk of the district. [1916]

It was a dark close night and the door of his tent stood open, for he was a lover of air. He had read on for some time when his attention was drawn to a movement of his tent wall. It seemed to him as if someone or something was rubbing along the side. He put down his book and got on to his feet to see what it could be. As he was about to step forward, the head of a tiger loomed in the doorway, the eyes gleaming brightly. Sir M. stood motionless with surprise and "Stripes" stepped into the tent. He was a fine specimen of a Royal Bengal tiger, and M. forgot everything in his admiration of the noble animal.

The table with the lamp upon it stood between Sir M. and the tiger, and each stood on either side of it gazing at each other. As the silent seconds passed, Sir M. realized that he was in danger and bethought him of his rifle which was almost within reach of his hand; but he dared not move and so continued gazing steadfastly at his visitor. The tiger too stood, surveying his vis-a-vis and then began to move round the table. The lamp either attracted or annoyed him and he raised his paw to the table. The weight of the huge paw tilted the table, the lamp toppled and fell with a crash. The terrified tiger gave a mighty roar, turned tail and fled.

The camp was aroused. Everyone shouted and rushed out into the night, armed with some weapon or other. Sir M. related to his brother guns what had happened and they all enjoyed a good laugh and rather envied him for the fine sight he had of such a superb specimen of the kings of the jungle. {1916}

THE TIGER AND THE SAMBAR | E. P. STEBBING

The night was a perfectly still one, the leaves hanging motionless from tree and shrub in the bright moonlight which fell full upon the small glade in which the salt-lick was situated. Our zareba lay in dense shadow as did the greater part of the surrounding forest, patches of moonlight appearing only in one or two places beyond the clearing. The forest was alive with sound; the crickets were shrieking as usual, night bush warblers and other nocturnal birds were voicing their sibilant or harsh notes, whilst at intervals the hoarse haunting hoot of owls rose on the night air, sounding like the cries of lost souls in purgatory. Weirdly uncanny are some of the night cries and sounds in an Indian forest. For an hour, perhaps longer, I sat and watched the little glade listening to these varying night sounds with

VALMIK THAPAR

always that persistent under note of the crickets. Once a khakar suddenly and silently appeared out of the darkness of the forest and stood ghostly grey in the clearing. For a brief space he remained as though carved in stone, intently listening, and then vanished as quietly as he had come.

I was beginning to wonder whether the vigil was to be a blank when I suddenly saw two round beads of fire, twin stars set close together in the darkness of the forest on the other side of the clearing. I first thought of fire-flies, to dismiss the idea as quickly as it had flashed across my mind. An animal, and from their height probably a sambhar, I surmised. No sound had I heard and for minutes nothing happened, only at times the stars disappeared as the wary animal moved its head from side to side and nosed the air for enemies. For a full minute the points of light disappeared altogether, and I was beginning to fear that the animal had retreated when I suddenly heard a slight rustle a little to the right of where they had appeared, and immediately afterwards a fine sambhar stag stepped quietly out into the clearing. Stepped out and came to a halt, head erect, muzzle pushed forward, nostrils dilated, and ears flicked to the front. He stood there as if carved in bronze, the moonlight turning to silver his antlers and upper parts, the rest being in dense shadow.

I had not come out to kill so much as to watch, and I had not made up my mind as to whether I should fire or not when fate intervened, and one of the tragedies of the forest was enacted before my eyes. Almost without a sound a mighty black shadow, coming from our right rear, hurled itself through the air, and with a startled appealing bellow the lordly stag was borne to earth. A struggle of wildly kicking hoofs, a few gasps and gurgles and a rifle shot awoke the quiet depths of the forest.

As the dark shadow hurtled through the air I gasped with amazement, and was conscious of a sudden frightened ejaculation from my companion. With the fall of the stag I came back to the realities, and keeping my fascinated eyes fixed upon the drama being enacted before them raised the rifle and so far as it was possible in the medley of conflicting black and silver shadows on the ground sighted on the black shape and fired. The sharp report was answered by a deafening roar, a roar which I afterwards interpreted as one of fright and rage, and a black and silver form leapt across the clearing and disappeared into the forest opposite, almost at the point from which the stag had issued. The briefest interval of crushing and rustling bushes and then a deep silence ensued. The stag lay inert, evidently dead.

I drew a deep breath. The shape was a tiger, and I wondered whether it had been stalking us when the sambhar had so opportunely appeared on the scene, or whether it was as unaware of our presence as we were of his.

These were my first speculations, but they were soon succeeded by the tantalizing hopes and fears as to whether I had hit him or not. The whole drama was one of seconds only—could not have been longer. It had all occurred in a flash—the hurtling shadow, the felling of the sambhar to the ground, the report of the rifle and retreat of the tiger. And yet it had left different conditions behind it in the little clearing. The crickets, it is true, soon restarted their séance if indeed they had ever interrupted it, but otherwise a deeper silence pervaded the forest for other night sounds had ceased. We ourselves were very much on the alert and not a little uncomfortable, and passed the rest of the night sitting back to back very broad awake with our cocked rifles, for I luckily had two weapons with me, ready for instant use. My mind was in a whirl of anxiety as to the result of my shot and my inexperience led me to fear that I might have made more sure of my shot had I waited till the struggle was over. But I had fired without stopping to consider details. It was with a feeling of great relief that at length I perceived the waning moonlight give place to the first pale note of the dawn. Soon the trees began to stand out dim and grey from the surrounding twilight, and with the wonderful abruptness of the East the dawn arrived. Cautiously and quietly we left the zareba and walked up to the dead sambhar. It lay on its side, head and neck outstretched and throat torn open and, as we soon discovered, with a bullet through the heart. So my shot had missed the tiger or, at any rate, had killed the sambhar, if it was not already dead at the time I fired, which appearances seemed to indicate. We made a short survey of the neighbouring grass for blood, but found none, and then I deemed it to be more prudent to get back to camp and fetch the elephant. I spent the morning searching for that tiger, but found no traces of blood. It appeared evident that, as ill luck would have it, the bullet aimed at the struggling mass on the ground hit the dying or dead victim and missed the marauder, which is exactly the kind of mischance which so often happens in sport, and probably accounts for half its elusive attraction and charm.

The incident proved, however, a most cheerful and exciting piece of news to give to the guests of the Christmas party on their arrival, and I feel sure that each man retired to roost on the first night with the conviction that he would meet a tiger during his first day's sport in such a delectable region. {1920}

The jungle was at our doors and on one occasion a member of the Staff met a tiger purring by the roadside not four miles from the house. Inspired by this adventure I sallied forth down the same road the following evening, and though His Excellency had in the interval shot the tiger, I did not go unrewarded. It is a delicious, twisty, switchback road through the heart of the forest, sometimes enclosed on each side, sometimes rising to give you such a view of immense distances as to remind you that Gwalior alone is as large as Scotland and Wales; and though we did not in actual mileage go very far, yet Sivapuri itself is remote and once away from the little bazaar and off the high road you are swept into a vast solitude. That lovely flowering tree, so well named the "Flame of the Forest", is in its full glory in April; partridge and quail were feeding to right and left, plover, a more elegant fellow than our own but with the same sad "peewit", curved aside as we passed, and every few minutes sounded the harsh warning of the peacock, the alarmist of the jungle. Presently I stopped the car and informed a sceptical A.D.C. that I had seen a pig, a hyæna or else a porcupine of gigantic proportions, and that I must straightway discover which. Cautiously we descended and stalked the bush in which I insisted the monster lay concealed. I was right! We were only about fifty yards off when a large and quite unconscious hyæna emerged, and strolled unconcernedly off upon the evening's business. He is the scavenger, the four-footed vulture of the forest, and I do not know which, the bird or the beast, is the more repulsive. But at [the] sight of him our hopes of tiger rose, for he fattens on his kill, and on almost every tiger beat you first see a hyæna. {1926}

ONLY WITH THE ELEPHANT | NIGEL WOODYATT

I had a steep rise to manipulate. Just as my elephant's head reached the top, and while I was hanging to the handrail of the howdah to keep my balance, the tiger moved forward again. I could see it, but was quite unable to fire from the position I was in, and the elephant was on its knees.

As the elephant rose the tiger charged, striking out with its paws. Half a dozen of the nearest sportsmen fired. One, immediately behind me, with a heavy rifle with which I thought he had blown off my head. The explosion was deafening!

All the elephants were now very excited, and making a tremendous noise. The tiger stuck to mine, but although unhit, the hail of bullets had disconcerted it, and it had no real hold. My elephant was trying to get the tiger under its feet, and actually kicked it over on to its back.[11] In this position the tiger tried to claw the old lady's belly by striking upwards with its hind feet, but was unsuccessful.

All this time I was endeavouring to get a shot, but my wife and I were being shaken to bits. At last, leaning right over the side of the howdah, I got one, but the muzzle of my rifle was wobbling up and down with the

[11] *I reproduce a picture of a somewhat similar incident in Nepal.*

VALMIK THAPAR

elephant's movements, like a cutter in a choppy sea.

After this shot the tiger disappeared, sneaking somehow through the confused circle of elephants. We never saw it again.

Such incidents are very disconcerting. One never knows what the end may be. This I can best illustrate by the account of an adventure, which befell Sir John Campbell in the Kumaon Tarai in 1912, when he was forward as a "stop," to a line of elephants beating a tiger up to him.

Sir John wounded the tiger as it passed him. The animal went on a short distance, then turned and broke back through the line. The beat was reformed the reverse way, Campbell joining the line. He had seen, more or less, where the tiger had gone into the long grass, and made for the spot, the line conforming to his elephant's movements.

As they neared the place, Campbell heard spitting and cursing like the noise of an angry cat, but he was then too close to draw a charge from the tiger by using his shotgun.[12] Therefore he told the man behind him to throw a bottle of barley water into the place where the noise came from.

Out charged the tiger, but turned to Campbell's shot and galloped down the line, where it clawed a small female elephant. After this it went off, and lay down near one of the "stops." This sportsman could not see the tiger, but directed Campbell to where it was. The latter, spotting it under some bushes, inflicted a mortal wound, just missing its spine.

Then the little elephant which had been scratched by the tiger (she was carrying a load of soda-water, as well as the man told off to keep it cool by wetting it) lost her head completely. Charging out of the line she went straight for the tiger trying to kneel on it, and butt it with her head. The result was that she got badly bitten in the trunk and mouth, while the soda-water man and most of the bottles were hurled into space.

Next she tried to roll on the tiger, with all her four feet in the air. A very thrilling spectacle for the line, which stood looking on, agitated but helpless. At the first attempt to roll she got the mahout's leg between her weight and the tiger. This snapped the limb in two. The mahout, poor devil, did not tumble off, as the other leg being hung up in the stirrup saved him from falling.

At the second attempt the elephant planted the broken leg into the tiger's mouth! As she got up the tiger came with her hanging on to the mahout's broken leg with its teeth and claws.

Then the tiger let go, and the elephant ran back to the line. {1922}

---

[12]*A sure way of making a wounded tiger charge, so as to get a fair chance at the animal.*

THE TIGRESS'S FURY | A. E. WARDROP

At last I got tired of this sort of work and proposed to my men that we should visit the patch of grass where she first showed herself, and see if the cubs were really there; so back we went, and had not gone far into the grass when the Sholagas exclaimed, "Here are her cubs, sir."

I just caught a glimpse of one or two woolly things in the grass when I heard a growl from behind me, followed by an ear-splitting roar, from the tigress, which sent the men running back. Instinctively I faced round, but when I saw her come charging down on to me with [her] mouth open, emitting savage grunts, I thought it was all up, as I could not believe she would leave me alone now that I was standing by myself beside her cubs. As she came on I heard the Sholagas behind me yelling for all they were worth to scare her from me; but she never paused in her rush till she was within a few feet of me. I was so petrified I had no more idea of firing than the man in the moon, simply depending upon frightening her by holding my ground, when she swerved clean round, still at the same speed, and galloped back on the track she came. I beckoned to the men to come on with my other rifle, and followed her, with the hope that she might be visible, but there was not a sign; so we then got to the other side of the cubs by a roundabout way, on some higher ground, and finally I decided to get up a tree that was immediately overlooking the cubs; but first I sent a man up, intending to hand him one of my guns and climb up after him. Hardly, however, had he got well up the tree when Stripes came charging at us again, and this time I made up my mind to give it [to] her...

We then went back to the nursery and caught her three cubs alive. I should say they were about three weeks old, eyes open, but no teeth; their claws, though, were very sharp, as my hands could testify when feeding them. [1923]

Both camps, that is to say, H.R.H.'s and that of the Maharaja, were completely surrounded by palisades and guarded by Nepalese troops. Great fires were lit at night to keep away a possible marauding elephant or wandering rhino or tiger. Such unwelcome visitors were always a possibility in a spot where wild animals abounded. A further provision against incidents of that description was a huge machan, termed very aptly the "Funk Machan," designed as a haven of refuge in the event of a stampede of elephants or the visit of a wandering rogue.

The greatest attention to detail was displayed in the lay-out of the camp, and every provision was made for the comfort and convenience of the guests. The roomy tents, which were beautifully furnished and fronted by garden terraces, flanked an open lawn scattered with chairs and tables where people might sit in the evenings. Here also a huge bonfire flared all night, and a giant log blazed—quite the biggest I have ever seen. The whole camp, both inside and outside, was lit with electricity, from the great arc lamps, which hung picturesquely from the trees (under which all the trophies shot during the day's sport used to be shown before being handed over to the ministrations of the skinning camp), down to the little reading lamp by one's bedside, which one could switch off before turning in.

The Royal suite of apartments was simple, yet all that could be desired, and ornamented, as befitted the occasion, with emblems and trophies of the chase. The floor of the mess tent was carpeted with leopard skins, pieced together as a great mat; the effect, as can be gathered, was extremely rich and striking. The very appointments of H.R.H.'s writing table were all mementos of sport in Nepal, being made up from rhino hoofs, horns and hide, and even the waste-paper basket was made from the lower joint of a rhino's leg. The albums on the tables of the mess tent held the photographic record of many a famous shoot in the Nepal Terai. The camp had a well-appointed post and telegraphic office attached to it.

DINER   *Bikna Thori, 14th December, 1921*

Consommé Printanière, Saumon a la Grand Duc, Suprême de Poulet Mascotte, Selle d'Agneau, Perdreaux sur Canapés, Haricots verts à l'Anglaise, Crème Viennoise, Petites Rissoles Nantua, Dessert, Café.

The menu card [above] shows the lavishness and wonderful care taken in everything by the Maharaja of Nepal to entertain the Prince of Wales. This dinner was served in the impenetrable jungles of the Nepal Terai, miles... [from] civilisation. [1925]

VALMIK THAPAR

The next moment I was arrested by a deep growl close at hand, coming from I knew not where—from where I was I could not see the lip of the cave in which she really was hiding. After a short interval, a thought suddenly passed through my mind of what I had been told of the disinclination of a wounded animal to charge uphill; it seemed desirable to regain the position I had formerly held on higher ground—to re-ascend the hill once more. But this could not be, as my consequent movement seemed to have the effect of bringing the wounded tigress across the short distance that separated us in a flash; I was young and inexperienced in those days, or I would have known that any movement I made, especially one which might be interpreted as a retrograde movement, was dangerous under the circumstances. There was a roar, and something large and yellow seemed to spring out of the ground and hit me a crushing blow on the shoulder. The rifle flew out of my hand, and I found myself on the ground trying to lift a huge weight from my thigh, something which was hurting me most terribly. I had instinctively seized the tigress by her ruff with a hand on each side of her head, and was straining with all my might to make her let go the huge mouthful she had taken of the upper part of my leg. I was a little above her on the hillside, and in the struggle the eyes of the human and the beast approached to within about twelve inches of each other, and met.

I was conscious of a pair of furious yellow orbs staring at me, but only for a moment; their angry glare quickly died out and their expression changed. It was fear that [had] unmistakably become imprinted there, and, all in one motion, she let go and hurled the terrifying human body from her. She had had one forepaw underneath, and it was a flick of the wrist and forearm that sent me flying through the air, as it seemed to me to land on some hard stones a few yards away. Her mighty power was thus brought home in a most impressive way, and I then felt how futile it had been to pit my comparatively puny strength against such an antagonist. I am sure that I felt just as powerless as a mouse must feel in the claws of a cat. {1927}

A LIGHTNING CHARGE | W. HOGARTH TODD

At this time of the year the bed of the river was dry with the exception of a few pools of water here and there. Large boulders of rock stuck out of the sand at places, and dense jungle came close down to the edge on both banks.

As we got near to our friend the peacock, which was still making the quiet evening hideous with his outcry of "Mia-a-oo—Ah-oo—Lo-ooka-aout!", we discovered that he was sitting on one of the trees at the far end of a small island in the middle of the river, or at least what would be an island in time of flood. It was now merely a long narrow strip of higher ground with large trees and boulders on it, about two hundred yards long and lengthways to the direction of the stream—the river here, including the island, was not more than one hundred yards wide, and had steep banks.

It was getting late, and the level beams of the setting sun were touching the tops of only the highest trees as we reached the nearest end of the island, and then proceeded to stalk our quarry along its edge. We had not, however, gone more than eighty yards or so when we were arrested by a deep, rumbling note, presumably proceeding from a place in the thicket below the bird.

Now, what could that be? We stopped to consider the matter in whispers—wild pig or possibly a bear was all that I could think of.

As we stood together a couple of young tiger cubs suddenly broke into view close by, coming from the island and making across the sand for the mainland—they were male and female, about the size of collie dogs. Very pretty they were to watch as they passed within about twenty yards of us. However, our enjoyment of watching them was suddenly and rudely interrupted by a series of terrific roars, which broke out from the farther end of the island. We then caught glimpses of a full-grown tigress charging at us, with bristling ruff, along the wooded bank.

This was too much for my wife, and she started running towards the island along the way by which we had just come. She covered the five yards or so which separated us from the island, and then went up the bank. I shouted to her: "For God's sake, stop!" for I saw that if she continued farther she would inevitably be caught by the tigress.

I don't know if my voice was especially insistent, I expect it was, or else the instinct of self-preservation asserted itself—anyhow, the great thing was that she did stop. I then implored her to stand still on the top of the bank where she was and not move; the one way to daunt a tiger is to stand still.

He is naturally not accustomed to anything standing up to him; he takes all his game on the run.

It was a very high test of courage; I might almost say as high a test of its kind as any Englishwoman has ever undergone. But she pluckily stood it, and thereby probably saved her life and my own as well. The tigress came along making her ghastly noise until within fifteen yards of her, when she suddenly crouched down in the long grass. She then continued to growl and snarl for what seemed to us like an eternity, but which in reality was probably only some two or three minutes. During that time my wife and I stood stock still eight or ten yards apart, and I continued to exhort her not to move. I thought that if I spoke aloud in my ordinary voice the courage would slowly ooze out of the brute, because another thing to which a tiger is not accustomed is the sound of the speaking human voice. I therefore told my wife this as calmly as I could as we waited, but also with the object of giving her confidence at the same time. The plan seemed to work, for the tigress was certainly kept at bay for an interval. On the other hand she was primarily, of course, out to frighten us, to attract our attention from her cubs and to give them time to make good their escape. She also succeeded beautifully in her little plan, for our attention had certainly been diverted all right! We had never had any intention whatever of doing her darlings any harm, although, of course, she did not know this. We now sincerely wished we had never seen the little brutes.

At the end of the distressing interval, when I suppose she thought that she had held us spell-bound long enough, she once more sprang to her feet with a final roar, bounded to within a yard of my wife, dug all four paws into the earth together, stopped, and then turned round and bolted. My wife almost fell down the bank, arriving close to the place where I was standing.

I fully expected the tigress to follow her. As I said before, I only had a gun loaded with shot in my hand, but this at the range of a yard or two might have served; it would of course have been necessary to kill the animal or blind her instantaneously, and this might have been possible at close range. However, having attained her object in thoroughly frightening us, the tigress evidently did not want to force the issue to extremes, but only to go off and rejoin her offspring.

As she faded away into the gloom of the trees on the island, I took my wife by the arm and together we hurried down the river-bed in the opposite direction, which was towards the end of the island from which the tigress had originally charged. As we passed the great trees on its farthest extremity, I thought I heard a laugh echoing from the top branches. Of course it must have been the peacock that was amused at the bird's-eye view he had literally had of the whole episode, and was now watching us scurrying past like frightened rabbits below. He must have said to himself: "Well, anyhow, they can't say I didn't try to warn them, but all the fools thought of was of adding me to the pot!"

I thought at the time that this was a perverted sense of humour and, partly to relieve my feelings and partly to frighten our friend the tigress, I fired two shots into the air in rapid succession; at the same time I realized grimly that this was the first time I had ever fired off a gun to frighten a tiger away. I expect that the two reports helped to accelerate the happy union between the mummy-tigress and her dear babies, while we wended our way back to camp through the gathering gloom of the evening to where we had two of our own whom we had left in charge of Nurse earlier in the afternoon. {1927}

They are sometimes in touch with a jackal who acts as a sort of "chela" [follower]. There is a common story that a jackal utters a peculiar cry called "pheal" when in the company of a tiger. The only one I ever heard calling in the company of a tiger did make this peculiar noise, but I have often heard them do so when there was no tiger within miles. The call is probably one of alarm or suspicion irrespective of the cause. I once saw three full-grown male tigers walk out abreast in a beat, only a few feet separating them, and a jackal was scampering in and out between the tigers quite obviously "sure of his ground." The jackal is a cheeky, intelligent, adaptable and insignificant animal, in no danger from the tiger, but to whom it is quite conceivable that he might be useful. The jackal referred to above and which uttered this peculiar cry did so on becoming aware of my presence of which the tiger was ignorant. The jackal is very much alive to his own interests, and one attached to or adopted by a tiger would have a very easy time, and he is the only animal which has anything in the nature of friendly relations with the tiger. All other animals fear and hate and shun him. His progress through the jungle either by night or in the daytime is advertised by the screams of alarm of peafowl, monkeys and all the deer.

It is not every tiger that will attack a large wild boar, and natives sometimes give one most circumstantial accounts of the tiger being worsted. This is conceivable, the pig's neck is almost unbreakable and as a large jungle boar may weigh as much as 300 lb. the fight is not so unequal as it might appear. Porcupines, judging by the frequency with which one finds quills sticking in tigers' paws, are probably killed by a blow of the paw. An instance of a tiger having been killed by a porcupine's quills has been recorded.

Tigers, when disturbed on their kills, will usually abandon the same without protest; but if the kill happens to be a pig or a porcupine, they will often defend it, and it is not safe to drive a tiger off one of these animals. Whether this conduct is due to their being inordinately fond of this fare, or whether the difficulty they sometimes experience in killing these creatures enhances their value, I cannot say; but this attitude of the tiger, which I have personally experienced, cannot be due to mere coincidence. {1931}

Lower down the river I encamped amid what was indeed the Empire of Nature. The forest was beautiful beyond description. Giant trees—the growth of ages—stood upon the river bank, their topmost branches dotted with vultures and their nests. The river flowed with serpentine course in a rocky bed strewn with great boulders and containing broad reaches, where crocodiles lay like logs upon the surface, and otters disported themselves in pursuit of fish. Sometimes the stream narrowed to a silver thread between stretches of sand or murmured over pebbly shallows. On the margin, kept green by perennial moisture, grew thick brakes of cane and grass jungle; graceful bamboos bowed their feathery branches to the water, and beyond the level the hillsides were thickly grown with teak and other trees. Shady nullahs, containing here and there a pool of water, wound their way to join the river.

In the forest was an infinite variety of animal life. Bison, though scarce, were to be met with. The great sign-manual of the tiger lay upon the paths and the margins of the pools. The half-devoured body of a four-horned antelope, placed for concealment in the fork of a tree, indicated the presence of a panther. Claw-marks all the way up the bole of a giant pipal-tree showed where a bear had climbed in search of honey. The bark rubbed off trees told of stags polishing their antlers—sambar on the hill-top, and spotted deer which frequented the river banks, where their graceful forms were reflected in the water. Wild dogs standing in a glen represented the vermin, which were unable to make any impression on so vast a quantity of game. From almost every thicket a little four-horned antelope rushed out with white scut in air; pea-fowl filled the shady places, and monkeys with black faces grinned and chattered overhead.

Here on every side resounded the voices of the forest. In the glades and on the banks of the stream the spotted deer were seldom silent. Constantly the belling of the stags or the shrill bark of the hinds resounded in the woods. In the evening the harsh, grating cry of a panther came from the neighbouring hills, and at morn and at the setting of the sun the resonant "Miaou! Miaou!" of the pea-fowl struck upon the listening ear. The deep purr or distant roar of a tiger, answered by the voice of fear in the jungle, might sometimes disturb the silence of the night. The chattering of monkeys, the monotonous shriek of the coel, the brain-fever bird, the ceaseless stridulation of cicadas, completed the chorus of Nature's orchestra; all these and other sounds struck upon the ear and gladdened the solitude of the woods. {1928}

Presently there was a rustle of wings, and a huge vulture swooped down beside the kill. Ten seconds later there was another, then a third—then a perfect cloud of them, volplaning in like airplanes. Their numbers out of nowhere and their simultaneous arrival will always be a mystery to me. I can only guess that one high-soaring scout had located the kill, and as he wheeled down fifty others noticed his descent and converged in a hideous swarm. There were several species, naked-headed and horrible—the most ruffianly gang of creatures.

Nothing but a motion-picture film, with sound equipment, could adequately portray the scene. Some of the birds stood at the outskirts of the throng, and the raised shoulders of their wings made them seem the very symbol of death. Two monsters perched on the carcass; the others scrabbled and hopped and pushed and tugged, one moment all fighting furiously in a shapeless pile of feathers and jerking heads and clawing feet, the next moment all standing quite motionless while a strange hissing chorus rose from the flock.

Fortunately, the tiger had not yet opened the deer carcass, otherwise those cruel beaks would have stripped the bones clean in a matter of minutes. Fighting each other, they could not make a concerted attack, and had to be content with picking out the eyes of the dead animal, and attacking the vents of its body.

As I watched and listened, I wondered if the tiger was listening too. If so, he would naturally be concerned over his dinner. For once, I guessed right.

There was a sudden roar from the thick grass behind the kill... And the next instant the tiger, in all his splendour, sprang out of the jungle.

I shall never forget his magnificent entrance on the scene. The vultures rose with a thunder of wings. How the ugly, awkward brutes, with a naturally slow take-off, escaped those whizzing paws I do not know. But an instant later there was not a vulture in sight, only that savagely beautiful beast, standing there by his kill, slowly turning his head and surveying the scene with his huge yellow eyes.

He was full in the open, and in the sunlight. I had never had a finer view of a tiger. {1947}

The ravine was about ten yards wide and four or five feet deep, and as I stepped down into it a nightjar fluttered off a rock on which I had put my hand. On looking at the spot from which the bird had risen, I saw two eggs. These eggs, straw-coloured with rich brown markings, were of a most unusual shape, one being long and very pointed, while the other was as round as a marble; and as my collection lacked nightjar eggs I decided to add these to it. I had nothing in which to carry the eggs, so I made a cup of my left hand, placed the eggs in it and packed them round with a little moss…

…This rock about which I have said so much I can best describe as a giant school slate, two feet thick at its lower end, and standing up not quite perpendicularly—on one of its long sides.

As I stepped clear of the giant slate, I looked behind me over my right shoulder and—looked straight into the tigress's face.

I would like you to have a clear picture of the situation.

The sandy bed behind the rock was quite flat. To the right of it was the smooth slate fifteen feet high and leaning slightly outwards, to the left of it was a steep bank also some fifteen feet high overhung by a dense tangle of thorn bushes, while at the far end was a slide similar to, but a little higher than, the one I had come down. The sandy bed, enclosed by these natural walls, was about twenty feet long and half as wide, and lying on it, with her forepaws stretched out and her hind legs well tucked under her, was the tigress. Her head, which was raised a few inches off her paws, was eight feet (measured later) from me. On her face was a smile, similar to that one sees on the face of a dog welcoming his master home after a long absence.

Two thoughts flashed through my mind, one, that it was up to me to make the first move, and the other, that the move would have to be made in such a manner as not to alarm the tigress or to make her nervous.

The rifle was in my right hand held diagonally across my chest, with the safety-catch off, and in order to get it to bear on the tigress the muzzle would have to be swung round three-quarters of a circle.

The movement of swinging round the rifle, with one hand, was begun very slowly, and when a quarter of the circle had been made, the stock came in contact with my right side. It was now necessary to extend my arm, and as the stock cleared my side, the swing was very slowly continued. My arm was now at full stretch and the weight of the rifle was beginning to tell. Only a little further now for the muzzle to go, and the tigress who had not once taken her eyes off mine was still looking up at me, with the pleased expression on her face.

How long it took the rifle to make the three-quarter circle, I am not in a position to say. To me, looking into the tigress's eyes and unable therefore to follow the movement of the barrel, it appeared that my arm was paralysed, and that the swing would never be completed. However, the movement was completed at last, and as soon as the rifle was pointing at the tiger's body, I pressed the trigger.

I heard the report, exaggerated in that restricted space, and felt the recoil shock. But for these proofs that the rifle had gone off, I might, for all the immediate result the shot produced, have been in one of those awful nightmares in which rifles refuse to be discharged at the critical moment.

For a fraction of time the tigress remained perfectly still, and then, very slowly, her head sank on to her outstretched paws, while at the same time a jet of blood issued from the bullet hole.

The two men who were following a few yards behind me, and who were separated from the tigress by the thickness of the rock, came to a halt when they saw me stop and turn my head. They knew instinctively that I had seen the tigress and judged from my behaviour that she was close at hand. Madho Singh said afterwards that he wanted to call out and tell me to drop the eggs and get both hands on the rifle. When I had fired my shot and lowered the rifle, Madho Singh came forward to relieve me of it. Very suddenly my legs appeared to be unable to support me, so I made for the fallen tree and sat down. Even before looking at the pads of her feet I knew it was the Chowgarh tigress I had sent to the Happy Hunting Grounds.

Three things, each of which would appear to you to have been to my disadvantage, were actually in my favour. These were (a) the eggs in my left hand, (b) the light rifle I was carrying, and (c) the tiger being a man-eater. If I had not had the eggs in my hand I should have had both hands on the rifle and when I looked back and saw the tiger at such close quarters I should instinctively have tried to swing round to face her, and the sudden movement would have caused her to spring. Again, if the rifle had not been a light one it would not have been possible for me to have moved it as I did and then discharged it at the full extent of my arm. And lastly, if the tiger had been just an ordinary tiger, and not a man-eater, it would, on finding itself cornered, have made for the opening and wiped me out of the way; and to be wiped out of the way by a tiger usually has fatal results.

While the men went up to free the buffalo and secure the rope, I climbed over the rock and went up the ravine to restore the eggs to their rightful owner. The eggs, which all this time had remained safely in the hollow of my left hand, were still warm when I replaced them. When I again passed that way, half an hour later, they had vanished under the mother whose colouring so exactly matched the rock that it was difficult for me, who knew the exact spot where the nest was situated, to distinguish her from her surroundings. {1948}

VALMIK THAPAR

THE HIMALAYAN BEAR AND THE TIGER | JIM CORBETT

On two occasions I have seen Himalayan bears walk off with tigers' kills. On both occasions the tigers were not present. And on two occasions I have seen bears walk up to feeding leopards and, after shooing them off, carry the kills away. But on this occasion the tiger—and a big male at that—was present at his kill and, further, he was not an animal to be shooed away like a leopard. At the back of my mind was the thought that surely this bear would not be so foolish as to try to dispossess the king of the jungle of his kill. But that was just what the bear appeared to intend doing, and his opportunity came when the tiger was cracking a bone. Whether the bear had been waiting for this moment I do not know; anyway, while the tiger was crunching the bone, the bear drew himself to the edge and, gathering his feet under him, launched himself into the hole with a mighty scream. The object of the scream I imagine was to intimidate the tiger, but so far from having this effect it appeared to infuriate him, for the bear's mighty scream was answered by an even mightier roar from the tiger.

Fights in the wild are very rare and this is only the second case I know of different species of animals fighting for the sake of fighting and not for the purpose of one using the other as food. I did not see the fight, for the reasons I have given, but I heard every detail of it. Waged in a hollow of restricted area the sound was terrifying and I was thankful that the fight was a straight one between two contestants who were capable of defending themselves, and not a three-cornered one in which I was involved. Time stands still when every drop of blood racing through a rapidly beating heart is tingling with excitement. The fight may have lasted three minutes, or it may have lasted longer. Anyway, when the tiger considered he had administered sufficient chastisement he broke off the engagement and came along the open ground in front of me at a fast gallop, closely followed by the still screaming bear. Just as I was aligning the sights of my rifle on the tiger's left shoulder he turned sharp to the left and leaping the twenty-foot-wide ravine, landed at my feet. While he was still in the air I depressed the muzzle of the rifle and fired, as I thought, straight into his back. My shot was greeted with an angry grunt as the tiger crashed into the *ringals* behind me. For a few yards he carried on and then there was silence; shot through the heart and died in his tracks, I thought.

A .500 modified cordite rifle fired anywhere makes a considerable noise, but here, in the ravine, it sounded like a cannon. The detonation, however, had not the least effect on the maddened bear. Following close on the heels of the tiger he did not attempt to leap the ravine, as the tiger had done. Storming down one bank he came up the other straight towards me. I had no wish to shoot an animal that had the courage to drive a tiger off his kill, but to have let that screaming fury come any nearer would have been madness, so, when he was a few feet from me, I put the bullet of the left barrel into his broad forehead...

At that moment I caught sight of a movement on my right and, turning my head, saw the tiger unhurriedly cantering along on the open ground over which he had galloped a minute or two earlier and looking, not at me, but at his dead enemy. {1954}

THE TIGER, THE BOAR AND THE ELEPHANT

GEORGE HOGAN KNOWLES

Under the intense brilliancy of a magnificently jewelled sky dawn was breaking, and under that serene spell in the early hours—so spiritually absorbing—we were moving leisurely along a broad fire-line that crossed a flat plain covered with high grass. We had scarcely gone two miles when suddenly we heard two or three sharp barks on the road ahead of us that sounded like wild dogs. We were interested at once and hurried forward. We left the road and stalked round to the spot through the high grass. It was getting sufficiently light to see, and we were suddenly surprised to find two wild boars standing in the middle of the road and defending themselves against a pack of jungle dogs. To suddenly come upon a jungle battle is something not to be missed—an opportunity of a lifetime—and we took up a very careful position on our elephants to watch the proceedings. All the inhabitants of the jungle being accustomed to wild elephants our presence passed unnoticed.

The two boars were on their mettle and kicking up clouds of dust. Suddenly there was a yelp like a war cry from the dozen or more dogs present, and they rushed upon the pigs. For a moment the sturdy defendants seemed to be entirely overwhelmed, but with the burly obstinacy of their race they ripped to the right and left, trying to push forward at the same time. Two dogs were actually carried along a short distance on the back of one of the boars, while some two or three dogs were lying on the road *hors de combat*.

It seemed evident that the boars would soon be borne down by the little bloodthirsty creatures, when suddenly one boar broke away into the high grass on the far side of the road. Some dogs followed, but after a short interval they came racing back. This struck us as being very strange, for the wild dog has no mercy and will run his victim down to death. Suddenly bright crimson rays shot across the grassy plain from the great fiery globe that reddened the eastern hills and hung over their summits. Surrounded and torn by the merciless dogs, the poor boar on the road had his head poised up in the agony, as it looked, of a last effort.

We decided to shoot at the dogs in order to save the poor pig. The elephant on which the Raja and I were riding suddenly became restless, and up went Major B.'s rifle; but, before he could fire, we saw the mahout quickly grip his arm and point to the right, into the grass, over the struggling mass below. Major B.'s rifle went up again and we followed the direction anxiously, but could see nothing in the dense high grass. A few seconds and a tongue of flame darted out of the cold steel barrels with a crash, followed,

TIGER FIRE

187

to our great surprise, by the deafening roar of a tiger!

The red dry grass in front of us is immediately a rustling and shaking expanse of stampeding animals, and with the exception of a few of the bolder dogs standing at the edge of the road and panting with their tongues lolling out, looking fiendishly at the poor boar, all have disappeared.

We hear the loud savage growls of the tiger continuing, and we move in that direction. We push our two elephants over the forest-line, where some dying dogs are struggling beside the collapsing boar, and have moved forward about a hundred paces through the thick grass, when in a small open clearing we suddenly come face to face with the tiger, hit apparently by Major B.'s shot, in a death-struggle with the boar that had escaped. We could now understand the reason why the dogs that had followed him had so promptly returned.

Both the tiger and the boar seemed to be badly wounded, and in pain and rage are tearing fiercely at each other. In the surprise of the moment our elephants swerve badly; but the mahouts are plucky and know what to do, handling them firmly and silently. It strikes us instantly that it is a tigress, from her size and general conformation. She is on top of the boar, who throws her off suddenly, with a wonderful exhibition of strength, rushing forward immediately and ripping her terribly in the bowels. With fierce gasping roars in rapid succession the tigress springs again—but she is facing us, and we are immediately seen! There is no possibility of a shot from off our turning and twisting elephants; and now as quick as the sweep of a sharp-edged blade she leaves the pig, and we see the gorgeous flash of black and red flaring in front of us, while a few chance shots pass wide of the mark! Instantly—before we can realize what has occurred—she alights on the trunk of Major B.'s swerving tusker. As her huge open claws and teeth are embedded in the frantic elephant's soft flesh, a loud shriek of pain escapes him. The tigress seems to be clinging savagely just below his forehead, and the mahout, looking down upon her furious steam-spitting jaws, is close enough to be spluttered with reddened froth.

The next instant, a deafening roar from Major B.'s maddened elephant shakes the very ground, as he swings round on to his hind legs. He stands bolt upright for a few seconds, and then comes down with a great thud on the ground with his fore-feet in his mighty effort to shake off the huge cat. The mahout and Major B. are clinging desperately to the pad as they are hurled up and then twirled round with the fury of the elephant. Major B.'s rifle is flung out of his hand, and it crashes into the high grass.

Suddenly the infuriated tusker turns his blood-besmeared trunk towards us, dripping with the hideous mess from the awful wounds in the bowels of the tigress, and falls on to his knees to crush her. The spectacle is a terrible one, and the mahout is now in imminent danger of his life. He can hardly keep his seat at the steep angle of the tusker's suddenly conceived and frantic stratagem; and Major B., with his left arm around the mahout's neck, is trying his utmost to keep him from tumbling off and being crushed to death along with the tigress, who now must sooner or later let go her grip.

My heart beats like a sledgehammer as we see the huge tusker about to stand on his head, as it seems, and it looks as if he must take a somersault! We shout to Major B. to try to jump off to one side, while we are doing our best to persuade our elephant up to rush the tigress when she springs away, as we expect her to do any moment in order to save herself.

But no! The tigress is fighting with the ferocity of a mother that has cubs. Suddenly, as we expect the worst to happen, the tigress loosens her grip and falls under the trunk of the elephant! Streams of blood pour down the tusker's forehead and trunk, and splash the white fur which the tigress shows underneath as she lies struggling on her back with her protruding claws striking the air in fury. Her hindquarters seem to be under the kneeling weight of the tusker's head and trunk, and she is apparently pinned. {1932}

ELEPHANT:

Elephant flesh, when carefully cooked, makes an excellent stew—tender and of good flavour. It has been mistaken for good beef. The tongue and trunk are not recommended; they are as tough as some rubber tyres. Sanderson recommends the baking of the feet in a hole in the ground under a wood fire, but we have had no experience of this.

BUFFALO AND BISON:

Only undercut and tongue can be eaten, while the tail and shin bone can be used for soup. The tail also makes an excellent brown stew.

BARASINGHA AND CHITAL:

The saddle and chops are good eating. For roast saddle, slit open the fleshy parts and let in slices of bacon, and roast in the usual way. The tongue boiled, and the tail either stewed or made into soup, are both appetising. The shin bone also makes excellent soup.

SAMBHUR AND NILGAI:

Except the tongue and undercut, the flesh of these animals is coarse eating, but the tail and shins make quite good soup, while the marrow bones would be hard to beat. The marrow or thigh bones are 12 to 18 inches long; these should be broken in two in the middle and the broken ends covered over with a thick layer of ordinary flour (*atta*) dough and bound firmly over with a piece of muslin or other cloth available, to prevent leakage of the marrow during the boiling operation. Boil for four to five hours and serve up hot, with salt and pepper to taste.

Barking deer, Blackbuck, Chinkara and Chaursingha are all good eating—legs, loin, saddle, undercuts, liver, etc.

The suet of Barking deer and Chaursingha is useful for cooking.

A "hot-pot" made of any part of the smaller animals and of small game is excellent, always stewing slowly. [...] No vegetables should be put into the stew as they would make it sour.

BEAR:

Some hungry people have eaten bear steak with relish, but our experience is that the undercut, chops and liver made into a pie with short pastry is the only possible dish.

PIG OR WILD BOAR:

In the cold weather the head and trotters make excellent brawn. Clean the head and trotters of all hair; from the latter remove the hoofs and put on to boil, using sufficient cold water to cover it. When sufficiently boiled to leave the bones easily, place in a hot pan and, while hot, remove all bones and such parts as are not required, viz., the eyes, ears and snout, and cut up the meat into small pieces as quickly as possible to prevent the fat settling in it. Now add the necessary seasoning, such as salt, pepper, cayenne pepper, cloves and a few leaves of sage or other scented herb if available, all pounded and mixed together previously. Stir briskly and place in a cake tin or mould, and press down, and keep pressed down all night with a heavy weight placed on top. Should a cake tin or mould not be available an ordinary aluminium *dekchie*, with the cover of the next smaller size *dekchie* placed over and weighted, will suit the purpose. The brawn will have cooled and set by the morning and should cut quite firm. The suet of the jungle pig can be used for cooking purposes, preferably mixed with *ghee* or Cocogem.

PORCUPINE:

This small animal is considered quite a delicacy and is certainly good eating; the flesh is white and tender and is a welcome addition to the larder.

SMALL GAME:

Stew, jug, grill or roast. Cold pies are always good. Any small game is useful for the hot pot.

SNIPE:

An excellent stew can be made of snipe and potato and onions. Never roast too brown—many people prefer them very lightly cooked. Serve on fried bread, with lemon and red pepper. Can also be eaten cold.

PEAFOWL:

[Peafowl] is, as a rule, dry eating, but can be considerably improved by the addition of a little bacon. Always hang the bird for two to three days if possible and, when roasting, slit open the breast in places and let in slices of bacon. This will improve the flavour considerably.

Mulligatawny made from peafowl, and served up with boiled rice and sliced lemon, is perhaps one of the most palatable dishes the sportsman can indulge in on his shooting excursion; and as peafowl are always plentiful, he should see that his cook is not a novice in preparing this dish. The following is a good recipe:

Ingredients to a pound of meat:

Turmeric (haldi)—about one inch [in] length.

Dry chillies (mirchi)—two or three in number.

Green ginger (adrak)—about one inch [in] length.

Gram, either roasted or boiled and husked—two or three tablespoons.

One small onion and salt to taste. {1932}

VALMIK THAPAR

THE ALLEGED CRUELTY OF TIGERS | F. W. CHAMPION

Why is it that novelists so commonly liken their most horrible and objectionable characters to tigers, and is it really true that the much-maligned tiger can justly be considered as the embodiment of cruelty and malignant ferocity? I reply at once that such a comparison, made ninety-nine times out of hundred by persons whose knowledge of tigers is confined to an occasional visit to a zoological garden, is a gross libel on what, in some ways, is one of the finest of wild creatures.

I do not pretend to claim that the tiger is as gentle and harmless as the lamb, or even the symbolical dove, the latter being, by the way, a distinctly quarrelsome bird; but I do say that cruelty for cruelty's sake is a vice practiced only by the self-styled lord of creation, *Homo sapiens,* and is totally unknown to wild creatures or the so-called 'brutes'. Now the ordinary dictionary definition of cruelty is 'delighting in, or callous to the pain of others'. Who, except possibly an occasional author of a 'popular' jungle book, could justly accuse the average wild tiger of exhibiting signs of great pleasure as he watches the struggles of his victim, which dies almost instantly; who could state that a tiger is capable of inventing tortures such as those practised by the Spanish Inquisition or the Chinese or the present-day Russian ogpu; who can point to a tiger indulging in even the petty cruelties which are so often to be seen in modern life; what tiger has ever performed an act of cruelty in any way comparable to the slow burning at the stake which our own countrymen, our own ancestors, did in the name of religion—in the name of God, the merciful!—only a few centuries ago? Yet the second-rate writer of novels, when he wishes to create a vivid impression of some monster masquerading in human form, who has sunk far below the level of creatures of the wild, seems incapable of finding any better simile than that of the tiger, who is positively merciful in comparison to the debased type of human being to which he is likened.

So much for cruelty—that is the deliberate and premeditated infliction of pain. Why, a tiger's brain does not rise to such refinements! The second dictionary definition of cruelty is "callous to another's sufferings"; and here, perhaps, one might make out some sort of a case against the tiger, but it would not be a strong one. A tiger kills horned and hoofed animals because he must have meat if he is to live, and the desire to live is the strongest impulse amongst animals. We human beings also kill other animals because meat is an important item of our food, although we can live without it, whereas a tiger simply cannot exist on a vegetarian diet. Hence our sin, if there be a sin in destroying life for the sake of food, is greater than that of the tiger.

Then, again, let us compare the methods by which the taking of life is carried out; let us see if we can justly claim that we are less cruel than the average tiger. A sambar is browsing happily in the full glory of life and freedom, deep in the beautiful forests which he has frequented from his earliest youth. A tiger on a hunt, passing stealthily nearby, hears the sound of the contented munching of his intended prey. He crouches instantly, and the sambar remains completely in ignorance of his arrival, or of the certain death which is so near. Stealthily the tiger surveys the ground, after the manner of the born hunter that he is, and then, having carefully chosen the best line of approach, he gradually draws nearer and nearer, taking the greatest care that the sambar shall remain totally unaware of his presence— for once the intended victim is warned, the stalk is ruined. Nearer and nearer draws Death in feline form and yet the sambar passes the last few moments of his happy life in the peace and contentment of his chosen home. At last the tiger, after an infinity of care, has reached sufficiently close to enable him to make his final rush; he pauses and braces himself for the last act. Then he makes a lightning rush, so fast that the human eye can barely follow, and launches himself on his prey, using such terrific force that frequently he breaks his victim's neck almost instantly, and in very few cases do the struggles of the sambar last for more than a few seconds. Surely this is not cruelty in its worst form! The tiger must have his food, and he has been provided by the Creator to assist in maintaining that "balance of nature" which is so essential to life in this world, and without which man himself would find his position extremely precarious. [1933]

The dense white mist of early morning lies like a huge sheet of cotton-wool caught in the elevated mountain-fringed plateau which forms the doon. All around, dimly visible in the all-embracing mist, stretches a dense carpet of fantastically tall grass, festooned with the glittering white brilliants of a thick deposit of hoar-frost; while vaguely here and there can be seen the phantom outlines of the surrounding hills, the apparent height of which is greatly magnified by their soft enveloping mantle. At intervals stands a bare shisham tree, which has already dropped its leaves rather than wait until Jack Frost shall nip them off; but the hardy sal trees are less wise, or perhaps one might say, more brave. In front, bordering the edge of the mountain stream which drains the water from the doon down to the plains below, lies a thick belt of trees shaped like the familiar Lombardy poplars of Europe. Their numerous short branches are covered with dark glossy green leaves, whereas from their crowns stand up, cold and naked in the mist, a number of bare dead limbs which vividly suggest the antlers of a stag. The leaves near the base have recently turned a rich brown for a few feet above the ground, showing the height to which their enemy has already risen this year, and the antler-like crowns indicate that, a year or two previously, the trees were entirely enveloped in the annual frost belt. Yet these sal trees, which are truly more at home in a warm damp climate like that of Bengal, still struggle on and show a wonderful example of Nature's persistence against overwhelming odds—an example which we human beings might emulate with advantage to ourselves.

The continuous song of the rippling stream now catches the ear with its sweet melody, and so clear is the intensely cold water, with the mist eddying and swirling like smoke above it, that every stone lying on the bottom stands out sharply defined from its neighbours. On this bitter winter's morning the mahseer, for which the stream is famous, are not visible; they dislike the cold and are now lying dormant on the sandy bottoms of the deepest pools. A Himalayan whistling-thrush, sometimes known as "the whistling schoolboy" and very like an English blackbird dressed up in a coat of dark purple, is already on the move. It is not yet the mating season, and his wild melodious whistle, so wonderfully suggestive of the glorious freedom of Nature's mountain fastnesses, is for the moment stilled; but he evidently believes in the old maxim of the early bird catching the worm, for he is the only sign of the abundant wild life as yet to be seen, beyond the fresh otter-tracks on the belt of sand at the edge of the water.

The sun is by now rising above the high hill to the east, but it has not yet penetrated through the dense blanket of mist and appears only every now and then as a yellow ball of light, hanging in a fluffy white curtain which eddies to and fro with the gentle morning breeze. Faintly from the top of the hill comes the moaning roar of a tiger, who has gone to bask in the warmth of the sun after his cold night's hunting in the dew-soaked forests of the doon below; whereas, away to the south, the shrill piercing cries of cheetal suddenly ring out in intermittent bursts as they catch fleeting glimpses of one of their bitter enemies—the family of leopards which, a constant menace, has lived in comfort for many years in their chosen domain. The leopard, who is the father of the family, is not, however, interested in the cheetal at the moment, for he is padding silently along a man-made path fully occupied with some business of his own and soon passes out of sight— and out of mind so far as the cheetal are concerned, for an all-merciful Nature has endowed them with short memories, without which their lives would be passed in perpetual fear and trembling.

At last the sun, as though tired of dallying with the fog, bursts through with unexpected strength, and almost at once the glittering fairyland of hoar-frost changes its form to another that is, if possible, even more beautiful. For the giant grasses become covered with large drops of water, which, catching the early morning radiance of the sun, shine back its brilliance as though it were from a thousand diamonds hanging in the air. Then comes a slight stirring of the breeze and the dew-bespangled spiders' webs, which stand out here and there glittering like miniature baskets of jewels, shiver and shake as they scatter their gems to the ground beneath them. Surely Browning, that great lover of mountain scenery, must have been captivated by some such scene, viewed after a storm, when he wrote those beautiful lines—

> "But morning's laugh sets all the crags alight
> Above the baffled tempest: tree and tree
> Stir themselves from the stupor of the night
> And the strangled branch resumes its right
> To breath, shakes loose dark's clinging dregs, waves free
> In dripping glory."
> {1933}

THE CAR, THE TIGER AND THE ORDERLY | F. W. CHAMPION

Another incident showing how inquisitive tigers can be recently occurred in the foothill forests of the United Provinces.

The story as related to me was as follows. A certain sportsman drove his car out into the jungle one afternoon with the intention of sitting up in a machan over a tiger-kill. When he had reached within a reasonable distance of his machan, he left his car on the road-side in charge of an orderly and went off to the kill. The tiger did not put in an appearance, and on returning to his car he was astonished to find that the orderly left in charge had apparently disappeared. He called loudly but received no reply, until he thought of looking inside the car, where, to his amazement, he found the still terrified orderly crouching down beneath the dash-board. On questioning the man, it transpired that he was sitting quietly inside the car, when to his horror he saw a tiger walking towards him. He had no weapon of any sort, so he crouched down inside the car, hoping that the tiger would pass on. But his hopes were not fulfilled. The tiger paused, gazing at the weird object which obstructed his road, and then decided to come nearer to investigate. First, he walked round and sniffed at the various parts of the strange vehicle, apparently quite unaware of the presence of the quaking orderly inside. Then he put his fore-paws on the bonnet, and looking in at the wind-screen, saw his own reflection in the glass. This gave him a shock, and he started to growl and paw at the reflection, quite unable to understand why his growls elicited no response, while the orderly, luckily for himself, remained hidden inside—comatose with fright. Finally the tiger gave a snort of disgust and departed, much to the relief of the most unwilling but undetected spectator. This was the story, as told by the orderly on his master's return, and from the clear pad-marks on the sandy road round the car and on the dusty bonnet, it could not have been very far from the truth. {1933}

The intimidating roars increased in volume as the maddened brute drew rapidly nearer, but still I could see nothing but the shaking of the undergrowth as she rushed towards me. There could be no doubt about her intentions, but I had no opportunity to stop her. The first view I got of her was when she bounded over the scrub straight at me. All I had time to do was to snap both barrels of my gun at her as she was in the air. Before I had time to lower my weapon, a snarling fiend loomed through the smoke from my cartridges and I went down. My gun was sent spinning from my grasp, and though none of the blows aimed at me struck me fairly, their force hurled me backwards. This probably saved my life, as the upper part of my body fell away from her when she collapsed, her back broken by hasty shots. Unfortunately for me, she still had the use of her fore-paws with which she caught me by the legs and dragged me towards her, then bit through my left foot.

It has been said that in moments such as this all the sins and omissions of one's past life flash through the brain! Though I was perfectly conscious all the time, I have no recollection of this being the case, and my one thought was: "How long is this chewing-up process going to last?" Perhaps my subconscious brain realized the futility of attempting to rake up all my "sticky past" in the time at its disposal and gave it up as a bad job!

I had no feeling of fear, and felt comparatively little pain from the wounds inflicted by the tigress. On the report of a rifle shot, however, a red-hot iron seemed to pass through the foot which was in the brute's mouth, and I am afraid that I added considerably to the anxiety of my rescuers by shouting to them that I had been shot. At the report the beast sank inert and lifeless, but I was still held a prisoner, as her jaws were tightly closed upon my foot, and the claws of her left paw were sunk deep in the muscle of my right leg.

When at last her mouth was prised open, and the objectionable claws removed, I was able to get up and survey the damage that had been done. It was quite extensive enough, and I realized that my future prospects did not look particularly rosy.

There was a deep gash in my right arm extending from the elbow to the wrist, and every bone in the hand appeared to be broken, apparently by her teeth, though I was not aware that it had ever been in her mouth. One of her fore-paws had ripped my coat across the chest, inflicting minor flesh wounds. With the other she had struck at my head, but luckily only succeeded in leaving the impression of her paw and claws in my pith helmet, which was picked up some yards away. Though I have been told by fond relatives and friends that my cranium is of more than average thickness, I tremble to think what would have happened to it if that blow had struck it fairly! Her huge canine teeth had pierced the heavy shooting boot I was wearing at the time, and met in my left foot; and the bullet which had ended her life had at the same time made rather a mess of my big toe on its way through her head. There were also deep claw wounds in the flesh of my right leg. {1933}

THE COURTING TIGERS | ARTHUR W. STRACHAN

For some time the tail continued its slow up-and-down motion; then the low-crouching form of a beautifully marked tigress emerged. Stealthily she slunk across the burnt land to another grass clump about fifty yards from her original position, and here she again lay down, but this time in full view. I could watch her every movement. Her rich chestnut coat was liberally striped, and the beautiful gloss upon it—so seldom seen in a captive animal—showed her to be in the prime of life.

She lay facing the spot where the bullock had been pulled down, gazing intently in that direction. Occasionally she raised her head to sniff the air, as if suspicious that her victim had been tampered with.

While she lay thus, my attention was again attracted to the spot where she had first appeared, and I turned my eyes towards it, just in time to see a magnificent tiger—undoubtedly her mate—emerge from the jungle.

The sense of danger depicted in the cautious movements of the tigress was entirely absent in the bearing of her lord. He stalked, boldly and majestically, into the open. On he came, straight towards me, his tail waving a challenge to any who should dare to dispute his sovereignty, till at last he stood on the edge of the drain within a few yards of where we were sitting. With his great head raised, and the tip of his tail twitching spasmodically, he silently scanned the surrounding country—a picture of dignity and grandeur such as few have the privilege of witnessing. To him the words of the poet Blake were indeed applicable: "Tiger, tiger, burning bright."

It was perhaps a minute or two before he appeared to be satisfied with his survey; then, making in his mighty throat a sound which was probably the equivalent of a human sigh of satisfaction, he lowered his head.

I could easily have shot him dead as he stood, but as there was still an hour of daylight I preferred to watch.

Now he turned and walked slowly in the direction of the tigress, whom I had almost forgotten in the intense excitement of watching the movements of her mate. She was still lying in the same position, and at first took no notice of his approach, but as he drew nearer she turned to face him, then crouched as if to spring. The male strode slowly on as if in studied indifference to her presence, while the body of his spouse seemed to sink gradually into the ground as she flattened herself as a cat does on the near approach of its prey.

With blazing eyes, ears laid back, and twitching tail, her attitude for the moment was anything but that of the loving wife. Waiting till the tiger was within a few paces, she sprang towards him as if bent on his annihilation, lifted a fore-paw, and gently patted him on the side of his face. Then she raised her head and obviously kissed him.

To these symptoms of affection the male at first seemed rather indifferent, but when she rubbed herself against his legs and playfully bit them, he condescendingly lay down and gently struck at her with his huge forepaws. Thus encouraged, the tigress also lay down, and a mock battle ensued between the two beautiful animals. This was conducted in absolute silence, save for the occasional soft "click" of teeth meeting teeth when the widely opened jaws came in contact with each other.

Sometimes locked in a close embrace, playfully kicking each other with their hind-feet, sometimes daintily sparring with their fore-paws, they rolled about thus for nearly a quarter of an hour, and I would cheerfully have given all I possessed to have been armed with a cinematograph camera instead of a rifle.

Never shall I forget the sight of these magnificent beasts playing together like a pair of enormous kittens, with the black background of the burnt land setting off their colouring to the best advantage, and the first faint opalescent glow of approaching sunset adding an indescribable beauty to the picture. Few, indeed, are the sportsmen who have been privileged to witness such a scene. [1933]

Rounding a boulder they came across the tiger stretched out dead, and to their surprise they found their friend in a very bad condition lying close to the tiger but apparently not mauled—one side of the man's body seemed to have been blown off. He was immediately taken to hospital in a semi-conscious condition and on his death-bed he gasped: "The tiger shot me." Reconstructing the scene of the accident it seems the tiger was waiting round the boulder and as the man appeared it sprang at him. Finding no time to fire his rifle he [had] jammed the butt down the tiger's mouth but the tiger, in clawing, had released the trigger and had blown off the man's side; at the same moment the tiger died from previous wounds. {1933}

Another strange story comes from the Sunderbans and is of a man who was saved, by a tiger from drowning. Two brothers were conducting some diving operations in the Sunderbans; one of them was seated in a small boat with his diving apparatus on but without the air pipe; he felt an impact which knocked him into the water. He realized that unless he could remove the helmet he would drown. Struggling in vain he felt himself pulled through the water and bumped on the shore. To his surprise he heard a rumbling sound close to his ear and this turned out to be the angry roars of a tiger. The animal had seen him sitting in the boat, [and] regarding him as a possible dinner, knocked him into the water, saved his life from drowning by dragging him ashore and then proceeded to try and make a meal of him, but the heavy rubber of the diving suit was too much even for the jaws of a tiger. In rolling the man over the tiger growled in anger and must have realized that it had got hold of a "tough old bird". The brother saw from the ship what had happened, fired a shot which scared the tiger away and our friend was released. [1933]

ON A BOAT WITH A TIGER | ARTHUR MUSSELWHITE

I have frequently seen them swimming in the big rivers of India. During floods on the Brahmaputra, a tiger exhausted from swimming in the river clambered on a raft; man and beast called a truce in face of the common danger, the tiger keeping to his corner and the men, women and children to the other side. After the waters had subsided and the tiger had recovered from his exhaustion, he returned to the water and swam towards the nearest land. {1933}

VALMIK THAPAR

THE TIGER'S RANGE | RICHARD PERRY

Even thirteen thousand feet may not, however, be a tiger's altitudinal limit. In 1934, a tiger, having killed a mule on the Sikkim road between Gangtok and the Nathu La pass, almost certainly went over the pass at a height of over fourteen thousand feet and down into the Chumbi Valley, where later a large domestic bull yak was found dead, though not eaten, with fang-marks in its throat. Inevitably the killer was believed to be a "*mirta*", an abominable snowman, though this was not by any means the 'first yak to be killed by a tiger. {1964}'

THE WILD DOGS OF MADRAS | RICHARD PERRY

To this day there are still no first-hand accounts of an actual kill by dogs, but Anderson was satisfied of the authenticity of at least three such kills in the forests of Madras, when packs of thirty or more dogs ringed tigers and tore them to pieces; and he himself was a witness in Mysore of all but the actual killing. 'One evening,' he writes, 'at about five o'clock, I was a mile from the bungalow. Suddenly I heard a medley of sounds whose origin I could not at first define. There were cries, yelps, and long-drawn bays, interspersed with grunts and *whoofs*! that puzzled me. Then I knew that the noise was that of wild dogs, which seemed to be attacking a pig or a bear. Grabbing my rifle, I ran in the direction of the din. I may have covered a furlong, when around the corner dashed a tigress, encircled by half a dozen wild dogs. Concealing myself behind the trunk of a tree, I watched the unusual scene.

'The dogs had spread themselves around the tigress, who was growling ferociously. Every now and again one would dash in from behind to bite her. She would then turn to attempt to rend asunder this puny aggressor, when a couple of others would rush in from another direction. In this way she was kept going continually, and I could see that she was fast becoming spent.

'All this time the dogs were making a tremendous noise, the reason for which I soon came to know, when, in a lull in the fray, I heard the whistling cry of the main pack, galloping to the assistance of their advance party. The tigress must also have heard the sound, for in sudden, renewed fury, she charged two of the dogs, one of which she caught a tremendous blow on the back with her paw, cracking its spine with the sharp report of a broken twig. The other just managed to leap out of danger. The tigress then followed up her momentary advantage by bounding away, to be immediately followed by the five remaining dogs. They were just out of sight when the main pack streamed by, in which I counted twenty-three dogs, as they galloped past me without the slightest interest in my presence. Soon the sounds of pursuit died away, and all that remained was the one dead dog.

'Next morning I sent out scouts to try to discover the result of the incident. They returned about noon, bringing a few fragments of tiger-skin, to report that the dogs had finally cornered their exhausted quarry about five miles away and had literally torn the tigress to pieces. As far as they could gather, five dogs had been killed in the final battle, after which the victors had eaten the tigress, and even the greater portions of their own dead companions.' [1964]

A completely inexplicable and unparalleled incident was reported in 1948 in the *Journal* of the Bombay Natural History Society, and concerned a hunter, Willoughby Grant, who after shooting a young tigress in a shola in the Nilgiris found many other pug-marks nearby. At 5.30 the following evening he wounded a tiger in the same shola. When the latter tried to crawl away seven or eight tigers appeared without warning and began to tear it to pieces! So far as he could distinguish them individually in the general mêlée, these comprised one tigress with two half-grown cubs, a second tigress with two full-grown cubs, and two tigers. There must, therefore, have been not less than nine tigers in the original party. After a while the seven or eight remaining tigers left the carcass of their dead fellow and rolled down a bank out of sight; but a few minutes later one came up again and was shot by Grant. Immediately, all the rest appeared and fell upon this one; and again in due course all rolled over the bank out of sight. After another five minutes or so a third tiger came up and was also shot, and was immediately set upon by the rest. The following morning one dead tiger was found intact, one half eaten, and the third completely eaten except for its four pads and one side of its head. {1964}

THE TIGER AND THE CAMEL

SAHIBZADA ABDUL SHAKUR KHAN

At about eleven in the night, my bullocks, all of a sudden [were], so frightened that they pulled the *tonga* with which they were tied after them and came nearly upon the sleeping driver. This unexpected disturbance awakened all and the driver began to cry in his excitement. We could not make out at the time what was the reason of all that but I guessed it might be owing to the presence of some tiger or panther. We made some precautions and again went to bed. In the dead of night, a *Reybari* came running and shouted to us. We were aroused by his shouting. He reported that a tiger had just fallen upon his camels and killed the biggest of the lot. They shouted after him, threw burning fuel towards him and thus they could only get the dead body. We replied we were unable to do anything at that time but promised to look to it in the morning.

We then slept for the remaining of the night. I could detect in the morning the big footprints of the tiger along the pathway that runs sidelong to the river bank at about 25 yards from the bullocks. Just under the bank there was a deep water of the river about 6 or 7 yards down that pathway. Those footprints were traced up to a place where the tiger might have seen the bullocks...

Having no nala or up and down [sic] to give him a good concealment, while the wind had been blowing against the tiger, he had hidden himself behind a bush about 20 yards from the animal. Then suddenly pounced upon the camel giving him a blow at his thigh which turned him right to come face to face with the brute. He gave another blow on his shoulder and then caught him by the neck so completely that the kilas (long teeth fongs [sic]) penetrated deep to the back of his head. He felled him down after a great struggle because though the ground was soft, still the footprints of the tiger appeared to have gone 4 to 6 inches deep at places. The camel was [a] strong one. The *Reybaris* shouted after him and threw burning sticks at him, but he had sucked the blood before he actually left the body. {1935}

VALMIK THAPAR

THE TIGER AND THE BAIT | R. G. BURTON

In the stillness of the night the moon shone down upon the scene, flooding all the open spaces with its soft effulgence, outlining the trees which spectral-like stretched their branches bare of leaves to the cool night air. But the great tree over the pool in the jungle covered with deep shadow the water beneath, where one solitary star was reflected peeping through the leafy canopy above. On the brink of the pool the tethered buffalo calf stood chewing the cud, all unconscious of the striped destroyer approaching from the river bank. Twenty yards off, the skeleton of the slain tiger, picked clean by vultures, lay white and ghastly with crimson streaks in the bright light of the moon. A fugitive breeze stirred the dry leaves and passed on to die in the thickets at the foot of the adjacent hill. The buffalo looked up, turned in the direction from whence the breeze had come and stood at gaze.

Perhaps he scented danger; the midnight air might well have brought him a taint of impending doom, for from the same direction a great beast of prey, grey in the moonlight, passed almost like a shadow from glade to glade. It paused for a moment motionless on the bank of the nullah, a thing of terror yet of splendour. The buffalo moved, stamped his hoof, and then bent down to get a mouthful of grass, and the tiger instantly crouched, watching the unconscious beast that stood chewing the cud. Then he approached behind the shelter of a bush and from a few yards' distance rushed upon his prey. With his paws and extended claws he seized the beast round the neck and shoulder, his jaws closed on the back of the neck, he tugged and turned his victim over and as it fell the neck was broken.

The tiger dropped his prey for a moment and then again seized it and with a wrench broke the rope that tethered it by the foreleg. He did not suck the blood from the jugular vein; he picked up the calf as a cat picks up a mouse, and with the hind-legs dragging and leaving a trail along the ground, he walked off towards a patch of bush. He came to the spot where lay the skeleton of his luckless predecessor, shot the day before, and dropped his burden. He sniffed at the remains, turned, and fled like a spectre into the depths of the forest, reached the river bank, and went away across a stretch of sand, making for some distant haunt.

Meanwhile another tragedy was being enacted higher up the watercourse at the place where the second buffalo was picketed, and a more unusual one than that just described. A great bull bison came down to the water to drink, for here too a little moisture had as yet not been dried up by the heat of the summer sun. As he approached the pool he saw the wretched beast tied up there and stood for a time gazing at this unusual intruder. He stamped his hoofs, snorted, pawed up the ground, apparently filled with sudden rage, as a bull bison behaves when drinking near a tiger's kill. Then he rushed upon the tethered animal, gored it with his massive pointed horns, trampled on it with all his great weight, and did not desist until it lay inert and lifeless; then seemingly satisfied with his work, the great beast drank his fill at the pool and departed slowly into the shadows of the forest. The story of this night's happenings was plainly seen in the marks on the ground.

At seven o'clock next morning we started for the forest across the river. From a distance we observed the buffalo under the big tree by the pool and at once saw that it was dead. But examination through the binoculars disclosed that none of the carcass had been eaten. This seemed curious, but the tiger may have been feeding well and not wanted to eat again yet; he might be lying close by, although we could not see him; but a tiger is rarely visible in such circumstances. We found tracks made on his approach and other tracks leading away towards the bank of the river. We followed these as far as possible and saw that without doubt the tiger had made off. His tracks were on a sand bank down to the stream and there he had crossed to the other side where the water was shallow; and sometimes galloping, as was evident from the impressions of his paws, had fled to distant haunts. The shikaris declared that the ghost of the dead tiger haunted the spot and warned other tigers of their danger.

We now went on to look at the other buffalo higher up the watercourse, and discovered the havoc wrought by the bison; thus the story of two extraordinary incidents was written in the book of Nature in tracks and other signs during one night as already described. Bison were protected in this part of the country as their numbers had been greatly reduced by an epidemic of foot-and-mouth disease; there was, therefore, no object in pursuing this ferocious bull, so we continued on our way up the nullah. Here, near another pool, we found tracks of a tiger, apparently the same animal, for the measurements corresponded with those of the footprints near the kill, although they were two days old, so Bhima said. Certainly they were not at all clear-cut like those of the night. The tiger had eaten a number of crabs whose remains were scattered in the water and on the brink: still more curious was a large python bitten in two and fished out of the pool on the point of Bhima's spear. The tiger had bitten a large piece out of its middle, but apparently not caring for the taste of it he had flung the remains into the water. {1936}

HUSBAND, WIFE AND TIGER | E. A. SMYTHIES

When we were both comfortably ensconced, the orderly went off to place the stops, and we waited for the beat to begin. Presently away in the distance I heard the elephants moving through the grass and trees, and almost at once a stop started clapping and a tiger roared twice. Just in front of my machan was a patch of very heavy *narkul* grass about twenty-five yards in diameter; after a few minutes I heard the tiger coming through this patch, and presently it broke cover in a fast slouch. I fired and, quite inexcusably, clean missed one of the easiest shots imaginable—a tiger broadside on at about twenty-five yards!

Instead of dashing away he turned round and bounded back into the patch of *narkul*, with a second shot (also a miss) to hurry him on his way, and lay up—invisible but quite close to me—snarling hideously. When the elephants came up to this patch, things began to get painfully exciting.

The tiger refused to break again, and vented his anger in continuous and terrific roars, one of the elephants of a somewhat timid nature was trumpeting shrilly, and both were crashing down young saplings and poles to try and drive him out. Then one of these saplings crashed down right on top of the tiger, and with another terrific roar he charged the two elephants. The timid one tried to fly, but was gallantly stopped by her mahout, while the other, as staunch an elephant, with as brave a mahout as one could wish to have, surged forward to the attack. Whereon the tiger turned and once more galloped past me; and yet once more I made an exhibition of rank shooting and missed him clean.

He went flashing past my wife, about thirty yards away, and as it was nearly past her, she fired and I saw the brute drop, the bullet just missing the spine. I saw her fire again, but the second shot appeared to miss.

It is here that the incredible part of the episode begins, which lifts it from the commonplace into the region of the unique. As she fired the second shot, apparently some movement attracted his notice, for with a crescendo of the most appalling roars I have ever heard he turned round and charged towards her, climbing the tree for all the world like a colossal domestic cat, with his gigantic forearms almost encircling it!

"Good God," I shouted a warning, "look out, it's climbing your tree," and as I turned round hurriedly, I knocked all the loose cartridges out of my machan to the ground.

As things were, I had no option but to take the risk of hitting my wife. I fired at the brute, when it was half way up the tree, but only grazed it. As

I looked down to work the bolt and re-load, I realized I had one cartridge left, and looking up again I saw my wife standing up in the machan with the muzzle of her rifle in the tiger's mouth—his teeth marks are eight inches up the barrel—and he was holding on to the edge of the machan with his forepaws and chin.

In this position she pulled the trigger *and had a misfire.*

~

You must realise that at least two-thirds of the tiger's weight was now on the machan, for except for his back claws, he was hanging out from the tree by the width of the machan which was rocking violently from his efforts to get on to it. The next thing I saw was my wife lose her balance and topple over backwards, on the side away from the tiger.

The beast did not seem to notice her disappearance, and as I again aimed at him, I saw him still clawing and biting the machan—the timber was almost bitten through, and the strings torn to shreds. I fired my last available cartridge, and by the mercy of Heaven, the bullet went true…

All I knew was that my wife had disappeared from the machan on one side of the tree, and the tiger on the other, that I had no cartridges left; and that I was helpless for the moment to give any further assistance. In fact, I expected every second to hear her screams, and to hear the awful noise of a tiger killing his prey.

~

WIFE'S OWN STORY

Whether my predicament was as bad as my wife's can be judged from her view of the incident. I quote her words: "As I fired again, apparently my movement caught the tiger's eye, for he turned round and charged straight at my tree, roaring worse than ever. I thought he was dashing past, but *suddenly realised he was climbing up the tree vertically under my machan,* and had just time to scramble to my feet, when his huge striped face and paws appeared over the edge, and he was evidently attempting to climb into the machan itself.

"His great mouth was open and all his teeth were bloody, and bloody foam came up at me with his roaring and spattered my hat and clothes. I pushed the barrel of my rifle into his open mouth and well down his throat (his teeth marks are eight inches up the barrel to this day) and pulled the trigger, and *had a misfire.*

VALMIK THAPAR

"Then I really began to feel desperate, and did not know what to do. We were having a regular tussle with the rifle, and he was shaking me about with it, when suddenly his huge paw came up through the bottom of the machan, cutting the strings to shreds, and in stepping back to avoid it, I must have stepped over the edge, for the next thing I knew I was falling.

"I thought I was falling straight on to the tiger, and it flashed through my mind, 'surely I am not going to be killed like this.'

"I never felt hitting the ground, but my next conscious impression was that I was running madly through the grass and undergrowth and over fallen trees, expecting at every step to feel the tiger leaping on me and (I don't mind confessing) feeling absolutely terrified."

~

Meanwhile I was yelling myself hoarse for an elephant, when suddenly my wife appeared at the foot of my tree apparently unhurt, and we stared at each other speechless. Almost simultaneously one of the mahouts arrived, who had rushed up his elephant regardless of wounded tigers or anything else, and she hastily scrambled up, and cleared off into safety, unhurt but for a slightly sprained wrist and a few minor scratches and bruises from her fourteen-foot fall.

One of the back-stops, who had seen the whole incident (and in consequence climbed up to the topmost twig of a sixty-foot tree) was shouting that he could see the tiger lying dead, and went off with her to the bungalow, leaving the stops to bring in the tiger. {1936}

It would be difficult to visualise a tenser moment than stretching your leg under an office desk and touching a tiger which had strolled in from the jungle for some extraordinary reason.

The following unusual incident occurred at Iskagundam on July 19, 1928, in the Nallamalai Hills of Kurnool district in the Madras Presidency, where the writer was camping with Rao Sahib K. R. Venkataramana Iyer Avergal, Conservator of Forests, and Messrs. B. K. Roy and S. Raghunatha Rao, the District Forest Officers of South and West Kurnool divisions.

~

Suddenly Mr Venkataramana Iyer appeared, in a state of some excitement, saying that a tiger had just walked into his room. The statement sounded singular if true, but investigation as to whether the "pi dog" had merely passed through his room or was still there seemed to be indicated. A rifle was standing handy, so after loading it, more as a sign of respect for Mr Venkataramana Iyer's veracity than with any expectation of using it, two of the officers proceeded to investigate through the door leading on to the back verandah which, luckily, was *propped open, about nine inches, by means of a stone.* That truth is stranger than fiction was proved by the unmistakable fact that the tiger was underneath the office table diagonally opposite to the back door. It was examining the window behind the table which, though open, was protected by bars. It did not present a perfect shot owing to the fact that it was partly screened by the office chair and a table leg.

However, the petrol lamp gave a good light. A few inches of shoulder, though not the neck, were clearly visible. A shot was, accordingly, taken which was followed by a brief moment of pandemonium, after which all was still. The pandemonium resulted in the extinction of the petrol lamp and, as was found afterwards, the disposal of most of the Conservator's office work.

~

A fairly lengthy consultation then ensued as to what was to be done next. All concerned were extremely anxious to have dinner, but the feeling that the tiger might also be in the same state ruled out any idea of asking the servants to take the dishes backwards and forwards between the kitchen and the house.

The supposition was that the tiger was dead, so the only natural thing to do seemed to be to try to verify this supposition. Fortunately, another petrol lamp was available, so one officer with the rifle and another with the lamp approached the door and peered in.

No tiger was to be seen, so with a walking-stick the brick which was preventing the door from opening more than *about nine inches was pushed further in*. As the door opened a tiger's tail became visible on the floor. As the tail did not move, the door was pushed further open with some confidence. It immediately became apparent that the tail belonged to a live tiger which was squatting on its haunches more or less behind the opening door.

This presented a quandary which led to a discussion as to what on earth had ever induced the officers to join the Forest Service. Something, however, had to be done, so after considering all possibilities, including that of making a hole in the *thatched* roof, it was decided to go and fetch a crowbar from the Ranger's camp close by and make a hole in the mud wall separating the two rooms. {1936}

AN AMAZING CONTEST
SHUJA UL ISLAM AND COLONEL JOHN H. ROUSH JR.

After eating a heavy meal of meat tigers develop an incredible thirst. We made a little blind on the ground from shrubbery cut further away. Tigers are nocturnal animals, and during the day they usually lie in the shade by some pool, or amidst the reeds fringing the course of a river. Therefore we anticipated that she might be nearby.

We hadn't waited long that morning when we smelled the fetid odour. The tiger has a peculiar, pungent smell. We knew it was approaching.

We saw it come out just as a large boar approached from the opposite direction, intending to drink. Both wanted to get at the ten foot wide muddy water hole.

The boar, grunting furiously, displayed his substantial tusks and stood his ground. Apparently the tiger was extremely angry, protective of her kill, roaring and wanted to shove the boar away. We gathered that the dead buffalo was hidden nearby. But the boar was tough and faced the tigress with hair and bristles erect. They appeared to be nearly equally matched in weight. We estimated they might each weigh about 300 to 350 pounds.

The tiger had her ears back and crouched low. It circled the boar trying to get at the rear. Suddenly she sprang forward, endeavouring to land a crippling blow with her front paw. However, the boar attacked the tiger. She was not a big one, but rather a small female.

There followed a ferocious battle. The pig slashed at the carnivore in short runs and then retreated. We saw blood appear on the sides of both the tiger and the boar. The tigress responded with claws and fangs. It was apparent that this was an uncompromising affair.

I must say, I trembled with excitement and didn't raise my rifle. The boar kept his rear away from the tigress. He would run in, slash and then run off. Each parry and thrust generated a cloud of dust that obscured the action. Fire in their eyes showed all-consuming hatred that had little attention for anything but their opponent. They didn't see us.

We saw that there was no doubt that the boar is a courageous and daunting adversary. Although the boar was dripping blood and had shreds of skin hanging from his flank he was not ready to give up. The boar still kept trying to disembowel the tiger with his flashing, sharp tusks.

The fight went on for some time, while we were absorbed in watching the melee. Pandemonium raged with roars and squeals and gruff threats. We saw the belly of the tiger had been ripped open. Both were severely wounded we could see, yet still facing each other. We visualized that the terrible wildlife dance could have only a tragic ending. Shortly they retreated into the thickets. We didn't get a clear impression of which was first to limp away into the forest. That evening we followed up, found the mortally wounded tigress and put her out of her misery.

The boar was found on the third day. The shikaris had been attracted by an accumulation of vultures circling overhead of the carcass. We got the tusks. They are very sturdy weapons, even though relatively short. Others have witnessed similar battles. Mr F. C. Champion, known as Chief Conservator of the Forests in India, related his experience in watching another duel of tiger and wild boar. Neither would yield. They fought to the death. {2001}

At the edge of the water hole we found traces of a recent tragedy—disturbed soil and blood stains. It was easy to read—a tiger had crouched in a patch of long grass and pounced on an unsuspecting sambhar when it came for a drink. Very cautiously, we followed the trail made by the tiger dragging the animal, and eventually located the body in a clump of bamboo at the mouth of the ravine.

In the meantime the vultures had collected, but instead of settling round the carcass they alighted on the trees, an indication that the tiger was nearby.

My brother and I were arguing whether we should go back to the village and collect a few men to scare away the tiger so that we could collect what meat was left, when he drew my attention to a movement in the long grass halfway up the hill on the right. We watched carefully and saw something red. My brother whispered to me *bakri* (barking deer), but I told him to be quiet and then we saw another and another and still another, until on that hill alone we counted twelve. It then dawned to me that they were not *bakri* but wild dogs, and we decided that we had better withdraw. To our horror we found a dog stationed alongside the path we had come by, and then discovered that we were surrounded. We immediately climbed up a large fig tree and sat very quietly. We had never heard of wild dogs attacking men before, but we knew that if they treed any animal they would surround it for several days until hunger or weakness caused the animal to leave its shelter, and then of course its fate was sealed.

From up the tree we had a very clear view of what happened. The dogs were stationed about thirty yards apart along both hills facing the ravine, as well as on the farther side of the nala. We counted 22 dogs altogether. The strangest part about their behaviour was their absolute silence and, when one moved, all move, gradually closing in.

Suddenly with a snarl a tiger appeared, and the dogs closed in still further until there was a ring of them round him, about forty to fifty feet in diameter. They were apparently driving him into the bed of the nala where he could get no cover, but where their paws could get a firm footing, with no obstructions such as twigs or scrub. This was very evident from their action. When the tiger faced the way they wanted him to go, the line of dogs withdrew but closed in behind, but when he faced the opposite way, they stood up to him, bunching together and making stiff-legged rushes of a few feet.

The dogs, however, left a large *mahowa* tree out of their calculation, for when the tiger saw it he made for it with a rush, scattering the dogs in his way. He gained the shelter of the tree and sat down with his back firmly against it and his tail curled round over his forepaws. The dogs closed in round the tree until the nearest was within ten feet; the majority crouched on their haunches with heads between forefeet as if content to play a waiting game. There were three or four half-grown pups which frisked round playing with each other too.

For the first half hour the tiger sat quietly, merely snarling occasionally, but then he began to lose his temper and gave vent to a couple of full-chested roars, but the only effect on the dogs was to make a few of them prick their ears.

The tiger then fell to lashing his tail, but one of the pups slipped round to the back of the tree and gave it a painful tweak. This brought the tiger round with a roar, he let loose with a 'haymaker', the pup threw itself on its back, paws in the air, slipped between the tiger's legs and got away unscratched. This move left the tiger's flank and rear uncovered, and a full-grown dog leaped in from the left, and snapped at the tiger's neck just behind the ear.

It was slow in retreating, with the result that it received a blow on the ribs which hurled it ten feet away, stone dead.

The tiger sat down again, but presently the blood from the bite in his neck started to trickle down his chest. This made him very uncomfortable and when he could no longer endure it he lowered his head to lick the blood off. This momentary inattention cost him dear as, the instant his eyes were off them, the whole pack rushed in and a few hectic seconds followed; the tiger was completely hidden under a mass of snapping, struggling dogs, as they fastened on to him everywhere biting and tearing. It is impossible to give an accurate description of the struggle, as all the eye could see was a seething mound of red, with glimpses of yellow and black. The dogs suddenly withdrew leaving five of their number dead or seriously injured. The tiger had fared very badly—one eye was closed, the corner of his mouth torn away, his ears in tatters and numerous gashes all over his body. The most serious injury seemed to be to his right forepaw as he was unable to place it on the ground.

The dogs reformed their circle, much closer this time and, whereas at first they waited for the tiger to make the first move, they now started making tentative rushes and kept the tiger on the alert. This continued for nearly an hour, while the tiger was fast losing strength. Again the dogs rushed in and there was another confused struggle. When the dogs drew off this time the tiger was in a very bad shape, and it was with a great effort that he kept himself erect. Presently his head began to droop and again the dogs attacked, one fastened on to the tiger's throat and, although immediately beaten to a pulp, its jaws remained locked and its hold could not be broken. In a supreme effort the tiger reared up on its hind legs with the dead dog still at its throat and others draped all over him. Even from this glimpse we could clearly see that he had been disembowelled; he toppled over backwards and was immediately covered with dogs; there were a few more convulsive struggles and all was stillness.

At this stage my brother and I slipped down from the tree and went back to the village. We told our story and collected a crowd and returned to the scene of the fight. By the time we got there the dogs had gone, leaving the vultures in possession. All that was left of the tiger was bones, sinews and a few tufts of blood-stained fur. We counted twelve dead dogs and could see where others had dragged themselves away. {2001}

THE TIGER'S DIET | J. D. INVERARITY

On opening the stomach of an old tigress I shot last month, I found in it the tail-end of a snake that the tigress had bitten off and swallowed whole; the portion swallowed measured two feet three inches in length. Though quite fresh, the pattern of the skin was rather spoiled by digestion, and I am not sure what kind of snake it was, but it appeared to be a python. There were no teeth marks on it, nor was there any breakage of the bones. It seems somewhat remarkable that an object of this length could be bolted whole.

The native thought that the tigress had caught it in the water when she went to drink. I should estimate the piece bitten off to be about one-third of the snake's length. The tigress had also made a heavy meal from a bullock. {2001}

THE TIGER AND THE PORCUPINE

SARDAR BHUPENDRA KUMAR

I am inclined to believe that the porcupine attracts the attention of the tiger due to the tastiness of its meat. For the tiger the porcupine is a toothsome morsel, and in spite of the protection afforded by the pointed spines and quills the tiger does not hesitate to face the dangers involved. I have myself seen the peculiar way in which the tiger goes about killing a porcupine. After his victim has been stalked to a convenient distance, the tiger with a powerful stroke tosses the porcupine in the air, and may even give it another blow if necessary. The porcupine usually hits a stone or some other hard object, becoming unconscious and exposing its vital parts.

In the process of attacking its prey in this manner, accidents are likely to happen. For example, while striking the animal small quills may get lodged in the tiger's pads which may be very difficult to extract by means of his teeth. Subsequently, these may penetrate deeper into the festering wound and disable him after a time.

Another likely place for wounds from a porcupine's quills is the mouth, or even the intestines. On many occasions I have found in tiger's droppings small quills which had passed through the alimentary canal. All the same, there is a danger of some pieces of quill sticking in the intestines and causing ulcers. In fact, one such tiger was found dead on the banks of Shikarghar Tank, near Banbihar Sanctuary in 1943, reduced to skin and bone by starvation. {2001}

THE WHITE TIGER | J. C. DANIEL

The Bombay Natural History Society recorded no less than seventeen cases of white tigers shot in India between the years 1907 and 1933. One of these was shot in the Dhenkanal State, Orissa, in 1909 and described as follows: 'The ground colour was pure white and the stripes were of a deep reddish black colour [*JBNHS* 19(3)].' Another was shot in the Bilaspur District of the then C. P. in 1910 and is described in the *Journal* [24(4)] as 'cream-coloured throughout but paler on the head and the stripes were chocolate brown.' Another was shot in the district of Bhagalpur in Bihar, and was described [*JBNHS* 32(3)] as: 'pure white with black stripes on her body and russet brown ones on the tail.' The taxidermists to whom the trophy was sent report that during the year 1926 they received three white tiger skins including mine (mine was shot on 6 December, 1926), but my skin is the only pure white one, the other two being cream coloured. As recently as 1958 a white tiger was shot near Hazaribagh in Bihar, and the skin was on view at a Calcutta taxidermist's.

A number of white tigers [have] from time to time been reported from Assam. In March 1889 one was shot in upper Assam and is recorded by

Lydekker. Lt. Col. F. T. Pollock in his book *Wild Sports of Burmah and Assam* published in 1879, wrote: 'Mr Shadwell, Assistant Commissioner in the Cossyah and Jyntiah Hills, also had two pure white skins, but when turned about in a strong light only a faint mark or two could be seen to indicate that they belonged to a tiger at all...' Bogabagh Tea Estate in Upper Assam is so called from the two white tigers found there at the beginning of this century, and one of them had 'a lemon-coloured patch on the back of the neck, otherwise it was white with faint stripes.' The two light-coloured tigers shot by W. G. Forbes of Hathikuli Tea Estate in 1929 were described at the time of curing by Messrs. Van Ingen as 'red tigers'.

Now back to the Rewa white tigers. There have been eight cases of a white tiger in this old state during the last fifty years, during which time diaries have been kept at the palace. These include a two-year old male captured near Sohagpur in December 1915, and kept for some years in captivity. H. E. Scott of the Indian Police saw this animal five years later (December 1920) and described it, in a Miscellaneous Note in the *Journal* [27 (4)], as follows: '*Body Colour*: pure white. No cream colour visible. *Stripes*: indistinct or light black: whilst some of the stripes, particularly the face markings, are truly black, the majority are ash-coloured owing to white hairs being mixed in with the black. *Nose*: mottled grey-pink (instead of pure pink as in normal tigers). *Eyes*: the colourings of the eyes are very indistinct. There is no well-defined division between the yellow of the cornea and the blue of the iris. The eyes in some lights are practically colourless, merely showing the black pupil on a light yellow background. *Eyelids*: pinkish-black. *Ears*: practically normal in colour and markings. The ground black is however slightly ashy. *General description*: the tiger is, of course, underdeveloped owing to years of captivity, but in height he is probably slightly above normal and in a wild state would undoubtedly have been an exceptionally large animal.'

The former Maharaja of Rewa shot a white tigress in 1937. In 1946 a white tigress was shot by the Administrator, and when skinned was said to have been found to have six unborn cubs—described as white, but I believe this was not substantiated. {2001}

THE SNAKE AND THE TIGER | FRANK NICHOLLS

Some years ago, I was in charge of an estate in lower Assam. I was going round the property with the visiting agent of the company, when an old man came to us from a village on the other side of a wide river, with the following story. For the past two days, he said, a large python had been holding on to the hind leg of a tiger. The python was fully stretched out with its tail round a tree... A month or so later I saw the man again and asked him what had happened to the python and tiger. He said that on the night after he came to inform me, the tiger had turned on the python and clawed it to pieces and had then cleared off. Why the tiger had not done this in the first place I cannot say.

A few months after that, I met an old and very experienced shikari friend of mine, named Percy Briscoe. During his early days in Assam, twenty years previously, he had spent much of his time roaming the Assam jungles, as I did on my free weekends, instead of going to clubs. I told him of the python and tiger episode which I have just narrated and he related the following tale. 'I was on my elephant riding through some grassland, miles from anywhere. There were a few trees scattered about and I suddenly came to a spot where the grass had been flattened out in a semi-circle in the centre of which was the skeleton of a huge python. The old mahout said, on seeing the skeleton, that the python had probably struck a tiger or leopard and having embedded its fangs in it, was unable to withdraw them and was subsequently killed in the struggle.' {1970}

A TIGER SNIFFS AT A BOOT | RICHARD HILTON

Jimmy therefore decided that he would sit up for the tiger *on the ground* rather than waste the chance. He had the sense to sit with a good stout thorn bush immediately behind him, so that he could not be stalked from behind. There he sat facing the dead cow with his rifle laid on the ground beside him. Unfortunately, like me, he fell asleep, and woke again to find a tiger sniffing his boots!

He dared not move a finger, even to pick up the rifle lying beside him, for the tiger would have been upon him long before he could fire. He had to sit absolutely motionless till at last the great brute, tired of the smell of dubbin, mooched off into the jungle. {1955}

VALMIK THAPAR

TO CALL A TIGER | A. N. W. POWELL

Once there, I began calling, and continued to do so for about half an hour, but without any answering call from the tiger. This was most disappointing, and now, of course, it was difficult to guess which direction the tiger had taken. To find any tracks in those grassy surroundings was impossible. Staying where we were was useless, so it was now a toss up between going on or going home. Finally, I decided to go on, but very soon found myself regretting this decision. Every step seemed to take us further and further into a tangled mass of grass and undergrowth, until eventually we were literally fighting our way through to get along. My men, who were all very much shorter than myself, seemed to avoid most of the branches and cobwebs which seemed to catch me every time in the face! We went down the far side of the hill, up a deep ravine, and up the side of another hill, and then, to my great joy, emerged on to a long grassy slope, with fewer trees and no undergrowth. As I stopped to mop my brow and admire the view, I realized that this would be an ideal spot for calling up. My call from there would be heard in the deep valley below, and in the range of hills beyond, and if the tiger did condescend to come towards us, it would be far easier for us to see him than for him to see us. Telling my men to hide themselves in the grass, I called. Imagine our delight when, at about the third call, we heard the tiger answer from the hills beyond. He was more than a mile away, but at each call he seemed to be coming nearer. Our excitement grew intense. Call answered call until at last the tiger was only about half a mile away. Here, however, he apparently decided to stop, and nothing we could do would persuade him to advance any further towards us. But although he refused to come any nearer, he still continued to answer our call. Leaving a shikari to continue calling, I then went forward with the intention of stalking him, or of intercepting him if he eventually changed his mind, and started coming towards the call. Unfortunately for me, what looked like a perfectly straightforward hillside was in fact a series of small ridges separated by deep nullahs, and by the time I had waded through the waist-high grass and gone up hill and down dale half a dozen times, I had fully realized that to see the tiger in that grass would be very nearly impossible. Besides, the tiger too had got fed up, and had ceased calling...

While sauntering homewards I stopped occasionally to call, but it was not until we had been going nearly an hour, that the tiger suddenly started calling again, away back in the hills, whence we had just come...

On rounding the first spur we realized that the tiger was calling about a mile and a half away from a hill to our right front. We therefore quickly decided to go obliquely up a hill from where we hoped to be able to answer the call. My shikari was not a local man, and neither of us knew the jungle, but our luck was in. After we had panted up the hill we found ourselves at the beginning of a long narrow plateau covered in grass. The plateau itself had very few trees, but there was dense jungle on the slopes on either side, and a narrow pathway led straight through the middle of the grass in the direction of the tiger, who, judging by the volume of his roar, was coming towards us. We now answered each other call for call. The shikari and I ran along the pathway towards the tiger, stopping only from time to time to answer him when he roared. There was no doubt at all now that we were both approaching each other very fast. It was amazing how many chital and sambhar sprang up out of the grass and bolted for their lives.

When eventually we had got to within two hundred yards of the far end of the plateau, we halted to take stock of our surroundings, and also to regain our breath. While we were doing this the tiger called about a furlong away. I answered immediately. A moment or two later we were delighted to see the tail of a tiger, held straight up in the air, moving, like the periscope of a submarine through a sea of yellow grass, towards the dense jungle to our right. The body of the tiger was completely hidden from view. The shikari and I now moved to our right, and got behind a small tree, about fifteen yards from the edge of the dense jungle, into which the tiger had disappeared about one hundred and fifty yards further away.

Between us and the edge of the plateau there was a small bare patch, devoid even of grass, marking the upper end of a narrow ravine, which a few yards further on entered the dense jungle, and then descended abruptly towards the valley below. Standing behind the tree with the shikari crouching in the grass beside me I now leant my rifle against the tree trunk, and eagerly scanned the edge of the jungle through my field-glasses, hoping the tiger would soon reappear coming that way towards us. He had ceased calling, and as minute after minute went by, my hopes sank lower and lower, until at last in sheer desperation I decided to call again. But even this failed to produce any response, and I had almost given up hope when my shikari whispered hoarsely that he could smell the tiger. The wind certainly was blowing from the jungle towards us, but, for all that, I could smell absolutely nothing at all, and was just thinking to myself how ridiculous it was of the shikari to talk such utter rot, when from the jungle about twenty yards to our right front out walked a tiger straight on to the open patch ahead. I still had my field-glasses in my hand. As I put them down to seize my rifle, the tiger saw me, and immediately crouched facing me. {1957}

After a short reconnaissance of the jungle, I selected a small promontory, which overlooked a nullah, and faced a densely wooded hillock about a hundred and fifty yards away. Between me and the hillock the ground was pretty open and about fifteen feet below my level. Everywhere else the jungle was extremely dense, and the undergrowth and young trees in the coppice made it difficult to see more than a few yards. The idea at the back of my mind was that by calling up from the promontory I could persuade the tiger to cross over from the hillock, where I imagined he was, and come across the open space towards me. At the end of the promontory, there was a dried up tree stump, about four feet high, which I selected as a back-rest. My men had orders to do the calling up from behind bushes a few yards to my rear.

Everything went beautifully. The jungles echoed to the call, which seemed to be in capable hands. The evening sun, however, was just above the tree-tops, and was shining into my left eye. We had called only three or four times when I saw the shadow of an animal moving across the hillock. I watched it carefully, and, when it stopped, I imagined I could see the head of a tiger, but in that dark dense jungle, it was impossible to be quite sure about it, and presently the shadow moved on and disappeared. I was convinced, however, that this was the tiger, and I kept careful watch on the open patch, hoping to see him creeping through the grass ahead of me.

I must have been watching for about five minutes, when I suddenly realized my men had stopped calling, and I turned my head round to signal them to go on doing so. As I looked over my right shoulder, I had one of the biggest shocks of my life. There, not more than five yards away, was the tiger sitting up on his haunches like a dog. We saw each other simultaneously, and I have never seen a tiger look more surprised in my life. I could not have fired at him except from my left shoulder, and as that was something I would not have risked doing in such circumstances, I scrambled to my feet. While I was doing this the tiger got down on to his elbows, and at the same time got up off his haunches, so that he was down in front and up behind, and in this extraordinary position started moving backwards. Then by swinging to his right he bounded away. By this time I had found my feet and just had time to let off one barrel before he disappeared. He went through that coppice like a train, and the frantic alarm cries of the deer showed that he had gone about a furlong at full speed. Well, that was that and for the second time that day I felt I had had a miraculous escape. {1957}

THE BISON AND THE TIGER | A. N. W. POWELL

'I had gone into the hills early one morning, together with another man, to try and shoot a sambhar. While we were sitting on a spur watching the opposite hillside, in the hopes that we should catch sight of a sambhar grazing somewhere, a big bull bison appeared, grazing peacefully, and moving slowly across a grassy clearing. He did not see us, because we were hidden in the grass, and were sitting absolutely still. Presently, to our horror, we saw a very large tiger come out of the jungle behind the bison. The tiger began to stalk the bison, who was quite unconscious of his presence. We were very frightened, and wanted to run away, but our blood was turned to water, and we could not run even though we wanted to do so. Suddenly the bison must have smelt the tiger, for he gave a very loud snort, and the tiger immediately ran back into the jungle. Then the fun began. The tiger showed his face from behind the trunk of a tree, and the bison put his head down and charged, hitting the tree such a mighty smack, that he himself was thrown over backwards, and the tiger ran quickly away to one side. Again the tiger showed himself from behind another tree, and again the stupid bison charged and hurt himself without doing any damage to the tiger. This went on for a very long time, and sometimes when the bison refused to charge, the tiger used to come out into the open to annoy him, so that he would charge again. It was a terrible tragedy, for the bison had no sense. After about four or five hours he was completely exhausted, and blood was flowing from his forehead. His flanks were heaving, and he was too tired even to turn round. Then the tiger attacked him from behind, and tore open the veins of his hind legs with his teeth and claws. The great bull sank down backwards, making a bellowing sound.' {1957}

THE TIGERS AND THE LIVER | A. N. W. POWELL

It was a glorious afternoon. The rain clouds had disappeared and the sun was shining brightly. The leaves of the trees had been washed clean by the rain, and, instead of looking dusty and dull, they were now glistening and green. The whole jungle looked beautiful. I had been gazing into this lovely woodland for about ten minutes, when I heard something coming noisily down the hill behind me. I imagined it to be a troupe of monkeys. A minute or two later, however, I caught a fleeting glimpse of a tiger, moving through the bushes towards the foot of my tree. Leaning over to have a good look, I discovered it was a cub, a bit bigger than a large Alsatian. It sat down right at the foot of my sloping tree! A minute later it was joined by another of about the same size. They were in a playful mood, and I wondered when they would start running up the tree trunk to start playing with me! Then they rolled over and over each other on the ground, and indulged in quite a fair amount of all-in wrestling, quite regardless of the noise they were making. I realized then that the noise I had mistaken for monkeys must have been these two playing on their way down the hill...

The two of them behaved like little savages over their meal, snarling and growling at each other, and competing for the best titbits hidden inside the carcass. It was when both dived in together that the fiercest arguments took place. I was so engrossed watching this gruesome savagery that I had not noticed the arrival of Mama, but there she was now, a fine big tigress, sitting up on her haunches, proudly watching her cubs fighting over their supper. All the same, she was very much on the alert, and kept looking all round, obviously doing sentry [duty] while the cubs were feeding. When, however, they had more or less finished their meal, she approached the kill, and, seizing it by the exposed rib with her teeth, lifted it off the ground, and tried to drag it away...

What worried me now was that a whole liver weighing several pounds was lying a few feet away from the kill, but neither the tigress nor the cubs had noticed it. I kept wondering how long this juicy morsel would remain undiscovered, and which of the three would be the lucky one to find it. When, however, the tigress had more or less satisfied her hunger, and had given up making quite such vigorous tugs at the kill, the liver caught her eye, and, after bending down to sniff it, she picked it up in her mouth, gave it a couple of hearty chews, and swallowed the whole thing in one big gulp. This then was the savoury!

Just before dusk, with the tigress and cubs still lying about near the kill, I was delighted to hear the full-throated roar of a tiger about half a mile away. Surely, this was Papa, coming along to have his dinner. For the first time now my thoughts flew to my rifle. But when the tigress heard the roar she sprang to her feet immediately, and the two cubs at once dashed to her side. In absolute silence, they stood looking in the direction of the roar. When the tiger roared again, the tigress's body literally heaved as she tried to suppress an answering roar. She was obviously dying to answer the tiger, but her motherly instinct made her refrain from doing so. The tiger, still roaring, went down the forest road about a furlong away, but did not come to the kill, and I firmly believe he did not know anything about it. He, however, put the wind up my shikaris who were waiting further down the road. Needless to say they had all climbed trees, and stayed in them till the danger had gone by!

It had been interesting to see how the tigress and her cubs behaved when they heard a male tiger roaring. It is generally accepted that a big male tiger will kill a small male cub if he comes across it. A tigress therefore takes good care to keep her cubs out of Papa's way while they are young. Actually, she always separates from her mate before the cubs are born, and goes away to some remote jungle, as far away as possible from the beats of all other tigers. This is done primarily to avoid the notoriously bad temper of her spouse, who is intolerant while the cubs are young and at the silly stage. Later, when they are well-grown and have learnt how to behave properly, they return with their mother to her old haunts, and sometimes even rejoin Father, who then does not take exception to his well-behaved children. It may even be considered a pity that this system is not more universally adopted! It is not uncommon to come across tiger families of Papa, Mama, and two or three cubs, all living happily together, but this does not happen until the cubs have reached the age of reason.

I cannot describe what infinite pleasure it gave me to see these two cubs, the tigers of tomorrow, at home in the jungle with their mother. I wished over and over again that I had had a camera with me in my machan. {1957}

THE TIGER, THE LEOPARD AND THE BOAR
J. E. CARRINGTON TURNER

A leopard is undoubtedly the most beautiful of all the Indian carnivora; he certainly captures the eye for the longest time and claims the most admiration. His coat is truly a most fascinating one, far more so than the tiger's.

This was one of the largest we had seen. He stood on the bank gazing in the direction of the galloping deer, a big meal lost, but a purely temporary disappointment; sooner or later he would make up for it. Having drunk, he evidently intended continuing his stalk, for he quickly crossed over to the other bank and, assuming a semi-crouching attitude, went off in the direction the deer had taken, now taking cover, then showing a little of himself when he wanted to look down the river-bed to see how far his quarry had gone. Then he disappeared from sight, but from the last we saw of him there was evidence of his determination to succeed. Of all the denizens of the jungle there is none to match his cunning, his skill and stealth while stalking. He stands in a class by himself.

The leopard and his stratagems were banished from our thoughts as soon as a wild boar strutted out of the scrub; on seeing him, my companion, astounded at the size of the animal, violated our pact of absolute silence throughout the vigil, and whispered: "Oh, what a monster!" I, too, was amazed, for I had never seen the equal of this boar in bulk, height, size of head and tushes (tusks). He was a mighty boar, greyish-black in colour, a row of bristles beginning between the shoulders and continuing down to his tail. His thick neck, the pair of sabre-like tushes, and the strength and weight of his enormous body made him the personification of invincibility.

There was no nervousness in his movements and he proceeded straight to the pool where, having satisfied his thirst, he calmly sat down in the water and wallowed and wallowed, dispelling the awful heat of the day, and cleaning his massive frame of irritating parasites. His was a supreme self-confidence born of sheer strength, and the possession of weapons which, once they struck, meant grave injury if not certain death. There he lay in the pool as if it was solely his. He seemed to be proclaiming to all whom it may concern:

This small pool in sand may one day dry,
I alone, till then, shall in it lie.

Having cooled himself he ceased his wallowing, slowly left the water and rolled in the pure sand about four paces away, almost in the middle of the river-bed. He rolled again and again. He was evidently feeling increasingly refreshed. Suddenly he arose, as if an electric shock had gone through him, and stared at the bushes fringing the bank, facing them squarely, absolutely motionless.

After a moment or two, from those very bushes, there appeared the menacing head and shoulders of a thirsty tiger. But to the quenching of his thirst there was now an obstacle. Momentarily daunted, he slunk back amongst the bushes and reappeared about five yards further down. It was easy to follow his movements amongst the bushes by watching the successive positions the boar took up, always facing the tiger head-on. Stripes was manoeuvring, realizing instinctively that here was an opponent with whom he could take no liberties. The boar continued to stand firm.

The tiger walked down the bank on to the soft sand, and circled the boar who wheeled to face him. The circling and wheeling continued three or four times until suddenly the tiger charged the boar, striking him with all his might, and, with the greatest agility leaping aside after his blow. The boar met the onslaught by turning dexterously and taking it on the side of his shoulder. In this manner the tiger delivered blow after blow; he was so agile in every limb that he easily avoided contact. His blows told their tale, for the boar was dripping with blood from his shoulders downwards.

Whenever the boar showed the least tendency to charge, the tiger would step backwards. There was no doubt that, in agility, the advantage lay with the tiger. Charge, strike and leap away: it was clearly attrition that he depended on for his victory. Nevertheless, neither the blows nor the flow of blood appeared to daunt the courageous boar.

This was clearly a fight to the death. We wondered how long the combat would continue. Neither tiger nor boar appeared exhausted. The former, always saved by his agility, was unscathed; the latter an increasingly bloody spectacle, his goriness forcing us to conclude that he would very soon be an exceptional meal for his enemy. While such a thought was passing through our minds, something wholly unexpected and highly dramatic happened. The tiger, in striking and endeavouring to jump away from the boar, either lost his balance and landed awkwardly, or skidded in the soft sand. Seeing his opportunity, and astonishingly quick to grasp it, the boar charged straight into him, and, burying his razor-edged tushes in the tiger's belly, ripped and ripped again, reinforcing his thrusts to the fullest by his stupendous might and enormous weight.

With the greatest difficulty the tiger succeeded in extricating himself and stood apart. In this momentary truce the boar also stood still but ever watchful, awaiting the next onslaught. But...it never came. A changed and disfigured tiger now stood before him. He was disembowelled, with much of his entrails dangling low and heavily from his belly. Slinking towards the bank, with his dragging intestines, he ascended it and disappeared in the thorny scrub bordering it.

The bleeding boar stood rock-like; breathing heavily, with heaving flanks, he watched his enemy disappear and continued facing that direction. Satisfying himself that there was no likelihood of further attacks, he rolled repeatedly in the soft sand, on the very battle site. Then rising and shaking himself, he walked downstream, and up the other bank, disappearing into the dark of the forest. {1959}

Having decided to break back through the beaters the tiger charged one of them and caught him by the shoulder in his jaws. It so happened that the man's brother, the next beater in the line, was standing quite close and seeing what was happening ran up and took a tremendous swipe at the tiger's head with his iron-bound *lathi* or stave. He hit the animal a resounding crack and then took to his heels and never looked back until he had joined a group of beaters some distance away.

When this happened I was about one hundred yards away down the beating line. I heard the sound of the tiger snarling and the coughing roar before he charged and then voices shouting that a beater had been seized. Doubling in the direction of the sounds I came on the bodies of a man and a tiger lying side by side. I was surprised because there had been no report of a firearm, and even more surprised when the beaters, plucking up courage, came clustering round and explained what they had seen. The poor man who had been attacked was quite dead, and so was the tiger. Examining the beast's head I found that the blow from the *lathi* had crushed the skull in a way that would have made survival for more than a few moments impossible.

Needless to say the thing was a most fantastic fluke. In general a man has no more hope of killing a tiger with a cudgel than with a fly-swat. {1959}

In addition to the Maharajah and myself, the party consisted of a lad called Serje Rao Shetole and two military officers, Colonel Bhow Sahib and Captain Sultan Hussain—he who shot the bold tiger that seized his elephant's tail. After we had walked a short distance I asked the two soldiers to go off in a slightly different direction towards a point where I hoped they might get a chance if the buck broke back while the rest of us continued in the wake of the little herd.

Shetole, who was formally engaged to the Maharajah's daughter, walked between his prospective father-in-law and me. He was not more than about twelve years old and naturally quite inexperienced, so that I did not instantly take notice when he whispered that he could see a tiger. All boys begin by seeing tigers all over the place when they are first taken out after large game and besides this we were in open country dotted with small bushes, the last sort of terrain where one would expect to find a tiger. In Rajasthan it is essentially a creature of the jungle and close cover.

However, when the boy muttered his absurd fancy to me I muttered back, mildly teasing and making a joke of the thing. The Maharajah wanted to know what we were being so confidential about, and when I told him stopped short and asked Shetole to show us what he had seen.

Shetole walked back a few paces and when we had joined him pointed to his right where, about a hundred yards away, a tigress, accompanied by two smallish cubs, was sitting on her haunches watching us.

Had I known as much then as I know now I should not have been so confident that we should not encounter a tiger away from tiger-country; nor should I have allowed the boy to point, or any of us to look directly at the animal. As it was, we all followed his outstretched arm with our eyes and stared blankly at the tigress, who, as soon as she realized that her cubs had been seen, let out a regular roar and came for us in great bounds, at the same time lashing her tail in great semi-circular sweeps like an angry domestic cat. Meanwhile—though we had not much inclination to worry about them at the moment—the two cubs must have slipped into some low cover nearby, for we did not see them again.

There was no tree in sight and the nearest vegetation more than boot-high was a small thorn bush about three feet tall, a pace or two to our left. As we moved to step behind this meagre protection the unfortunate Shetole, thinking perhaps that we were going to take to our heels, turned and began running back the way we had come. This of course attracted the tigress' attention and she changed course and went after him. Throwing away the little rifle he was carrying, the boy ran as fast as he could until after a few yards he caught his foot on a stone and pitched head first into a clump of dwarf thorns.

This fall was, to put it mildly, providential, for the tigress who was still some little way away lost sight of him and at once turned back towards us. For our part the Maharajah and I, having nowhere to go, stood firm beside our ridiculous bush and awaited events. The maharaja had the small bore Mauser with which he had intended to shoot antelope and I had the case with his cartridges. As she came the tigress made an absolutely deafening noise and I for one was convinced that here stood a couple of sportsmen who would never harm another tiger.

However, seeing us stand firm, she suddenly stopped short about fifteen feet away and crouched as if for a final spring, twitching her tail, swaying her snarling head from side to side, and now and again tearing at the ground with the extended talons of her forepaws. We for our part kept watching her without moving. It was a very bad moment indeed.

After she had been terrifying us in this manner for perhaps half a minute I suddenly swung the cartridge bag round my head and shouted, telling my employer to fire at her. This no doubt relieved my feelings and mercifully for all of us the Maharajah disregarded the ill-conceived advice. As it was, my behaviour proved to be the right course of action, for having no doubt come to the conclusion that we stood at bay and were not unduly frightened of her, the tigress suddenly remembered her cubs and wheeling abruptly round went galloping back to where she had left them.

When she was some eighty or ninety yards away the Maharajah coolly raised his Mauser and took a shot at her. Fortunately it was a clean miss: speaking very quietly I begged him not to shoot again, since if she was hit the chances were that she would return and make an end of us without further ceremony. Unless the shot were more accurately placed than is usually possible with a rapidly moving target it was highly improbable that one of his small calibre bullets would kill or disable her.

We were undoubtedly well shaken, for it was a moment or two before we remembered Shetole. After a little looking around I saw a thin leg sticking out of a thorn bush and going up to it bade the owner come out. It did not move, so I leant down and touched it, at which it reacted with a sort of extraordinary tremor. The poor boy told me afterwards that he was sure in his panic that the tigress had taken hold of him...

But our troubles were by no means over. We had only been walking for a few minutes when we again heard the menacing cough of a tiger not far off. Uncertain of the direction from which it came we halted and looked circumspectly round. After a little [while] the unpleasant realization that the noise lay directly ahead was borne in on us and about a minute later a very large male tiger emerged from behind some low cover perhaps a hundred yards away and almost immediately charged. It was like some dreadful dream. I remember that the thumping of his pads as he galloped towards us over the hard baked ground sounded oddly like the ringing noise of hoofs. This was no doubt due to his exceptional weight.

As before we stood close together waiting for him, and this time the lad stood between us solid as a rock. Again, exactly like the tigress whose mate he undoubtedly was, the animal stopped about fifteen feet away and menaced us, swaying his great snarling muzzle from side to side close to the ground and switching his tail, making up his mind to pounce. To forestall this, I took a quick aim between his swinging ears and fired. Providence was with us that fantastic morning, for not only did I miss, but the report and the cloud of dust raised by the bullet which hit the earth close to his head, as well as the shout which I let out, evidently discouraged him. After another two or three snarls he turned and cantered back to his cover.

The extraordinary way in which we had been attacked twice within a matter of minutes by two unprovoked tigers, coming from different directions, had given us something of the sensation of being surrounded; moreover our constant changes of direction had left us a little disorientated.

We knew that the tiger was certainly ahead of us and that in all probability the tigress was still somewhere not far off to our rear. On our left we could see a low hill and on our right a river. The best chance seemed to be to make for the hill, although there was enough cover there for the tigers to stalk us, in the hope that the country on the other side would be open and we should be able from the higher ground to find a route back to the shooting brake. In fact this proved to be the case and within an hour we had reached it unmolested. Bhow Sahib and Sultan Hussain who were waiting for us were chagrined to see us return empty-handed. {1959}

VALMIK THAPAR

FATAL ENCOUNTERS | KESRI SINGH

Ten minutes after we had started our progress up the riverbed the tiger came out of some bushes about twenty yards in front of Mohammed Khan's elephant—a species of beast he can never have seen before—and stood blocking the way. His manner was perfectly calm and collected and he offered an excellent target to the shikari, who at once shot him in the chest. I could see the tiger, but was unable to fire because my elephant was passing under the branches of a tree at the crucial moment.

The moment the tiger was hit he uttered a tremendous roar and charged the elephant before him. The elephant could not face this and swung round to fly. As she swung the tiger leapt at her flank and clawed his way on to her back where Mohammed Khan was sitting in the kind of low howdah called a charjama. With a blow of his forepaw he crushed Mohammed's head and then, tumbling on top of him, died.

In these extraordinary and terrifying circumstances, with the tiger on the howdah behind him, the mahout behaved with the most praiseworthy coolness. He stayed in his place and as soon as the noise of the tiger had ceased got the elephant under control and made it crouch, so that both the bodies could be removed from the charjama. Mohammed had been killed instantly. His bullet had penetrated the tiger's heart and the beast had charged, mounted the elephant and killed him during the half minute or so of life which remained to it. {1959}

THE TIGER THAT TOOK ON A BOAR | KESRI SINGH

A tiger I knew took on a boar,
And there never was a beast so woefully sore,
For after the fight and as sure as sin,
There was more of that tiger out than in.
See how he flashes his fiery eye,
Ready to cut, to thrust, to die.
A boar that will charge like the Light Brigade
Is the bravest beast God ever made.

I thought that the boar, after receiving this warning, would slink away into the jungle, but here I was mistaken. He looked round in all directions carefully and, when he saw the tiger, simply grunted with the bristles raised

VALMIK THAPAR

vertically on his back. The tiger approached and roared back in reply.

All this we were watching through the holes in the screen quite unseen by the animals. I could have dropped the tiger with a single shot if I wanted to, but I was so engrossed with what I saw that I held my fire for the time being.

On hearing the roar of the tiger, the boar repeated his Hoo! Hoo! in rather a more aggressive and defiant manner. Not content with this, he actually advanced with short steps in the tiger's direction.

The tiger was now crouching low, moving stealthily round and round the boar. The boar changed his front with every movement of the tiger, keeping a determined face with his deadly tushes always towards the treacherous enemy. The bristles on the boar's back standing up at right angles magnified his size in the moonlight.

The tiger had narrowed down his circles and come nearer and was now growling and showing his teeth. He crouched still lower till he seemed almost flat on the ground and, gathering his limbs, he suddenly sprang on the boar with a loud roar. The struggle for a brief minute was fast and most thrilling. The tiger with one sweep of his strong paw landed a terrific slap right across the face which made the boar reel. At the same time the boar with a hoarse grunt collided with the tiger, slashing him with his sharp tushes. Now both the combatants were streaming with blood.

The tremendous sweep of the tiger's claws had torn flesh and skin away from the boar's forehead, leaving a flap of skin hanging over his face, which half-blinded him. Even with this disability the boar with another hoarse grunt again rushed straight at the tiger who very cleverly eluded the charge and quick as lightning alighted on the boar's back, tearing him with his sharp claws. I almost thought the game was over but it was not so. The boar, regaining his balance, gave a few ripping gashes with his sharp white tushes which almost disembowelled his foe. The tiger now slunk to a nearby stone and the boar, completely exhausted, staggered aside and laid down on the ground still champing his tushes in defiance to the last. The tiger with the blood pouring out of many rents made by the boar and with his entrails protruding from his skin also laid himself down for eternal rest by the side of the big stone. The mutually disabled combatants now lay aside and I thought it was high time to put them out of their agony. {1963}

I started to creep forward and kept going for about ten minutes. Then, while edging round a bend, I was suddenly stopped dead.

Just in front of me and apparently asleep under a patch of shade was a large leopard stretched on the sand. But there was something wrong. A closer look showed that its attitude was unnatural. The head was twisted grotesquely and one forepaw was slightly bent and held drunkenly in the air. The leopard was dead.

As I started to approach it my nose told me that it had been dead for some time. A swarm of blue flies buzzed up as I came nearer and wafted the sickly-sweet smell of death more strongly to my nostrils. Something had eaten a small part of the hind-quarters and the sand all round the leopard was wildly churned; the sand was too dry to show what animal had been feeding.

I began to look around me and almost at once spotted something else. A little farther down the nullah, hard against one bank, were the remains of what had once been a chital stag. All that was left now was the head, a few pieces of skin and splintered bone, and two almost whole ribs.

Both animals had been dead for about two days, and I was just beginning to wonder what had happened when I noticed that a small *flame-of-the-forest* tree had fallen across the nullah some ten yards farther down. It was blocking the nullah completely, but starting not far in front of it I could see in the sand the mark of a drag which disappeared into the foliage of the fallen tree; something heavy had been dragged through to the other side. I went up to the tree and, after tearing away some of the leaves and smaller branches, saw something black lying within two yards of me. It was the dead body of a huge wild boar.

I climbed over the tree and looked down at it. The mask was set in a ferocious snarl, and the one tush I could see was stained brown with congealed blood. The remains were fresh, the meat hardly tainted; but the body of the boar had been horribly ripped and torn and once again a little had been eaten off the hind-quarters. This was the work of a tiger, and if that bloodstained tush meant what I thought it did, the tiger had not had the fight all his own way.

As I got up from examining the boar I suddenly realized that the jungle around me was strangely quiet. I looked up at the trees for vultures and found not a single one in sight. The truth came to me the next second. Somewhere close at hand the tiger was lying up. It *had* to be: with the dead leopard lying pretty much in the open that was the only explanation for no vultures.

It was now just six o'clock and a little darker than usual. The black clouds I had noticed when leaving the house had crept up overhead and muffled thunder was vibrating in the stifling air...

As I stood on the bank listening, I was a little uneasy. To be so near the kills at a time when the tiger might come back to feed was asking for trouble, and I should have liked to know if it had already either seen or heard me. I was still thinking about that when, without the slightest warning, the tiger appeared about five yards in front of me.

It came from behind a small cluster of teak like a conjurer's illusion. At first it did not see me for it was moving obliquely away, but I must have given some slight start of surprise which caused it to stop and turn. I saw then that it was a tigress and she was looking straight at me. I can still see those eyes even today; but why I remember them so clearly is not because they held the threat of sudden death, but because they were vacant and not seeing me at all. I might have been some usual piece of jungle scenery, and when the tigress had gazed for several seconds she turned calmly away and then passed out of sight behind some cover.

As she went I saw that she was plastered with dried mud and along her left flank ran a long, bloody gash; and she was moving with a marked limp.

The moment after the tigress disappeared from sight I recovered my wits. It had been an odd encounter and there was much I still did not understand; but there was no doubt that she was a badly crippled animal and if I was quick there was still a good chance to put her out of her pain. After the blistering heat of the day she should now be making for water. She had certainly gone in the right direction; there was a pool in a larger nullah about fifty yards away. If I could surprise her there she would be a sitting shot from the bank above it...

The tigress's roar seemed to burst in my ear. Then I heard her crashing towards me from the high ground a little to my right. The next second she hurtled into view and with a mighty bound landed in the clearing some thirty paces in front of me.

The shock and surprise were so complete that the ball cartridge fell from my fingers as I was putting it in the breech. I know now that this mishap undoubtedly saved my life; for if the gun had been loaded I should have used it at once before I'd had time to appreciate the situation.

It took me perhaps fifteen seconds to realize that the animal before me now was not the tigress but a tiger. That he was bent on mischief there was no doubt. The moment he landed on his feet he whipped about to face me and then began weaving quickly from side to side across my front. At the same time he was throwing up his head and shattering the air with bellowing roars. Then he began to make quick feint attacks. He'd dart in, crouching low to the ground with his hind-quarters slightly raised and ears laid hard against his head. All at once he would check with his lips mouthing a vicious snarl that spat out between gleaming fangs. The next second he would break his feint with a great sideways leap to start weaving and roaring again.

At any second that tiger was coming in. He was playing like a cat with a mouse and the real attack could not be delayed long. Each time he threatened my eyes went to the end of his tail. The moment that flickered he would spring.

All this time I had been creeping slowly backwards, fascinated by that prancing yellow body. The shotgun still hung open over my left arm. Should I suddenly snap it shut and try for his head with the buckshot in the right barrel?

Before I could make up my mind I saw something that ruled this idea right out. From the corner of my eye I had spotted the tigress. She was under a small tree just a few yards to my right, sitting up like a big cat before a fire. On her face was a pleased smile as she watched the scene before her.

When I found her so close I suddenly knew what was really going on. These two were mating. That would explain her extraordinary behaviour earlier when she had ignored me so near the kills; for it is not uncommon when the female's in season to find her going about in a kind of dazed, ecstatic trance.

After that diversion for the fraction of a second my eyes snapped back to the tiger. There was no ecstatic trance about him! He was right out for business and getting more excited every moment. This encounter was just what he wanted: a chance to show-off before his sweetheart, and if that charnel-house in the nullah was anything to go by, this tiger had had some practice...

Help came from the most unexpected quarter. A thin tongue of lightning flickered down in a brilliant violent flash. Hard on it came a deafening crash of thunder from right overhead. It stopped the tiger dead in his tracks. Then came the rain. At first just a few large drops spattered against my hat and bare arms. Then, to another crash of thunder, a deluge roared down from the leaden sky.

A solid sheet of water was suddenly cascading before my eyes and soon splashing up from the ground in a fine mist. Quickly taking advantage of this heaven-sent diversion I moved farther behind my tree. But the tiger had given up. As the rain rattled and bounced off his streaming back it seemed as though all the ardour had soaked right out of him. Watching him closely, I put another buckshot cartridge in the empty chamber and then slowly clicked the gun; as it snicked shut I slipped off the safety-catch.

But the game was over. With a great shake of his rain-soaked body the tiger suddenly wheeled about and then trotted away. Almost at once he was joined by the tigress. The last I saw of them they were bounding away together towards some broken land where they probably found shelter in a cave...

That was undoubtedly my lucky day for several reasons. Firstly, if I had met the tiger instead of the tigress near the small nullah I do not think he would have hesitated for a single second. He would have come for me at once because I was far too near his kills and a tiger's temper is always short whenever he is mixed up with a tigress.

The tiger, of course, had killed that leopard. As I see it, the tiger must have surprised the leopard soon after *the leopard* had killed the chital stag. But the leopard—and some are very bold—must have refused to give way over his own kill. Then the tiger went for him, not so much for the possession of the carcase but to show off to his mate. The tiger had attacked the boar too; but it is not unlikely that the boar proved such a tough antagonist that the tigress had waded in to help. In the fracas she got that long gash down her side.

The two reasons that might have proved fatal if I had shot at the tigress? Nothing is more certain than the fact that I should have given her the choke barrel if I had fired the moment she appeared—and merely peppered her with number 6. That would have been enough to bring her straight at me. After that, from such close quarters, I doubt whether I should have killed her with a single charge of buckshot in time. But even if I had there was still the tiger about which I still knew nothing. I don't think I would have got away a second time if he had caught me unawares bending over the dead body of his lady love. {1960}

Towards the closing years of British rule in India there was real concern for the game. A lot of animals now were scarce and some kinds of them already well along the road to extinction... A tightening of forest rules and stricter enforcement, a low limit to any individual's bag, more and larger game sanctuaries and—above all else—much more plain common sense [was needed].

Sound enough. In some other countries where the animals had been hunted as hard as they had been in India, prompt and energetic action had not only saved most of the game but seen it increase. The same thing would work here.

Then it was 1947, and with Independence times really *did* change. Old-time sportsmen, had they seen it, would have been speechless with amazement, for almost overnight an entirely new kind of hunter had started to roam the jungles. There had of course been black sheep before, but most hunters had obeyed the rules and shot in conventional ways. Not so the new men. Forest rules for them just did not exist and they shot neither on foot nor from a machan. Instead, they rode in a jeep, and as it sneaked along forest roads at night they picked off everything that showed up in the headlights from the comfort and security of the front seat.

At much the same time the old 'water-hole gunner' really came into his own. The satanic government that had imposed those harsh measures to keep muzzle-loaders and twelve-bores out of irresponsible hands was gone. Now, almost anyone that cared to apply for a license, was sure to get one. In no time at all freshly killed venison was on display in the bazaars.

Indian sportsmen were aghast, and their letters of protest were soon flooding into newspaper offices. But they did little good; these sportsmen were a tiny minority and nothing they said or tried to do made the slightest difference: they were cranks from the bad old days.

This change came fast and its effects were noticeable almost at once. Indeed, looking back now it seems as though the animals disappeared overnight. All of them, of course, had not been shot. It was just that they were not seen about so often, and when they were seen there was something about the way they fled that showed them sensible of the constant threat now abroad both by day and night.

It was not like this ten years ago. Then, herds of chital and nilgai were a common sight on any dawn round of the estate. Sambur would be about too if you were early enough and in the right place, and there was hardly a morning that showed no glimpse of barking deer and four-horned antelope and the dainty chinkara sporting about the more open ravines.

Then the shots started to echo through the nights. Most of them were the long-drawn-out *Boo-o-oom!* of muzzle-loaders using the always-slightly-damp bazaar black powder. For the first few nights I believed it was just a sudden increase in the occasional poaching that has always worried us. But when the shots continued night after night it was obvious that something unusual was going on.

A few inquiries soon showed what was happening. A lot of the small cultivators around us had acquired guns 'to protect their fields'. But they were not sitting over their crops. After dark most of them were roaming the forests in bullock-carts and shooting at any animal they met by the light of a torch. Along the main road that runs two miles from the estate matters were even worse. At night this road is used by a lot of animals which come out of the jungle on each side of it. Now, after them, went trucks and private cars creeping along in low gear with headlights blazing and a spot sweeping the sides—and perhaps as many as four gunners ready for the first pair of eyes to flash back at the lights.

These mechanized rogues had better weapons, shotguns with a sprinkling of old rifles. With these the kills came easily. So did the money for the skins, meat and horns. This was too much for the passengers in the local buses: such easy money could not be ignored and so these, too, began taking their weapons in case anything showed up along the way. Something often did, and then an obliging driver—for a hunk of meat—would stop the bus and allow the shot to be taken through the window.

Most of the sportsmen that saw what was going on sent in reports. At first, though, they were not really worried for something like this was bound to happen when the old ban on firearms was suddenly lifted. Such flagrant poaching would of course not be allowed to go on; just let a few offenders be fined and have their arms confiscated and the abuses would stop. The authorities, when reports reached them, were bound to act quickly.

That the authorities did nothing was perhaps the biggest shock of all. The slaughter went on and there was not the slightest evidence that anything was being done to stop it. Nobody seemed to care, and as things got worse *The Times of India* came out with this:

'The Uttar Pradesh conference on the preservation of wildlife has very appropriately drawn the country's attention to the depredations of poachers and trigger-happy shikaris. Herds of *chital*, *chinkara* and spotted deer have become rare and the reason for this, according to U. P.'s chief game warden, is the use of buckshot by shikaris who fire into a herd. For every animal that is killed on the spot several others are injured by buckshot, and these beasts suffer a slow death from festering wounds. In parts of Uttar Pradesh poaching has apparently become organized business: in some towns of Lakhimpur, Kheri district, people seldom buy mutton; they prefer venison which is cheaper and readily available in the bazaar thanks to the very private enterprise of the poachers. Professional bird-catchers are playing havoc with winged fauna and the conference was told that partridge and quail are on the verge of extinction. The Uttar Pradesh Government can be expected to accept the conference's recommendation that a two-year ban be imposed on the use of buckshot and that the U.P. Birds and Wild Animals Protection Act be amended to put an end to the malpractices of the professional bird-catchers. But this will not be enough. Strengthening the law is no substitute for enforcing what is already on the statute book, and the conference revealed that the enforcement aspect has been neglected to an incredible extent. What is one to make of the official admission that a large number of poachers are Government servants? It is fair to assume that what is true of Uttar Pradesh is more or less true of other states. Government officials attending the Naini Tal conference were unable to suggest steps to put an end to this deplorable state of affairs. Divisional Commissioners and other senior revenue and police officials have promised to dissuade their subordinates from poaching, but persuasion is a curious method of enforcing the law.'

Right from the start the poachers on our own land became an unmitigated nuisance. Very early on they got Leggy, a four-horned antelope, who screamed home one morning with a back leg hanging from a sinew after a meeting with a sneaking bullock cart in the big nullah. Not long after they got Sammy [the barking deer]...

I saw some of the tragedy that was now getting into its stride from my wooden armchair above the pool in the nullah. This chair is built permanently into the fork of a giant tree and has been there nearly ten years. It is thirty feet above the pool and commands wide sweeps of the jungle beyond both banks. I use it a lot throughout the year and often spend whole nights in it watching the animals coming down to drink. The best time is towards the end of the hot weather. By then the other pools in the nullah have dried up and this one holds the only water for a long way around.

The first hot weather after the change brought some of the tragedy now going on after dark into sharp focus. That year the *mowha* flowers were late. When at last they started to fall from hundreds of trees in a long strip of jungle near the pool, that was the only water for a considerable distance. At once that strip became a death-trap. The sweet fleshy petals of these flowers draw herbivorous animals like a magnet, and when the sickly sweet scent brought them to the strip, the bullock-carts were waiting in the darkness under the trees and on the road through it were the crawling trucks and jeeps.

The deer and antelopes were the hardest hit and brought to the pool the saddest stories of all. I would see fawns which had been with their mothers a short time before suddenly appear alone, their eyes big and frightened in the moonlight; or a frantic hind, mad with anxiety, would come dashing down to the water searching desperately for a baby which would never nestle into her side again.

Nothing was being spared, and for every animal killed outright, several more got away wounded. Some of these staggered to the pool at their last gasp for a last drink. Others, not so badly hit, would come trembling with terror to quench a burning thirst. After doing that they would limp painfully away—perhaps to weeks of agony unless they were found and destroyed in the morning. For no shot is ever fired from the chair; the pool is a sanctuary and I like to believe that the animals know it.

It was late one night when I first saw the cub. He seemed to have come to the pool alone although he was obviously a very young tiger. By now, however, that was nothing unusual and he was very likely searching for a mother he would never find. Under the hard light of a full moon I watched him flitting about by the water's edge. He seemed quite happy, and if his solitary state concerned him he was not showing it. He was not thirsty either for he made no attempt to drink but just played with the dead leaves rustling on the sand in the light breeze.

I was just wondering how to catch him in the morning when his mother materialized from the shadows under the left bank of the nullah. As she came another cub was playing with her tail. She went straight to the pool and drank, then the three glided away as silently as they had come.

The next evening I was up in the chair early. The night before, those cubs had looked young enough for that outing to have been one of their first. If that was true, it suggested a hide-out close to the pool and the tigress would certainly come again. But as the moon was bright and she would come up warily, I had taken Bimbo with me and tied him in the branches above my head.

Bimbo is a langur monkey who hates all the big cats. For this reason he often earns his keep because the merest glimpse of a tiger or leopard sets him screaming his lungs out and dancing about the tree like a drunken dervish. That kind of performance is often useful to put a suspicious animal at ease if it has either seen or heard anything unusual from where you are sitting. But once Bimbo starts his act there can be no doubt—it was only a monkey after all.

The tigress came soon after nine o'clock and Bimbo was off the moment she appeared. But this time it didn't work for when the tigress looked up she must have spotted me at once. She did not come to pool again for more than two months; rather than expose her cubs to a possible risk she drank at the river some way to the south. It was on a night much later when I did not expect them that the three glided down to the pool again. That was the last time I saw the tigress alive. When I saw her next she was stretched on the concrete floor of a garage twenty miles away. A truck driver had shot her the previous night.

~

When I found the tigress in the garage I was on my way to Jubbulpore for three days. Had it been possible to skip my appointment I should have gone straight back to look for the cubs. As it was, I could only wonder what had become of them all the time I was away. If they had been close to their mother when she was killed either of two fates could have overtaken them: they might have been shot or captured. The last possibility was the more likely. Tiger cubs are a rich prize and they are not difficult to round up because all young animals suddenly losing mothers will hang about the spot where she disappeared from for several days.

Those cubs had been so much on my mind that I went down to the pool shortly after I got home and began to search along the water's edge. I was not really expecting to find any sign of them, but almost at once I found their small pug marks and near them, half buried in the sand, a chewed peacock's feather with traces of blood. An hour later I had found more feathers and the remains of a full-grown peacock.

The cubs were safe after all and obviously needed no help from me. The wily peacock is difficult to surprise, and to have got one, the cubs must already be using 'big tiger' tactics and haunting the game-paths leading to the water. They could safely be left on their own, but to keep an eye on them I meant to find their hide-out.

It was a good place. The tigress had chosen well and was rearing them in a deep cave with a narrow slit of an entrance well screened with thorns on the side of a hill. It was, as I had suspected, not far from the pool; yet I might never have found it but for the lucky accident of seeing, from some high ground a little way off, one of the cubs coming out.

Once I knew where they lived I got to know them well with glasses from that high ground. They grew fast, and it was not long before they were hunting bigger game; nor was it long before they were roaming farther afield. Then they started staying away from the cave for days at a time. I was sorry about that; they had been a source of endless delight and this meant that they would not be staying much longer for they were now big enough to split up.

At last I thought they had gone. More than a week went by and there had been no sign of them near the cave... Then one evening they were back and I knew that they had killed something near the entrance to the cave. The clue was vultures waiting patiently on a silk-cotton tree half-way up the hill.

I enjoy stalking, so I set off to get near enough to watch them on whatever they had killed. After some time I picked up the young tigress lying on some grass in a patch of shade. But of the tiger and the kill there was no sign although I spent another fifteen minutes looking around for them.

I was just starting to turn back when I felt that something was wrong. For a few seconds I thought that sixth sense was warning of danger; the tiger now was big enough to be rough if he caught me near his kill. Before moving I glanced all round me and then climbed higher up the hill. There was still no sign of him, but from my new position I saw on the ground below me some vultures I had not noticed before. A moment later I realized the truth. There was no kill and the vultures were hopping slowly towards the tigress because she was dead.

Her body was still warm. She could not have died much more than an hour before. Her white stomach, still bearing traces of her baby-coat, was swollen and had been punctured by buckshot in a tightly grouped pattern. The grass all around had been flattened by her final struggles; her lips were drawn back in a snarl of pain hurled at the last cruel agonies of a lingering death.

Where was the tiger? Was he too, either dead or dying of wounds somewhere near the cave? It was not unlikely. The cubs would almost certainly have been met together, and if they had been met with dazzling headlights, the glare would have 'fixed' them long enough for the second barrel. I searched until dark but couldn't find him.

Early the next morning I knew that he was not dead. He had drunk at the pool during the night, and when I saw the vultures keeping to the trees, I knew that he was lying somewhere close to the dead tigress.

Soon after lunch I was up in the chair above the pool. The day was warm enough to send the tiger to drink early. But in case he was late I had mounted a torch on a rifle. Yes, I was going to break the no-shooting-from-the-chair rule if he showed any signs of a wound serious enough either to kill him after days of agony or leave him so crippled that his life would be a misery and perhaps a danger to man and beast.

The afternoon was indeed hot and drowsy and I am ashamed to admit that the droning jungle soon lulled me to sleep. It was five-thirty before I finally struggled out of warm hazy dreams and with a sudden start saw the tiger on the far side of the water.

Fortunately he missed the startled movement as I woke for he was looking away as he lay on the sand by the water's edge. When the sleep was off my eyes I saw that he was staring intently at a leaf blowing over the surface and drifting towards him. When it came within reach he started to dab at it with his right front paw, but with a touch so gentle that his pad was the merest caress on the tiny tip of its curled-up sail. From that moment I always called him the Lonely Tiger. His expression was so forlorn that there flashed into my mind the vision of a small boy pondering the cruel fate that had killed first his mother and then his sister, and so condemned him to the heartache of loneliness and unexciting games played on his own.

All at once he smashed his little boat into the water with a sudden splash. *Just a silly kid's game!* Then before I quite realized what he was doing he had reminded me why I was at the pool by starting to lick at his left front paw. From my perch thirty feet above him I saw it at once: a small patch of red flesh licked clean of fur. I leant forward to watch. But he licked nowhere else so that seemed the only wound he had. I wondered whether it would be just a single pellet from the second barrel.

I waited till he got to his feet and started down the nullah. He went slowly and with a limp, but the wound in his paw still seemed to be the only injury he had. I let him go; from that he would recover with few or no ill effects.

He was to limp for the rest of his life. On wet sand and damp earth which held the impressions of pug marks well, the left front paw always showed a little twisted with the outside toe pressing harder than the others. This was to tell me in years to come when the Lonely Tiger had been round...

The tiger never used the cave again and many months passed

without a sign of him. Then he came back, but now he was only a casual caller because he had settled down on a regular 'beat' which took him about ten days to get round. The wound in his paw evidently had healed well and he seemed a normal tiger living on jungle game, for no report of a cattle-kill ever came in when he was about.

Sometime later he disappeared completely for nearly a year. Where he went I never knew, but it was most likely a wife that kept him away from his old haunts; when they finally called him back he probably left a family in some distant jungle.

When at last that familiar pug mark appeared in the nullah again it was an unexpected visiting card from an old friend. Once more he had come back to settle down on a beat, so whenever he was expected I started to sit over the pool for I badly wanted to see what he looked like now.

He came at last on a night when there was no moon. But even a tiger cannot pass silently over dry leaves and I heard him crunching across the thick carpet of them I had spread on the nullah bed. When the torch flicked on he stopped dead and started back at the beam. He was a magnificent animal, his coat glossy and but lightly marked with stripes. The light held him for more than a minute before he started to edge away. That night I should have taught him a lesson, a shot near his nose then might have given this story a different ending. But neither I nor the Lonely Tiger knew then that the sands of his life were running out and that he had only eight more days to live....

For the past two weeks I had been hearing a great deal about the man shooting in the block a few miles to the north. 'One of the richest men of all, sahib,' Bhutu told me. Certainly something unusual was going on. From all accounts the camp arrangements were fantastic: luxuries galore and enough servants to astonish an old-time Viceroy. But in spite of luxuries, hundreds of beaters, and a dozen or more young buffaloes for baits, no tiger had been shot up to the beginning of the third week.

I thought I knew what was going on. Since Independence there have sprung up in India firms to deal with visiting sportsmen from overseas. A few of these are excellent and they do their clients well; they also observe all the forest rules and make sure that animals are shot by fair means. There are other firms not so good and some that should not be allowed to operate at all. These last ones are interested in nothing but money and if they know the forest rules they seldom obey them; and as their hunting experience is usually nil their safest best to get trophies is to allow their clients to shoot from jeeps.

The camp I had been hearing about was a show run by perhaps the worst of the bad firms. When this shoot was nearing its end I happened to meet the client casually one day on the road. He hailed from some country 'south of the border' and spoke English with a strong American accent. He was very disgruntled about no tiger for he had just come from Africa where animals 'grow on every bush'. On parting he asked me if I could sell him a tiger skin in the event of his shoot ending with no tiger in the bag.

But the shoot was not yet over. If it had started slowly this probably was only because the man in charge of it had no intention of making things appear too easy. He had charged a great deal of money, and it was therefore necessary at first to make some show of getting a tiger by normal hunting methods. From what I heard the attempts had been pretty pathetic; so now, with the shoot drawing to an end, it was time to start using the jeeps at night.

They got him on the fourth night. The jeep had left camp soon after midnight for the best time was 'towards morning'. On this trip tiger was top priority, but if anything else showed up it was not to be neglected. Nor was it. Twenty minutes after the start an immature sambur stag fell to a .375 magnum. It was covered with leaves and left where it dropped to be collected in the morning for it was too early yet to clutter the rack at the back of the jeep: 'You just never could tell when you might want the room.' Wise counsel as it turned out, for later the rack held a chital hind.

By now time was getting on. But the night was not yet over, and just a little farther along the road another victim was waiting. As the first fingers of dawn reached up for the sky his brilliant eyes blazed back at the headlights. For a few seconds the animal was indistinct. Then the jeep was juddering to a crawl as the guide pointed excitedly ahead with *There he is!*

A tiger stood across the road. As the jeep purred nearer it sounded no note of danger. His puckered mask held only a puzzled expression as the bright eyes stared at the oncoming lights. The jeep closed to a few yards. The tiger at last turned slowly towards the side of the road. As he moved, the bullet smacked into his belly, low and far back.

The tearing pain of the bullet kept him moving for almost a mile. Then the shock brought him down beside a patch of thorns. He was mortally wounded and in terrible agony. Left alone he would have gone no further; but the first grey of dawn had now changed to lemon-coloured light and through it he saw two men, still some distance away, moving along his trail. He staggered away without being seen and then rested again where the jungle borders Bhutu's field on the northern boundary of the estate.

At dawn that morning I was not far away from this boundary with Bhutu and two other men helping to stamp out the last smouldering patches of a fire which had burnt all night. We heard Bhutu's wife shouting long before she reached us with the news that a tiger had just crossed their field and had growled when it saw her.

We found the two men first. They were examining a fresh patch of blood under a tree. One was armed with an old single barrel 12-bore, the other had an axe. When I had found out who they were they readily told the whole story and then amazed me more by explaining how they had been left behind 'to find the dead tiger'. The rest, with One-Shot Sam, had gone comfortably home to a hearty breakfast.

When the men were forbidden to search farther the one with the gun started to argue. The tiger, he said, had to be found. The foreign *burra sahib* badly wanted the skin and would make trouble if he didn't get it. I sent Bhutu and Jaganath to see them on their way and make sure that they did not slip back.

When I started to follow the blood trail I was still unaware that I was after the Lonely Tiger. He ought to have been miles away on his beat for he was not due back for another two or three days. But where the trail left the leafy carpet of the forest for a path through scrub I suddenly found that twisted pug clearly printed in the fine dust. This, although a shock, was also a help. A strange tiger would have been making off at random and any cover that offered the slightest security might have concealed it. But not this one. At least I was ready to bet that when thinking of a safe place to hide he would be making for the cave.

The trail was easy to follow. The tiger, still losing blood, had kept to a path which winds diagonally across the side of a wooded hill. Near the bottom of this, the path forks, the right branch curling down to the nullah, the other going on over boulder-strewn ground under heavy jungle to the tiger's old cave. The blood turned away to the right. My guess had been wrong, but once that idea had been tossed out of my mind I realized that the pool in the nullah was the obvious place for the tiger to make for. What he must need now more than anything else was water.

I should find him by the pool. That was certain; for he had been forced to rest at two places on the way down from the top of the hill and that had slowed him up considerably; now, he could not be very far ahead. From the fork I crept to within fifty yards of the nullah and then left the path to make a detour through the jungle which would bring me out above the pool from a flank.

I regretted doing this at once. The noise of my progress now was dangerous. The surface of the path had been powder-soft and dead silent, but the ground here was strewn with dry leaves and I seemed to be treading on them all. There was no time to go back. Having once started it was best to keep going as quietly as I could and make for a screen of bushes ahead that edged the bank just above the pool. At last I reached them and paused briefly; then I inched forward the last two yards and looked down at the pool.

The nullah bed was empty. One quick sweeping glance took it all in. Then a sudden chill swept through me when I saw what I had walked into. The water in the pool was cloudy with slow swirls of muddy sediments still settling to the bottom. The tiger had only just left. Across the dry sand I could see the deep pocks left by his pugs still ringed with a thin wet line. The tracks led from the water to where the path sloped up the bank…the path I had just left.

There could be little doubt that he had heard me coming. But now, instead of running away, he had turned to meet the threat and had come up the path to fight. From somewhere very close he was watching me. I kept quite still, ears straining, eyes searching frantically for some sign: attack might come at any second—the only warning a sudden noisy charge over the dry leaves from wherever he was hiding.

I saw him first from the corner of my eye. He was crouched by a teak tree twenty yards off and a little behind me. The next second the foresight was racing towards him.

But I was too late. Death was staring straight back at me from the tiger's eyes even as I swung towards him. As I stared back I heard the pounding of my heart and the frantic cries of monkeys which had just spotted him from the trees along the nullah. They were very excited. But then they didn't know as I did that the Lonely Tiger was dead. {1960}

THE STORM | HUGH ALLEN

The weather now looked ugly indeed and there was something about the sky that alarmed me; overhead, the clouds seemed to be boiling as they lashed out the rain. A few seconds later I had forgotten them when, above the smashing of the deluge, I suddenly heard the roar of the rising river four hundred yards away. It was a sound that sent me hurrying back to my raincoat and gumboots.

The river of course always rises when the rains start and it often rises fast. But this rise was too sudden and suggested abnormal conditions which had not been there when I visited the river bank fifteen minutes before.

When I reached the river the roar of the racing waters was deafening. Far upstream I could see nothing of the causeway that takes the main road across the river-bed; in its place was a frothing, muddy-white line stretching from bank to bank. That meant a rise of nearly twenty feet in perhaps as many minutes: somewhere up in the mountains about Pachmarhi where the Denwa has its source, there must have been a lot more rain that even we'd had. After watching the river for some minutes I squelched across to the big nullah.

I found the water here already over the banks and flooding the land on both sides; the current down the centre was like a raging millstream. From force of habit I started to splash through the water as near to the bank as I could judge. I was looking for the obstruction until I realized that there probably was none; the nullah just wasn't big enough to carry away the tons of water falling from the skies.

At three o'clock in the afternoon it was nearly dark and a high wind was rising steadily. The cattle, which had gone out as usual in the morning, had been brought back at midday and put in their shed. After that I had sent all the men back to their quarters; in this weather there was nothing anyone could do outside, and by the signs in the sky we had not yet seen the worst of it. The skies were getting darker, and as the rain pelted down the wind was rising to a high wailing shriek.

The typhoon struck soon after six. There was little warning, though a fiery blast of shattering thunder may have been its herald. A few seconds later, the elements went mad and the world was suddenly a howling inferno struck through with violent flashes of vivid violet light. The fury of the wind was frightening. It was roaring through the trees with a speed that appalled and the whole house was shuddering to the screaming impact. Above the deafening roar we could hear loud *snaps* as branches were torn from the trees and the grinding crashes as forest giants slammed down before the onslaught.

Within fifteen minutes of the first blast the roof of the cowshed was torn off bodily. We heard it start to tear loose, then came the rumble and rattle of falling bricks. Hard behind that rose the frantic cries of terrified cattle and the clatter of stampeding hooves on concrete. All at once the clatter stopped, bitten off by the wind with alarming suddenness.

As I looked at the damage the torch was hardly needed. The wreckage was brilliant under the almost continuous lightning. The roof had reared upwards and then levered down one entire longitudinal wall. The debris had fallen on the cattle and three of them were still writhing under a mass of splintered rafters and rubble; of the others there was no sign.

With four men carrying lanterns I set off to look for them. The force of the wind now was such that the driving rain really hurt our bare hands and faces. We had scarcely gone two hundred yards to the north of the house when we were pulled up short. Stretching away into the night was a solid sheet of water. It covered the field in front of us to disappear into the trees fringing the far side; as far as we could see to the right and left of us there was water everywhere flooding up from the nullah.

We turned left and skirted along by the water. Almost at once we found the cattle. They had not gone far and were huddled together under some trees with the water lapping their legs. By now they had calmed down and gave no trouble when the men started to drive them home.

I left the men to it and then set off to find out how bad things really were. The rain was still slashing down, but even so the extent of the flooding from the nullah had come as a shock to me. What about the river? That was a much more formidable force and as I hurried across to it the first tinge of anxiety rose about the safety of the house.

The house is on a part of the estate which is roughly triangular. One side of the triangle is formed by the river. The other side is the nullah which, after running diagonally across the estate, meets the river to form the apex; about the centre of the base, between the river and the nullah, the house stands on a slight rise.

With my head down I turned into the wind and fought towards the river in a straight line. Even today I can recall vividly almost every step of that journey. It was like a waking nightmare with the wind nearly strong enough to lean on as it tore past with its unearthly shriek. Long before I should have reached the river, my way was barred by its flooding waters coming to meet me. This was far worse than the nullah; you could see the water creeping up to the thunderous roar coming from behind the line of trees that marked the river bank in the rain-obscured distance.

I was just starting to move on to where the river meets the nullah, three-quarters of a mile from where I was standing, when I caught a sudden flurry of movement across the water in front of me. I switched on the torch quickly. Through the silvery rods of the rain smashing through the beam I saw a pack of wild dogs scampering towards me. They came on and then jumped to the dry land. They were within a few yards and all round me, whimpering and uttering sharp little cries of alarm; for all the notice they took of me I might not have been there.

As I walked on I kept the light sweeping across the waters. After a few minutes I switched it off; the lightning was better, the almost continuous flashes lit the scene around me like daylight.

Not far on from where I had left the wild dogs I saw a small herd of spotted deer, four hinds and a stag, splashing out from a wood which in normal times is a hundred yards from the river; now it was an island of trees. They must have seen me as clearly as I could see them, but they splashed on, away from the greater danger of the rising water. When they had passed only a little way behind me, I went on. There was still no sign of the storm abating and the wind was driving the pelting rain as strongly as ever; the thunder was still crashing with scarcely a break. After another fifty yards I stopped again.

This time there was no going on. The waters now were not only on my left but on my right as well, and just in front of me they met. The river and the nullah were now a single sheet of water. For a few moments I just stood still staring at the floods. The danger to the house now was very real. From where I was it was only a quarter of a mile away and the waters were creeping towards it from two sides.

I turned quickly and started back. Almost at once I found myself in another nightmare of a different kind. Across my path there was suddenly a great sounder of pig standing motionless. To get past them I had to skirt to one side in spite of a great throat-tearing shout to move them. Then animals were everywhere. In the flashes from the skies I could see them all around me, some standing still while others moved slowly as though in a dream. I did not know then that we were all on an island only some ten acres in extent which was rapidly growing smaller.

When I got back to the house, Babs had some coffee waiting on the stove. When I had gulped it down I went out again to see the cattle. They had been put in an old and long disused 'country' shed. The roof was of rough thatch, the sides built of light stakes lashed together with strips of bamboo; the only reason why this was still standing was probably because the wind had no 'push' against its openwork sides.

The cattle were very restless. Now that they were locked up again the collapse of the roof in their old shed was obviously still a vivid memory. They were milling around wildly, barging into one another and crashing against the flimsy sides. If this shed collapsed it would not be the wind but the cattle which pulled it down. But there was nowhere else to put them, the three other sheds were some distance from the house and were already under water when I passed them on my way back.

Half an hour later I went out again. The swollen nullah was now within a hundred yards of the house and the river had swept across the base of the triangle to join it. The area of our island had now shrunk to about three acres—and there was still no sign of the rain stopping.

On my way back to the house I had another look at the cattle. They were still very restless but still safe inside. That hardly seemed to matter now. I was going to give the rain another hour and if it had not stopped then I should let them out to take their chance in the floods.

Some twenty minutes later, as we were sitting in a room at the back of the house, it seemed to me that the rain had suddenly slackened. I got up and went out towards the front veranda. When I reached the door leading to it I stopped and looked out. There was no light outside and none in the room behind me. Beyond the veranda the lightning was vivid, the scene beneath it as light as day. The rain *was* stopping. Then, as I stared out at it, a slight movement from the left turned my eyes.

A tiger was standing at the end of the veranda. It had been the merest flash of a picture but clear beyond mistake. The lightning flashed again and it was still there.

A moment later I was in the back room grabbing for the rifle. The magazine was full and a torch mounted on the barrel for I had only recently put it down. Back again at the veranda door I peered round. The tiger was still there and I snapped on the light. But he didn't wait a second. As the light hit him he sprang...out of it and away into the night. The bullet I sent after him was wide and smacked into a concrete trough in the garden.

It was the last straw for the cattle. In his flight, the tiger streaked past their shed. That was all they needed: a strong whiff of tiger slammed into their nostrils by the wind. They were stampeding wildly before the echoes of the shot died away. There was a violent crash and the shed was match-wood. Then the cattle were out and thundering away, snorting with terror.

As the sounds of their flight faded I suddenly realized that the rain had stopped. All at once the main sound of the night was the mighty roar of the river. A good sound now. One that told that the dangers of the floods were over. The river falls just as fast as it rises and that loud booming proclaimed that the waters were receding and racing away to the sea.

What the extent of the damage was I could not even guess, but that was something to worry about in the morning. In the meantime, we had to round up the cattle again and somehow bed them down for the rest of the night. {1960}

FIGHTING FOR THE KILL | PATRICK HANLEY

I once saw this happen when I was watching a tiger's kill on which a leopard was feeding. The leopard, loath to leave the carcase, roared and snarled at the tiger in fury, when it broke cover and approached it, in an attempt to drive the tiger away. While a tiger never seeks a quarrel in the jungle, except with another tiger during mating time, he is still the King of the jungle, and no leopard could get away with this impertinence.

As the leopard stood there snarling and roaring, the tiger sprang at it. For a few moments the roars and snarls of the two animals resounded in the jungle, but it was a short battle, for within a few moments the tiger had tumbled the leopard over and was astride its back, biting deeply into its neck behind the head, severing the spine, and killing it. Then I saw it do a thing which I have never seen a tiger do before or since. After walking around the carcase of the leopard, sniffing it, the tiger threw itself down beside it and started eating it. For nearly an hour he gorged on the flesh of that leopard, until he had consumed the whole carcase with the exception of the head and legs. Then, getting up, he sniffed at the carcase of the sambhar, his original kill, on which he had returned to feed, and walked off into the jungle. {1961}

BATTLES BETWEEN COURTING TIGERS | PATRICK HANLEY

W hen the tigress called beside me, she was answered almost immediately by a tiger a short distance from where I was standing, and within a few moments two more tigers answered her. Since the tigress was so near to me, and it was only the wind factor which had prevented her getting my scent, I thought it would be wise to climb up a tree which I had spotted as a suitable look-out, growing a few yards from where I stood and, having safely accomplished this, I sat hidden by leafy branches, hoping that the tigress would come out into the open and hold her court there in the glade so that I could get photographs of her when she and the tiger she was calling met. I was fortunate that day. Within a few moments she walked out into the glade, and stood within forty feet of the tree on which I was hiding, calling incessantly to the tigers which were answering her. Their answering calls had agitated her, and she kept repeating her calls now at almost minute intervals.

Three tigers were answering her now, all coming closer every moment, and I looked forward to the time when they arrived in anticipation of seeing a stirring jungle drama, filled with jealousy, hatred and savagery, being played before me in that forest glade. Presently I saw the first tiger, a magnificent beast, at least ten feet long over curves, walking out from the jungle into the forest glade on my right, about twenty yards from me. He stopped a moment to gaze at the tigress, which, as soon as she saw him, put her ears back and dropped into a prone position on the grass, flicking her tail from side to side, showing her excitement. The tiger gave a peculiar call a deep-seated, hollow "grr-aounch", and advanced slowly towards her.

But he did not get far. Quite suddenly, from a thicket near him, I saw a flash of black and red flying through the air as a huge tiger, nearly as large as he was, almost landed on top of him. The first tiger sprang nimbly aside to avoid his attacker, and, snarling and growling with rage, he crouched low to face his adversary, which quickly sprang around getting ready for the fray. Both animals were now crouching low, getting the measure of each other, the evidence of their fury showing by the eyes narrowed to slits, the ears turned back flat on their heads, their tails lashing furiously from side to side as they faced each other. In a moment they came to grips, and the jungle resounded with the noise of their growls and roars as they fought.

It was a battle of giants, terrific in fury and intensity, and while it continued the cause of it all, the sleek young tigress sat placidly watching the fight, cleaning her fur with her tongue, while she gazed serenely

unconcerned at the contestants struggling for her favour, quite at her ease, while the rest of the jungle animals in the vicinity trembled with terror at the noise of the battle. It was inevitable that the tigress would accept the victor as her lord and her mate, a story as old as the jungle itself.

I was so busily engaged watching the fight and taking photographs of it, that I had failed to notice that tiger No. 3 had arrived on the scene, until I saw the tigress get up and walk away into the shade of a tree growing about ten yards from where she had been reclining. Presently she raised herself on her haunches, and began staring at a thicket at the edge of the jungle opposite her, her tail flicking from side to side in an agitated manner. I followed her gaze with my binoculars, and quickly saw the cause of her agitation. Tiger No. 3 was sitting beneath a low jungle shrub which hid him from view, watching the tigress and the two tigers fighting. How long he had been there I could not tell, but he made no effort to come out of his hiding place, or to take part in the fight.

The situation was now more intriguing than ever, and I sat on my tree fascinated, watching the little jungle drama being played out before me, wondering how it would end, now, with the advent of the third tiger into the picture.

The fight went on probably for another five minutes, and both tigers were bleeding freely from the wounds they had inflicted upon each other, for they were evenly matched, and the contest was fierce and deadly. They wrestled savagely standing on their hind legs, biting, clawing, roaring angrily, snarling at each other while they fought. Presently they fell to the ground, locked together in a deadly embrace, and tumbled about, giving and taking cruel punishment, flinging up great divots of turf and grass into the air as they tore up the ground in the intensity of the struggle. It was terrific. Suddenly, one of the tigers tore the neck of the other open with its claws, giving its opponent a vicious wound which compelled it to break off the fight and limp away hurriedly towards the jungle, followed by the victor roaring at it savagely as he drove his opponent off. Soon, however, he returned, and I could see that he also was limping badly, and had great weals across the ribs where he had been torn by the claws of his opponent, together with many severe scratches on his head from which he was bleeding. Presently he threw himself on to the grass and rolled on it, wiping away the blood and torn hairs from his face and body. Then, getting up, he walked towards the tigress to claim her for his mate.

When she saw him approaching, the tigress rose from her prone position and, glancing towards the thicket in which the third tiger was hiding, she advanced about five paces and stood awaiting the victor of the fight. Presently she went down on her haunches, her tail flicking swiftly from side to side. I have often wondered since, whether that tigress knew that the tiger, which had fought so fiercely for her favour, would be denied it. It was the nature of a tigress to accept the victor without question as her mate, but in this case the situation was complicated by the entry of the third tiger into the contest, and the victor of the battle was too severely wounded to fight for her favour again, against a fresh contender. And he would certainly have to fight if he wished to keep her as a mate. That was the inevitable law of the jungle, of which the tiger is king. It was a cruel situation, and I felt sorry for the wounded beast.

As he came within five paces of the tigress the third tiger sprang. The wounded tiger bared his teeth and attacked the usurper immediately, but he was incapable of fighting for long, and in a little while he was chased away by the third tiger, which was fresh and unwounded, and stronger than the wounded beast. I saw him limping away into the jungle as quickly as he could, and for a little while he was hidden from view. Then I saw him again at the edge of the forest glade, about two hundred yards away, standing sadly [and] watching his enemy winning a mate which should have been his. Life in the jungle is filled with disappointments such as this, for it is one of its inevitable laws that only the strongest can win a mate or a meal.

After driving the wounded tiger off, the third tiger came back to the tigress, and as he approached her she threw herself on to the grass and rolled on it on her back. Then she became kittenish, and started playfully clawing her newly found mate as he came up to her and licked her on the neck. They played there happily for a while, then suddenly she sprang up and bounded away swiftly into the jungle, and he followed, racing after her at terrific speed. I last saw them tearing along together, bounding over huge tussocks of pampas grass, disappearing deeper into the jungle until they were lost to view. The Queen had found her mate! {1961}

VALMIK THAPAR

PROTECTING THE YOUNG | OLIVE SMYTHIES

In the rains Tanakpur is deserted. The climate is extremely unhealthy, so bad that the entire population leaves; the hill people go back to the hills, and the forest contractors go to their homes in the plains. The flooded river cuts off all communications with Nepal.

Late one evening, when we were staying in the Forest bungalow, we were watching three men fishing with nets in the waters of the Sarda. Suddenly two tigers and a half-grown cub emerged from one of the grassy islands close by. We heard the men shout, whereupon the tigers moved off across the dry bare bed of the river towards the forest on the right bank, a quarter of a mile away.

Simultaneously we heard from this forest the trumpeting of a wild elephant, and soon after the terrifying roar of a charging tiger. We got our field-glasses, and were astonished to see a big male tusker elephant come out on to the bare river bed, being furiously attacked by two tigers.

Spellbound we watched this titanic battle, which raged up and down the river bed in full view of the bungalow. Presently it grew too dark for using field-glasses, but the moon rose, and we could still watch the fight. The noise was appalling. The elephant trumpeted and bellowed, the tigers roared hideously. About 11 p.m. the noise died down and the tigers disappeared.

Next morning we found the elephant lying dead at the foot of the bank just below the bungalow. There was no sign of the tigers. We examined the marks on the elephant. The trunk was quite untouched, but both eyes had been clawed out, and there were deep scratches round the eyes. There were terrible bites and scratches on the top of the head and neck, back and rump, and the throat had been torn open—evidently the *coup de grâce.*

We wondered what could have provoked the tigers to attack the elephant. It is inconceivable that they made a senseless and unprovoked attack on a full-grown tusker, and equally inconceivable that the elephant started the fight. It is probable that the tiger cub was the cause of the trouble.

He may have blundered into the elephant and received a kick which made him yelp. The tigress's maternal fury would have been aroused, and she would have come to the help of her cub; the tiger would have joined in the affray.

It was interesting to note how the wounds on the tusker indicated the tactics of the two tigers. It was evident that no frontal attack had been attempted, or the trunk of the elephant would have been mauled.

We surmised that one tiger had threatened in front, enabling the other tiger to leap on the elephant's back and start biting and scratching. At some stage of the battle one of the tigers must have managed to crawl on to the top of the head and scratch out the eyes, perhaps deliberately, for it seems a natural instinct of the cat tribe to go for the eyes.

The poor elephant, blinded, had staggered on, tortured with the fiendish laceration of his back, stumbling along in agony over the boulders of the river bed falling at last over some obstruction, and exposing his throat to a fiendish mauling by the other tiger, finally dying from loss of blood, or severance of his windpipe. The tigers had taken a terrible revenge for any possible injury to their cub. The tusks were small and looked old.

Evelyn had a consultation with the Ranger as to what should be done with the carcase. It was not possible to dig a pit deep enough to bury it in the river bed, which was full of boulders. The Ranger employed a gang of coolies to collect boulders, and this being accomplished, they built them up in a huge cairn round and over the carcase. This, however, proved to be a failure. An appalling stench came through, and jackals and stray dogs managed to creep between the stones, and pull out pieces of flesh.

Evelyn decided that the only thing to do was to try and burn the whole thing. The Ranger poured about 100 gallons of kerosene oil over the body, and made a huge bonfire of the dry driftwood from the river bed. He then set fire to the funeral pyre, which burned for several days, by the end of which time only the bones and the skull of the tusker remained. {1961}

VALMIK THAPAR

THE ANANTAPURA TIGER | M. KRISHNAN

Anantapura was a small forest village in a valley at one end of Ranthambhor. Some of the villages inside it were moved out when Ranthambhor was set up as a tiger reserve, the villagers accepting alternative sites well outside the reserve, and offered amenities for giving up their old holdings; Anantapura was such a village. Now only the departmental outpost and a rest-house remain, an imaginatively built rest-house in the old, rural style, washed terra-cotta with red earth, with the walls of its hall zestfully decorated with contour-frescoes in white *chunam* by the departing village women, with figures of camels and deer and peacocks and village belles, and among them a tiger that would have delighted Picasso, so elemental and free from petty concern for realism in its morphology, the Anantapura tiger, in short...

I was in this rest-house late in April. The days were hot and the nights cool, even chill after midnight. There is no electricity at Anantapura and our stock of kerosene being low, we did not keep the hurricane lanterns burning long. By 7 p.m. it would be quite dark and I would be busy writing up the day's field notes, by 8 p.m. I would have had my dinner and a little later, with nothing to do, retire to my cot in the open, just outside the verandah. For a while I would lie awake listening for animal sounds, but there were hardly any. Then, tired with the day's work and replete with dinner, I would fall asleep to be up well before four o'clock in the morning.

An hour before dawn, announced by the loud mewling calls of peacocks and the chirps of little birds, I could hear a tiger from the base of a nullah only half-a-kilometre from the rest-house. This nullah ran straight up the hillside and, crossing the crest, descended down the other side—the motor road took a circuitous 9 kms. to reach the same spot on the crest where the nullah crossed it, and then went beyond that point to another rest-house.

What puzzled me about this pre-dawn tiger was that interspersed with the usual tigrine moans, I heard a repeated resonant, musical sound, like the vibrant twang of steel wire stretched taut across a resonator and plucked sharply. After listening to it for several nights, I was sure that this sound, too, was made by the tiger—towards daybreak the tiger evidently went uphill along the nullah, for his moans and also the musical resonant twangs would diminish in audibility, and then cease altogether. I have never heard, or heard of, a tiger coming out with this curious sound, nor read of it in any book.

One day, as soon as there was light enough to see by, I went to the nullah and scouted around soon after the tiger had ceased calling. On the fine dust outside the mouth of the nullah there were clear footprints of an adult male tiger, and these went up the nullah as well, but I could make no sense out of the criss-crossed trails of pugs. Next morning, I took a local with me to the spot, a man better at reading animal spoors than I, and after much scrutiny and a stiff climb up the nullah we were none the wiser. However, the pugs, old and new, clearly showed that the tiger used the nullah both for going uphill and for returning to the purlieus of Anantapura.

It took me days to realise that as the nullah led straight up to the hilltop road, I should look for pugs in and around the road. When I did so, I could find few footprints on the sandy surface of the road: though our valley was secluded, the hilltop was very windy and footprints had only a brief life on that windswept road. Further, the nullah branched into three arterial nullahs before reaching the road, and all of them were stony and covered with much dead leaf and grass and shrubs, but I did find a few clear pugs in them.

I had only one more day in reserve, and decided to wait in the evening at a point on the hilltop road where it took a bend, in the hope of getting a look at the musical tiger. We got to this point on the road later than planned, and rounding the bend found the tiger right in front of us in the middle of the road and proceeding in the same direction as we were, a tall, rangy, dark, full-grown tiger.

He did not turn to look at us, but accelerated to a shambling trot and then leaped lightly down to a patch of dry, tall grass stems beneath the road, to our right. By the time the jeep could be stopped on the slight decline of the road, we were right alongside the tiger—he stood broadside on to us just below the road, turning his head to look steadily at us, but though he was so close, hundreds of reed-like tall grass culms were between us, obscuring him. I signed to the driver to reverse and take the jeep back, and he did so with the minimum of noise and fuss and stopped beyond the bend.

The light was failing fast and anyway the tiger, hidden by the bend, was out of sight but I was not depending on sight. For about two minutes, there was utter silence, and then we could hear the crunch-crunch of dry grass stems being trodden upon as the tiger left the patch of tall grass. We went forward and now he was in plain view, some 50 metres away from us, on the open slope of the hill, rim-lit by the sinking sun. A silhouette picture was still possible and would have an appeal of its own, but still the grass stems right in front barred it. The driver pointed to where, a little ahead, the hillside seemed level with the road and suggested we should turn in there for an unobstructed view; gently he eased the jeep forward and turned to the right—and with a sickening crash we were jerked right out of our seats as the front wheels sank through the treacherous cover of grass into a deep ditch. I was watching the tiger all the time, and as we crashed into the ditch, he gave a convulsive leap forward, and then slid down the hill into bush cover and disappeared.

It would be dark quite soon and the jeep, jammed hard in the ditch, could not possibly be pulled out by the three of us, and we were far from home. However, in the opposite direction, there was a rest-house only 4 kms. away and in it the officer in charge of the reserve and his jeep. We sent our local guide there to summon help, and the driver and I sat on as best as we would in the uncomfortably slanted jeep.

With darkness, a cold wind sprang up to add to our discomfort. The alarm calls of chital and sambar announced the progress of the tiger down the hill, but ceased after some time. We sat on, hugging our knees with our hands, for there was nothing else we could do.

After about half-an-hour, a sambar belled suddenly: the repeated explosive *dhanks* seemed to come from quite near. Apparently the tiger was coming up the hill. Then we could hear him, first a long-drawn, sighing moan and then the musical twang so peculiarly his own announcement. We could not see him, but no doubt he could see us perfectly with his vastly superior night vision. We heard the vibrant twang again, but this time from behind us and beyond the road, and again from to the right of us, and then from in front. He was circling us.

"He is circling us!" whispered the driver to me. He seemed positively shaken but oddly enough, for fear is infectious, it never occurred to me that we could be in danger. Tigers have their share of curiosity, and apparently our continued immobile presence there intrigued him. Anyway, I tried to reassure my companion, and then listened intently. I could not tell how far away the tiger was, but could hear the occasional rustle of dry grass as he passed over it, so that he seemed near enough. Systematically he circled us for what seemed an age and was certainly at least ten minutes, no longer moaning but punctuating his circuit of the jeep with his plucked-string call from time to time.

Then, all at once, there was silence. My companion touched my arm and mumbled a question. Risking my reputation as a naturalist, I told him what I felt was the explanation of that sudden silence. "The tiger has gone away," I told him, "The rescue jeep is coming!" Sure enough, a minute later we could hear it coming up, but the exquisite hearing of the tiger had warned him of its approach much earlier. {1985}

A BATTLE ROYAL | KENNETH ANDERSON

'Nothing happened till about eleven o'clock, when a tiger started roaring on the other side of the river. Judging from the sound, he was within a couple of hundred yards of where I was sitting.

'Almost immediately, an elephant began to trumpet—you know, that high-pitched note of anger and fear they make when they can't decide just what to do. And every time the tiger roared, the elephant would scream in return.

'It was amusing and exciting, too, for although the tiger did not appear to be coming any nearer, there was no doubt that the elephant was. The tiger continued to roar and the tusker to scream as he came closer and

VALMIK THAPAR

closer, and very soon after that, with a mighty crashing and swishing of bamboos behind me, Jumbo announced his arrival on the scene.

'Things began to happen after that! Why this elephant was so upset at the tiger's roars I cannot imagine, but there was no doubt he was either scared stiff of Stripes or in a right royal rage—perhaps a mixture of both...

'I thought of shooting the elephant, but it would have led to a hell of a lot of trouble with the forestry people, as he was not a proscribed rogue at that time. I would have lost my licence, with a heavy fine into the bargain.

'The next moment the problem was taken out of my hands and transferred to the elephant in a most unexpected way. For who should step out of the undergrowth... but the tiger himself...

'The tiger was the first really to lose his temper. With a coughing roar he charged the elephant, but as he reached to within a few feet and was about to spring upon its head or back, the elephant reared on to his hind legs, as we see them do in circuses, and then descended to earth again in an attempt to crush the tiger beneath his forefeet or catch him with his trunk.

'But Stripes was too quick! He jumped aside nimbly, stood on his hind legs in turn, and flailed the elephant's trunk with a rapid right and left with the outstretched talons of his front paws.

'Jumbo squealed, curled in his trunk out of harm's way, and madly charged the tiger in turn, trying to impale him with his single tusk.

'But it was a vain hope. Once again the tiger side-stepped, and this time leaped over that threatening tusk directly on to the elephant's forehead, where he clung tightly, holding on grimly with his teeth and the talons of his forepaws in the thick hide of the elephant's neck, while the claws of his hind legs raked the upper sides of the unfortunate beast's trunk.

'The fight was lost and over then, but for the fact that, in his desperate attempt to get rid of the intruder tearing at his neck and trunk, the elephant now did the correct thing. Bending down, he practically stood upon his head, bringing the enormous weight of his body to bear upon the tiger.

'In a last-minute endeavour to escape that terrible pressure, the tiger let go, now concentrating all his efforts in trying to wriggle out from underneath. He succeeded to a degree and was half-free, when one of the elephant's groping forefeet came down upon him.

'Feeling his victim at last beneath his foot, the infuriated elephant took full advantage of the situation. He jerked his head free from the loosened grip of the tiger, at the same time putting his remaining front foot down upon the other end of the tiger's body. He now had his victim helplessly squashed beneath him.

'The tiger's roars had changed to horrible, gurgling gasps when that terrible trunk uncurled itself [and] got underneath the body of the tiger between the two ends that were pinioned to the earth beneath those mighty feet, and heaved upwards with a sudden tremendous tug.

'The next moment I saw a sickening sight. So great was the rage and strength of that elephant that he tore the tiger's body into three pieces, that portion held in the folds of his trunk parting from the other two ends under his feet, and coming away in a red, gory mass.

'Still trumpeting…and with blood pouring down the sides of his own head and neck, the monster thrashed the middle section of tiger furiously against the ground while not attempting to remove either of his forefeet from the remaining two sections…' {1976}

THE FIRST SCIENTIFIC STUDY OF THE TIGER

GEORGE B. SCHALLER

'A solitary gaur bull snuffles nearby at 2050 hours, but he senses the tigers and bolts. The female returns to the carcass with her cubs at 2130 hours, and one or more feed until 2320 hours. All rest for half an hour, and then the tigress eats alone for 45 more minutes. After another silent spell, the animals feed off and on from 0230 to 0415 hours. The female growls harshly several times, and there is much breaking wind.

'A tiger roars once in the distance at 0330 hours. At 0430 hours the tigress roars twice and is answered by a roar and 15 pooks. Between 0430 and 0620, the tigers rest by the kill. The female then rises, first attempts to drag the carcass away, and finally feeds with the cubs. Several times she emits rolling growls, twice culminating in a harsh "aaarrr" as she jerks her head with exposed canines at a cub beside her. She walks 50 feet from the kill at 0635 hours and sniffs the ground there. One cub rubs its body from shoulder to rump against her foreleg. Back at the kill, she gives an explosive snarly "tcho" at a cub which crowds her. All feeding stops at 0655 hours, and the animals rest beside the kill until 0710 hours, when the cubs go in single file 150 feet up the ravine. They lie down there at 0735 hours and are joined by their mother at 0755 hours.

'The male tiger appears suddenly along the bank of the ravine. He passes the remains of the gaur and approaches the tigress and cubs. They rise and watch him. The female steps toward him, and they meet behind a clump of bamboo, only their hindquarters visible to me. They face each other for 3 minutes before the male ambles off without looking back. She follows him 50 feet, squirts scent once and then returns to her cubs.

'The female goes to the kill at 0835 hours and gnaws on a gaur leg. The cubs cluster around her, one climbing over her back. After a brief snack, she rises abruptly and lies down in the shade 30 feet away, where she is joined by the cubs. At 0850 hours she charges 20 feet at several crows which sit in the branches above the carcass. The young move out of sight at 0900 hours, but the tigress is restless, finally settling down at 1030 hours. At 1655 she is still reclining, her hindquarters in a pool. Every so often she swishes her tail up, showering herself with water. She rises at 1712 hours and looks at the gaur bones and the few scraps of skin; she glances to the right, then to the left, checks a few bones 50 feet away, and apparently having decided that nothing edible is left, walks steadily into the forest, leaving her cubs behind.'

'A prolonged period of play among the cubs, as described above, was seen on only one other occasion, in the evening of May 31:

'The tigress rests with her 4 cubs in a shallow ravine near the remains of a chital buck at 1835 hours. The cubs are 110 feet from her, and when she approaches them, all bound up and crowd around her. One places its forepaws on her neck, but she bares her teeth, shakes her head, and emits several deep growls. She lies down, first on her side and then on her back with all 4 feet in the air. A cub lies by her, a second cub chews on the ear of the first one, and a third cub rolls onto its side and claws at the grass; the fourth cub, a male, worms itself close to the female, reaches out with one paw, and strokes her head; he then holds her head between both paws and licks it. One cub rises and rubs the top of its head against the tigress' chin. Another young [one] comes up, flops on its side, and strokes the head of the female with a forepaw. When she turns on her side, a cub drapes itself over her neck. She purrs with open mouth. Two cubs wrestle, one mock-biting the other's head. The female rests once more on her back, now with a cub lying across her face gnawing on an ear.

'It is dusky at 1915 hours. Two cubs lie near the tigress. One steps over her body. When another one follows, she cuffs it lightly with a downward swing of her paw. A third cub crouches in the grass and suddenly rushes at another cub 15 feet away; they wrestle. Two cubs face each other, rear up on their hindlegs, and swat with their paws; then 3 of them wrestle vigorously. One bumps into the tigress, receiving several light cuffs in return.' {1967}

VALMIK THAPAR

THE TIGER AND THE HYENA | R. D. MACKAY

This gentleman reported that a village shikari had mentioned that he had seen a hyena following a tiger, and that, from the general appearance and gait of the tiger, all was not well with him. He thought nothing of the story as hyenas, not infrequently, do this at a respectable distance. It 'pays off' because they often get a bite from what the tiger leaves. He thought also that the tiger may have been maimed but banished any suggestion of it being a man-eater, since it had not come to notice as one. Some days later, the village shikari came to report that a hyena had killed a large size cow-calf and asked if the Sahib would come and shoot the hyena as it would probably repeat the killing if it were allowed to go scot-free... The Sahib said that he would oblige and accompanied the shikari to the kill. A jackal slunk away from the kill on their arrival. Not very much of the kill had been eaten, so they decided there and then to sit concealed on the ground.

They got into a bush and, for an hour, nothing happened but then to their astonishment they saw a Tiger tottering towards them, the hyena following behind and, from the short rushes he was making every now and then and on either side of the tiger, it appeared that the hyena was giving him direction. It finally edged the tiger on to the kill, and then sat down at a distance from it. The gentleman recognized that the tiger was blind. He shot the tiger because it seemed to him to be the most humane thing to do. He couldn't say if the tiger had gone blind from natural causes; but his personal opinion was that someone had blinded it with small shot. {1967}

The tigress walked slowly towards me, all the time keeping close to the bank and hugging its shadow. The cubs were walking by her side, almost between her legs. Only one of them, the restless one, would sometimes stray into the open, tarry behind, and then run to catch up with the others. They reached a small cut in the bank, a sort of opening into the stream that marked the end of a narrow gametrack running back into the grass and beyond into the forest. The tigress stood near it and so did the cubs. I could see all of them very clearly from my hideout as they were only twenty yards away and the place that straddled across a narrow sandbank had a thinner and little less dark evil of shadows enveloping it.

The tigress was big for her sex, approximately a nine-footer, and temptingly close, almost at a point-blank range. I picked up my rifle and drew a bead on to the base of her neck as she stood facing me, a little quartering to the left, looking aside towards the jungle. A perfect target, I could not have asked for a better one, and a little flick of my finger's tip on the trigger would have stopped her. But I had no intention of killing her. She had the sanctity of motherhood and the privilege of a creative artist. I had no heart to destroy her and was not enough of a scoundrel to expose the helpless little ones to a slow death by starvation or even worse, death in the jaws of hyenas and jackals. I dismounted my rifle from my shoulder and replaced it on its rest.

The tigress sat down on the sandbank, stretching her fore-paws full in front of her and touching the ground with her belly. The cubs started playing around her, almost like kittens, jumping on one another and also on the back and neck of their mother. Sometimes they would stalk one another, sometimes they would rub themselves against the body of their mother and sometimes they would lick her face and be licked by her in return.

It was a beautiful sight, a most enchanting picture done in the tradition of classical art and washed in the colours of the abstract school. I sat spellbound with fascination, and lost myself in watching them with immense pleasure. All the three cubs were of the size of a small bull terrier. One of them had a heavier body and a bigger head than the other two. Perhaps it was the male cub. And it was this one that was full of little pranks and the most amusing tricks. They must have been about one year old, or perhaps a little more, and had reached the stage when after a period of vigorous training and instruction they started helping the mother in securing the prey, first by driving it towards her, and then pulling it down under her watchful eyes. {1967}

AN ERA OF CONSERVATION

By the 1970s, Project Tiger was in full swing and the pen and the camera had replaced the gun. However, it was still extraordinarily difficult to observe wild tigers as they continued to fear man as they associated him with death. But, as the years rolled by, encounters became more common and the narratives changed once again. I think the best years for observing wild tigers were the 1980s since, by then, a new generation of cubs had grown up who were not used to being wary around humans. Science was also making its first inroads into the natural world. Unfortunately, by the time the twentieth century ended, tigers were once again caught up in a crisis that stemmed from both poaching and poor governance and that had led to a serious decline in their numbers.

~

The warm sand of this bank was a different world from my bower in the coarse grass. I sank down, and a wonderful sense came over me. This was now my home too. Why should I not indulge myself in a bit of sunbasking as was the right of stork and lapwing, python and crocodile? Surveying the river from this new view I found emerging from the muddle of driftwood a second Prehistory. [...] Now a great bird flew straight at me, head swung to the side he looked upon me with an awful eye.

But the living distractions were so many. Among them a pair of crows, raucous in the woods behind the sand apron. I considered these protests when new circumstances put them from mind.

If I could have asked the blessing of this place by some godly messengers, I should have asked (since this was India) for such a flight of great casqued hornbills as now broke from cover at the far downstream bend of the river. Toward me they came, a ragged formation of black wings and improbably white heads, immense bills compounded by the upperdeck casque surmounting all. They paused in a distant tree and then in ones and twos beat their way through the forest and upriver, all the while calling up a clamour in affirmation of their own wondrous reality.

Nearly behind me now was this day marked delicately with portents. Against the pressure of time I held myself in check—a few ruckuses in the woods did not necessarily mean... Our own rooster at home could call up a storm at any passing pussy cat. Yet there was this elation that would not beat down.

The casqued hornbills, in themselves such a charge, coming downriver straight on like a flight of black angels—at once exciting, even a little sinister, they simply exploded my self-discipline. I fought a last round with my inherent pessimism, a screen for an optimism that bruises so painfully. For self-protection I stuff pessimism back in mind to be called for if needed.

Something was coming.

Whereas I usually moved my glance in a manner to cover all possibilities, I now fixed my entire attention upon an arch of tree, a bent trunk without foliage at the far edge of the sand apron. With a forest wall and hundreds of feet of riverbank to choose from, I homed in upon the most aesthetically perfect point of entry to the river world, not for reason of art but because every fiber of my being was drawn magnetically to that place.

I adjusted [the] binoculars.

I squirmed more deeply into the sand below the summit of my small dune.

I adjusted the camera, increasing exposure as the day dimmed. Focus. Focus. Contain the uncontainable elation. It is an afternoon scene like the others, yet nothing can convince me of this. It is quiet, peaceful, yet my interior responds as if an express train is bearing down upon me. Where? When? And then where-when becomes there! Now!

With concentration, sand-grain intense, naturally I could not record normally. Suddenly there were two feet, two fore-legs, very white with tawny and black lines incising the white in delicate striping from the outer edge of the legs, fading to leave the leg mainly white. I think this was through the camera lens, but perhaps it was simply naked eye. How I was seeing did not register. Why did I not see the entire animal? He was certainly a hundred feet away. Perhaps it was protective hysteria that guarded me, gave me only this bit until I could handle the simple fact that a tiger was standing where I had wanted it to be, willed it to be, expected it to be, beneath the arch of branches. "Life doesn't happen this way," ran a little river of thought deep behind the frozen log-jam of my external mind.

The tiger stood with the self-possession of an actor making a stage entrance in a human theatre. He looked straight before him, apparently directly at me, his glance traversing the sand apron, the river. Motionless I in my motionless dune must have been as a shadow in a vista he knew well. Now he accepted that nothing was amiss. Because I was there first, all was well.

He lay down where the sand was strewn with the last of winter's tawny leaves. His pink tongue protruded an inch or two in rosy wellbeing as he cooled himself. This pink-tongued presence laid the lie to the whole company of men, men who were experts, lifelong residents in the world they shared with tigers. Perhaps their skepticism had infected me during the moment of this very morning when I had questioned the worth of coming on this part-spent day.

While I concentrated on absolute immobility before the eyes of the tiger, my senses were returning rather like scattered birds to a roost. One thing to be alone on a lovely river, I thought—an incredibly elemental experience to be alone on a lovely river in the presence of a tiger. I was surprised that it wasn't fear I felt, only rending excitement.

The camera was on my chest, before my lower face. For all the fiddling I had done it did not seem in focus. I made fingers work. Rana Jung had warned, "If you *do* see tiger"—and how unlikely his tone had made *that* possibility—"move with great slowness. Your first shot must work, for you won't have a chance for a second." How much easier to say than to act upon. But they settled, those words.

I was myself again. Yes it was most certain that he was looking at me, the shadow in the dune. Staring and intently. I pressed the shutter release which sounded like a cannon and he continued to stare, the very pink tongue continuing to cool him. I wrenched a new film forward with a hideous grinding sound. Tiger still there, staring. I performed this sequence three times; now that my eyes were focusing better I could see a small clutter of leafless twigs creating a tracery before the tiger's face. But now he turned to look toward the river. This movement brought him free of the twigs. I shot two more pictures and since he seemed oblivious to camera noise, apparently deadened by its passage across the water, I wondered if I might risk trading [the] camera for binoculars.

With infinite slowness I accomplished this. Using the human powers closest to the flowing action of [a] python, I made [an] effort to reposition myself to the right.

Suddenly above and behind my head came a snort of alarm; something had come to the top of the dune. Something. A deer I should think had been coming to water and had seen me or the tiger or both of us. I could not resist a slow partial turn of my head before realizing how futile such a gesture was, for whatever had been there was now certainly fled.

Eventually the tiger stretched full length. He was at peace and it produced a kind of peace in me as well. How could I have imagined so much? Five, six, seven minutes in the presence of such a one as this.

But I couldn't stop being human when the test came. In the human way I began to look beyond what had been granted me. Of course the light was going fast. Self-mastered, I would have let it go.

I hardly know what I did—crawled some, crouch-walked some, conspicuous in the soft sand, somehow negotiating the perhaps fifty feet that brought me to the grass patch that until today had been my hide. All this in hope of bringing myself in view of the tiger's side, into full view before the sun left him.

Folly substituted for peace—how typically human. The tiger was of course by now fully aware of me and drawn into a tense crouch. He stared at me in smouldering readiness, ears flattened back.

I had to refocus as best I could, attempt to hold a three-hundred-millimetre lens unsupported at a sixtieth of a second. Lunacy. Made shots and faded from view behind the grass bank, hoping he would forget about me. All this is embarrassing to admit. I can only offer lamely that being alone in the presence of tiger is extraordinarily unsettling.

When I made my way behind the screen of grass the traverse to the other end was made difficult by two-foot-deep potholes monsoon-dug around each grass clump. By the time I reached the end nearer to the tiger and the bridge tree, he had vanished. {1993}

THE IMPACT OF A TIGER'S ATTACK

FIONA AND MEL SUNQUIST

Number One exploded out of the grass with a shattering roar. She made one leap up the tree and in a split second was on top of Kirti. He saw her coming and tried to ward her off with the antenna, but she flung it aside without noticing. She sank her claws into his thigh and buttocks and bit deeply into his leg. The force of her acceleration ripped Kirti off the branch and they both tumbled to the ground fifteen feet below.

VALMIK THAPAR

No one could believe what was happening. Kirti's wife Pat repeated "Oh, my God" over and over again, her voice rising in hysteria, but everyone else was dumb with shock. Before anyone could move the tigress charged again, her roars blasting through the silence. The elephants spun on their heels and bolted in blind panic ahead of the enraged tigress. Nothing could stop them. Equipment flew everywhere in a wild confusion of screaming and trumpeting. People clung to ropes or whatever they could find, trying not to be swept off the elephants in the headlong dash through the bushes.

Seconds later Mel's elephant slammed to its knees; it had fallen into one of the hidden ditches. People pitched forward, then back as the elephant rose and lunged ahead, only to drop into another ditch a few yards further on. Mel flew over the elephant's head into the bushes, where he lay stunned while the elephant continued its escape. After about fifty yards Bodai, the driver, somehow managed to get the trembling beast under control and circled back. Mel, who was trying to stand, heard Sagar pleading with him to climb up, get back on the elephant because the tiger was coming, but he was dazed and unable to respond. Bodai finally managed to get the elephant to *cul* or put her foot out to form a step, and Mel scrambled up the ten-foot wall of the animal's backside.

They reassembled the elephants a hundred yards from the tree. Pat was quiet, wide eyed, and everyone else was dazed. Regrouping, still in shock, everybody suddenly realized that they would have to go back in and face the tigress again. They had to find Kirti, whether he was alive or dead. The antennas were broken, and the other radio-tracking equipment was scattered all over the area. Now they had no way of knowing where the tigress was, and to get Kirti out meant that someone would have to be on the ground...

Six hours after the accident, Kirti was in Shanta Bawan Hospital in Kathmandu being treated by the best doctors in Nepal. He spent ten weeks fighting infection and received several skin grafts. His long and painful recovery took five months, but nine months after the accident he was back at work in Chitwan. {1988}

There were large windows opening down to the floor of the verandah and through one of these the estate manager retired. After entering his room, he had just closed the window and was gazing out for an instant, when he saw a dark mass land on the verandah, right onto his friend, and then heard sounds of a scuffle and a cry for help.

Seizing his rifle, to which a sword-bayonet was attached, and flinging up the window, he rushed out, in time to see his assistant walking down the steps that led up to the verandah from the garden alongside the tiger and with his hand in the latter's mouth.

The manager was afraid to fire lest he should hit his colleague, so running after him and with admirable presence of mind, he went up to the tiger apparently undetected and plunging his bayonet into the animal's body, at the same instant fired.

There was a roar and a scuffle, and the assistant took advantage of the moment to release his hand. {1992}

THE MAGICAL TIGER OF THE MAYADWIP

KALYAN CHAKRABARTI

A motor launch was gliding smoothly into the calm and crystal-clear waters of the mighty Mayadwip river. It was the season for honey collection and the entire atmosphere was surcharged with the sweet fragrance of Khalasi (*Aegiceros majus*) flowers with numerous swarms of rock bees busy collecting honey. But the searching eyes in the launch were riveted on a black, moving object in the middle of the river.

The launch was heavy, fitted with a steel hull and manned by a crew of ten. The serang (pilot) steered the launch towards the moving object which ultimately appeared to be a full-grown tiger crossing the river. The Sundarbans tigers are said to enjoy immunity from fatal shots while in water, because only their nostrils keep peeping above the surface even in rough weather. A strong wind had started in the meantime and the launch had a violent rocking on the crests of the waves. Attempts were made to shoot the animal. Five shots were fired in quick succession from the unsteady launch. But the rocking diverted the bullets well away from the animal which was closely watching the proceedings.

The crew then started aiming lumps of coal at the swimmer which casually blocked the few accurate missiles by its broad left paw. Long bamboo poles, the normal equipment of a launch, were thrust at the tiger, but the ends were gripped and the animal caught hold of the pointed end with both paws and chewed [it] up until the pole was reduced to shreds. The exhausted crew grew more and more nervous at the animal's daring ingenuity.

The serang repeatedly rammed and overran the animal to suffocate and drown it, by driving the launch over its head. The cook then splashed hot water on the animal. But neither any injury nor any exhaustion was noticed. This mesmeric existence of the tiger caused a section of the superstitious crew to bolt themselves in a cabin below.

The serang was perplexed but the animal temporarily solved the problem by getting itself air-borne, by raising its body in mid-air and then effecting a smooth landing on the small dinghi attached to the launch. Having climbed the dinghi, it lay its head below the wooden planks to register its tiredness and fear. Fear, in turn, struck the crew like an electric shock with the premonition that the dinghi might now be used as a platform to climb on to the launch. To stave off such an eventuality, the tow rope was considerably extended with the help of another rope.

The battle of nerves was reaching its climax. The panic-stricken crew became petrified. At long last it was decided to drag the dinghi along with the tiger to the timber coupe of Herobhanga where the animal could be brought under control with the help of the coupe staff in possession of rifles. It was a long way and Matla, a mightier river, had to be crossed. As the launch entered Matla, its rushing waves overturned the dinghi and the tiger was tossed back into the water. It swam ashore, completely fagged, outwitted by the helpless and curious crew of the launch, and leisurely walked away, turning its head at the launch several times before vanishing into the mangrove forests.

It had fought a grave battle single-handed for three hours against men and machines and ultimately did not suffer any setback. {1992}

TIGERS IN THE MIST | K. ULLAS KARANTH

It was a cold morning in May 1994. I drove my battered 4X4 along the grass-covered forest track cleaving through the curtain of mist that still enveloped the forests. Dew dripped heavily from the foliage. A jungle fowl puffed up his silver hackles and crowed: *Kick yaa. Kick-kick*, he announced his intentions boldly to rival cocks, from a safe perch on an *Erythrina* sapling. With me were two men from a British television crew, hoping to film tigers. We were in Nagarahole, a green jewel of a wildlife park at the foot of the Western Ghat mountains in the Indian state of Karnataka. Teeming with deer, pigs and gaur on which tigers prey, this dense jungle is a paradise for the big cats. However, I thought our chances of actually seeing a tiger, let alone filming one, were pretty slim; unlike in the open forests of some north Indian parks, where tourists can view some habituated tigers, the cats of Nagarahole are secretive and shy.

I was proved wrong soon enough. As we came up a rise, I spotted a bulky form silhouetted against the mist, about 250 ft (75 metres) ahead. A tigress sat on the road, facing us. Her two cubs, slightly smaller than leopards, were playing in front of her. Tigers in the mist! It was a marvellous family portrait of the great cats, their rich ochre and black colours subtly showing through the white veil swirling around them. I stopped the vehicle and cut the engine.

The tigress lay down, still facing us. She was alert but calm. The cubs gambolled in the short grass. Blue-winged parakeets and black hill mynas screeched around us. An unwary peacock walked towards the tigress from behind, spotted her suddenly, and flew away, emitting raucous alarm calls. Nothing seemed to bother the tigers; we watched them for over 40 minutes and the TV crew, feeling ever-more confident, had their fill of exceptional footage of wild tigers.

The cubs, still playing, got closer and closer to us. Suddenly, something—maybe the whir of the video camera—alarmed the tigress. She stood up and started cantering towards us: eyes blazing, ears erect, strides quickening. I realized that she was going to charge; but, having spent nearly a decade studying tigers, I also knew that we were perfectly safe inside the vehicle, and that she would veer off during the last second of her mock charge. She was merely warning us to get away from her cubs.

My hitherto confident companions, however, were in a panic. It was the first time they had seen a charging tigress—surely their last one too, they seemed to think, certain that the open vehicle provided no protection against her fury. Whispering, I managed to calm them, and they restrained themselves from jumping off the vehicle.

Within seconds the tigress charged, emitting blood-curding growls and bounding to within 10 ft (3 metres) of us, before swerving off to the left. She continued to growl menacingly from within the dense bamboo cover, as her cubs scurried back up the track. I reversed the vehicle a few yards to reassure her, and the growls subsided. While my companions had become nervous wrecks, I had enjoyed the spectacular show of feline ferocity; not because I was any braver than they were, but because my perception of the moment was shaped by what I knew about tiger behaviour. The TV crew had merely reacted with the elementary fear most people instinctively feel for the great cat. {2001}

THE MATING PAIR | ARJAN SINGH

Early in the morning I crept silently to the River Bend hide, and from it, on a sandpit opposite the Leopard Haven spillway, I saw the bulky form of the male lying down. Through my binoculars I also made out the slimmer shape of Tara reclining beside him under the shade of some jamun trees. After a while she got up, walked to the edge of the water, and crouched with her tail to one side, clearly in invitation, keeping up a hollow, vibrant growling as a sign of her receptive condition. The male promptly rose and mounted her, but no sooner had he taken the nape of her neck in a symbolic grip than she whirled round on him with an explosive snarl, and he hastily backed off.

After this preliminary attempt at copulation, Tara lay on her back with her paws in the air, while the male went sedately back to his old position. Soon, however, she got up again and walked over to him. Then she tantalized him by brushing provocatively against his head, flicking his nose with her tail, and presenting her hindquarters in front of him. When there was no immediate response, she seemed to become even more restless, and walked into the river. The tiger followed, with a bemused expression on his face, and as he passed her, she rubbed her head against his, before rubbing her entire sinuous body against his bulk. So far all the preliminary, flirtatious advances had been hers...

He sat on in the water, and with soft, moaning grunts summoned his tigress back. She soon appeared on the bank and presented herself, whereupon he got out of the water and mounted her. With each powerful thrust, his nasal moan increased in volume and vibrated like a dynamo, until at the climax she turned on him with an explosive roar and his tail shot up in the air as he hastened to dismount. Tara then lay on her back, and later moved into the water with him. Soon after that they went back under cover, and the sounds of their courtship continued unabated... {2005}

As I walked down a forest track in Nepal one day, a tiger stepped from the bushes some distance ahead. I moved quietly behind a tree to watch. The tiger sat down and gazed in my direction. After a while he rose, sniffed a nearby tree, turned to eject scent, and began to walk towards me. About 30 paces away he turned once more into the bushes. My jeep arrived and we drove close to the undergrowth, trying unsuccessfully to spot the tiger. One of my companions suddenly said: 'Look behind!' The tiger was standing again on the track, looking curiously at us. Then he walked on with majestic unconcern.

On another occasion, this time in India, I was on an elephant searching for a tiger whose kill was nearby. We came upon him in a dry river bed, sprawled comfortably on his back in a shady spot, just like a pet cat on the hearth. He raised his head to glance at us, then sank back, closed his eyes and drifted off to sleep. Dappled sunlight illuminated his rich, black-striped, golden fur, his white chest and belly. With a massive paw, he brushed a fly from his nose.

Another time, a tiger emerged from behind a boulder and faced my open jeep. I examined him closely through binoculars. His shoulder muscles

rippled as though he were about to spring. A shiver of fear ran through me. But he turned and disappeared into the jungle.

I have had many close encounters with tigers, but these incidents illustrate some of their outstanding characteristics: an aloof, self-sufficient air; sheer beauty; and raw power. They left me with a sense of awe. It is impossible to see a tiger in the wild without a quickening of pulse. Few people in the past had the experience, unless they were actually hunting. {2002}

THE KING OF THE BEASTS

GEOFFREY C. WARD AND DIANE RAINES WARD

In the meantime, the tigers of Ranthambhore had only Fateh Singh. He had worked within the sanctuary for nearly twenty years, and his success had several times led his superiors at Jaipur to promote him to a desk job. He always turned them down. He planned to stay in one place—and in charge—until he retired. 'I know this place,' he explained, rising in his seat to peek over the top of the thorn bushes. 'I'm not happy anywhere else. I've bought myself a farm at the edge of the forest so that every day until I die I can drive over and visit my park.'

He clutched my shoulder. 'Tiger in the road,' he said. Perhaps forty feet ahead of us a tiger sat in the middle of the track—filled the track, in fact, and seemed somehow to fill the forest that stretched away on either side as well. Nothing had prepared me for his size or for the palpable sense of menace and power that emanated from him. 'His name is Akbar,' Fateh whispered, beginning to softly hum with pleasure at the sight of him. 'About five hundred pounds.'

The tiger rose slowly to his feet. Everything about him seemed outsized: his big, round, ruffed face; his massive shoulders and blazing coat; his empty belly that hung in folds and had finally forced him into the open to hunt; his long twitching tail. It seemed inconceivable that such a big vivid animal could have stayed hidden in this drab open forest for so long.

We sat very still in the open jeep as the tiger stared at us. 'He's a good boy,' Fateh said, still humming. I devoutly hoped so. The tiger turned and cocked his huge head to listen as a sambhar called from a clearing off to our left; then, after fixing us with one more steady glance, he slipped silently into the grass. Neither his smiling protector nor his protector's wary guests had been worth so much as a growl. {1993}

THE TIGRESS THAT KILLED A CROCODILE | JAISAL SINGH

Two years of severe drought had taken its toll on almost all of Ranthambhore's wild inhabitants. The picturesque lakes with Mughal pleasure palaces at their banks, usually full of lotus and water lilies with sambhar deer grazing on them, had dried up and the harsh sun had cracked the earth. The hundreds of muggers that lived in these lakes had been forced to fight for whatever remained of them; mostly just a small puddle. Most migrated over the craggy Aravalli hills to the Chambal and Banas rivers that surround the reserve on two sides.

It was a tough time in this dry deciduous-dry thorn forest. I guess that was nature's way of weeding out the weak and thus ensuring the survival of the fittest.

No other tiger, or animal for that matter, in Ranthambhore embodied that tag of 'fittest' better than the resident tigress of the lake area, Machhli. Seventeen and still going strong at the time of writing this, she was bringing up a litter of two cubs when the drought hit her realm in 2002.

On a cold and dry December afternoon I entered the park through the Jogi Mahal gate with a few friends in my jeep. This medieval entrance to one of the finest wilderness areas in the world lies in the shadow of the legendary eighth century fortress of Ranthambhore. Machhli and her cubs had been seen moving into the area that morning by a forest tracker. Taking that report into account I decided to take the road that runs behind Padam Talao, with the hope of finding them. About a hundred yards past the magnificent banyan tree at Jogi Mahal, there she was—feeding on a freshly killed chital doe. But the cubs were not with her. We had hardly taken a photograph or two when she dragged the kill into a small bush to protect it from scavengers and started to walk in the direction of the Mahal. We followed. About thirty yards away she disappeared into the tall grass. I was sure that she would eventually walk the cubs this short distance for them to feed. Nearly an hour later, one cub peered out of the undergrowth at our jeep. Then a second. Shortly thereafter Machhli strode out and the cubs followed her as she walked them confidently on the jungle track towards the kill offering us a lovely view and, though the light was fading fast, a few photographs.

What happened next jolted us out of this calm and happy scenario we were witnessing. As the family of tigers approached the carcass, Machhli shot like a bullet away from us, roaring loudly. Of course, we presumed the worst; a transient male tiger must have come along and was trying to appropriate her kill. And if so, he would definitely kill the cubs, who now scampered towards our jeep for safety. With our pulses racing, we reversed the jeep a little and through a small clearing saw a hitherto unrecorded happening.

It was not a transient male, but a large mugger who had come out of the small puddle that was all that remained of Padam Talao. Machhli and the crocodile were going at each other. The tigress was putting herself and the cubs at a huge risk by taking the crocodile on. The slightest error on her part and the crocodile would have sunk its teeth into Machhli. Or gravely injured her with its powerful tail. The cubs would probably not have survived without their mother being able to hunt and feed them. Letting out blood-curdling roars that were echoing off the battlements of the fort, she was running circles around the crocodile, waiting for an opportune moment to strike. The crocodile was swishing its tail and trying to take a bite out of her in its own quest for survival. She finally found a chance and jumped on it from the rear, sinking her canines into the nape of its neck and grabbing the reptile with her powerful paws. The mugger tried to fight back but the determined and courageous matriarch fought on till the crocodile gave up. It was almost dark when we left them, Machhli having walked back to comfort her terrified cubs. She had mortally wounded the crocodile, who died a cold and painful death when the temperatures dropped to nearly zero degrees later that night. In the morning, she had dragged the crocodile a little and had started to eat from near its neck.

At the time, I was using a digital video camera with which, even in extremely poor light, I managed to capture this incredible encounter. It was the first recorded encounter of a tiger killing a crocodile in the wild. {2002}

The early 1980s were a very interesting time for Ranthambhore. Its wild population of tigers had not only increased but had also become comfortable with the presence of human beings observing and photographing them from inside an open-topped jeep. That coupled with the reserve's dry deciduous flora and natural topography afforded photographers and observers alike superb viewing of these magnificent big cats.

In 1984, a large and extremely courageous male tiger had taken over the area of the lakes. Sambhar deer, attracted to the lotus, lilies and other aquatic plants thronged the area, and spent a considerable amount of time in the water, feeding—even with the ever present danger of an Indian marsh crocodile silently clamping its jaws into them, and pulling them down to a dark, watery grave. Wild boar stayed on the shallow, marshy edges where waders drummed about and chital fed on the verdant banks. Owing to the tall khus (vetiver) grass that surrounds these lakes, they were, and continue to be, a perfect hunting ground for large predators. Genghis, the resident male, adopted a hunting technique that had never been witnessed before. He would move into this tall grass, carefully pick his quarry, and charge fearlessly into the water, catching a panic-stricken sambhar while it tried to swim across the water.

I must have been five years old when I first saw Genghis. The scene around the lake was idyllic. Genghis had silently moved into the tall grass unnoticed and was sitting camouflaged at the edge, picking out his sambhar. On choosing a fawn, he charged, sending both animals and birds into utter panic and confusion. Keeping his eyes on the quarry, he followed it into the deep and finally sunk his canines into the helpless fawn's jugular while the area echoed with alarm calls from an assortment of animals. He then dragged his kill out and into the tall grass to feed. My father, Tejbir, using his sixteen millimetre Bolex camera, captured the entire sequence on film. It remains, even today, one of the finest sequences of tiger behaviour ever captured on moving picture.

Wild tigers killing their prey have rarely been captured on film, unlike other big cats in Africa like the lion and cheetah. I am given to believe that there are possibly only nine or ten sequences that exist.

Thus I was elated when history repeated itself, coincidentally on the same lake, twenty-nine years later. It was mid-December and temperatures at that time of the year drop to almost freezing at night, and a lovely fifteen to twenty degrees during the day with crisp sunshine. The fourteenth was a perfect day and I had driven into the park just after daybreak. It had been reported that a male had been seen moving towards the area of Malik Talao the previous evening. Scanning the tall grass with my binoculars yielded nothing. The sun had now come up and we were about to pour ourselves a coffee and dig into scrambled egg sandwiches when a single chital alarm from the direction of the Tambakhan road caught my attention. Though a single call does not confirm the presence of a predator, I nevertheless decided to investigate. On reaching the tiraha (junction), I saw some movement in the dhok jungle to my right. It was a tiger walking right towards us. We reversed on to the paal (embankment) which had water on both sides. The tiger, by then identified by us, was actually a tigress (T-17). Walking on the paal, she suddenly paused, and stood motionless. A group of sambhar in shallow water to our right had got her interest. I switched my camera on to high-definition video mode and quickly changed lenses. Half a minute later, she bounded away, going down the slope at lightning speed and into the water. Before the sambhar had time to react, she had a young fawn—one almost as big as the one Genghis had caught twenty-nine years earlier—in the grip of her powerful jaws. She then waded through the lake with her kill in the direction of a dry nullah which would have taken her directly to the gorge in which her young cubs were resting. As we repositioned the jeep, she walked right by us and disappeared into the dry, rocky stream bed. {2012}

VALMIK THAPAR

TRADITIONAL ENEMIES | DHARMENDRA AND DIVYA KHANDAL

Tiger T-24 knows how to be in the news; this incident of T-24 with the leopard is an amazing encounter in natural history, one that I was fortunate to capture and document. It happened one morning when most vehicles had gone inside the park routes that some people sighted T-24 on the roadside, sitting under a huge banyan tree. Since it was a Wednesday, an auspicious day for the locals, there were more number of worshippers going to the Ganesh temple than tourists going to the park. On sighting the tiger, the locals on motorbikes and private vehicles created a ruckus. A ranger called up Dharmendra to reach the spot and try to control the situation. I went along with him to find out what was going on.

T-24 was climbing up a hill when we reached, and as we looked in his direction, we saw a leopardess running upwards and quickly climbing a tree with T-24 chasing behind it. Realizing that the leopard was a difficult target for him, he did not try too much and continued to move forward. It was a thrilling moment for us as witnesses.

The tiger and the leopard are two big cats with equal charisma and magnificence. There is always a curiosity amongst naturalists regarding how these two species interact with each other and how they share their prey base. In Sariska, when all the tigers were poached in 2005, the leopards' activity, even in day time, rose as they roamed fearlessly in the entire habitat.

And it wasn't just the leopards: the movement of hyenas and jackals during the day went up around that time as well.

The year 2005 was also a time when poaching was rampant in Ranthambhore, and the tiger numbers had gone down. During this time, the legendary tiger conservationist, Fateh Singh Rathore, observed that there was an increase in the number of leopards sighted, which itself was an indicator of a decrease in tiger numbers. However, there is no scientific study to prove this; these are mere observations used by experienced individuals to gauge the changes affecting tigers in a sanctuary. Indian male tigers on an average weigh about 220 kilograms, whereas the Indian male leopard weighs about 63 kilograms. An average tigress weighs about 139 kilograms while a leopardess weighs about 32 kilograms.

The tiger is about three or four times heavier than the leopard; hence, there is no equal confrontation between the two. However, there is one trick up the leopard's sleeve which always saves it from the tiger—its ability to climb trees. Yet, a few leopards are killed each year due to tiger attacks; in Ranthambhore, the figure is about two to three leopards. Most of the times these are sub-adult leopard cubs that get killed by tigers as they move out to find their own territory and lack the experience to tackle such situations. For instance, in 2010, a leopard cub and his mother were seen climbing two separate trees while confronting a tiger. The young cub, however, was afraid and impatient to get to the mother, so he tried climbing down soon. When he was halfway down, the tiger managed to attack him and he was killed in front of the mother who stayed back on the tree.

The tiger does not look at a leopard as food, it looks at it as an enemy or intrusion: one that competes for the same prey base and hence needs to be taken out. Often the tiger ends up snatching the leopard's food when it gets a chance to steal it. However, very few people have actually seen this happen. {2012}

VALMIK THAPAR

THE LEOPARD THAT FELL INTO THE TIGER'S LAP
GOVERDHAN SINGH RATHORE

Goverdhan had an amazing encounter with a tiger when he was with an old friend, Geoffrey Ward, who is a writer of international repute and a great supporter of Ranthambhore. Geoff had, over the years, played a vital role through his writings in keeping Ranthambhore at the forefront of attention across the world. His book, *Tigerwallahs*, provides a memorable account of some of the key characters who played a role in India's battle to save her tigers. In Goverdhan's words, 'It was March 2009, and I was in the forest with Geoff, Diane, and my son, Yudhveer, on an early morning safari. We were at the beginning of Bhakola, coming via Kachida, just enjoying the morning sun and beautiful early morning light. Just happy to be in Ranthambhore with no one around. Yudhveer and I had just returned from Kanha. He was beginning to get interested in wildlife and had acquired his first camera, which was given to him by his grandfather Fateh. He was busy clicking anything and everything, thinking like most kids his age that each click was going to be a masterpiece. I was just happy to be there, watching him. As we drove farther along Bhakola, the light grew better, catching the amazing green of the jamoon leaves, and shining through the tufts of grass. The valley was silent except for the odd sound of birds. Just as we were about to reach the last water patch on the road, before we climbed to get to Lakarda, Yudhveer, who was looking for beehives in trees, shouted, "Leopard!" Sure enough, there was a large female in the tendu tree right above us. She did not seem happy and was very restless. We tried to find out what was bothering her, and just then, Yudhveer shouted, "Another leopard!" That is when we saw the semi-adult cub across the nullah in another tree. He was even more restless, and looked really scared, moving up and down the branches, and constantly looking down at the ground. We could see the mother above us calling to the cub, probably asking it to calm down. Until then, we could not really know why this was happening, as we had not seen the tiger sitting at the base of the tree where the cub was. Before we could even ascertain this fact, the cub became extremely nervous, and started sliding down the tree, urinating as though in absolute panic. In seconds, there was a huge growl as if a fight were taking place, with sounds of splashing water. In my mind, the whole thing was over within a few seconds, and then there was total silence as though nothing had happened. The mother looked on helplessly as the tiger sat on the dead cub and started eating it. She just kept moving up and down the tree, not knowing what to do while we sat in our car mesmerized, listening to the sound of bones breaking as the tiger dug his canines into the leopard cub. This was the most spectacular event I had ever witnessed in the wild, having been in Ranthambhore for nearly forty years. It was getting late and we had to get out of the park, and so we left the mother leopard, the tree, and the tiger eating the cub well-hidden inside a thicket of jamoon trees. The drive out was one of complete silence, as none of us could believe what we had just seen. Yudhveer looked very pleased as he had been the first to spot the leopards and we were glad that he was searching for beehives because otherwise we would have just driven past, oblivious of what was about to unfold.' {2009}

VALMIK THAPAR

THE BATTLE BETWEEN EQUALS | ADITYA 'DICKY' SINGH

In the morning safari, some jeeps saw a pair of tigers walking from Zone 1 of the Ranthambhore national park towards the Kalapani anicut in Zone 6. In the evening, I booked a jeep for Zone 6 and we found the mating tigers (T-24 [male] and T-39 [female], both young adults) in the rocky plateau across the anicut.

The plateau had some short grass cover and low trees. The sun was behind the tigers, so the back light was very strong. For a time, the tigers were in the shade which was no good for photography. After about half an hour, however, the tigress suddenly got up and started stalking towards the edge of the plateau.

A mother bear with two small cubs riding on her back was walking towards the pair of tigers and the tigress had gone to confront them. By the time the bear became aware of the tigers, the tigress had got very close to her and her cubs.

The bear appeared to be in serious trouble and we expected her to bolt away but she had other plans. The bear cubs flattened themselves against their mother's back while she charged at the approaching tigress. I think the tigress was taken by surprise at this move and tried to get out of what was quickly turning into a messy situation. However, the bear blocked her path and stood up on her hind legs to confront her while the tigress kept backing off. It is possible she did not have the experience to take on a desperate mother.

The bear started screaming loudly and got increasingly aggressive. Soon there was a loud slanging match between the two, which the bear won. The tigress beat a hasty retreat while the bear stood her ground.

By this time the male tiger, who had been observing the drama from a distance, decided to get involved. T-24 was about four years old and had just come into dominance. We were worried for the bear.

We had seriously underestimated the power of an angry mother. T-24, the young male star of southern Ranthambhore, could not even budge the bear. These two had another loud slanging match that once again went in the bear's favour.

T-24 soon realized that the fury of an angry mother was hard to overcome and started backing away from a now one-sided fight and did not stop till he had reached a safe distance.

All this happened in exactly two minutes and ten seconds. When the clock started, it seemed that the mother bear had got herself into a very serious spot. In ten seconds she had taken control and, two minutes later, she had forced two tigers to back off. The victor walked off, leaving behind two sheepish cats. {2011}

VALMIK THAPAR

In February 2011, a tigress in Ranthambhore National Park died of natural causes, leaving behind two small three-to-four-month-old female cubs. It took four days to locate the cubs hidden in a narrow crevice with a natural spring at its entrance.

The forest department officials debated whether to secure the cubs in an enclosure within the park or transfer them to a zoo as their survival in the wild was next to impossible. As the debate carried on, the cubs were fed on meat and remote cameras kept an eye on their activities. The cubs seemed content and took the feed given to them. The cameras captured them indulging in normal juvenile activities, even playing with the trap cameras when they discovered them.

In March, for the first time, the cubs disappeared from the 'den' area, much to the consternation of the monitoring team. They reappeared in a few days to the relief of the observers. This activity was recorded often over the next couple of months: the cubs would disappear and reappear after a few days. Once they were away from their den area for almost a week. During the absence of the cubs from their den, the trap cameras captured a leopard and even a hyena visiting and sniffing around the site. When the cubs were present, however, other predators and scavengers were conspicuous by their absence.

On 14 May 2011, to the amazement of all of us monitoring the cubs, a camera trap nearly three kilometres away from the den captured a large male tiger walking with one of the cubs on the main vehicle track to Kachidah Chowki. This, then, explained the disappearance of the cubs regularly from their hiding area. The male was taking them out on territorial walks. Since they were always seen in good health, it was obvious that he was sharing meals with them too. This kind of behaviour had never been observed by any expert up until now. Ranthambhore was once again set to reveal new secrets of the lives of tigers.

Forest Department officials monitoring the cubs saw the male playing and even sharing kills with them. It was assumed that he was their father. In one instance, when the cubs were ten months old, the male killed a small buffalo bait and let the cubs open and feed on it while he watched and this was observed by the Divisional Field Officer, Y. K. Sahu.

I sought and was granted permission by Mr Sahu to monitor the cubs' activities. It was in January, nearly a year since their mother died, that I saw one of the cubs with the male while he was taking it on a territorial walk.

The cub was following the male and observing scent marking and making phlegm on smelling the spray. This was the first time anyone had captured this activity between a male and a cub on camera.

Three months later, there was more surprise in store for me when I came upon Zalim the tiger, sitting at the Goolar Kui watering hole, accompanied by one cub. Upon hearing a series of monkey alarm calls, Zalim, followed by the cub, retreated to the cover of a bush around thirty yards away. A tigress, Sundari or T-17, who had mated with Zalim in January approached the watering hole and sat down in the water, unaware of the two tigers nearby. The cub decided to take a walk and was observed by Sundari, who immediately went into a stalking position. The cub quickly returned to where the male was and Zalim got up and started walking menacingly towards the now cowering female. The cub watched for a while and retreated into the bush. Zalim, meanwhile, walked up to the tigress who had gone into a completely submissive pose. He came nose to nose with her and there was loud vocalizing before Zalim turned away, scent-marking bushes and trees as he marched towards where the cub had disappeared. It was an amazing natural history moment which left me breathless. This male was truly protecting and bringing up the two female cubs. {2011}

VALMIK THAPAR

THE BABYSITTER OF BANDHAVGARH | KIM SULLIVAN

Pyari the Chakradharra tigress, born in 1996, is pictured with her first litter male cub, Challenger, born in 2000, who is two years old, along with her second litter of four six-month-old cubs born in 2002.

For over a month I had the privilege of watching this family interact. The young male Challenger had adopted the role of babysitter as for many long days he would tend to his younger siblings whilst Pyari was off hunting or resting, probably getting some much needed peace. He would play, fight, swim, eat and even try to suckle with them. He did not just show up and then leave again—he actually lived and moved with the family. He remained with the cubs at all times not even following his mother to hunt. He was their guardian and protector in her absence. Challenger was very tolerant with the cubs, often appearing even tender and loving to them if one can impose human emotion on wild tigers. His mother Pyari allowed him to live and move and even eat with the family even though he was well past the age a cub separates from his mother. When he would try to join in the suckling she usually gave him a bit of a snarl and he moved off and just lay next to the family. She was seemingly very comfortable with his role as the babysitter. Toward the end of the month, his father, B-2, was seen fighting with him, presumably to let him know that it was time for him to leave, which he did shortly afterwards. Challenger had naturally started to spray-mark the territory and this was not tolerated by his father. However, in the next year and a half he would return to challenge his father and the other dominant male, Bhoka, for a small chunk of the Tala zone. We also know what happened to all the tigers pictured here, which in itself is remarkable, as more often than not the sub-adults and cubs of the Tala zone disappear and we do not know their fate. Their behaviour was fascinating to observe and gave me an insight into this supposed solitary life of tigers. I concluded they were much more familial than previously believed. {2012}

THE FIRST DAYS IN A TIGER'S LIFE
RAGHU CHUNDAWAT AND JOANNA VAN GRUISEN

It is next to impossible to tell if a wild tigress is pregnant or not, except maybe a couple of days before the birth. Even among captive tigers, Sankhala records that there are no obvious signs to indicate pregnancy in tigers. However, in Panna, since we were monitoring tigresses with radio collars, we could interpret their movements better. This remote monitoring taught us that a pregnant tigress starts checking out sites before she decides where she wants to give birth. Once she settles down for birthing, she remains there for the first five to six days, hardly moving out at all. This is the first definite sign of the birth of a litter.

We have only a few fleeting observations of cubs during their first week of life, but we had a wonderful opportunity to watch and film cubs and their mother (F-120) during their second week. At this early age, the mother still spends seventy to eighty per cent of her time with the cubs but she will occasionally move a few metres away and rest nearby. For the first two weeks she is like a milk bar for the cubs. They suckle and sleep, suckle and sleep, occasionally even while still attached to the nipple. Sankhala also noted how extremely careful captive mother tigers were about cleanliness. Every time the tigress suckled her cubs, she would clean them and herself.

After eight to ten days of no feeding, a female will leave the cubs to go hunting. Monitoring tigresses during such hunts we noticed that they seemed unusually nervous and any sound might alert them to abandon the search and return to the cubs. When a tigress makes a kill far from her litter, that is, about two to three kilometres away, she will eat quickly and head straight back to her cubs; she may not even return to the kill again. We have even seen one tigress make a kill but return to the cubs without feeding at all.

The mother exhibits this extreme caution for several weeks, rarely leaving the cubs unattended for long. On one occasion, F-120 killed a large male nilgai and tried to bring it as close as possible to the cave where she had kept her cubs. She dragged it for almost 600 metres, then dropped it over the cliff into the gorge below. She was so nervous about leaving the cubs that she left the carcass twice and climbed all the way down to check on them before returning to her efforts. It is not easy dragging along 250 kilograms of dead antelope; we were impressed by her foresight to drop it from the cliff so she didn't have to climb up every time to reach the kill.

While watching F-120 with her new cubs, we witnessed something particularly remarkable: a visit from the resident male we knew to be the cubs' father. As he moved down the gorge towards the cave, F-120 came out to greet him and they settled down together about twenty metres from the cubs. He may have remained there most of the day as our team saw him in the vicinity in the evening. Unfortunately, we could not stay to watch their behaviour as he only arrived as we were leaving and already in the open. We could not return to our hideaway spot without disturbing them so we had to leave. This seems to somewhat gainsay the accepted belief that the father has nothing at all to do with the female and cubs after birth.

The tigress usually moves the cubs within ten days of their birth but she does not take them far. F-120 had only moved her cubs around 100 metres from her birthing place. Occasionally we observed them move the cubs only after two weeks. By the time the cubs are three to four weeks old their mother will make longer forays and she may occasionally be away for twenty-four hours or more. She will start patrolling different parts of her range and spend more time on her kills. Other than these forays, over seventy per cent of our locations were within 500 metres of the litter.

We also noticed that tigresses never used the same locations for birthing. The cubs first move out with the mother between the ninth and tenth week, although on one occasion it happened even later than this. It is amazing how much distance these young cubs can cover at this tender age. The furthest we recorded was over four kilometres although usually they cover a couple of kilometres at a stretch. It is around this time that we see them on the prowl for the first time. {2012}

BOOK THREE

THE
SECRET
LIFE OF THE
TIGER

—

When the year 1976 turned over, I was desperate to get away from Delhi. I was bored with city life and exhausted by the tiresome marriage I had entered into at the young age of twenty-two. I was convinced that somewhere in my early twenties I had got everything wrong. By March, I had decided to escape the horrors of Delhi; within hours, my train hooted into a station and I was transported into another world—the district town of Sawai Madhopur in Rajasthan that lies adjacent to Ranthambhore. I didn't know then that it would become more than a home to me. It is this world that still engages me thirty-seven years later, fills up my senses and remains deeply embedded in my soul.

When I first arrived in this very special bit of tiger turf, I was not sure where I was going or what I was doing. All I knew was that it would somehow help change my rather drab and routine city-based life. Even to this day, I am not sure what made me visit Ranthambhore in particular or why the tiger and jungles beckoned to me, although I can make an educated guess. At some point as a child, the forests of the tiger must have made an impact on me like nothing else. I had an uncle who ran the forests of Uttar Pradesh in North India, and I would always end up in Corbett National Park following the trail of tigers with a bunch of cousins. I vividly remember watching tigers from the back of an elephant, and these childhood adventures must have become ingrained in my memory; as a result, in my moment of crisis, these remarkable memories resurfaced, and I decided to go back to the forest to see if the magical place of my childhood could restore my inner self. On the face of it, my failed marriage aside, I had no reason to be so disenchanted with myself. After a stellar academic career and international success as a filmmaker and photographer, I should have been on top of the world. Yet, I was an angular, awkward individual, given to depression and filled with an emptiness that always left me frustrated and unfulfilled.

Maybe this is why I was destined to be devoured by Ranthambhore. Who knows? All I can say is that during those very special days of March when the seasons change and winter turns to spring I was completely dazzled by the sheer beauty of Ranthambhore—its landscape, its lakes, the massive fort echoing with the endless memories of man. Crumbling ruins of a glorious past dotted the forest and were slowly being enveloped by nature. It was like watching an embrace between nature and history. The

This tigress was stalking me as I walked, before I quickly retreated to my jeep.

lotus flowers, the enormous banyan trees, lake palaces and the invisible tiger created a magical mosaic that enveloped my senses and filled me with a spirit of life that I had never experienced before. I fell in love with that extraordinary mosaic of the natural world interlaced with history stretching back more than a thousand years. Weeks went by without catching a glimpse of the tiger, but the challenge of searching for it was an enthralling experience. In the meantime, I got to know the incredible man who ran the national park—Fateh Singh Rathore. I had never before encountered someone like him. He was full of colour and richness, music and song; a man who loved his whisky, he had an earthy understanding of both nature and life. He, like the forests of Ranthambhore, remained a part of my being till he died in 2011.

In those first weeks that I spent in Ranthambhore I relished my privacy and complete anonymity in the forests. There were no visitors and no one to be seen. I lived in Jogi Mahal, a little forest rest house below the ramparts of Ranthambhore Fort that stood at the edge of a lake filled with lotuses, and faced a vast banyan tree. I regularly slept under the branches of the banyan tree and woke to the shrill calls of animals and even the shadow of a leopard as it slunk by. In the day, the terrace of Jogi Mahal served as a perfect observation post to watch birds as they dived into the lake for fish, or crocodiles as they glided through the water.

On the twentieth day of this first trip, I was ready to do anything to get a glimpse of what was then the really elusive tiger. I had seen its pugmarks on forest paths, heard the alarm calls of animals as it passed by and once, far in the distance, I even heard its roar, but it always evaded vision. I searched for it mainly between dusk and dawn when the forest fell silent and the people who lived in the villages went to sleep. The tiger was entirely nocturnal and avoided any human contact. The villages in the park were full of livestock and there was so much disturbance that the tiger, when it had to, slipped in and out of the forest silently.

Strange as it may seem, it was on my last night that I had the encounter I always longed for. After dinner that night, I slipped into the jeep with the two trackers, Laddu and Badyaya, and the driver, Prahlad Singh. It was my last night and my fingers were not just crossed but felt welded together. The sky was pitch black with a brilliant array of stars. Our first job was to check two live baits that had been put out to attract the tiger. (These were days when baits were used to find tigers; even with them it was tough to encounter the animals as their movements were unpredictable.) The first bait that we went to check was tied to a large banyan tree at Singh Dwar. It

VALMIK THAPAR

A leopardess with her one-year-old cub. Shy and nocturnal, they keep away from tigers.

had been killed. My heart missed a beat, but I could see nothing around the dead animal. As I flashed my torch around, I spotted a leopard curled up in the banyan tree watching the carcass.

Other than the crickets playing their orchestra, there were no other sounds. Suddenly, the booming alarm call of a sambar deer rent the air. I knew instinctively that a tiger had killed and the sound of our jeep had forced it to flee. The leopard was watching from its perch on the tree. The atmosphere was electric. The leopard decided to creep down the tree and cautiously made its way to the carcass. It was taking a chance as its hunger dictated its steps. It nibbled at the carcass for five to ten minutes but when the sambar called once again, he was forced to retreat. I waited for a while but the tiger was not coming. Our presence discouraged it. I did not realize it then but it would be years before the Ranthambhore tigers would lose their fear of man.

I quickly drove off to the second bait. Gone. Not a sign of it anywhere. I tried to search the area thoroughly but an old ruined wall hampered my visibility. I was sure the tiger feasted behind it. I was desperate to see it and the only person I could think of who might help was Fateh Singh Rathore. I raced out of the park to Sawai Madhopur where he lived. It was nearly 11 p.m. when I arrived at his house. On banging on the door, I found Fateh a little groggy but awake. When I explained the situation to him, I caught a glint in his eyes. He picked up his Stetson hat and jacket and we raced back into the park. With Fateh at the wheel, we reached the old wall at the edge of the lake close to midnight. He drove all around the wall, cramming the jeep into every crevice and corner. We directed our searchlights into every conceivable place we could think of. I was sure that the elusive tiger of Ranthambhore would have fled the scene because of all the pandemonium.

As I had suspected, we found nothing, but as Fateh reversed I saw the rear wheels of the jeep entering the water and soon the back of the vehicle was in danger of being submerged. I shouted to Fateh that we would soon be afloat and all he said was to keep the torch trained on the wall. And that is how I saw my first tiger in Ranthambhore—from a floating jeep while I flashed the searchlight around. There was a sudden sharp cough and snarl. Framed in front of me and watching the commotion with its huge head above the wall was the tiger.

I watched my first tiger for two minutes in hushed silence, and it was a sight I have never forgotten. The two minutes seemed like two hours and its beauty as it peered at us that night had a magnetic power that was incomparable to anything I had ever known. As suddenly as it appeared, it vanished behind the walled enclosure at Rajbagh and I had to rub my eyes to believe that I had seen it. Fateh and I exchanged a look of sheer delight and he quickly summoned help on his wireless; at about 2 a.m. we were towed out of the lake. It was a night to remember and I knew I was hooked. I had to see more of this animal and discover its secret life. My affair with Ranthambhore and its tigers had begun, and in the encounters that followed, my adrenalin flowed like never before. For me, I suppose, the tiger was *the* great symbol of freedom and a total contrast to the 'chained' human spirit. Watching tigers became an all-encompassing passion and so exciting that everything else seemed dull and dreary in comparison. That first magical sight of the tiger drew me deeper and deeper into its realm. Each subsequent encounter created its own impact. Yesterday, thirty-seven years later, I watched a young tigress stalk a sambar and I was still mesmerized by the scene—as much as I was by that first encounter.

If I was to track back and recapture memories of some of my favourite tigers, the first that comes to mind is Padmini and her calm, mature and intelligent behaviour as she tried to raise five cubs and successfully managed to raise four. Amongst her cubs, Akbar and Babur were the most curious and confident, coming to within a few feet of us, especially in the middle of the night. I loved every minute of my moments with them. I also spent much time with little Laxmi, the smallest of this litter, as she grew to adulthood.

By the early 1980s, one of my all-time favourites, Noon, appeared on the scene. She controlled the exquisite area of the lakes in Ranthambhore and earned her name because of her intense activity in the middle of the day. In fact, when the late Prime Minister Rajiv Gandhi visited the sanctuary in 1986, she performed for him by killing a sambar at the edge of the lake. A few years earlier, my favourite male tiger, Genghis, was a regular sight around the lakes as he mastered the ability of killing sambar in the water—a kind of predation seen for the first time in Ranthambhore. In fact, he taught Noon the art of this kind of hunting, and these were the tigers that started rewriting the natural history of the species for the world to learn from.

There was also the very aggressive Nasty, who would emerge from nowhere and charge my jeep; the very calm and gentle Nick Ear whom I spent many delightful years with; Broken Tooth, the big male with the calm temperament, whom we saw repeatedly for nearly ten years (between 1979 and 1989).

Tigers are very individualistic—each one has its own nature just like humans do. In the 1990s, there were the stars of the sanctuary—Lady of the Lakes and her daughter, Machli, who is today nearly eighteen years old and still alive. Machli has given great pleasure to thousands of visitors from across the world by her confidence and comfort around vehicles. In the late 1990s, I named a male Bumbooram, and had a splendid time watching him for long hours. He was also the star who performed when President Clinton visited Ranthambhore just as the century turned.

In the last decade, the naming of tigers got phased out and was replaced by numbers from T-1 to T-52. I think the last names that I remember were Broken Tail and Jhumroo, and the enormous Charauli tiger. Many of Ranthambhore's star tigers and their offspring were shifted to Sariska to repopulate it after its tigers got poached. Now the catch words are T-17, T-19 and so on.

The emotions have gone but in the pages that follow are some of my best experiences with the tigers Fateh and I knew and named. During these early years, we got to observe their lives and I will always feel privileged that it was revealed to me in such detail.

Over the years, I must have watched 200 different tigers in Ranthambhore, and as I traverse the park, each one of these incredible encounters comes back to me as if it happened yesterday. It is from observing tigers in Ranthambhore that many new facts of tiger behaviour were established. Along with my tiger guru, the late Fateh Singh Rathore, I had the immense privilege to record, with pen and camera, some of these

remarkable observations. From 1976 to 1988, we pursued the tiger to discover its secrets and narrated in the pages that follow are some of the unique encounters we recorded in our diaries—encounters that changed field biology and gave new insights into the world of the tiger.

FIRST ENCOUNTERS: RANTHAMBHORE'S
MAGICAL WORLD

It was a cold crisp winter morning in 1976 when I caught the train to Sawai Madhopur in Rajasthan. I had heard about the Ranthambhore Tiger Reserve but had no idea what to expect. That is one of the hazards and one of the joys of travelling in India—you never know what is lurking beyond the next milestone.

Sawai Madhopur certainly provided no clue. It was a typical district town mushrooming around the railway track, which was obviously its only reason for existence. My heart sank a little as I thought of the endless train whistles which must surely frighten any tiger. My apprehension increased as I stepped on to the platform and received the stares of people around me. It was almost like a reversal of roles, with myself as the tourist attraction. I went outside and took the first tonga I could see. We jolted along to the forest headquarters through the dismal mess of concrete and brick structures put together haphazardly, dangerously innocent of ecology or environment, which is the mark of every small town in India today. Volumes of smoke from the cement factory in the distance clouded the sky.

At the barrack-like office of the forest department, I met Fateh Singh Rathore, the wildlife warden, and asked him for the necessary permission to spend some time in the Ranthambhore Tiger Reserve. He looked me up and down, as if assessing whether the animals would approve or not. I passed the test, hired a jeep and a driver and was on my way by the afternoon. A metal road ran parallel to a range of hills and, after a few kilometres along it, we turned off on to a dirt track between the rise of two hills. And then it came, the first excitement. Below a sheer rocky stone cliff, an ancient gate which once must have had supporting fort walls, long since crumbled. It was a royal entrance to the tiger reserve, almost as if it had survived just for this. As we passed through, the vegetation thickened on either side of the road. The sounds changed; birdsong invaded the silence, mixing incongruously with the groan of the jeep. And it was in the glow that I saw the Ranthambhore fort extending upwards from one of the cliffs, as if man had decided to just chisel a bit of nature, the upper fringe of the rock, but not disturb or fight it.

The driver explained that we had arrived at our destination. I tried to look around me, through the trees as it were, for signs of life, but my eyes were not accustomed to seeing in the forest, which requires a tension and skill not easy to come by. But I could see the peepal and the spreading banyan and wondered whether any of them had lived through the days of

Ranthambhore's glory. My speculations were disturbed as the jeep braked suddenly when a male blue bull (from the antelope family) sauntered across the road with a quiet majesty. We were now speeding below the massive fort standing on a gigantic rock which seemed to extend for many miles. As we crossed the last rise the scene in front of us changed dramatically, the hills giving way to an expanse of lake land interspersed with low hills and large sheets of water, the largest clothed almost entirely in giant pink and white lotuses. It was the pink of the pichhavais and innumerable folk paintings, a pink I had never believed was possible before. It was too much to take in all at once, this mix of history and nature. Suddenly, we branched off the road and I thought we were plunging straight into the largest banyan tree I had ever seen. Two of its hundreds of roots formed a natural gateway to the forest rest house which was a structure rising out of a miniature painting with its arches and low domes. The driver explained that Jogi Mahal had once been the residence of a temple priest. I rushed up the steps leading to the wide terrace and then through the arched doorway and at my feet as it were, lay that lake of lotuses which I had glimpsed earlier. The water lapped against the walls of the rest house, in the distance crocodiles lay sunbathing, one with its jaws open as if yawning. A herd of spotted deer grazed at the edge of the far side of the lake and a large group of sambar were moving downhill towards the water. Some were already standing there, nibbling at the lotus leaves. To the right of the lake were the remains of old palaces and guard posts. I turned around on my feet, looking backwards and there was the spreading banyan tree with the fort as a backdrop, filling the horizon with its imposing presence. It was a hypnotic moment of great intensity, of indescribable beauty which was, suddenly, quite exhausting.

Fortunately, the rest house was simple, appointed without fuss and without the usual garishness of most rest houses. Thankfully, electricity had not yet reached Jogi Mahal and it was still safe from the onslaught of modernization, though one wondered for how long. By now, the forest staff had collected around: Laddu, the tiger tracker; Ramu, the wireless operator; Prahlad Singh, the driver. The forest was linked with wireless at various points for better watch and administration.

We lit a fire as darkness descended and the crackling of the firewood joined the nocturnal sounds of the forest. The crickets, the nightjars and the Spotted Owls had woken up to the dark. Small bats swooped out of their hiding places and the large wings of the flying fox flapped above us, Laddu sat talking about his encounters with tigers—how you could spot them in darkness of the night—Ramu, about the spirits and ghosts that inhabited the forest and Prahlad about ancient spears that lay embedded in the fort walls.

It was my introduction to the life of the forest and the forest alphabet. Without warning, this relaxed atmosphere was unexpectedly, for me at least, shot through with a loud boom that echoed off the fort walls, sustaining itself for five to ten seconds. This was the scare-call of the sambar deer, I was told. I took fright and jumped up, much to the amusement of the forest staff. For them it was normal, the sambar warning their families in the area that a tiger or a leopard was on the prowl. The predator had been smelt and the others should seek safety. Again and again it came, that booming sound. Torches were flashed into the darkness just in case the predator was lurking around the rest house. Then the spotted deer's shrill screech echoed across the waters of the lake which meant that the predator had moved on from wherever he had been. Everyone was automatically on the alert and I felt little shivers run down my spine as the tension mounted.

The deer is gifted with a keenly sharpened sense of smell, far more sensitive than that of the tiger or the leopard, so its warnings go out well in time. The predators, on the other hand, have a vision which burns through the darkness, enabling them to stalk for food with ease. This is the interdependence of the forest, the way nature finds its balance and ensures the survival of the fittest, sad though it may seem.

The silence deepened, the calls died as suddenly as they had started. The predator had obviously moved out of the area, the forest relaxed once again, the nocturnal sounds resumed their fury and one already felt a part of it all, although a very small part. In fact, it was a kind of metamorphosis from Delhi where, basically, one lived in total isolation from nature. In the forest, though, you are suddenly put in your place. You are not alone but you cannot afford to be wayward.

We were up with the sun the next day and the light was startling to begin with. It seemed to blind the eyes after all the straining of the night before, which now I thought I had all but imagined. I wondered which unfortunate creature had crossed the predator's path. We set out in the early morning glow, through the roots of the banyan, past the peacocks pecking at the earth, talking to each other in that most incredible tone, on towards the small habitation at the base of the fort. There was a tea shop and a few huts which belonged to the priests who manned the Ganesh temple up the hill. Large numbers of pilgrims wound their way up laboriously for spiritual elevation. Suddenly, the jeep was brought to a halt by a man gesticulating wildly. He told us that in the night a leopard had driven a young male buffalo up the road.

We jumped out of the jeep to verify the story, because this was headline news. Sure enough, the leopard's pug marks were clearly visible in the dirt track. This is how the movement patterns of the animals can be tracked. They are quite easily distinguishable—the deer, the wild boar, the sambar, the cheetal, the peacock and, of course, the tiger. We followed the pug marks for one furlong. The buffalo's tracks were ahead of it. The poor thing must have tried to gallop down with the leopard close at heel. At the end of the furlong, the tracks stopped and an occasional one was seen branching off into the forest. There was a patch of blood, some buffalo hair—the leopard had certainly killed.

Cautiously, we followed the increasing trails of blood and there, a hundred metres up, lay the half-eaten carcass of the buffalo. The leopard must have dragged it up, to eat in comparative peace and security. Vultures hung overhead, jackals were edging closer to the kill—for it is over the carcass that all the predators and scavengers meet, in a way. In a couple of hours, nothing would be left of the buffalo except for a few bones and scraps which would be consumed by the hyenas at night. I was asked to take a closer look at the carcass. The tooth marks of the leopard were clearly visible, the buffalo's belly had been split open, a sure sign of a leopard kill. It takes some getting used to—this conflict in the raw, the hunger, the chase, the kill, the scavenging, in an endless cycle.

The dirt track meandered around the lake. Behind us, ever present, was the backdrop of the Ranthambhore fort, silent with its memories of battles and wars which once raged around its ramparts.

Just then we came upon the second lake, larger than first, called Rajbagh. In the centre of it stood a palace with a road leading up [to it]. There was the usual courtyard with chattris and terraces at the four corners. I sat in one and looked out, savouring the sounds of the parakeets and treepies, the cool breeze wafting up the lake, crocodiles basking in the early morning sun, a group of wild boar digging in the wet soil, the spotted deer and the sambar grazing peacefully without fear. Perhaps this scene had remained unchanged for hundreds of years.

As we set out again, we were able to see the animals at closer quarters. The spotted deer is forever on the alert, limbs ready to dart away at a second's notice; the sambar has long ears and a doleful expression in his eyes and this one stared at us wide eyed with curiosity; the blue bull wears a coat of steel grey and the male, particularly, has a regal gait. The wild boar snorted past, almost as if ashamed of its looks. In the distance we spied a solitary chinkara, the gazelle, petite, elegant with its large, sensitive eyes, poised for imminent flight, an example of physical perfection.

The Ranthambhore forest is a dry deciduous forest, turning a rich, lush green during the monsoons and reduced to dry, parched twigs under the hot summer sun which drinks up every drop of moisture, except for the lakes. The terrain is unique, with its black, rocky cliffs and the forested hills, sprinkled here and there with old walls and crumbling palaces, relics of a forgotten glory. At the far end, you can see where the Vindhyas thin out and the Aravalli hills surface above the ground, extending all the way to Delhi. It is ideal tiger country, I was being told, when suddenly the jeep screeched to a halt. Prahlad Singh had seen tiger pug marks. We jumped out and there they were, large and clear. We followed them on foot with mounting anticipation but after three kilometres, they branched off without a trace. I was to learn later how evasive the tiger is and how difficult to sight, requiring great reserves of patience and perseverance.

The first ten days just rolled by, ten days of initiation into forest rites. Waking to the sound of peacocks and other birds, watching the ungulate population grazing as if without a care in the world, the crocs basking forever in the sunshine and we chasing not butterflies but pug marks, pug marks of leopards and tigers, studying all the signs, the indications of kills from the hovering vultures to the hungry jackals and the sounds of the crows.

The evenings were as spectacular, with the animals coming down to the lakes for a drink, the peacocks flying off to their perches in the trees to sleep, in constant fear of the cat family, the crickets becoming vocal and resounding scare-calls of the deer telling us that the predator was on the move and so were we, looking, searching, peering, walking, straining for that one encounter with the tiger or the leopard but seeing instead only the other nocturnal animals: the jungle cat, the civet cat, and the amazing porcupine with all its quills upright in self-defence.

We would return exhausted and defeated, huddle around the fire, eat vast quantities of whatever was available and listen again to stories of the forest, of other encounters, which only added to the acuteness of my frustration. I had two nights of possibility left and hope was fast ebbing when a sharp sambar call startled me from my tea-drinking. I turned around and flashed my torch and just twenty-five feet to my right two sharp green eyes were reflected in the beam of light. The tiger at last! But no. It was a hyena, loping past the rest house. No wonder this was the first and last call of the sambar, just a mild warning for mothers to keep their babies close in case the hyena snatched them away because that is all the damage it can inflict. I felt good. I had seen the hyena, my first, and the forest was full of the invisible presence of the tiger and leopard, just a flashing glimpse of them as I have described earlier.

At the end of my second trip, I decided to make one last determined attempt and set off in the jeep with Prahlad and Laddu. The jeep was open, the air chilled us to the bone as we sped through the forest flashing our torches on either side. As we came down an incline in between two sharp cliffs we switched off the engine to listen, to listen to every sound that came to us. This is the best way to gauge the presence of the predator from the direction of the call. And the call came, of the deer, wild and shrill, shattering the night with its intensity. It came again and again, forty-five times in all. Its nearness confirmed that the predator could not be far from us. We moved slowly forwards flashing the torch and there it sat in all its splendour, a leopard, feasting on a female spotted deer. We stopped the engine. It looked at us with disdain and continued eating, unperturbed by our presence. It was about seven-and-a-half feet in length, with the spots on its glossy coat glowing in the torchlight. Suddenly, as if satiated, it got up and walked towards us, or rather, towards the banyan tree, climbed a branch, settled down comfortably, and watched. Leopards are very shy and keep away from jeeps. We may have disturbed it.

I was told that it is rare to see a leopard feeding on its natural kill. We were mesmerized by the scene and sat deathly still, not daring even to breathe because the slightest movement might make the animal suspicious. But Prahlad was taking no risks and decided to drive away: disturbing a predator at its meal is just not on. We were intruders and had interrupted the most important moment of the leopard's day because stalking and killing is a complex operation requiring planning, skill and physical effort of some proportion. It was clearly my lucky day and although it may sound like pure fantasy, I did see the two top predators in that one night.

It was not very long after we had left the leopard that straight ahead of us, on that very road, we saw a tiger walking. Just walking. I could only see its back, but what I saw cast a spell which was to become a passion in the coming months. We followed slowly and it stepped aside and into a clearing about ten to fifteen feet away, watching us intently, completely relaxed. We switched off the engine and caught it in the light. It was gorgeous, however cliché the word may sound, the yellow and the white and the black. I felt fear draining out of me and longed to get out of the jeep and just stroke its coat. But I knew that would be disastrous.

Transfixed though we were by the scene, we knew we had to leave

A tiger inside the palace pavilion of Rajbagh.

before we disturbed the whole area. That one long glimpse, in a sense, was the beginning of a long relationship which, I hope, will be a fruitful one for the tiger. What this species has suffered at the hands of man, of rajas and poachers alike, is too sordid a story to be recounted. Wanton destruction for the sake of that grotesque photograph of the maharaja standing, gun in hand, beside the bullet-ridden body of this king of the jungle, or selling skins to adorn a human body, has nearly destroyed the species.

We were to learn a great deal from Fateh Singh who had an uncanny rapport with the forest and its animals, the tiger in particular, and a reservoir of knowledge and experience. These were to guide us on subsequent trips when we descended on the Ranthambhore Tiger Reserve, armed with cameras and notebooks so that something of what we felt and learnt could be communicated to others. {Ranthambhore, 1976}

PADMINI

We were back in Delhi, the feel of the forest still with us, odd bits of information buzzing in our heads, waiting for our next opportunity, the call, as it were. It came soon enough with the new year—1977. There was a ring at the doorbell of my house—a telegram for me, from Fateh Singh. 'Come immediately,' it said. It was a mad rush as Tejbir Singh and I organized ourselves to leave in the morning. We took the train and were met by an excited and jumpy Fateh at the other end. His first words (and I still remember them) were, 'A tigress has been spotted with five cubs.' Fateh Singh then spent some time explaining. His experience had begun several months ago when he first set eyes on the tigress, whom we now decided to name Padmini.

The year in which her story starts is 1976. Padmini was then a four-year-old tigress in the Ranthambhore Tiger Reserve of Rajasthan and Fateh Singh was the assistant field director, when he sighted her in a very pregnant state, her belly bulging hugely. This is cause for great excitement to any field man in a forest: a new lot of tiger cubs to be born.

Driving his jeep near the vacated Lakarda village on an evening in December 1976, he sighted some pug marks. A careful examination of the tracks immediately revealed that a tigress was moving with a large brood—unbelievable in many ways and rare for any tiger reserve in India. A mother and five cubs! He could tell the approximate age from the size of the marks and was beside himself with excitement. Some time ago, this would have been the most unlikely place for the find. When still inhabited, the noise of the cattle, the shouts and cries of men, women and children kept all the animals miles away. There was no possibility of shelter as all the grass and trees around had been destroyed by the villagers. But Lakarda was now deserted; after the shift, the grass had come up slowly and nature had taken over the deserted settlement. Animal life moves freely in and around it now. It is here that we believe Padmini gave birth to her family.

An immediate problem was keeping track of the movements of the tigers for, so far, no satisfactory method has been evolved to do this. (An experiment was conducted in neighbouring Nepal to determine the movement of a tiger by collaring the animal. A collar with a transmitter attached to it emits signals which allow one to track the animal's movement. In India, this experiment was conducted on other animals such as the nilgai, cheetal and sambar; the first attempt with a tiger resulted in a casualty, and the experiment was abandoned. Also, the major concern of Indian wildlife experts has been on keeping man's interference with the ecological system in the forest down to a minimum.) Fateh's only recourse was to keep track of the movements of the tigress by following her pug marks and her kills, thereby attempting to establish her territory and pinpoint her presence in different areas.

As though aware that she was 'marked', Padmini began a game of hide-and-seek with him, complicating an already difficult situation.

Although Fateh Singh had been seeing masses of fresh pug marks—indications of a large family of tigers—no actual sighting had been made. Somehow, Padmini's excessive caution had to be broken down, and some kind of rapport developed between her and her human observers.

It was in early January 1977 that the tension was broken and Padmini first showed herself. Fateh was sitting in a hide near the village, hoping for some sign of the family which had been active in the area during the morning. It was twilight; the first stars were appearing in the sky. The crickets and the nightjars had started their chatter. An icy wind was blowing. Suddenly, the stillness of the night was shattered by the shrieking death cry of a buffalo. Immediately afterwards, a brooding silence enveloped the forest. Not a sound was heard in the dark.

Fateh moved off quickly towards the noise of the buffalo when the lights of the jeep caught Padmini head-on. Approximately nine feet in length, with a beautiful coat and in the best of health, she stared at him and snarled. Suddenly, in a flurry of movement, five young tigers ran across the road, disappearing into the bushy country around. It seemed as if the cubs had rushed into hiding on their mother's indication. Padmini watched Fateh carefully and with a measured tread walked away, leaving his heart beating faster at this first sighting of the complete brood. It was also the first sign of success after a patient wait of many days. The dawn brought Fateh back to the same area in the freezing cold. Early morning frost covered large stretches of the forest; his hands were numb driving the jeep, his eyes smarting with the chill, but there she was, at the spot of the night before, sitting over her prey. To her right lay a full-size lame buffalo which she had killed the night before. Only a portion from the hind legs had been eaten. None of her cubs were in sight. Padmini watched Fateh suspiciously. This was amazing behaviour for, during the day, tigers will normally find dense shelter to sleep in. But Padmini sat alert—she was guarding the meat. She knew that every ounce mattered and she would have to keep continuous vigil to prevent it from being scavenged by vultures, jackals or hyenas. Because of the special situation her whole pattern of behaviour had undergone a change: she was spending the day alert instead of asleep.

At about mid-day when Fateh heard a jackal call from the left of the tree, he realized that this was a definite sign that the cubs were moving towards their mother. The jackal alarm call is warning of the presence of a predator. Sure enough, within ten minutes two cubs appeared under the tree. Fateh was unable to photograph them because of the awkward angle: the branches obstructed his vision. The tigress suddenly lifted her head and seemed to signal to her offspring, who vanished instantly. Once again the jackal called, after which silence prevailed. The tigress relaxed. During all this, Fateh had stuck to only observing the scene. Now, keeping a certain distance, he perched on the branch of a tree to keep watch and to photograph. On the first click of the camera, Padmini made a threatening charge, stopping directly under the branch where Fateh sat. For a brief moment, the thought of man and tiger confronting each other on the same branch crossed Fateh's mind. But tigers very rarely climb trees, unlike other members of the cat family. Secure in this knowledge, Fateh clicked on. Padmini charged again but half-heartedly, demonstrating the tremendous power that this magnificent animal is capable of. Convinced that the man on the tree meant no harm and confident of her own prowess, she seemed to be ignoring him. She snoozed, dozed, yawned, rolled over, nibbled the meat. The suspicion had worn off. It was as though she had started accepting his presence and was behaving naturally. For five days, from early morning to late evening, Fateh sat watching her, but all through she kept guard with no sign of her cubs, who obviously only came at night after he had left. The carcass of the buffalo slowly diminished and on the last day hardly anything was left, but she still sat guard. All her actions conformed to the needs of her cubs. Not an ounce of flesh was to be scavenged or wasted as long as her cubs could continue feeding on it undisturbed.

This is when we came into the picture, to add to the mounting excitement and tension. Were Padmini's young ones determined to remain invisible to us or were our efforts going to prove successful?

During the months of January and February we saw Padmini often. She was a picture of confidence and less and less bothered by our presence so long as we maintained a certain distance. The cubs kept out of sight but we were fortunate enough to get fleeting glimpses of them as they rushed by and scattered. But noticeably longer stretches of observation were possible each successive time as the cubs seemed to be more secure in our presence.

We were now able to distinguish between the sexes and found that Padmini had three male and two female cubs. But the real question was, could Padmini manage to hunt and kill for herself as well as provide for five growing tigers, and for how long? It was a mammoth task under any circumstances. An approximate idea of the total consumption of meat would be an excellent indication of the problems facing a tiger family: Padmini had to ensure an average-to-minimum consumption of sixty-five to eighty kilograms of meat every few days.

The young ones were of slightly different sizes. There was one dominant male cub, tougher and fitter than his brothers and sisters. He seemed more venturesome, confident and courageous, especially in our presence; we decided to name the male cubs, Akbar, Hamir and Babar.

The female cubs were more fragile: smaller than Akbar and a shade smaller than Babar and Hamir, they seemed definitely more delicate and feminine. There was a slight difference even between the two of them. The smallest, whom we called Begum, was not in the best of health and gave us some worry. During our first few glimpses, she was always lagging behind the rest of the family. Poor little Begum—she was part of a very natural phenomenon in the wild where the youngest in a family is totally dominated by her brothers and sisters. It was obvious that she was getting the smallest share of the meat after a kill and that she was the shyest, eating last of all. It was a sad situation and we were worried about her chances of survival.

The other female, whom we called Laxmi, was in much better condition but always one step behind her brothers.

Now that the entire family had been identified, the complex task of assimilating and analysing the different behaviour patterns of each member began. Normally, much confusion could arise in studying such a large family and distinguishing one from the other. What is important to note is that Padmini, Akbar, Babar, Hamir, Laxmi and Begum all had different characteristics, facial expressions and most important of all, different markings. Tigers can be distinguished by the markings on their foreheads and around the sides of their faces. This is a sure method of recognition. After taking a series of photographs, it was possible to enlarge the face, study the pattern of stripes around the mouth and forehead and slowly be able to tell the difference between the members of the family. The stripes on the body also vary considerably.

Our worst suspicions regarding little Begum were confirmed during the last week of February. In the evening, we had spotted Padmini moving through the area and had decided to camp out on the incline in the hope of seeing some developments. This was an important area for water and we felt

Padmini's cubs strike different poses around us. We spent one year following this family.

the family might come to drink before their siesta during the day. We had spent the night at an observation post in the hope of viewing the family in the early hours of the morning. It was a beautiful spot with patches of tall grass interspersed with shrubs, not thick enough to obstruct the vision and right below us was a dried riverbed next to which there was a waterhole. The family had been extremely active here; it was very close to Lakarda village where Padmini had first been sighted.

We woke up with the dawn. The birds had started their chatter, the morning was cold and crisp. We crept along the ground to the edge of the incline and looked below. And there they were: Padmini walking through the grass even before the first rays of the sun were out behind her, with Akbar, followed by Babar and Hamir and then Laxmi—but not a sign of little Begum. Had she got lost somewhere or was it possible that in the last week she had been unable to cope with the pressure of living and had given up and let nature take its course? We kept putting the thought out of our minds as we watched Padmini and her four young ones disappear into the forest. There was still a faint hope that Begum had strayed and might join them later. In any case, we decided that this was an important development and we must somehow confirm it. So, by evening, we tied a buffalo near Lakarda to study the pug marks and view the family closely. The time was 5 p.m. When we returned around 11 p.m., the buffalo was dead and partly

eaten. On hearing the sound of jeep, the family had moved away to a more secure position in the grass.

Using our powerful searchlight we identified Padmini sitting beside her female cub, Laxmi. Nearby, with a slightly snarly expression on his face, sat dominant Akbar. A little behind were Babar and Hamir. Of little Begum there was no sign. What we feared had obviously happened. Little Begum was no more; nature had eased her out. She had been the littlest in the family and her health was affected by her position in the family hierarchy. She had not been able to get enough food and had probably just wasted away.

THE NILGAI KILL

The most exciting encounter I ever witness involving tiger and nilgai takes place on a chilly November morning in 1982. We are driving around the third lake when, in the distance, we see a frantic tracker on a bicycle, gesticulating wildly as he approaches us. He shouts, 'There is a tree full of crows and I have just seen a tiger feeding on a blue bull by Rajbagh.' We rush off and, sure enough, come to a tree with nearly fifty crows on it. Below it sits Padmini with three fourteen-month-old cubs around her. Nearby lies the carcass of a huge adult male bull which must weigh at least 250 kilograms, possibly more. The carcass is far too heavy for her to move and Padmini is nibbling at the rump, a small portion of which has been eaten. The two cubs sitting behind her get up in an attempt to approach the kill, but as they come close, she rises, coughs sharply and slaps one of them across the face. The cub submits, rolling over on its back, and settles down near her restlessly while the other cub starts to eat from the rump. Padmini seems to be saying, quite clearly, 'One at a time.'

At 7.30 a.m., Padmini gets up, grabs the nilgai by the neck and tries to drag it away, but its foot gets stuck in a forked tree root. She settles down to eat some more, and half an hour later tries again—this time dragging the carcass about eight metres. Now she permits the second cub to eat. The third lies some thirty metres away in the distance. Crows chatter incessantly and a group of vultures circles while others sit on a nearby tree. The crows fly in and around in an attempt to pick up scraps of meat but twice Padmini charges them. A single vulture flops down but in a flash he, too, is charged and takes flight.

Soon after this, Padmini drags the carcass about ten metres further up the rise of a hill. We follow quickly as the terrain is easy here and accessible to a jeep. The great advantage of the dhok forest is its excellent visibility, and scanning the area we now see Laxmi, Padmini's female cub from her litter of 1976. We now have five tigers spread out at different distances around the carcass, with Padmini and Laxmi closest to it. There is much getting up and sitting down and Laxmi twice marks the trunk of a tree. Now Padmini gets up, sniffs a tree, spray-marks it and walks towards her nearest cub, nuzzling it briefly. She then turns around and walks past Laxmi, snarling at her before grabbing the neck of the nilgai and pulling it farther up the hill. Two of her cubs are sleeping in the distance, but soon all three rise and circle out of sight. Padmini and Laxmi are lying side by side near the carcass.

A few minutes later, Padmini gets up and walks down the slope of the hill towards the lake. Laxmi moves towards the carcass and starts to feed.

It is 11.00 a.m. We follow Padmini as she moves towards the edge of the second lake and flops into a patch of water. She drinks a little, rolls around and gives herself a good soaking. After twenty minutes she rises and moves into the long grass. Sounds of snarling and growling are heard and the faint outline of two tigers can be seen moving in it. Padmini soon emerges from the grass and sits by the roadside.

We leave her there and go back to the nilgai. Laxmi is eating but, surprisingly, there is now another adult tigress sitting nearby. It is Nick Ear, a female from Padmini's second litter. At noon, Padmini appears from the rear, marks a tree and moves towards the kill. She and Laxmi cough at each other. Padmini sits and snarls at Laxmi who moves off towards Nick Ear and settles down on her side to sleep. Padmini also dozes off but with a watchful eye on the crows perched on the branches. At 12.30 p.m., the dominant cub returns from the lakeside and sits at the kill, nibbling at the fast-diminishing rump while Padmini watches alertly.

At 1.00 p.m., the cub moves off and rolls on his back before flopping onto his side to sleep. Padmini gets up and chews on the carcass for some fifteen minutes, then she too moves off again towards the lake. Laxmi rises and settles near the carcass. At 2.00 p.m., Padmini returns to her original position and a grimacing Laxmi moves back. From our rear, two more of the cubs emerge. There are now six tigers in front of us. The sight is unbelievable.

But more is to come. About forty-five metres away, amidst growling and snarling, yet another female, Nasty, appears, growling continuously as she approaches the carcass. She is the seventh tiger, but this time one without any kin link to Padmini. Time seems to stand still, but then at 3.00 p.m., we spot a large male walking along the edge of the hill. He sits down some distance away, and after carefully studying him with our binoculars, we discover that it is Akbar, the dominant male of Padmini's first litter. And behind him, with thudding hearts, we see yet another tiger, but at this range we cannot identify it.

Fateh and I look at each other in near hysteria. Nine tigers surround us at varying distances from the nilgai. Hardly daring to breathe, our eyes switch from tiger to tiger. No eating is taking place. Four are sleeping, two are grooming, and two are watching the kill. One is on its back, paws in the air. Padmini seems to be completely in command of the group and is obviously the one who killed the nilgai. Soon after 3.30 p.m., Nick Ear moves towards the kill and eats for some twenty-five minutes. She then moves off and Padmini's dominant cub arrives to feast. Laxmi also decides to eat but a sharp snarl from Padmini sends her off. After the cub has eaten for fifteen minutes he moves off, and Laxmi comes in to eat.

So far, we have seen five different tigers eating, but only one at a time and all strictly controlled by Padmini. There seem to be one male and two females in her third litter. Laxmi now moves off towards a dry stream bed from where cheetal alarm calls are sounding. Perhaps her own cubs are hidden there as we have seen no sign of them. She vocalizes six times before moving out of sight. The time is 4.30 p.m. and the shades of evening are taking over. At 5.20 p.m., we leave the hill after some ten uninterrupted hours of quite extraordinary observation. The next morning, on returning at 7.00 a.m., I find five tigers—Laxmi, Padmini and her three cubs—sitting around the kill with just the head and rib cage of the nilgai left. After chewing for forty minutes, they disappear over a rise and into a nullah.

Now only the crows are left, picking at bits of bone. We leave. It has been an incredible twenty-four hours. I have never come across a description of a scene like the one we have just witnessed—where nine tigers have fed on the same carcass, totally controlled by a dominant female. It would appear that Padmini had made the kill but as several other tigers were also present in the area, she took a decision to share the carcass. As it happened, all except two of the tigers were sons and daughters from her various litters. But she had total control and dominance over the situation. Not once did she permit two tigers to eat together, thereby preventing any conflict that could have arisen.

To find nine tigers around a kill is a rarity, and I think the fact that seven were related means that there is the possibility of strong kinship links among tigers and that these may be sustained over long periods of time. I think tigers easily recognize another individual, be it brother, sister or mother. A great deal more observation is needed for conclusive evidence on kinship links and their role, but this example shows that tigers can congregate without conflict around a natural kill—and with a female in full control of the feeding process. {1982}

THE AGGRESSION OF NASTY

Aggression between tigers occurs most commonly around food and the process of feeding, especially when adult animals feed together. However, such situations are rare.

Not surprisingly, there have been times when we, the observers, have attracted hostility. There was the time when the tigress Nasty became very aggressive towards human beings. This was during the first five months of 1983. Nasty charged us seventeen times during these months—and not always when we could see her!

I remember one occasion when a burst of alarm calls had me moving rapidly towards the sound. I switched off the engine near a patch of tall grass and scanned the landscape, listening intently. Sambar and cheetal alarm calls echoed around Rajbagh and the monkeys were chattering incessantly on a tree. Suddenly, I heard the grass rustling to my right and had a momentary glimpse of Nasty charging the jeep. I immediately started the engine and put the jeep into reverse gear. She stopped, snarling, tail twitching and ears held back, and I sat some hundred metres away, watching. Then, for no apparent reason, she charged again and chased me for another hundred metres, after which I decided to leave the area, almost paralysed by the shock of the charge. I still have not fathomed the reason for her aggression. Annoyance at a jeep? Her period of oestrus? An injury? Or just a moment of anger? It could have been anything. But her aggression ended during the middle of 1983 and she never charged us again. Genghis once charged our jeep, ending up only a metre or so away and I thought for a moment he might take over the wheel. But these charges were threats and never culminated in an actual attack. {1983}

GENGHIS, THE MASTER KILLER

During 1983-84, Ranthambhore witnessed an extraordinary and quite exceptional form of tiger predation when one particular resident male developed a technique for attacking and killing his prey in the water, concentrating his activities around the three lakes. Nowhere in the literature of the past have we been able to find any other account of a tiger behaving in this way. As a strategist, he was unmatched—an innovator. We called him Genghis.

By early March 1984, Genghis was a regular feature there and on many occasions we found him camouflaged in the tall grass that surrounds the lake. On one such occasion, a group of wild boar unsuspectingly approached him. In a flash, he leapt and pounced on a piglet and swatted another with his paws. Carrying them one at a time, he entered the grass to eat. We found him the next morning protecting the scraps of meat left over from his feast. He was exceedingly aggressive then and charged our jeep once, roaring in anger. By 11.00 a.m., after consuming the leftovers, he moved to Rajbagh where he went to sleep in the grass. A couple of hours later, four sambar came around the edge of the lake and as they approached him, he charged out of the grass, giving chase but unsuccessfully. He went back into the grass where he remained until sunset.

Late one morning a few days later, we found Genghis walking towards Malik Talao where he disappeared into the tall grass. One whole side of the third lake was surrounded by dense grass, growing right down to the water's edge. We decided to spend the day watching the lake and settled down in the cover of some bushes with our notebooks and camera equipment.

At 11.30 a.m., a group of four adult sambar approached the lake shore.

Genghis goes at full speed after a group of sambar deer.

Immediately, Genghis popped his head out of the grass and started moving diagonally through it in the direction of the deer. Just as he reached the edge of the cover, a peahen burst into flight nearby. Startled by the sound, one of the sambar turned—and spotted the tiger. As the deer started to stamp and bellow an alarm call, Genghis charged, but the bird had ruined his attack. The range was too great, and as the sambar leapt away, calling frantically, he broke off the charge and, with an expression of annoyance, padded slowly back into the cover of the grass thicket.

Despite the summer heat, the lake was strangely quiet for much of the afternoon. A small herd of cheetal grazed on the far side of the lake; a few sambar entered the shallows, grazed a while, and then drifted away, but there was little activity in our immediate vicinity. A Golden Oriole chirped away on a nearby tree and a pair of Paradise Flycatchers settled at the edge of the lake to drink. I had almost given up hope of the sambar returning. But then, just after 5.00 p.m., two groups of sambar appeared—approaching from opposite ends of the lake and wading steadily towards the centre, right opposite our observation point.

A slight movement stirred the tall grass at the far side of the lake where we knew Genghis lay hidden. A face appeared. He had moved right to the edge of the thicket and was peering out, studying the sambar with intense concentration. For several minutes he stood there, motionless, like a statue.

The next thirty minutes were some of the most tense and exciting moments I have ever lived through. Our sweating hands gripped our cameras and notebooks as we waited, with hearts thumping, for the tiger to make his move. With incredible patience, Genghis waited, measuring the distance separating him from the sambar grazing peacefully in the water. And then he charged. In front of our furiously clicking cameras he crashed through the few remaining metres of long grass and plunged into the water. The lake seemed to erupt in an explosion of spray. Bounding through the water he made for a small group of hinds and their fawns, then changed his direction to concentrate his attack on one terrified fawn that had got separated from its mother in the panic. The young deer was doomed from that moment. Covering the last few metres with swift, powerful strokes, Genghis pounced, driving his victim under the surface then reappearing seconds later with the fawn's neck clenched in a killer grip.

We watched in amazement. Never before had we seen a tiger even attempt to launch an attack in the waters of the lake, nor was it something we had ever come across in old accounts. Was this just a temporary aberration or were we seeing something new?

We left the lake at dusk in a state of elation. We had witnessed an astonishing feat, a successful hunt in water. Even better, we had captured the entire attack on film. Genghis was now making effective use of the area of the lakes and utilizing it fully as a hunting ground. He had somehow managed to use the water to his own advantage, unlike the surprised sambar which had lost vital seconds watching the tiger bounding after it through the water. The camouflage of the tall grass was perfect. Genghis was almost showing off. He was even ready to attack the sambar after having killed and eaten only a few hours earlier. And this was not just an unusual day. Genghis spent twenty-four days between the second week of March and the second week of April using the same strategy in Malik Talao. He killed six young sambar. This strategy was obviously effective on the younger animals who seemed to lose precious time in their confusion. But the summer heat was increasing and the water level in Malik Talao was dropping rapidly.

By early April, there was a wide gap between the grass and the water and Genghis's success was diminishing. He now had to cover quite a distance on dry land before hitting the water, and the sambar had more time in which to make their escape. In the second week of April, we witnessed one of the last successful kills that Genghis made in Malik Talao.

In response to the changing situation, Genghis switched his activities to Padam Talao, still using his new strategy of attacking in the water. Padam Talao was much larger than Malik Talao, and on most of its shoreline there was still the cover of tall grass thickets. Naturally, we followed, and soon discovered that the best vantage point from which to observe the attacks was Jogi Mahal itself, which is located on the edge of the lake. Besides charging into the water to kill, Genghis also tried two other strategies. In the first, he would see a group of sambar from the grass and then come right up to the edge of the water, out in the open, to watch them, causing the sambar to bolt in alarm. As this lake is large, it is not possible for the sambar to cross from one side to the other with ease. Instead, they invariably bolted towards the corners, and Genghis would attempt to cut off these exits and make his kill as the deer fled from the lake. To do this, he sometimes had to run nearly 150 metres, which at full pelt is an amazing feat and one that invited comparison with the technique of the cheetah. His other strategy was to swim out into the lake, pursuing groups of sambar with powerful strokes and causing much confusion. If, in this process, a single animal got separated, Genghis would overpower it with ease. He seemed to patrol all sides of the lake, constantly watching the entry and exit points. Sometimes in the terrible heat of the afternoon he would spot a group of sambar in one corner and then stalk them for some 200 metres before charging. If there was a jeep on the road watching the scene, he would stalk around the jeep, moving with it and using it as a cover for his final ambush.

But Genghis's hunting forays into the water were not without problems. Padam Talao had some sixty marsh crocodiles and as Genghis was killing in the water, he came into aggressive conflict with the larger ones. On one such occasion he was found sitting at the edge of the lake looking carefully at a spot in the water. He sat for several hours watching as crocodiles splashed and nibbled around what must have been the carcass of a sambar. Twice he swam back and attacked the spot where he thought there was a carcass, but in vain. On the third occasion, he went back into the water and in great fury smashed at the water with his forepaws. Dipping his head down, he quickly grabbed the carcass and made for shore. He had to swim at least forty-five metres and still managed to keep a grip on the carcass, which was of an adult sambar hind. While swimming, he wrapped a paw around the sambar's neck and used the other paw to stroke the water. Once, for a moment, he disappeared under the water with the carcass but quickly surfaced again and powerfully stroked his way to dry land. An amazing feat—a tiger swimming to shore with an animal weighing at least 200 kilograms. {1984}

THE INTENSITY OF COURTING AND MATING

I have never seen tigers mating. Fateh, who has now spent seventeen years in Ranthambhore, saw tigers mating for the first time on 9 April 1985. I had unfortunately left by then. But before describing this episode, using Fateh's notes, it is worthwhile going back to March when the two tigers seem to have met.

My diary notes for 6-7 March record that the large male tiger, Kublai, spent most of that forty-eight hour period in the vicinity of the lakes, and that pug mark evidence indicated the presence of the resident female, Noon, with him. It was the beginning of a long courtship, which we were to observe with mounting excitement and tension over a period of more than a month.

Every day we set out eagerly to search for evidence of the pair. Often we would find them together, sometimes lying contentedly a few metres apart, at other times nuzzling each other about the face. Sometimes we watched them interacting over sambar kills near the shores of the lake. And on one memorable occasion, they indulged in a mock fight—an incredible sight as these two magnificent animals reared up on their hindlegs, Kublai growling as he gently boxed Noon about the neck and head.

As the days passed, the pair became very vocal, often filling the night air with the widest range of growls, cries and moans I have ever heard. Kublai's interest seemed to be growing day by day. More and more frequently we would observe him nuzzling Noon or, when the two were apart, sniffing the ground where she had walked or rested. Their interactions seemed to be increasing in intensity all the time.

We could scarcely believe our good fortune. The pair remained in the area of the lakes through the rest of March and into April, providing us with a unique opportunity to observe the entire courtship without interruption. But the suspense was almost unbearable. None of us had ever seen the final act in this drama. Our one thought as we set off each morning was: 'Will this be the day?' But the days passed, and on 6 April, after thirty days of continuous observation, my time ran out and I was forced to leave Ranthambhore. Fateh's detailed notes provide us with a graphic account of the final chapter in this story.

The morning of 9 April is dark and stormy. Thick black clouds billow across the sky and a blustery wind kicks up swirls of dust along the shore of Rajbagh. A sambar carcass is floating in one of the pools, but there are no signs of tigers. Satisfied that Kublai and Noon are not in the immediate area, Fateh drives back to the resthouse, content to try again later. At four in the afternoon a radio message comes through, telling of alarm calls in the area of Rajbagh. Fateh rushes back to the lake and to the small pool where the carcass is lying. By now, a gale is blowing. Covered with a film of dust, he seeks the shelter of some trees.

At 5.20 p.m., Noon emerges from a thicket of grass and sits at the edge. She is soon followed by Kublai who reclines some metres away. Both tigers appear relaxed. Quite suddenly, Noon rises and strides rapidly to Kublai, who raises his head. Noon rubs her flank against him in an effort to get him to rise. He does, and she quickly settles in front of him, offering him her rear quarters. Immediately, Kublai mounts her and some fifteen seconds later, Noon growls sharply, followed by a few lower-pitched growls for another ten seconds. Then Kublai jumps off and Noon, after a sharp grunt, stands up and moves away. They both go and rest some metres away. Eleven minutes later, Noon rises again and moves quickly towards Kublai, seductively rubbing her head, and then her right flank, against his mouth. She then sits in front of him. Kublai stands again and mounts her. This time they are partially hidden by the grass thicket. Noon emits a sharp grunt and, in seconds, Kublai jumps off the snarling tigress.

Now Kublai moves right out of the grass and slowly walks around the edge of the lake. He pauses to stretch himself on the fallen trunk of a palm tree, and then walks on the trunk before moving to the edge of the water, close to the sambar carcass. He snarls viciously at a couple of crocodiles attempting to nibble at the carcass, and then settles down to watch against a backdrop of the red flowering tree, the 'flame-of-the-forest', with the flowers scattered around him on the grass. Fateh is astonished at the raw beauty of the scene from across the pool. Tiger, red flowers and sambar carcass are all reflected in the water, creating images of poetic intensity.

Noon quickly follows Kublai's path to the edge of the water. With a sharp snarl at a gliding crocodile, she encourages a response from Kublai by nuzzling him, sliding her flank against his and then sitting receptively at the edge of the water less than a metre in front of him. Kublai rises, seemingly aroused again by Noon's provocative position. He mounts her, sliding his forepaws down her back until they make contact with the ground near her forelegs. His head leans against the right side of her neck as if they were entwined. His hind legs remain half bent as his forelegs straddle Noon's neck. Her forelegs are fully stretched and the hind legs slightly bent. After fifteen seconds, Noon emits a sharp growl and Kublai grips the folds of skin around the nape of her neck. Some seconds later, she throws him off, snarling upwards aggressively. Carefully, they lick every inch of their rears, especially their genitals. Fifteen minutes later, Noon initiates another session of copulation in much the same way. The sun has set and the forest sounds change as the crickets take over. Way out in the distance, a Brown Fish Owl flies off in search of prey, and a pair of Golden Orioles flits across the sky, the bright yellow of their chests providing relief against a dull forest green.

Now Noon walks off around the edge of the lake. Kublai decides to follow, but he has gone only a few metres when the crocodiles return to the carcass and he decides to retrace his steps. Amidst much snarling, he settles down at the edge of the water, looking carefully at the carcass some three or four metres away. Noon is out of sight. After five minutes Kublai rises again as if to follow her, but the crocodile activity again forces him to retrace his steps. He seems caught between staying around the carcass and being with Noon. The light is slowly fading but minutes later Noon returns; again she rubs bodies with Kublai and they mate.

Kublai's interest in the sambar carcass is much greater than Noon's. She seems not in the least bothered about food. In the next half hour, they mate three more times. It looks unreal as their perfect reflections glint off the water. Night is slowly taking over. The time is 6.48 p.m. Fateh has watched eight copulations in eighty-eight minutes. It has been his most exciting observation ever of tiger behaviour. Awed by the power and beauty of the scene, he slowly drives back to Jogi Mahal. The next day there is no trace of the tigers. The saga is over.

Thirty-five days of regular interaction finally culminated in the mating of Kublai and Noon. Observations of matings are rare and very seldom recorded. Tigers obviously prefer privacy, free from the disturbance of human observers. In Ranthambhore, records show that mating occurs at all times of the year, with no definite or intense mating season. The tigress who conceives may not come into oestrus again for eighteen to twenty-two months, though there are exceptions to this. She spends a long period of time teaching and training her cubs. Those who do not conceive, or who lose their litters for some reason, will come into oestrus again anywhere between one month and three months later. However, these records are from zoos, and very little information is available on the tiger oestrus cycle in the wild.

FROM FATEH'S FIELD NOTES:
From 6 March to 9 April 1985, Kublai and Noon spent much of their time together. It was the preliminary phase of their courtship, and much of their

interaction was over food.

10 March, 1.20 p.m.: Noon drags ashore the carcass of a sambar hind she has killed in the shallows of Padam Talao. She has retained her vice-like grip on the throat, and the sambar's body trails between her forelegs and beneath her body. Once ashore, she pulls the carcass into long grass a hundred metres back from the lake in order to feed.

4.00 p.m.: Noon returns to the lake to quench her thirst and to soak in the cool water. Tigers often do this soon after making a kill, and also during feeding, particularly in hot weather. Noon is even more fond of the water than most and is often seen partly immersed.

4.20 p.m.: Noon suddenly rushes from the water and charges back to her kill, clearing a deep muddy wallow with one five-metre leap. She had probably seen a greedy treepie heading for the meat!

7.30 p.m.: A deep resonant 'aaoon' reverberates across the lake, soon followed by another. Kublai is moving towards Noon. Tiger sounds echo off the walls of the fort for another twenty minutes. Has Noon invited Kublai to the feast? Or has the male's appearance some days ago stimulated the tigress's oestrus cycle?

11 March, 6.45 a.m.: Noon is sitting some ten metres outside the grass and we suspect that Kublai has taken over her kill. She rises and moves tentatively towards the grass, but retreats again submissively in the face of a series of low rumbling growls. Later in the day, she tries to stalk another sambar but is unsuccessful, and for the rest of the day is kept away from the kill by Kublai, who remains in the grass, not even coming down to the lake to drink.

During this preliminary courtship, Kublai annexed at least four of Noon's kills, and only once was she able to snatch part of one back—while Kublai was taking a drink at the lake. He was firmly established as the dominant male and Noon's food intake suffered considerably.

9 April 1985 saw Fateh's seventeen years of painstaking observation rewarded when he was able to watch and record on film, the culmination of Kublai's month-long courtship of Noon.

5.30 p.m.: Kublai and Noon have already mated twice, but partly hidden in the dense grass. They now laze at the edge of the thicket indulging in protracted love-play. Noon nuzzles Kublai, they rub heads, and Kublai's paws touch the tigress's chest. She is standing while he remains sprawled on his side as she tries persistently to rouse him.

5.37 p.m.: Kublai leaves the grass and strolls off round the lake followed by Noon, who at one point overtakes him and leads the way. But their attention is caught by a sambar carcass floating in the water. They make no attempt to rush in and drag it out, but the presence of food so near brings their walk to an end and they remain on the shore nearby.

5.45 p.m.: Noon moves quickly to Kublai's side and with a brief nuzzling movement along his head and neck, she brushes her flank against him seductively. By this time, Noon was forcing a response from the male every fifteen minutes or so in her eagerness to mate.

5.48 p.m.: Noon has moved in front of Kublai and dropped into a receptive crouch. Immediately he moves into position over her.

5.49 p.m.: The pair mate, Kublai gripping the loose folds of skin on the side of Noon's neck with his canines. Coitus lasts some fifteen seconds.

The act is interrupted violently by Noon as she twists and snarls aggressively at the male, throwing him off before mating is completed.

6.12 p.m.: Yet another period of copulation takes place, despite the fact that Kublai has seen us and is watching us carefully. This time he does not grip her neck, and Noon is not aggressive; she lies at full stretch, her chin almost on the ground. Tigers copulate with some frequency and in this case the pair mated eight times between 5.20 and 6.48 p.m. {1985}

The tigress carrying her four-week-old cubs to a safer hideout. At this age, the cubs are helpless and require their mother's complete devotion.

THE DEVOTED MOTHER AND HER CUBS

Tigresses that do not conceive can come into oestrus again thirty to ninety days later. The gestation period is from ninety-five to one-hundred-and-fifteen days and the bulge of the tiger's belly is only clearly visible in the last few days of her pregnancy. At this point, she disappears from sight, and from our previous experience, sometimes remains unseen with her brood for ten to twelve months.

Early one morning, I was driving through the Semli Valley, wondering if Laxmi would show herself again. Dawn is a special time, with the play of light, wafting mist, the cool fragrant air, all clothing the forest with an unmatched perfection. Suddenly, I noticed the forest track was covered with fresh pug marks. I examined them. A large tigress with her tapering pad, followed by a mass of tiny pug marks—her brood—had walked ahead of us some minutes ago. They must be around. Could they be just ahead of me? It would be unusual for Laxmi to walk such young cubs down an open track. Usually this does not happen till the cubs are four to five months old. I inched the jeep forward, my eyes scanning both sides of the track for a glimpse of the family.

A few hundred metres ahead, I stop the jeep. It is time to wait for sounds of alarm. In the distance two sambar hinds move away gingerly, tails half-raised. A cheetal looks sharply towards the forest. It is motionless. My eyes are unable to pick out anything. The shrill alarm of a peacock breaks the silence. Another peacock picks up the call. After a few seconds the alarm call of the cheetal pierces my ears. Frenzied and frequent calling now surrounds me. Quietly, I watch the forest. It seems as if the tigers are walking towards the vehicle track. Suddenly, shades of tan and black emerge from the dull yellow of the forest. Laxmi appears with three tiny cubs. One of the cubs jumps across the road. It looks about two-and-a-half to three months old. I can hardly believe my eyes. It is my first glimpse ever of cubs this size. Laxmi settles down on the track for a few minutes. Her cubs look at me furtively from the cover of a bush. She soon rises and paces leisurely into the forest, followed by three scampering cubs. They move towards a network of ravines and disappear from sight. For me, it is a dream come true. I rush back to base, heart pounding with excitement. In near hysteria, I tell Fateh what I have seen. We sit down to plan strategies for the following weeks. The next morning, I find Laxmi sitting on a grass patch ten to fifteen metres from the forest track. Her three cubs surround her. One nuzzles her face, another rests against her back, the third watches us curiously. Very tentatively, it moves a little towards us before rushing back to the security of Laxmi. The cubs now turn their attention on each other, leaping into the air and knocking into each other. They then dash towards Laxmi. She licks one of them thoroughly, then lies on her side to suckle them. All three soon find the right teat and feed, stimulating the flow of milk with their tiny paws. I watch this remarkable spectacle for fifteen minutes. I have never seen such a display of love and warmth, such evidence of an amazing bond between a tigress and her cubs. {1985}

Noon picked up the art of hunting in water from Genghis. Here, she is in full flight after a sambar deer.

JOGI MAHAL: A DREAM LOCATION

Jogi Mahal was my favourite haunt and like home to me. I lived in this rest house on the edge of Padam Talao or Lotus Lake for years. The sweep of its balcony was probably the most impressive observation post to watch the natural world around. It was also utterly calm, peaceful and soul-stirring. I have watched many tigers from the balcony, both walking by and hunting in the shallow waters, but nothing could prepare me for the encounter I had in March 1985.

It was about 11 a.m. and I was sitting having a cup of coffee on the balcony of Jogi Mahal. I watched a Pied Kingfisher hover and then dive into the waters of the lake to pluck out a fish with an expertise unsurpassed by any living creature. In the distance, a crocodile glided by and an Osprey flew across, scanning the field below for fish. Above me, several Blossom-headed Parakeets made a delightful racket as their crimson heads glinted in the sun. The ramparts of the fort loomed behind me and a treepie suddenly came around me in search of crumbs. Such peace and a feeling of timelessness. In a flash, my reverie was broken as a bunch of cheetal alarm-called from the bushy edge. It was a sudden explosion of noise as five spotted deer raced out to the edge of the water followed by a tigress at full pelt. What a sight as the coffee spilled and the tigress brought down one of the deer. The other four deer reluctantly fled into the water. Normally they never enter the water as they fear the crocodiles. It is only sambar that enter because of their large body size and less fear of a crocodile attack. The cheetal are too fragile and delicate for these crocodile infested waters and as they swam out a few dozen metres the crocs gobbled them up like toffee! Within minutes, five spotted deer were dead and there was no sign of anything. The tigress was back in the bush and was quite clearly responsible for the crocodiles' feast. The waters looked calm with no trace of the cheetal massacre. The magic of nature. What an incredible encounter! So rare in the annals of natural history that I started jumping around in sheer delight. {March 1985}

Nalghati and her two four-to-five-month-old cubs with Kublai, the resident male. This was one of the first ever records of the male tiger in the role of the father.

FATHERING THE CUBS

On 29 April, Fateh found the Nalghati tigress and Kublai sitting some twenty metres from each other under the shade of a flame-of-the-forest tree. It was the first time that they had been observed together, but of the cubs there was no sign. Their absence was a trifle worrying. The male and female spent much of their time sleeping with little evidence of conflict. Sleeping or resting is typical tiger activity on a hot day. Energy is carefully conserved.

Fateh returned the next morning to find a pair of King Vultures perched high up on a tree and scores of White-backed Vultures at different points nearby. A pair of Egyptian Vultures circled low over a dense grove of bushes and shrubs. Above one of these thick bushes, several crows flew about in a frenzy. These were all certain indications of the presence of a carcass. Fateh decided to negotiate the difficult terrain in his jeep and soon found Kublai resting under the shade of a tree. Kublai is a medium-sized male weighing some 200-225 kilograms. He is probably three metres in length from tip of the nose to tip of the tail. Records of the length of tigers have been known to exceed three-and-a-half metres and nearly 275 kilograms in weight. The tigress is at least thirty centimetres shorter and forty-five kilograms lighter but these are estimates: our tigers have not been measured or weighed!

After much scanning with binoculars, Fateh glimpsed the Nalghati tigress deep inside a bush, guarding the carcass of a sambar hind. It was difficult to see, but it looked as if she had eaten a small portion of the rump. Again, there was no sign of the cubs. I joined Fateh and we spent the day under the branches of a tree, watching what turned out to be one of the most exciting encounters with tigers we had ever seen.

Early in the afternoon, the tigress spent half an hour feeding on the carcass. The heat was intense, nearly 45°C. A hundred metres away, there was a small waterhole surrounded by large boulders. We decided to position ourselves around it. The tigers had to come to the water at some point.

At four in the afternoon, Kublai lazily ambles towards the pool and slides into the water, hind legs first, soaking himself completely, leaving just his head visible. Tigers don't like water splashing in their eyes and most of them enter water backwards.

About twenty minutes later, Nalghati follows and they both laze around in the water. Minutes later, both my heart and Fateh's must have missed a beat. The male cub walks quite nonchalantly towards the pool, not a flicker of surprise or fear on his face, circles the two adults and enters the water near where Kublai is stretched out. Soon, following her brother, the female cub walks to the pool, entering the water to sit on her mother's paw. Nalghati licks her face. Fateh and I cannot believe our eyes—the tranquillity of the scene is extraordinary. One big happy family: Nalghati, Kublai and two five-month-old cubs all in close proximity, soaking themselves in this rather small pool of water. They lap the water at regular intervals. In half an hour, the male cub rises, quickly nuzzles Kublai and leaves the pool. The female cub follows him and they play, leaping at each other, slowly drifting towards a tree, clambering up the branches to play a game of hide and seek amidst the foliage. The two adult tigers watch. Soon, Nalghati leaves the water and disappears into the forest. The cubs continue to play with each other under the protective eye of Kublai. At dusk, Kublai heaves himself out of the water and moves towards the cubs.

The cubs rush up to him. He licks one of them. When we leave, Kublai is sitting a metre or so from the two cubs. We have witnessed what must be one of the most closely kept secrets of a tiger's life. It is the first photographic record of a resident male associating with a tigress and her cubs in his range. {1986}

One warm day in March, I arrived at the Semli waterhole to find the three cubs resting in the cool of the undergrowth. The female cub moved towards us as we arrived, in her normal way, passing very close to the jeep. There was no sign of Laxmi. The cubs lazed around for nearly an hour and at 4 p.m. one of them suddenly became alert. It darted off to the far side, followed by its siblings. The forest exploded with the sound of purring as the cubs exhaled in great bursts, probably indicating joy. We followed to find the cubs rubbing their flanks against Laxmi. All four tigers purred incessantly, as if orchestrated, as the cubs licked, nuzzled and cuddled their mother. Purring probably starts around the age of ten to twelve months. I, certainly, have not heard younger cubs purring. This is how the cubs greet their mother on her return after a long stretch of being away.

The purring continues for nearly ten minutes as all four tigers walk towards us. The cubs rub their bodies against Laxmi, expressing their delight at seeing her. They move to a waterhole and quench their thirst, then Laxmi moves some twenty metres away to rest in the shade of a tree. The cubs return to their original positions. It is nearly five in the evening and we decide to watch from a distance, hoping that some deer will soon come to the waterhole to quench their thirst. At 6 p.m., a group of fourteen cheetal emerge from the cover of the forest and cautiously approach the water. Laxmi is suddenly alert, watching intently. The deer have not seen her or the cubs. The cubs lie frozen, knowing the slightest movement will give the game away. Most of the deer have their tails up. They are suspicious, but they need water. Slowly, step by step, they approach. They are now between the mother and her cubs—a perfect situation for Laxmi. She crouches, moves some three metres forward on her belly as if gliding along the ground. Then one cheetal alarm call pierces through the evening. Laxmi moves in a flash; her cubs sprint from the far side and in the panic and confusion of the moment a fawn gets separated and flees towards Laxmi. Laxmi pinions it between her paws and grabs the back of its neck. The fawn squeaks and dies. A Stork-billed Kingfisher flies away from its perch, its blue wings glinting in the late evening light. Picking up the fawn, Laxmi carries it some metres away. Her cubs move in, hoping to feast on a few morsels. Laxmi drops the fawn to the ground and settles on it, covering the tiny carcass with her paws. She turns and snarls viciously at the approaching cubs. One of the female cubs moves off but the male and the other female settle down to face their mother a metre away. Both cubs start a low-pitched moaning sound, which

I have never heard before. It soon turns into a wail, as if they were begging for the carcass. Laxmi snarls and coughs sharply at them. The male cub rises and moves towards her but she growls, picks up the carcass and settles down again some three metres ahead, the fawn between her paws. All three cubs settle down around her, moaning continuously. She snarls back and this continues for fifteen minutes. Suddenly, two of her cubs 'cannonball' into her and all three tigers go rolling over in a flurry of activity, but the male cub snatches the carcass expertly and rushes away with it, followed by one of his sisters. Laxmi sits unconcerned and proceeds to groom herself. The male will not tolerate his siblings on the carcass and they return to Laxmi. They watch the male cub eating. They wait patiently for forty-five minutes until the fawn has been consumed. Then they all move off. I have found that, when the prey is tiny, the dominant cub asserts his right to eat most of it. He shares only when the kill is large. {1987}

VALMIK THAPAR

A MORNING WITH NOON AND HER CUBS

During the early part of 1987 we had several memorable encounters with Noon and her cubs. One day late in January we went off into a bitingly cold morning to look for them. The chill factor in an open jeep in this season is zero degrees Celsius. We stopped near Rajbagh and the barking of a langur monkey from the side of the lake spurred us on. The sun was just rising over the hill. Amidst a cacophony of cheetal, sambar and langur calls, we arrived at one corner to find Noon walking nonchalantly with a cheetal fawn swinging in her mouth.

Noon walks along the shore of the lake. A few peahens take flight. She is heading for a bank of high grass. Suddenly, two peacocks fly out of the grass, closely followed by two racing cubs. The male, in the lead, grabs the fawn and darts back to a clump of grass. Noon licks her female cub and they both recline at the edge of the grass. The male polishes off most of the carcass but towards the end Noon interrupts him. He snarls at her but she ignores him and picks up the remnants. The male cub moves away. The female cub joins her mother and they chew on the bits and pieces the male cub has left. An hour has gone by and soon mother and cubs leave the grass, walking across the edges of the lake towards Padam Talao. The cubs jump and chase each other as they walk around the lake. One charges into Noon and she snarls in annoyance. All three have now reached the edge of the first lake. The cubs turn a corner and disappear around the edge of the lake. Noon walks in front of us on the vehicle track. Two sambar alarms blast the silence near the cubs. They have been seen. Noon is now completely alert and darts forward on the track, realizing that the sambar is caught between the track and her cubs. The cubs are assisting her unintentionally. There is a thud of hooves and a noise in the undergrowth. Noon has settled down on her belly, frozen to the ground at a point where a narrow animal path leads out from the edge of the lake. She has judged the exit point exactly. A large rock hides her. In a flash she leaps into the forest and is out of sight. We hear a grunt. Moving ahead, we find her a few metres off the track, in the throes of killing an adult sambar hind. She has a perfect killing grip on the throat. The sambar's legs twitch in vain: the grip is firm. The cubs approach cautiously and watch her intently. The male cub moves to the carcass but a flicker from the sambar's hind leg forces it to retreat. In minutes the sambar is dead. The male cub rests his forepaw on the rump, while Noon still holds her grip and the female cub stands near her mother. Noon drags the carcass away to where a thick bush makes visibility difficult. The cubs jump all over the sambar and their mother. A kill of this size feeds mother and cubs for three days.

Noon's cubs had unintentionally helped their mother kill the sambar. Slowly, as the cubs grew, this process became more planned. The Semli cubs, now thirteen months old, were already working with their mother when she hunted. Not yet able to kill for themselves, they would take up three different positions and try to scare the deer in the direction of their mother. With four tigers circling an area the prey would invariably panic and the mother's chances of success seemed better. {1987}

AN INCREDIBLE ENCOUNTER:
NOON TRIES TO KILL A SAMBAR

Suddenly from where the tigers had disappeared comes one of the largest sambar stags I have ever seen, galloping out, closely pursued by Noon. My mouth falls open. I cannot believe it. Does Noon expect to kill such a large stag in a chase over open ground? Stag and tigress are out of sight some thirty metres ahead. Fumbling with the starter of the jeep I move ahead, heart pounding. A couple of metres from the vehicle track in the clearing the sambar stag stands motionless. Noon clings on to the side of its neck. Her canines have a grip, but they are nowhere near the throat. Both tiger and sambar are frozen in this position, staring at each other. There is not a sound or a movement. It is a scene I never expected to see in my life. Goverdhan, Fateh's son, wakes me from my daze: 'Come on, use your camera, we will never see this again.' My reverie broken, I swing into action, cursing myself in the process. In the rush of departure I simply picked up the camera nearest to me which only has an eighty-five millimetre lens and no more than twenty shots left; I have no more film on me. Such is jungle life sometimes. I take a few quick pictures, not sure how steady my hands are in the excitement of the moment. Goverdhan warns me to be careful. Sambar and tiger are still locked together. I decide to change position and move up to within three metres of them. They are not in the least bothered by our presence, too involved in their own struggle. I am so close that I feel I could touch them. I choose my shots carefully so as to not finish the film too soon. Noon seems unwilling to shift her grip, which might allow the sambar to escape. A few parakeets fly overhead, some Green Pigeons chatter in a tree nearby as tiger and sambar remain locked together.

In a few minutes, the sambar, with a great heave of his neck, shrugs the tigress off but in a flash she attacks his forelegs in an effort to break them. The stag jerks away, but Noon goes for the neck again, rising on her haunches with one paw on his shoulder for leverage. But in vain. The sambar swivels around and Noon now attacks the belly. With much struggling in the region of the belly and hind legs, she succeeds and the sambar finds itself in a sitting position while the tigress takes a firm grip on one of its hind legs. My film is slowly running out. Suddenly Noon's male cub appears and stands motionless observing the encounter. Noon and sambar are again frozen in position. The cub inches closer, perhaps sensing victory. Noon yanks at the hind leg, opening the skin and trying desperately to break it. This is the only way she will prevent the stag from escaping, as her grip is

Noon tried every possibility of bringing this enormous stag down and finally succeeded. Her cubs started to emerge in anticipation of a feast, but in the end the sambar shook her away and escaped.

not a fatal one. I am totally mesmerized. The cub must be learning a lot from watching the combat.

Suddenly, the sambar, utilizing every ounce of his strength, shakes Noon off, stands and runs. The cub flees in fear, and an exhausted Noon tries to chase the sambar. The sambar, with a burst of adrenalin, escapes in the direction from which he has come, towards the edge of Rajbagh. Noon lopes after him, but hasn't the energy to sustain any speed. Her cubs come around as if egging her on but she snarls at them in irritation. The cubs run ahead of her, following the sambar to the water's edge. The stag alarm-calls for the first time, a strange dull and hollow sound as if his vocal chords have been damaged in the attack. Seeing the approaching tigers he wades into the lake. Noon and her cubs now watch anxiously from the shore. The stag has great difficulty moving through the water. He stumbles forward and finds himself in a deep patch; he is forced to swim and nearly drowns. His head bobs up and down, his limbs move frantically as he struggles to reach the far bank. The tigers follow along the shore but Noon soon gives up and reclines at the edge, exhausted and panting. Her tongue is cut and bleeding. Her cubs jump around her but she snarls at them and they lie down to rest under the shade of a bush.

The stag limps towards the shore and stands motionless for many minutes in the shallow water. Noon watches for a bit but then decides against pursuing her quarry and walks away into the dense cover of Mori to

shelter. Her cubs follow. The sambar slowly hobbles out of the water on to a bank of grass. His right foreleg looks twisted and broken; patches of skin have been raked and a bloody injury swells on the side of his neck. How he had found the strength to escape I can't fathom. Now this magnificent stag is a sorry sight. [1987]

INDEPENDENCE AND LEARNING THE ART OF SURVIVAL

By October of 1987, all the cubs had grown. The Nalghati cubs were twenty-three months, the Semli cubs twenty-two and Noon's cubs in their seventeenth month. The three months of the wet season had been critical in the development of the Semli and Nalghati families. The cubs were now sub-adults and were probably mature and independent enough to go their own ways. The rains that year had been poor. Though the forest was green, Padam Talao and Rajbagh were about half full and Malik Talao merely a pool of water. The contrast with previous years was striking. The failure of a good monsoon two years running would cause havoc in the area. Lack of rain means that crops fail, little income is generated for the farmer, fodder is not available for cattle, and dried up wells create a severe water shortage. The pressures on a forest mount, as water is better conserved in the natural reservoirs of a forest, thick and shaded against the heat of the sun. Compared with the outside world, the forest offers many more possibilities for fodder, leaf litter and other nutrients that cattle can survive on. So man and his livestock are desperate to rush in.

Every year, the vehicle tracks in Ranthambhore are washed away by the rain, and road gangs are busy after September relinking the different areas in the forest. Sometimes late rain causes this work to stretch on to the end of October. That October, the roads to Semli and Nalghati were not ready and I could not trace the cubs. But late one evening around Malik Talao, a burst of cheetal calls indicated the presence of Noon and we soon found her in a clump of grass. Without warning, she leapt forward and there was a squeak. She emerged from the grass carrying a cheetal fawn and moved across to another bank of grass where both her cubs darted towards her, the male snatching the fawn. But the cubs were both large and the female cub also gripped the carcass; for a while both cubs remained frozen, holding on to either end of the fawn. Then began a frantic tug of war as the little fawn was rocked from side to side. Noon reclined a distance away as the cubs fought over their right to eat. Amidst several growls and snarls, the male finally won the bout and disappeared to eat on his own. When the cubs are this age, the mother will provide a regular supply of food for them, but for the rest of the time the cubs are left on their own, sometimes for as long as a couple of days.

The cubs are no longer rooted to a spot. They wander around their mother's range, keeping in touch with her movements through scent and the occasional sound. The cubs are forced to fend for themselves and attempt their first stalks for prey. They sometimes succeed with peafowl, monkeys and the fawn of various deer. It is a critical time in their lives when their ability to survive is put to the test. Has the mother's training been efficient and effective?

It was only sometime in November that we rediscovered the Semli family. We found the smallest and most curious female cub spending much of her time in the Lakarda Valley, within her mother's range. She seemed to have separated from both mother and siblings. The male and the larger female cub, now adult tiger size, were found together in the Semli Valley. Sometimes they were separated by several hundred metres, but they were still in the same vicinity. On one occasion, Laxmi arrived with the smaller cub and all four spent the evening together. We found evidence that their movements overlapped and occasionally they would share food, but Laxmi spent most of the time on her own, as did her small cub, although the other two chose to stay together. All the cubs had been seen with their own kills, so we knew they were able to hunt and survive independently.

The months of November and December were difficult for Ranthambhore and its inmates. Successive periods of drought had created tremendous pressure on the natural fodder and water that remained within the park. Thousands of cattle and their graziers repeatedly entered the park in an endless quest for grazing lands and timber for fuel. During this period, innumerable livestock fell to the predators of the park. This included camels, which tigers relish given the opportunity. In Kachida Valley, two leopards killed a cow and fed on it for a day; by the next morning, a tigress had appropriated the carcass. This invasion created unnatural conditions in which there was more interaction between predator and livestock. This meant that the wild ungulates and the predators would both suffer during the course of the year because of the damage done to the forest. Also, graziers tend to carry poison and when an animal is killed, they poison the carcass. The predators of Ranthambhore always remain around their kills and this could have fatal consequences. In fact, late in December, just near the main entrance to the park, a twenty-month-old tiger was found dead, apparently poisoned. He had been eating a buffalo that had entered the park the day before. It was probably one of the Basandhra tigress's cubs.

Fateh and I were extremely concerned about the situation but Fateh was limited to giving advice. A few months earlier, after twenty years of looking after tigers, he had been transferred to another area where there were no tigers. Choosing to stay in Ranthambhore, he was now on extended leave. We spent many hours discussing the problem of livestock with the new director of the park; Fateh's experience was extremely helpful and by 1989 more effort was being made to keep livestock out of the park—and it was proving effective.

It was during January that we noticed Noon's male cub developing a much greater degree of independence from both his mother and his sister. He could be found on his own, strolling around the area of the lake, though if Noon happened to kill, then suddenly the whole family came together to feast. Later that month, we were fortunate enough to witness a rare encounter between the tigers. Early one morning while driving through the gentle layers of mist around the lakes, we found an Egyptian Vulture circling a bank of high grass around Malik Talao. A few crows flew noisily around a patch in the grass. A treepie darted around, indicating a precise spot. The grass was too high for us to see anything and we decided to take the jeep through. A few metres in, we found Noon resting and both her cubs tearing at the hindquarters of a large sambar stag. The male cub had his own piece and the female ate from the carcass. The stag had probably been killed the previous evening. We had been watching the tigers for about half an hour when, suddenly, from a long way off, came the persistent alarm calls of a sambar. So frequent were they that it seemed to confirm that yet another tiger was in the area. We decided to investigate and from the rise of a hill we saw, padding along the vehicle track, a very large male tiger. I didn't recognize him: he seemed to be a transient male. At a junction between various tracks, he sniffed the ground and the bark of a tree repeatedly, and chose to move towards the bank of high grass. Maybe he had picked up Noon's scent from the previous evening. Now sniffing the air, he carefully circled the grass and then walked through it. Naturalists have often claimed that a tiger's sense of smell is slight and hardly put to use, but I have repeatedly seen tigers sniffing their way along in their efforts to unravel some of the secrets a forest might hold.

The male tiger has reached the far side of the grass, thirty metres from Noon's family, and at the edge of the grass he flops down and appears to go to sleep. By this time, Noon is carefully inching her way out of the long grass towards the male, her eyes peering anxiously in an effort to scan the area. She suspects possible danger but the grass is too tall for her to pinpoint the position of the intruder. She remains frozen for some minutes, looking carefully in the general direction of the male tiger. Suddenly the male flicks his tail, a few blades of grass move and Noon has located her quarry. Completely alert and tense, she starts to stalk towards him. It takes her fifteen minutes to move thirty metres. She moves so gently that you cannot hear the sound of her weight on dry grass. Head lowered, muscle bunched up near her shoulders, she comes to a halt a couple of metres from the male tiger. Now she remains frozen, watching him, clearly realizing his potential threat. She looks as if she will attack. The male has his eyes closed. I wonder if he is playing a game. Cautiously, Noon takes another step forward and suddenly the male swivels around, confronting her with a vicious growl, and in a flash both tigers rear up on their hind legs, literally standing to face one another. They keep their balance for a bit as they gently try and slap each other, then lower themselves with the most blood-curdling growls. They rise on their hind legs three times this way before sitting down to face each other. The forest goes silent.

Noon is soon up and quickly tries to return to her carcass. In the distance I see her male cub running away. The male tiger follows Noon. The female cub now leaves the grass and attempts to nuzzle the male but he snarls and mother and daughter watch him as he enters the grass and appropriates the carcass. Noon follows him but as she approaches, she is met by a series of low growls. She retreats with her cub to settle down at the edge of the grass in the shade of a tree. There is no sign of the male cub. After a while, the female cub attempts to enter the grass, approaching cautiously. She persists until she is within a metre of the male but his aggression soon forces her away.

Late in the afternoon, the female cub is again attracted to the carcass. Despite much growling by the male, she manages to snatch one of the legs of the deer but in the process she receives a swipe on her foreleg which causes a small gash. Unconcerned, she continues to chew on what she has retrieved. Noon remains out of the fray and reclines outside the patch of grass. Late that evening, a sounder of wild boar, attracted by the stench of the carcass, approach warily, see Noon, and trot off.

The next morning, we found Noon and her female cub chewing on the many remnants of the carcass. The male tiger had left the area after eating his fill. There was still no sign of Noon's male cub. Noon chewed at the flesh between the antlers while her cub stripped the last meat from one of the forelegs. By 11 a.m., they had finished feeding and mother and cub moved out of Malik Talao into a network of ravines. I didn't see the male cub till three days later when he had joined his mother and sister on another sambar kill. He was spending more time on his own and had avoided possible conflict with the male tiger by preferring to slip away. It was the first time that we had seen interactions between a transient male and a resident tigress.

The Nalghati cubs were over two years old and though male and female cub were sometimes together, there were few signs of the mother. Both cubs were able to kill, sometimes in tandem, but also on their own. Our study of them was over and we spent most of our time observing Noon and her offspring around the lakes.

At about 5 p.m., one day in February, three of the larger crocodiles in Rajbagh attacked a medium-sized sambar hind in about a metre of water. Fateh watched this encounter unfold. One crocodile made desperate efforts to yank the hind leg, while another tried to grab the neck, amidst much turning and twisting of their bodies. The sambar was frozen, unable to move out of the water. Other deer around the lakes alarm-called and within ten minutes the sambar was slowly sinking into the water, gaping wounds around its neck and rump. There was now a swirling mass of crocodiles around the sambar and it soon drowned amidst the onslaught. The crocodiles were having difficulty wrenching the carcass open to devour it. Suddenly, Noon and her cubs appeared on the scene.

The cubs sit on their haunches to watch while Noon circles the shore, moving towards the crocodiles. She stops to watch the activity for a few minutes and then enters the shallow water, slowly at first, gingerly picking her steps through the lake bed. Suddenly, with a burst of speed, she rushes straight for the crocodiles and the carcass. Snarling viciously, she slaps at the water and the crocodiles are forced to retreat. Fateh estimates that there were nearly twenty crocodiles around the dead sambar. A large one still guards the floating carcass but Noon rushes at him and smacks her paw into the water with such force that the crocodile glides away. Quickly grabbing the carcass by the throat she starts to pull it out of the water. It requires a herculean effort. The cubs, who have been watching attentively from the shore, now race across towards their mother, meeting her just as she is about to reach dry land. She stops as the cubs nuzzle her and jump about the carcass. She then proceeds to drag it back on to dry land, moving in reverse. Her male cub grasps her tail as if to say, 'I'll pull you, too' and then to Fateh's surprise the female cub also attempts to pull her brother's tail. This strange procession of tigers moves slowly to a bank of grass with the sambar, pausing every now and then to rest during this exhausting activity.

The water in the lakes was drying rapidly. For the first time in the history of the park, Padam Talao, the first lake, had been reduced to a large pool of water. Deer, boar and antelope grazed on the dry bed of the lake. It would be completely dry by May. A few crocodiles remained in the pool, but most of them had migrated towards Rajbagh. Rajbagh was a larger shallow tract of water but was also drying rapidly. What would be the fate of these hundred crocodiles? Where would they go? There was too little water in the ravines for them to survive. There would be few fish for them to feed on. The whole ecology of the area around the lakes was undergoing a change. The lack of water might create a severe problem. By early March, Noon's male cub was turning into a lake expert, following in the footsteps of his mother. He was persistent in his attempts to charge deer from banks of high grass, sometimes even racing into the shallow water in the lake to attack his quarry. The female cub was more reticent. She would join her mother and brother after their attacks or charges.

Noon and the cubs frequented the area around Jogi Mahal. I remember a group of us were sitting around a fire one cold winter's night, in a courtyard surrounded by a wall. Between a few drinks and a lot of chatter, I suddenly heard the grass rustling outside. I quietly left the group and looked over the wall; to my delight, I found Noon standing below on a forest track. We looked at each other for a few seconds, then I turned and signalled to the group around the fire, who were now quite noisy. They thought I was mad as I waved my hands up and down. It took them a moment to realize what I was trying to say, but then, in silence, they crept over to the wall. Noon had been joined by her cubs. One of the group couldn't control herself and exclaimed loudly. Noon turned and coughed, moving off towards the kitchen, her cubs scampering ahead. I couldn't believe it when I suddenly saw one of the forest guards carrying our dinner on a tray, walking towards the male cub. Fateh yelled to him. I had visions of the dinner in a mess on the floor and a man scurrying away, but the guard kept his cool and, realizing his predicament, turned and walked back to the kitchen. Noon and her cubs passed by.

The male cub spent most of his time around the rest house. One evening, he was seen calmly reclining around the area where the cars were parked. He had even walked through the kitchen towards a lower corridor of the building. Even though these tigers had never threatened a human being, this behaviour gave cause for concern. In fact, Fateh and I felt responsible for the close proximity the tigers enjoyed with the jeeps. Our fingers are crossed to this day that no untoward incident occurs. A lot depends on the care exercised by the men who drive the jeeps. Tigers that are irritated for some reason do charge the jeeps but they have always been mock charges and have never culminated in an attack. Nasty, for instance, had charged me over a dozen times in a period of a few months. It comes as a shock, actually.

The jeeps are open on the sides and top and to be confronted by a snarling tiger less than a metre away is paralyzing. It is only after years of experience that one learns to accept this possibility and an observer has to be careful to select the best position for a jeep without being intrusive or threatening. Our greatest concern was that if a group of people teased or chased a family of tigers, then they may have to face the wrath of a tigress. We humans have a certain sense of arrogance in such situations. An arrogance born of fear. This is what is dangerous.

In the summer of 1988, the Semli cubs were into their adult life. Usually when we saw them they were alone; we occasionally encountered them as a group. They seemed to sustain their links as siblings. Noon's cubs were nearly two years old. The male was spending most of his time alone, but continued to join his mother and sister over food. His sister spent more time with Noon. Unlike leopards, tiger cubs spend nearly twenty months in close touch with the mother. Leopard cubs tend to become independent between the ages of twelve and fourteen months. But with tigers, the process of becoming independent occurs differently for different cubs and depends on the nature and individual characteristics of the cub. I think it is also affected by the ecological system in which they live. If undisturbed and well managed, tigers can, as families, form temporary groupings in order to hunt and share food. There is, of course, much myth surrounding the tiger's solitary nature. I think tigers were forced into solitary and nocturnal lives in order to survive their endless persecution. In protected and undisturbed habitats like Ranthambhore, the tiger has flourished and revealed facets of its family life that few would have imagined possible. They live in family groups that maintain links even after the cubs reach adulthood, thus demonstrating the possibility of sustaining kin links over long periods of time. Throughout this period of two years we never observed or saw any evidence of conflict between the growing cubs and the resident male. There is no doubt that the resident male who fathers the litter plays a role in raising the family.

We had been fortunate to see the cubs of Noon, Laxmi and Nalghati, seven in all, reach a point of maturity where they could kill for themselves. The Basandhra cubs around the fringe had not been so lucky. One of the cubs had presumably been poisoned soon after feeding on a buffalo carcass. The Bakaula tigress who operated in the resident Bakaula male's range had been seen briefly with two cubs. But during a period of three months in early 1988, she suffered from a severe wound in her right paw that caused her much anguish and pain. Somehow she limped around and managed

VALMIK THAPAR

to kill the occasional cheetal and sambar for her cubs. But the state of the wound restricted effective hunting. She would lick it frequently, her saliva being an excellent antiseptic. I couldn't believe that she could cure it. It had been bloody one day, but improved and was soon back to normal. But during this period she had lost a twelve-month-old cub and was now seen with only one cub.

Ensuring the survival of the cubs is a difficult process. The mother loses a few cubs at birth and then when the offspring are six months old, with a burgeoning appetite, a lot depends on the availability of the prey, the size of the litter and the mother's abilities. This can be a vulnerable time and a cub can sometimes be lost in the frenzied quest for food. When sub-adult tigers are independent and hunting, they can suffer from a lack of skill and experience. This is a moment when their mother's training determines their chances of survival in the future. At this final stage, the father's role is minimal. From the time when the cubs are sixteen to eighteen months old, the father's presence is irregular and interactions with the sub-adult cubs are rare.

Our final observation of family life was late one afternoon during the middle of May 1988 with Noon in the Rajbagh area. It was a memorable evening. At that time of the year, the water of the lake had receded to a shallow tract in the centre. Cheetal herds congregated on the open ground to feed on the green shoots at the water's edge. At 5.30 p.m., the male cub emerged from a bank of high grass. Well-fed and fit, he walked leisurely towards the water. The cheetal herds alarm-called, watching him carefully. But he was in no mood to hunt. The herd moved to give way to him. A few sambar in the water alarm called and walked out. The cheetal watched the tiger at the edge of the water as he settled in to cool himself and quench his thirst. They then went back to grazing without further alarm. The tiger sat quietly soaking in the water. Thirty minutes later, Noon emerged from the far side and headed to the water, reclining in it opposite her cub. Soon afterwards, the female cub appeared and strolled up to the water, immersing herself in it some thirty metres from Noon. All three tigers sat. The cheetal herd grazed in the background. The sun was setting. The saga of the families was over. I wondered what the monsoons would be like. Would the crocodiles survive? What would the lakes be like? Would all three tigers be active the following season? Their level of predation around the lakes was high. Would the lakes be able to sustain enough prey after the rain? The key factor in determining their future would be the success of the rains. I prayed for it. {1988}

THE ROCKS OF NALGHATI

It was 5 p.m. in the evening that I encountered the two sub-adult cubs of Nalghati. They were sixteen months old and watched me curiously as I drove by. The mother was absent. A short track led off the road to a pool of water and at the edge of the track were two large greyish rocks. As I approached the rocks, the two cubs came in closer and one of them, the more dominant one, decided to jump on the rock and view us from a height. The perfect setting. It was a majestic scene as he towered above and my camera clicked away. His sibling remained a little in the distance. At 6 p.m., the sun was setting and I decided to head home but as I turned the ignition, the jeep stalled. I soon realized to my shock that we had run out of petrol. We were just ten feet away from tigers and truly stuck a few hundred yards off the main road. There were no jeeps around and I could feel my heart thudding. I decided to get out of the jeep and walk back before the light faded completely, but lady luck was on my side—a jeep came by and we tumbled into it, leaving our stranded jeep in front of the two tigers. Later that evening when a mechanic went to collect and restart the jeep, he discovered a tiger sitting in the back seat. The tiger leapt out and my jeep came back home but what a day it had been. These first twelve years from 1976 to 1988 were a critical learning process for me as I absorbed the very secret life of the Ranthambhore tiger through endless rich and incredible encounters. It was through Ranthambhore's tigers that the world was given a glimpse into the arcane lives of these magnificent predators. {1988}

VALMIK THAPAR

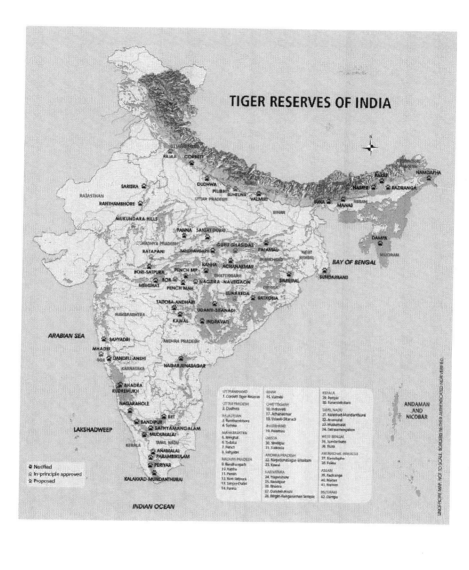

TIGER RESERVES OF INDIA

A NOTE ON STYLE

As the extracts in Book Two of the book are taken from books published across many different centuries we have avoided standardizing proper nouns, punctuation, hyphenation, italicization and so on. Although customarily we do not believe it is appropriate to supply translations to Indian words or phrases if these occur in the original excerpt we have left them in. In the rest of the book, we have standardized spellings and punctuation as per our house style.

Dates of first publication of the work and other information in the book from which the piece is excerpted, as well as biographical details about the author, may be found at the back of the book. While every effort has been made to check the accuracy of these excerpts with the original publication from which they have been taken if any errors have inadvertently crept in, we will gladly correct them in subsequent editions of the work if these are pointed out.

VALMIK THAPAR

APPENDIX

We have nearly 66,000 square kilometres of land that comes under tiger reserves in India and contains about 1,000 to 1,350 tigers. The rest of the tigers live in the wild on the outside. The all India estimate of tigers in 2010 as per governmental record is about 1,500 to 1,900 tigers, which I think is overestimated. These tigers are estimated in a series of different landscapes. The Shivalik-Gangetic landscapes include the Corbett National Park and adjacent areas which house a population of 200 to 250 tigers. This is one of the most important landscapes to the north of the country for the tiger. On the southern side, the Western Ghat landscape complex houses, on the Karnataka side, a very healthy population of 300 tigers between the Nagarhole and Bandipur tiger reserves and extends to the Tamil Nadu border. Several of our tiger reserves have very few tigers in them, some of them without even a viable breeding group. A few of the reserves may have some strays that come and go. The latest survey declared that Mukundra Hills has no tigers and will now be prepared so that the animal can be re-introduced there! The federal government declares, with the Planning Commission's approval, a fixed number of tiger reserves every five years. They believe it is better to keep such habitat protected even if tigers are few and far between. At a later date, they could decide to introduce more tigers into these areas or add tigers into areas that are short of them. These are intensively man-managed and in several cases, in my opinion, badly managed. Seventeen state governments manage this land and often poorly, the result of which is that the tiger suffers. Such landscapes for the tiger will only do well after we overhaul the Indian Forest Service and create new and innovative relationships with the non-governmental world, professionals and others including wildlife scientists, anthropologists, sociologists, afforestation experts, village panchayats, corporates and NGOs. This needs to be done urgently, before we find that we are only left with tigers on paper.

List of Core and Buffer Areas of tiger reserves in India, notified under the Wildlife (Protection) Act, 1972, as amended in 2006

(as on 3.6.2013)

Sl. No.	Name of Tiger Reserve	State	Area of the core / critical tiger habitat (In Sq. Kms.)	Area of the buffer/ peripheral (In Sq. Kms.)	Total area
1	Bandipur	Karnataka	872.24	584.06	1456.3
2	Corbett	Uttarakhand	821.99	466.32	1288.31
3	Kanha	Madhya Pradesh	917.43	1134.361	2051.791
4	Manas	Assam	840.04	2310.88	3150.92
5	Melghat	Maharashtra	1500.49	1268.03	2768.52
6	Palamau	Jharkhand	414.08	715.85	1129.93
7	Ranthambore	Rajasthan	1113.364	297.9265	1411.291
8	Similipal	Orissa	1194.75	1555.25	2750.00
9	Sundarbans	West Bengal	1699.62	885.27	2584.89
10	Periyar	Kerala	881.00	44.00	925.00

11	Sariska	Rajasthan	881.1124	332.23	1213.342
12	Buxa	West Bengal	390.5813	367.3225	757.9038
13	Indravati	Chhattisgarh	1258.37	1540.70	2799.07
14	Nagarjunsagar	Andhra Pradesh	3721.00	1175.51	4896.51
15	Namdapha	Arunachal Pradesh	1807.82	245.00	2052.82
16	Dudhwa	Uttar Pradesh	1093.79	1107.9848	2201.7748
17	Kalakkad-Mundanthurai	Tamil Nadu	895.00	706.542	1601.542
18	Valmiki	Bihar	598.45	300.93	899.38
19	Pench	Madhya Pradesh	411.33	768.30225	1179.63225
20	Tadoba-Andhari	Maharashtra	625.82	1101.7711	1727.5911
21	Bandhavgarh	Madhya Pradesh	716.903	820.03509	1536.938
22	Panna	Madhya Pradesh	576.13	1002.42	1578.55
23	Dampa	Mizoram	500.00	488.00	988.00
24	Bhadra	Karnataka	492.46	571.83	1064.29
25	Pench	Maharashtra	257.26	483.96	741.22
26	Pakke	Arunachal Pradesh	683.45	515.00	1198.45
27	Nameri	Assam	200.00	144.00	344.00
28	Satpura	Madhya Pradesh	1339.264	794.04397	2133.30797
29	Anamalai	Tamil Nadu	958.59	521.28	1479.87
30	Udanti-Sitanadi	Chattisgarh	851.09	991.45	1842.54
31	Satkosia	Orissa	523.61	440.26	963.87
32	Kaziranga	Assam	625.58	548.00	1173.58
33	Achanakmar	Chattisgarh	626.195	287.822	914.017
34	Dandeli-Anshi	Karnataka	814.884	282.63	1097.514
35	Sanjay-Dubri	Madhya Pradesh	812.571	861.931	1674.502
36	Mudumalai	Tamil Nadu	321.00	367.59	688.59
37	Nagarhole	Karnataka	643.35	562.41	1205.76
38	Parambikulam	Kerala	390.89	252.772	643.662
39	Sahyadri	Maharashtra	600.12	565.45	1165.57
40	Biligiri Ranganatha Temple	Karnataka	359.10	215.72	574.82
41	Kawal	Andhra Pradesh	893.23	1125.89	2019.12

42	Sathyamangalam	Tamil Nadu	793.49	614.91	1408.40
43	Mukandra Hills (including Darrah, Jawahar Sagar and Chambal Wildlife Sanctuaries)	Rajasthan	417.17	342.82	759.99
	TOTAL		36334.61	39708.46	66043.07

NOTES ON THE CONTRIBUTORS

A. A. Dunbar Brander (1877-1953) was a conservator of forests who spent more than twenty-one years in the British Indian Forest Service in the Central Provinces of India.

A. E. Wardrop* (1872-) was with the Royal Hose Artillery during the days of the British Raj. He was also a big game hunter.

A. I. R. Glasfurd* was a captain in the Indian army.

A. Mervyn Smith* was a shikari who spent most of his professional life in the jungles of India.

A. N. W. Powell* was a prolific big-game hunter.

A. Wimbush* was an I. F. S officer during the British Raj.

Abu'l-Fazl (1551-1602) was Akbar's vizier and one of the legendary Nine Gems of his court. He was the author of *Akbarnama*, the official history of Akbar's reign, written in three volumes.

Aditya 'Dicky' Singh is a tourism professional, traveller, wildlife enthusiast and photographer.

Alexander Hamilton* was a soldier and traveller who spent time in the East Indies between 1688 to 1723.

Arjan Singh (1917-2010) was one of India's foremost conservationists as well as a respected authority on the big cats. He played a crucial role in the creation and official recognition of the Dudhwa National Park.

Arthur Musselwhite* was an avid adventurer and photographer.

Arthur W. Strachan* was a connoisseur of Indian wildlife.

Babur (1483-1530) was the first Mughal emperor.

Balendu Singh is the honorary wildlife warden of Ranthambhore Tiger Reserve and Sawai Madhopur District.

Barbara Curtis Horton* was an Englishwoman in India.

Bernard C. Ellison* was a naturalist and the curator of the Bombay Natural History Society.

C. E. Gouldsbury* was a member of the late Indian Police Force.

Cuthbert Larking* was a soldier in the British Indian Army.

Daniel Johnson* was a surgeon with the East India Company in Bengal.

Dharmendra Khandal is a field biologist with Tiger Watch, an NGO that works to conserve wildlife in Ranthambhore. He is married to **Divya Khandal**.

E. A. Smythies (1885-1975) was an eminent forester and was known for his knowledge of the ecology of Nepal and Uttarakhand. He was once the Forest Adviser to the Government of Nepal and the Chief Conservator of Forests, Uttar Pradesh.

E. P. Stebbing (1870-1960) was both a sportsman and an avid naturalist.

Edison Marshall* was a big game hunter in India.

Edward Hodges-Hill* is an author with a keen interest in man-eating lions and tigers.

F. B. Simson* was a retired civil servant from Bengal.

F. W. Champion (1893-1970) served in the Imperial Forest Service of India. Deeply interested in natural history, he was famous for being one of the first wildlife photographers and authored the book *With a Camera in Tiger-Land*.

Fiona Sunquist is a wildlife photographer, writer and was the editor of the *International Wildlife Magazine*. **Mel Sunquist** is a wildlife ecologist and an expert on carnivores with many years of experience in the field.

Fitz William Thomas Pollok (1832-1909) was an officer of the British Indian Army and left various records of his adventures in the subcontinent.

François Bernier (1625-1688) was a French physicist who lived during the time of James I (of England), Louis XIII of France, and Emperor Jāhāngir.

Frank Nicholls* was a tea planter in Northeast India.

Geoffrey C. Ward is a writer, historian and documentary film-maker. He is married to **Diane Raines Ward** who is an environmental activist.

George B. Schaller (b.1933) is one of the world's foremost experts on wildlife behaviour and the winner of the 1973 National Book Award for the sciences.

George Hogan Knowles* spent more than thirty years travelling through India and was known for his unerring skill with a rifle.

Godfrey Charles Mundy (1804-1860) was the aide-de-camp to the British diplomat and military leader, Lord Combermere.

Goverdhan Singh Rathore is the son of legendary conservationist Fateh Singh Rathore and works closely with Tiger Watch, along with other conservation projects.

H. A. Leveson* was known as 'the old shekarry' in his time.

Henry Bevan (1796-1846) was a member of the late twenty-seventh regiment of the E. I. C. Madras Native Infantry who entered the service in 1809.

Hugh Allen (1911-1968) served in the British army during World War II, but when a bad head wound put him out of active service in 1942, he was hospitalized in India. He learnt to love the country and took up farming amongst the jungles, developing his skills for big-game shooting out of necessity, rather than entertainment.

Isabel Savory* (1869-) was an Englishwoman who travelled to India during the time of the Raj.

J. C. Daniel (1927-2011) was an Indian naturalist and the erstwhile curator and Director of the Bombay Natural History Society.

J. D. Inverarity* was a member of the Bombay Natural History Society.

J. E. Carrington Turner* served in the Indian Forest Service and spent more than thirty years in the jungles of India.

J. H. Rivett-Carnac (1839-1923) was a Fellow of the University of Bombay, the Royal Asiatic Society, the Geological Society among others.

J. Moray Brown* served with the late seventy-ninth Cameron Highlanders in British India.

Jahāngir (1969-1627), born Nur-ud-din Mohammed Salim, was the son of Akbar and the fourth Mughal emperor.

Jaisal Singh is an author and tourism professional who runs a chain of wildlife resorts including Sherbagh in Ranthambhore.

James Forbes* was a British official in India, whose duties included the administration of justice, the collection of revenue and the supervision of agriculture in five large towns and 150 villages.

James Gordon Elliot* was a soldier and a sportsman.

James Inglis (1845-1908) was a merchant and an indigo planter who lived in India for twelve years. He was fond of tiger hunting and pigsticking.

Jamshed Butt* was a prolific hunter, known by aboriginals as a 'wizard of hunting'.

Jim Corbett (1875-1955) is best known for stalking and hunting man-eating tigers and leopards, but he was also a sport-hunter, organizing a tiger beat as late as 1946, and continuing to shoot in East Africa where he emigrated after India became independent.

John Daniel St. Joseph* was an officer with the Indian Forest Service where he served for over twenty years.

John Finnemore* was a travel writer and the author of *Peeps at Many Lands: Japan*.

Joseph Fayrer* worked with the Bengal Medical Service as a doctor.

Julius Barras* spent twenty-eight years of his life in the army in India and was a keen sportsman.

K. Ullas Karanth is a conservationist and a leading expert on the tiger.

Kalyan Chakrabarti is a widely acclaimed wildlife writer and scientist.

Kenneth Anderson (1910-1974) was a hunter, writer and an Indian wildlife aficionado.

Kesri Singh (1892-1980) of Kanota was a soldier, shikari and close companion to the maharaja of Jaipur.

Kim Sullivan is a wildlife photographer and shares an unaffected, unaltered, actual moment in a tiger's life.

Lady Lawrence (1879-1976) was already a published author before she married Sir Henry

Lawrence, the former governor of Bombay, in 1914. She spent twelve years in India.

Leopold Grimstone Paget (1824-1892) joined the Royal Artillery in 1843 and was transferred to India during the Mutiny of 1857.

M. Krishnan (1912-1996) was a naturalist, writer and photographer who wrote a column called 'Country Notebook' for the *Sunday Statesman*. He was awarded the Padma Shri in 1970.

Maharanee Sunity Devee (1864-1932) was the maharani of Cooch Behar.

Mark Thornhill* was an English official in India.

Niccolao Manucci (1639-1717) was an Italian writer and traveller who worked in the Mughal court.

Nigel Woodyatt (1861-1936) was a soldier and big game hunter in India.

Olive Smythies was an Englishwoman who lived in India for many years.

Patrick Hanley* was a planter in India and a keen observer of wildlife.

Peter Jackson is the chairman emeritus of the World Conservation Union (IUCN) Cat Specialist Group and an expert on the tiger.

R. D. Mackay* had years of experience as a hunter, especially in the wild and untamed forests of Uttar Pradesh.

R. D. T. Alexander* and **A. Martin-Leake*** were fellow shikaris.

R. G. Burton (1864-1961) was a decorated British military officer and an authority of his time on the tiger.

Raghu Chundawat is a conservation biologist and an expert on the snow leopard and the tiger. His wife, **Joanna Van Gruisen**, is a wildlife photographer and conservationist.

Reginald Heber (1783-1826) became the Bishop of Calcutta in 1823.

Richard Hilton* served as a soldier in India for many years.

Richard Lydekker (1849-1915) was a geologist and naturalist, and served as the vice president of the Geological Society of London.

Richard Perry* was a wildlife enthusiast and the author of *A Naturalist on Lindisfarne, Shetland Sanctuary, At the Turn of the Tide* and *The Watcher and the Red Deer*.

Robert H. Elliot (1837-1914) was a British coffee planter in Mysore and wrote books on plantation life and farming.

S. Eardley-Wilmot* (1852-) was the Inspector General of Forests to the Government of India from 1903-09.

Sahibzada Abdul Shakur Khan* was a keen shikari from Tonk, Rajasthan.

Sardar Bhupendra Kumar* was a wildlife enthusiast from Dholpur.

Sher Jung (1904-1996) was an Indian freedom fighter. He commanded the Kashmir National Militia in 1947 at the time of the Pakistan invasion.

Shuja Ul Islam* and **Colonel John H. Roush Jr.*** were sportsmen and hunting companions.

Sir Samuel W. Baker (1821-1893) was a Fellow of the Royal Geographical Society, London.

Sir Thomas Roe (1581-1644) was an English diplomat, politician and scholar who lived during the reign of Elizabeth I and James I of England.

Sir William Foster (1863-1951) was the Register and Superintendent of Records at the India Office, which was created to oversee the Provinces of British India.

Thomas Bacon* served with the Bengal Morse Artillery.

Thomas Bowrey* (1713-) was a British sailor who wrote a Malay-to-English dictionary and the book *The Geographical Account of Countries Round the Bay of Bengal* during his travels across the East Indies.

Thomas Pennant (1726-1798) was a Welsh naturalist, writer and traveller.

Thomas Williamson (1790-1815) served with the East India Company in Bengal for more than twenty years.

Victor Jacquemont (1801-1832) was a French botanist, geologist and a traveller who came to India in 1828 and consequently settled here.

W. Connell* wrote for the Journal of Bombay Natural History Society.

W. H. G. Kingston (1814-1880) was known primarily as a writer of adventure stories for boys.

W. Hogarth Todd* was an Englishman in India and the author of *Work, Sport and Play: An Englishman's Life in India before the War*.

Walter Campbell* was a part of the Seventh Royal Fusiliers and the author of *The Old Forest Ranger*.

William Blane was an Englishman who hunted with Asaf-ud-Daula, the vizier of the Mughal Empire.

William Knighton (1824-1900) was a member of the household of Nussir-u-deen, King of Oude.

William Rice was a soldier and sportsman.

William Robert Foran (1881-1968) was a big game hunter and one of the first six European officers of the *British East Africa Police*.

Yvonne Fitzroy (1891-1971) sailed to India in 1921 with Lord and Lady Reading and wrote an account of her years in the country.

PHOTO CREDITS

Aditya 'Dicky' Singh: Page 307.

Balendu Singh: Page 310.

Dharmendra and Divya Khandal: Page 303.

Fateh Singh Rathore: Pages 229, 234, 259, 285, 289, 352, 354.

Gunter Zeisler: Page 341.

Jaisal Singh: Pages 302, 304, 329.

Judith Wakelam: Page 350.

National Gallery of Australia, Canberra: Page 26.

Private: Pages 2, 5, 6, 7, 9, 14, 15, 18, 33, 36,37, 38, 40, 43, 45, 47, 49, 50, 51, 52, 54, 56, 57, 63, 66, 67, 68, 69, 71, 73, 75, 77, 78, 79, 83, 84, 85, 86, 89, 92, 95, 96, 98, 100, 103, 104, 109, 111, 113, 114, 116, 117, 120, 121, 124, 126, 133, 138, 145, 154, 158, 160, 164, 165, 166, 170, 174, 178, 184, 189, 199, 202, 203, 204, 207, 213, 220, 221, 223, 241,242, 274, 286, 293.

Raghu Chundawat and Joanna Van Gruisen: Page 313.

Rosie Corcoran: Pages 70, 137, 172, 205, 215, 304, 315.

Sanctuary Photo Library: Pages 217 (Indranil Paul); 231 (John Santhosh); 298 (M. D. Parashar).

Sheikh Usman Tirandaz: Pages 30, 97,

Tejbir Singh: Page 226.

K. Ullas Karanth: Page 292.

Valmik Thapar: Pages 237, 279, 316, 319, 334-335, 362-363, 372.

Victoria Albert Museum: Pages 11, 23, 24, 142, 266.

Wikimedia Commons: Pages 61, 131, 151, 185, 192, 193, 200, 264, 268, 269, 295.

ACKNOWLEDGEMENTS

A. A. Dunbar Brander
'A Strange Alliance'. *Wild Animals in Central India*. London: Edward Arnold & Co., 1931.

A. E. Wardrop
'The Tigress's Fury'. *Days and Nights with Indian Big Game*. London: Macmillan & Co., 1923.

A. I. R. Glasfurd
'The Forest and the Tiger'. *Rifle and Romance in the Indian Jungle*. London & New York: John Lane: The Bodley Head, 1905.

A. Mervyn Smith
'Aladdin's Cave', 'The White Tiger'. *Sport and Adventure in the Indian Jungle*. Hurst and Blackett Publishers, 1904.

A. N. W. Powell
'To Call a Tiger', 'On Facing a Tiger', 'The Bison and the Tiger', 'The Tigers and the Liver'. *Call of the Tiger*. London: Robert Hale Ltd., 1957.

A. Wimbush
'The Tiger in the Rest House'. Taken from 'With a Tiger "In Camera"'. *Big Game Encounters: Critical Moments in the Live of Well-Known Shikaris*. Stanley Jepson (ed.). London: H. F. & G. Witherby Ltd., 1936.

Abu'l-Fazl
'Tiger Hunting in the Reign of Akbar'. *The Ain-i-Akbari*. H. Blochmann (trans.). New Delhi: Aadiesh Book Depot, 1871.
'The Shāhinshāh and the Wounded Tiger'. *Akbarnama (Volume I)*. H. Beveridge (trans.). New Delhi: Low Price Publications, 1989.
'Emperor Akbar Hunting Six Tigers'. *Akbarnama (Volume II)*. H. Beveridge (trans.). New Delhi: Low Price Publications, 1989.

Alexander Hamilton
'Sighting a Tiger'. *A New Account of the East Indies: Being the Observations and Remarks of Capt. Alexander Hamilton from the Years 1688-1723*. Edinburgh: John Mofman, 1727.

Arjan Singh
'The Mating Couple'. *A Tiger's Story*. New Delhi: Bahrisons and Tara Press and India Research Press, 2005.

Arthur Musselwhite
'Shot by a Tiger', 'Saved by the Tiger', 'On a Boat with a Tiger'. *Behind the Lens in Tigerland*. Calcutta: Thacker, Spink and Co., 1933.

Arthur W. Strachan
'The Tiger's Embrace', 'The Courting Tigers'. *Mauled by a Tiger: Encounters in the Indian Jungles*. London: Moray Press, 1933.

Babur
'Emperor Babur's Tiger'. *The Baburnama: Memoirs of Babur, Prince and Emperor*. Wheeler M. Thackston (trans.). Smithsonian Institution, 1996.

Barbara Curtis Horton
'The Ultimate Encounter'. *Tiger Bridge: Nine Days on a Bend of the Nauranala*. Santa Barbara: John Daniel & Co., 1993.

Bernard C. Ellison
'A Royal Dinner in the Jungle'. *H. R. H. The Prince of Wales's Sport in India*. London: William Heinemann, Ltd., 1925.

C. E. Gouldsbury
'The Ferocious Tiger', 'Tigers Attack Buffalo', 'The Tiger on the Elephant's Head'. *Tigerland: Reminiscences of Forty Years' Sport and Adventure in Bengal*. New York: E.P. Dutton & Co., 1916.

Customs' Officer from the North-West Provinces of India
'The Tigers in the House', 'Camp Food: A Gourmet Chef's Dream'. *Past Days in India: Or, Sporting Reminiscences of the Valley of the Soane and the Basin of Singrowlee*. London: Chapman and Hall, 1874.

Cuthbert Larking
'The Bombay Tiger'. *Bandobast and Khabar: Reminiscences of India*. London: Hurst and Blackett, Ltd., 1888.

Daniel Johnson
'Travelling through Tigerland'. *Sketches of Indian Field Sports: With Observations on the Animals; also an Account of some of the Customs of the Inhabitants; with a Description of the Art of Catching Serpents, as Practised by the Conjoors and their Method of Curing themselves when Bitten*. London: Robert Jennings, 1827.

E. A. Smythies
'Husband, Wife and Tiger'. Taken from 'A Tiger that Climbed a Tree'. *Big Game Encounters: Critical Moments in the Live of Well-Known Shikaris*. Stanley Jepson (ed.). London: H. F. & G. Witherby Ltd., 1936.
'The Tiger and the Black Bears'. *Big Game Shooting in Nepal (with Leaves from the Maharaja's Sporting Diary)*. Calcutta: Thacker, Spink & Co., 1942.

E. P. Stebbing
'The Tiger and the Sambar'. *The Diary of a Sportsman Naturalist in India*. London: John Lane, 1920.

Edison Marshall
'The Tiger and the Vultures'. *Jungle Hunting Thrills: Selected Stories from Shikar and Safari*. Montana: Literary Licensing, 2011(reprint).

Edward Hodges-Hill
'The Tiger versus the Bayonet'. *Man Eater: Tales of Lion and Tiger Encounters*. Heathfield: Cockbird Press, 1992.

F. B. Simson
'Tigers on Trees', 'The Mahout and the Tiger'. *Letters on Sport in Eastern Bengal*. London: R. H. Porter, 1886.

F. W. Champion
'The Alleged Cruelty of Tigers', 'Magnificent Forests', 'The Car, the Tiger and the Orderly'. *The Jungle in Sunlight and Shadow*. London: Chatto & Windus, 1933.

Fiona and Mel Sunquist
'The Impact of a Tiger's Attack'. *Tiger Moon*. Chicago: The University of Chicago Press, 1988.

Fitz William Thomas Pollok
'Chasing a Tiger in Assam'. *Sport in British Burma, Assam, and the Cassyah and Jyntiah Hills*. London: Chapman & Hall, 1879.
'The Tiger and the Python', 'The Tiger and the Girls'. *Incidents of Foreign Sport and Travel*. London: Chapman & Hall, 1894.

François Bernier
'The Islands of the Sundarbans'. *Travels in the Mogul Empire 1656-1668*. Oxford: Oxford University Press, 1916.

Frank Nicholls
'The Snake and the Tiger'. *Assam Shikari: A Tea Planter's Story of Hunting and High Adventure in the Jungles of North East India*. New Zealand: Tonson Publishing House, 1970.

Geoffery C. Ward and Diane Raines Ward
'The King of the Beasts'. Courtesy of the author.

George B. Schaller
'The First Scientific Study of the Tiger'. *The Deer and the Tiger: A Study of Wildlife in India*. Chicago: The University of Chicago Press, 1967.

George Hogan Knowles
'The Tiger, the Boar and the Elephant'. *In the Grip of Indian Jungles*. London: Wright & Brown, 1932.

Godfrey Charles Mundy
'The Tiger in the Mangroves'. *The Journal of a Tour in India*. Volume I, II. London: John Murray, 1832.

Goverdhan Singh Rathore
'The Leopard that Fell into the Tiger's Lap'. *Tigers: My Life*. Valmik Thapar and Fateh Singh Rathore. New Delhi: Oxford University Press, 2011.

H. A. Leveson
'Tigers Fight over a Kill', 'Rare Encounter between Tiger and Gaur'. *Sport in Many Lands*. London: Chapman and Hall, 1877.

Henry Bevan
'A Tiger Attacks a Boat in Sundarbans'. *Thirty Years in India: or, a Soldier's Reminiscences of Native and European Life in the Presidencies, from 1808 to 1838*. London: Pelham Richardson, 1839.

Hugh Allen
'A Forest Story', 'The Lonely Tiger', 'The Storm'. *The Lonely Tiger*. London: Faber and Faber, 1960.

Isabel Savory
'The Tiger and the Bear'. *A Sportswoman in India: Personal Adventures and Experiences of Travel in Known and Unknown India*. London: Hutchinson & Co., 1900.

J. C. Daniel
'The White Tiger'. *The Tiger in India: A Natural History*. Dehradun: Natraj Publishers, 2001.

J. D. Inverarity
'The Tiger's Diet'. *The Tiger in India: A Natural History*. J. C. Daniel (ed.). Dehradun: Natraj Publishers, 2001.

J. E. Carrington Turner
'The Tiger, the Leopard and the Boar'. *Man-Eaters and Memories*. Dehradun: Natraj Publishers, 2007 (reprint).

J. H. Rivett-Carnac
'The Tiger and the Cooking Pot'. *Many Memories of Life in India at Home and Abroad*. London: Blackwood and Sons, 1910.

J. Moray Brown
'Rare Observations of Tiger Stalking', 'Tooth and Claw'. *Shikar Sketches with Notes on Indian Field-Sports*. London: Hurst and Blackett, 1887.

Jahāngir
'Emperor Jahāngir's Tiger', 'Jahāngir's Tiger Hunt'. *Tuzuk-i-Jahāngiri*. Alexander Rogers and Henry Beveridge (trans.). London: Royal Asiatic Society, 1909-1914.

James Forbes
'A Royal Sport'. *Oriental Memoirs by J. Forbes, revised by his daughter Countess de Montalambert*. London: Richard Bentley, 1834.

James Gordon Elliott
'Christmas Dinner in the Jungle, 1800-1947'. *Field Sports in India 1800-1947*. London: Gentry Books, 1973.

James Inglis
'The Splendid Forest', 'The Tiger at Camp', 'Protocols and Rules for Hunters'. *Sport and Work on the Nepaul Frontier*. London: Macmillan & Co., 1878.

Jamshed Butt
'Man versus Tiger'. *Shikar*. London: R. Hale, 1963.

Jim Corbett
'The Chowgarh Tigress'. *The Mohan Man-Eaters and Other Stories*. New Delhi: Oxford University

Press, 1948. Reproduced with permission of Oxford University Press India, Copyright © Jim Corbett.
'The Himalayan Black Bear and the Tiger'. *The Temple Tiger and More Man-Eater of Kumaon*. Oxford: Oxford University Press, 1954.

John Daniel St. Joseph
'Man, Tiger and a Pack of Wild Dogs', 'The Tiger's Behaviour and Diet', 'The Natural Kill', 'A Worthy Opponent', 'The Tiger's Hunting Technique'. *Life in the Wilds of Central India*. Edinburgh: Empire and Commonwealth Museum, 1930.

John Finnemore
'The Alligator, a Nasty Opponent'. *Peeps at Many Lands: India*. London: Adam and Charles Black, 1907.

Joseph Fayrer
'A Blood-Curdling Attack', 'The Tussle with the Crocodile', 'The Records and the Superstitions', 'The Tiger and the Stag'. *The Royal Tiger of Bengal: His Life and Death*. London: J. & A. Churchill, 1875.

Julius Barras
'The Charge of the Tigress', 'The Furious Tigress'. *India and Tiger-Hunting, Series I*. London: Swan Sonnenschein & Co., 1885.

K. Ullas Karanth
'Tigers in the Mist'. *Way of the Tiger*. U.S.A: Voyageur Press, 2001.

Kalyan Chakrabarti
'The Magical Tiger of the Mayadwip'. *Man-Eating Tigers*. Calcutta: Darbari Prokashan, 1992.

Kenneth Anderson
'A Battle Royal'. *This is the Jungle: More Tales of the Man-Eaters*. New Delhi: Rupa Publications India Pvt. Ltd., 1976.

Kesri Singh
'Attacking a Tiger with a Lathi'. *The Tiger of Rajasthan*. New Delhi: Jaico Publishing House, 1959.
'The Boy and the Tiger', 'Fatal Encounters'. *One Man and a Thousand Tigers*. New York: Dodd, Mead & Company, 1959.
'The Tiger that Took on a Boar'. *Hunting with Horse and Spear*. New Delhi: Hindustan Times Press, 1963.

Lady Lawrence
'The Forest Dawn'. *Indian Embers*. Oxford: George Ronald, 1949.

Leopold Grimston Paget
'The Tiger's Forest'. *Camp and Cantonment: A Journey of Life in India in 1857-1859, with Some Account of the Way Thither*. London: Longman, Green, Longman, Roberts, & Green, 1865.

M. Krishnan
'The Anantapura Tiger'. *Nights and Days: My Book of India's Wildlife*. New Delhi: Vikas Publishing House, 1985. 'The Anantapura Tiger' is used courtesy the estate of M. Krishnan.

Maharanee Sunity Devee
'The Tiger and the Sahib', 'A Tiger in the Tent'. *Bengal Dacoits and Tigers*. Calcutta: Thacker, Spink & Co., 1916.

Mark Thornhill
'The Man-Eaters of Doon'. *Haunts and Hobbies of an Indian Official*. London: John Murray, 1899.

Niccolao Manucci
'Shah Jahan Hunts Tigers with Elephants and Buffaloes'. *A Century of Natural History*. J. C. Daniel (ed.). Mumbai: Bombay Natural History Society, 1983.

Nigel Woodyatt
'Only With the Elephant'. *My Sporting Memories: Forty Years with Note-Book & Gun*. London: Herbert Jenkins Limited, 1922.

Olive Smythies
'Protecting the Young'. *Ten Thousand Miles on Elephants*. London: Seeley Service, 1961.
P. T. Etherton
'An Elephant Takes Flight'. *The Last Strongholds*. London: Jarrolds, 1934.
Patrick Hanley
'Fighting for the Kill', 'Battles between Courting Tigers'. *Tiger Trails in Assam*. London: Robert Hale Ltd., 1961.
Peter Jackson
'A Few Close Encounters'. *Endangered Species: Tigers*. London: New Burlington Books, 2002.
R. D. Mackay
'The Tiger and the Hyena'. *Have You Shot an Indian Tiger?* New Delhi: Sikkson's Press, 1967.
R. D. T. Alexander and A. Martin-Leake
'Food in the Wild'. *Some Signposts to Shikar*. Calcutta: Fred. R. Grenyer, 1932.
R. G. Burton
'The Man-Eaters of Sagar Island', 'The Tiger and the Pony', 'Carried Off By a Tiger', 'The Attack', 'Superstitions and the Value of a Tiger's Parts', 'The Tiger in Military History'. *A Book of Man-Eaters*. New Delhi: Mittal Publications, 1984.
'Enchanting Forests'. *Sport & Wildlife in the Deccan*. London: Seeley, Service & Co., 1928.
'The Tiger and the Bait'. *The Tiger Hunters*. London: Hutchinson and Co. Publishers Ltd, 1936.
Reginald Heber
'The Magnificent Forest'. *Bishop Heber in Northern India*. New York: Cambridge University Press, 1971.
Richard Hilton
'A Tiger Sniffs at a Boot'. *Nine Lives: The Autobiography of an Old Soldier*. London: Hollis & Carter, 1955.
Richard Lydekker
'The Black Tiger', 'The Cherrapunji Tiger'. A *Handbook to the Carnivora*. London: Edward Lloyd Limited, 1896.
Richard Perry
'The Tiger's Range', 'The Wild Dogs of Madras', 'The Nine Tigers'. *The World of the Tiger*. London: Cassell & Co., 1964.
Robert H. Elliot
'A Tiger Family'. *Gold, Sport and Coffee Planting in Mysore*. Westminster: Dodo Press, 1898.
S. Eardley-Wilmot
'The Vicious Attack on the Elephant', 'The Bend of a Stream'. *Forest Life and Sport in India*. London: Edward Arnold, 1911.
Sahibzada Abdul Shakur Khan
'The Tiger and the Camel'. *Shikar Events and Some Useful Notes Thereon*. New Delhi: 1935.
Sardar Bhupendra Kumar
'The Tiger and the Porcupine'. *The Tiger in India: A Natural History*. J. C. Daniel (ed.). Dehradun: Natraj Publishers, 2001.
Sher Jung
'A Family of Tigers'. *Tryst with Tigers*. New Delhi: Hind Pocket Books, in arrangement with Robert Hale, 1967.
Shuja Ul Islam and Colonel John H. Roush Jr.
'An Amazing Contest'. *Hunting Dangerous Game with the Maharajas: Tales of Adventure on a Grand Scale that Took Place for the Most Part in the First Half of the 20th Century*. New Delhi: Himalayan Books, 2001.
Sir Samuel W. Baker
'Stealing Cattle', 'A Good Man and True'. *Wild Beasts and their Ways: Reminiscences of Europe, Asia,*

Africa, and America. London: Macmillan and Co., Ltd., 1898.

Sir Thomas Roe and Dr John Fryer
'Early Descriptions of Wild India', 'The Tiger and the Deer', 'Early Natural History Observations'. *Travels in India in the Seventeenth Century*. London: Trubner & Co., 1873.

Sir William Foster (ed.)
'Early Descriptions of Hindustan'. *Early Travels in India, 1583-1619*. Oxford: Oxford University Press, 1921.

Thomas Bacon
'The Tiger and the Palki'. *First Impressions and Studies from Nature in Hindostan*. London: W. H. Allen and Co., 1837.

Thomas Bowrey
'Catching Wild Tigers'. *A Geographical Account of Countries Round the Bay of Bengal 1669-1679*. Cambridge: Printed for the Hakluyt Society, 1905.

Thomas Pennant
'The Sundarbans Tiger'. *The View of Hindoostan*. Volume II. Printed by Henry Hughes, 1798.

Thomas Williamson
'Sensing Water Currents', 'Battling a Tiger'. *Oriental Field Sports*. London: Printed for Edward Orme, 1807.

Victor Jacquemont
'Hunting for Sport'. *Letters from India: Describing a Journey in the British Dominions of India, Tibet, Lahore and Cashmere, 1828-1831*. London: Edward Churton, 1834.

W. Connell
'The Tiger and the Wild Dogs'. *The Tiger in India: A Natural History*. J. C. Daniel (ed.). Dehradun: Natraj Publishers, 2001.

W. H. G. Kingston
'The Tiger and the Bird Lime', 'Hand-to-Hand Combat with a Tiger'. *Adventures in India*. London: George Routledge and Sons, Ltd., 1884.

W. Hogarth Todd
'Combating a Tiger', 'A Lightning Charge'. *Tiger, Tiger!* London: Heath Cranton Ltd., 1927.

Walter Campbell
'Jungle Life', 'The Tiger and the Wild Hog', 'Man and Tiger', 'The Tiger and the Drunk'. *My Indian Journal*. Edinburgh: Edmonston and Douglas, 1864.

William Blane
'An Elephant's Response to a Tiger's Presence'. *An Account of the Hunting Excursions of Asoph ul Doulah: Nabob of Oudh*. London: Printed for John Stockdale, 1788.

William Knighton
'The Tiger and the Rhino'. *The Private Life of an Eastern King*. New York: Redfield, 1855.

William Rice
'The Tiger that Killed a Cheetah'. *Tiger-Shooting in India*. London: Smith, Elder & Co., 1857.

William Robert Foran
'A Tiger Fights a Wild Buffalo'. *Kill: or be Killed*. London: Hutchinson and Co. Publishers Ltd., 1933.

Yvonne Fitzroy
'Inside the Emerald Forest'. *Courts and Camps in India: Impressions of Viceregal Tours, 1921-1924*. London: Methuen & Co., 1926.

SELECTED BIBLIOGRAPHY

Allen, Hugh. *The Lonely Tiger*. London: Faber & Faber Ltd., 1960.

Anderson, Kenneth. *The Tiger Roars*. London, New Delhi: Rupa Publications India Pvt. Ltd. in arrangement with George Allen and Unwin Ltd., 1967.

Babur. *The Baburnama: Memoirs of Babur, Prince and Emperor*. Wheeler M. Thackston. Smithsonian Institution, 1996.

Barnes, S. *Tiger*. London: Boxtree, 1994.

Barras, Col. Julius. *India and Tiger-Hunting, Series I*. London: Swan Sonnenschein & Co., 1885.

Batten, J. and Darro, P. *The Best of Tiger Hunting*. 1986

Bedi, Rajesh and Ramesh. *Indian Wildlife*. New Delhi: Brijbasi, 1984.

Best, James W. *Forest Life in India*. London: John Murray, 1935.

Best, James W. *Tiger Days*. London: John Murray, 1931.

Boparai, Shaminder. *Billy Arjan Singh: Tiger of the Dudhwa*. New Delhi: HarperCollins, 2011.

Bradley, Mary Hastings. *Trailing the Tiger*. London: D. Appleton and Company, 1929.

Brander, A. A. Dunbar. *Wild Animals in Central India*. London: Edward Arnold & Co., 1927.

Breeden, S. and Wright, B. *Through the Tiger's Eyes*. Berkeley: Ten Speed Press, 1996.

Burton, R. G. *A Book of Man-Eaters*. New Delhi: Mittal Publications, 1984.

Burton, R. G. *The Book of the Tiger*. London: Hutchinson and Co. Publishers Ltd., 1933.

Caldwell, Harry R. *Blue Tiger*. New York: Duckworth, 1924.

Champion, F. W. *The Jungle in Sunlight and Shadow*. London: Chatto & Windus, 1933.

Champion, F. W. *With a Camera in Tiger-Land*. London: Chatto & Windus, 1927.

Colonel Burton. *Tigers of the Raj*. Gloucester: Alan Sutton, 1987.

Corbett, Jim, Thapar, Valmik, Singh, Billy Arjan, Ward, Geoffrey C. and Ward, Diane Raines. *Tigers and Tigerwallahs*. New Delhi: Oxford University Press, 2002.

Corbett, Jim. *The Mohan Man-Eater and Other Stories*. London: Oxford University Press, 1948.

Corbett, Jim. *The Temple Tiger and More Man-Eaters of Kumaon*. New Delhi: Oxford India Paperbacks, 1954.

Courtney, N. *The Tiger Symbol of Freedom*. London: Quartet Books, 1980.

Daniel, J. C. (ed.). *The Tiger in India: A Natural History*. Dehradun: Natraj Publishers, 2001.

Eardley-Wilmot, S. *The Life of a Tiger*. London: Edward Arnold & Co., 1911.

Fayrer, J. *The Royal Tiger of Bengal: His Life and Death*. London: J. & A Churchill, 1875.

Fazl, Abu'l. *Akbarnama (Volume I, II)*. H. Beveridge (trans.). New Delhi: Low Price Publications, 1989.

Foran, W. Robert. *Kill: or be Killed*. London: Hutchinson and Co. Publishers Ltd., 1933.

Forsyth, J. *The Highlands of Central India*. London: Chapman and Hall, 1919.

Gee, E. P. *The Wildlife of India*. London: Collins, 1964.

Glasfurd, A. I. R. *Rifle and Romance in the Indian Jungle*. London: John Lane, 1905.

Gouldsbury, C. E. *Tigerland: Reminiscences of Forty Years' Sport and Adventure in Bengal*. New York: E. P. Dutton & Co., 1916.

Green, I. *Wild Tigers of Bandhavgarh*. U.K.: Tiger Books, 2002.

Hanley, Patrick. *Tiger Trails in Assam*. London: Robert Hale Limited, 1961.

Hewett, Sir John. *Jungle Trails in Northern India*. London: Methuen and Co. Ltd., 1938.

Hornocker, M. (ed.) *Track of the Tiger*. San Francisco: Sierra Club Books, 1997.

Horton, Barbara Curtis. *Tiger Bridge: Nine Days on a Bend of the Nauranala*. Santa Barbara: John Daniel & Co., 1993.

Inglis, James. *Tent Life in Tigerland and Sport and Work on the Nepaul Frontier*. London. Sampson Low, Marston, Searle, & Rivington, 1892.

Ives, Richard. *Of Tigers and Men: Entering the Age of Extinction*. New Delhi: Nan A. Talese, 1996.

Jackson, Peter. *Endangered Species: Tigers*. London: New Burlington Books, 1991.

Johnsingh, A. J. T. *On Jim Corbett's Trail*. New Delhi: Permanent Black, 2004.

Johnson, Daniel. *Sketches of Indian Field Sports: with observations on the animals; also an account of some of the customs of the inhabitants; with a description of the art of catching serpents, as practised by the conjoors and their method of curing themselves when bitten: with remarks on hydrophobia and rabid animals*. London: Robert Jennings, 1827.

Joseph, J. D. *Life in the Wilds of Central India*. Edinburgh: Empire and Commonwealth Museum, 1930.

Jung, Sher. *Tryst with Tigers*. New Delhi: Hind Pocket Books, in arrangement with Robert Hale, 1967.

Karanth, K. Ullas. *A View from the Machan*. New Delhi: Permanent Black, 2006.

Karanth, K. Ullas. *The Way of the Tiger*. Hyderabad: Universities Press India Pvt. Ltd., 2001.

Karanth, K. Ullas. *Tigers*. Scotland: Colin Baxter Photography Ltd., 2001.

Khan, Mutamad. *Tuzuk-i-Jahangiri*.

Knowles, George Hogan. *In the Grip of Indian Jungles*. London: Wright & Brown, 1932.

Larking, Cuthbert. *Bandobast and Khabar: Reminiscences of India*. London: Hurst and Blackett, Ltd., 1888.

Lt. Rice. *Tiger-Shooting in India*. London: Smith, Elder and Co., 1857.

Matthiessen, Peter. *Tigers in the Snow*. London: Harvill Press, 2000.

McDougal, Charles. *The Face of the Tiger*. London: Rivington Books, 1977.

McNeely, Jeffrey A. and Wachtel, P. S. *Soul of the Tiger*. New York: Doubleday, 1988.

Meacham, Cory. *How the Tiger Lost Its Stripes*. New York: Harcourt Brace & Co., 1997.

Montgomery, S. Y. *Spell of the Tiger*. Boston: Houghton Mifflin Company, 1995.

Mountfort, Guy. *Saving the Tiger*. London: Michael Joseph, 1981.

Musselwhite, Arthur. *Behind the Lens in Tigerland*. Calcutta: Thacker, Spink and Co., 1933.

Naidu, Kamal. *Trail of the Tiger*. Dehradun: Oxford University Press, 1998.

Padel, Ruth. *Tigers in Red Weather*. London: Little, Brown, 2005.

Peissel, Michel. *Tiger for Breakfast*. Bombay: Allied Publishers, 1966.

Perry, Richard. *The World of the Tiger*. London: Cassell & Co., 1964.

Pollok, William. *Sport in British Burmah, Assam, and the Cassyah and Jyntiah Hills*. London: Chapman and Hall, 1879.

Pollok, William. *Incidents of Foreign Sport and Travel*. London: Chapman and Hall, 1894.

Powell, A. N. W. *Call of the Tiger*. London: Robert Hale Limited, 1957.

Rathore, Fateh Singh, Singh, Tejbir and Thapar, Valmik. *With Tigers in the Wild: An Experience in an Indian Forest*. New Delhi: Vikas Publishing House, 1983.

Reddy, E. Ajaikumar. *Man-eating Tigers of Central India*. New Delhi: Indialog Publications, 2004.

Rice, Major-General William. *"Indian Game,": (from Quail to Tiger)*. London: W. H. Allen and Co., 1884.

Sainthill Eardley-Wilmot, C. I. E. *Forest Life and Sport in India*. London: Edward Arnold & Co., 1911.

Sankhala, Kailash. *Return of the Tiger*. India: Lustre Press Pvt. Ltd., 1993.

Sankhala, Kailash. *Tiger! The Story of the Indian Tiger*. New Delhi: Rupa Publications India Pvt. Ltd. in arrangement with Collins, 1978.

Schaller, George B. *The Deer and the Tiger: A Study of Wildlife in India*. Chicago: The University of Chicago Press, 1967.

Scindia, Madhav Rao. *A Guide to Tiger Shooting*. 1920.

Seidensticker, John, Christie, Sarah and Jackson, Peter. *Riding the Tiger*. Cambridge: Cambridge University Press, 1999.

Seshadri, Balakrishna. *Call of the Wild*. New Delhi: Sterling Publishers Limited, 1986.

Shah, Anup and Manoj. *A Tiger's Tale*. U.K.: Fountain Press, 1996.

Shahi, S. P. *Backs to the Wall*. New Delhi: Affiliated East-West Press Pvt. Ltd., 1977.

Shakespear, Captain Henry. *The Wild Sports of India: With Detailed Instruction for the Sportsman; to which are added remarks on the breeding and rearing of horses and the formation of light irregular cavalry.* London: Smith, Elder & Co., 1860.

Singh, Arjan. *A Tiger's Story.* New Delhi: HarperCollins Publishers India, 1999.

Singh, Arjan. *Tiger Haven.* London: Macmillan & Co. Ltd., 1973.

Singh, Kesri. *The Tiger of Rajasthan.* London: Robert Hale Limited, 1959.

Singh, Kesri. *One Man and a Thousand Tigers.* London: Robert Hale Limited, 1959.

Sinha, Vivek R. *The Vanishing Tiger.* London: Salamander Books, 2003.

Stebbing, E. P. *The Diary of a Sportsman Naturalist in India.* London: John Lane, 1920.

Sterndale, R. A. *Denizens of the Jungle: A Series of Sketches of Wild Animals, Illustrating their Forms and Natural Attitudes.* Calcutta: Thacker, Spink & Co., 1886.

Stewart, Colonel A. E. *Tiger and Other Game.* London: Longmans, Green & Co., 1928.

Stracey, P. D. *The World of Animals: Tiger.* New York: Arthur Barker Limited, 1968.

Sunquist, Fiona and Mel. *Tiger Moon.* Chicago: The University of Chicago Press, 2002.

Swaffham, John. 'Netting Tigers in the Jungle'. *The Wide World Magazine.* 1902.

Taraporewala, Soonoo. *Tiger Warrior: Fateh Singh Rathore of Ranthambhore.* New Delhi: Penguin, 2012.

The Oxford India Illustrated Corbett. New Delhi: Oxford University Press, 2004.

Tilson, R. and Seal, U. *Tigers of the World.* New Jersey: Noyes Publications, 1987.

Todd, W. Hogarth. *Tiger, Tiger!* London: Heath Cranton Limited, 1927.

Ward, Geoffrey C. and Diane Raines. *Tiger Wallahs.* New Delhi: Oxford University Press, 2002.

Williamson, Thomas. *Oriental Field Sports.* London: Printed for Edward Orme, 1807.

INDEX

VALMIK THAPAR

Portrait of a tiger in Ranthambhore. [Photo credit: Sanjna Kapoor].

Three five-month old cubs in Ranthambhore (January 2017). [Photo credit: Sanjna Kapoor].

The huge male tiger, Gabbar, in full flight after a tiny chital fawn, in Tadoba, Maharashtra. (Photo credit: Sanjna Kapoor).

Gabbar carries off the fawn he chased. (Photo credit: Sanjna Kapoor).

T3, one of the largest male tigers in Ranthambhore (January 2017).
(Photo credit: Valmik Thapar).

Nur, Ranthambhore's most stunning tigress, with her cubs (January 2017). (Photo credit: Sanjna Kapoor).

A snarling tiger in Ranthambhore. (Photo credit: Valmik Thapar).

A young male tiger races along a path in Ranthambhore. (Photo credit: Jaisal Singh).

Nur with her newest family in Ranthambhore (January 2017). (Photo credit: Sanjna Kapoor).

Nur dragging the carcass of a sambar for her cubs to eat.
(Photo credit: Sanjna Kapoor).

Gabbar, the big male, just before he pounces on a chital. (Photo credit: Sanjna Kapoor).

Top and bottom: Portraits of Noon with her cubs. (Photo credit: Sanjna Kapoor).

Ranthambhore's lake tigress, with her litter of three. (Photo credit: Valmik Thapar).

A male tiger sniffs the scent of another tiger. [Photo credit: Sanjna Kapoor].

T3, the big male. [Photo credit: Valmik Thapar].

A young tiger peers out of Ranthambhore's grass. [Photo credit: Sanjna Kapoor].

A male tiger approaches the jeep. (Photo credit: Jaisal Singh).

Made in the USA
Middletown, DE
05 April 2018